THE COMMON QUEST

THE
COMMON
QUEST

Theology and the Search for Truth

by
CHARLES A. M. HALL

THE WESTMINSTER PRESS
Philadelphia

COPYRIGHT © MCMLXV W. L. JENKINS

Scripture quotations from the Revised Standard Version of the Bible are copyright, 1946 and 1952, by the Division of Christian Education of the National Council of Churches, and are used by permission.

Acknowledgment is made to the following for the use of quotations:

John Wiley & Sons, Inc.: *The American College: A Psychological and Social Interpretation of Higher Learning,* ed. by R. Nevitt Sanford. 1962.

Doubleday & Company, Inc.: *The Theatre of the Absurd,* by Martin Esslin. Copyright © 1961 by Martin Esslin.

LIBRARY OF CONGRESS CATALOG CARD No. 65-19780

Published by The Westminster Press®
Philadelphia, Pennsylvania

PRINTED IN THE UNITED STATES OF AMERICA

To Marcia

and to my Athens and Jerusalem — North-
western University, McCormick Theological
Seminary, the University of Basel, Wellesley
College, Beaver College, and my mother the
Church, bride of Christ, wife of Hosea's Lord
— who have engaged me in the common quest.

Contents

Preface

This book begun in terror ends in humility. A preface represents the last substantive contribution of the author and thus, theoretically at least, may be expected to distill the wisdom achieved in the creative process. Here, as is also the case with works of art, the distillate accrues only drop by drop within the process of what follows. It is left me to record here two dimensions of *apologia pro opere meo,* my motivation and my purpose, and to express a few of the many dimensions of my gratitude. I am left to try to explain why I wrote this book, what I wanted to do with it, and who it is I have principally to thank.

To Kendig Brubaker Cully I owe the entire impetus for the formulation of this particular book. As general editor of the Westminster Studies in Christian Communication, he sought an author personally involved in the struggle to communicate the Christian Gospel in the academic world, as teacher and if possible as pastor as well, and I was at hand. He is not to blame that as my wrestling with the stuff itself taught me what this book had to be it grew too unwieldy for inclusion in the Studies. I can only hope that the book, now born as its irreducible, recalcitrant self, will do honor to the patient encouragement and critical appreciation by which he immeasurably contributed to its coming to birth.

In addition to the practical impetus and shape given the book by the project initiated by Professor Cully and The Westminster Press, there were internal reasons imparting the drive which caused it to come into being. The problems of Athens and Jerusalem are manifest today to all who are sensitive. Paul Tillich had sought to formulate a theology of culture, and others longed to return to a culture of theology, but though many were making determined efforts to exist and to reflect as specimens of " the Christian Scholar " the problem in its fundamental depth and its ever-increasing scope seemed to require a thoroughly fresh address. The resources have been available for some time, but who was to use them? The opportunity was presented to me — and that is where the terror began. It took not a moment's reflection to recognize my unworthiness, my unpreparedness to write such a book as I conceived to be required. It would take more of a philosopher, more of a scientist, more of an artist, more of a practical man — above all, it would take more of a theologian — than I to write such a book. The bare consolation which gradually came was that while *I* was not equal to the task, and while there are *many* who are highly competent and eminently qualified to criticize such a book, there seemed to be no one else at hand to write it. In addition, the abiding conviction that had grown from a lifetime in both the Academy and the Church would not allow me to stop short of the attempt *to see together* the ways in which each strives to discover and to bring into interaction what is true with what is human. Thus the book ends in humility, in humble gratitude that what I wished could be said has been said — not perfectly, but it has been said.

What was it that I wished to say? I was concerned to clarify the nature of human knowing, both as a resource for and as itself a form of human living. Such a statement necessarily implies fundamental conviction about knowing and living, about Truth and Humanity. I hold such convictions as a citizen of the Christian Church and as a citizen of Academy. Further, I believe not only that the methods of Church and Academy for discovering and creating truth and humanity are compatible but that they both serve the same Truth and the same Humanity. There is abundant evidence that neither of these human institutions, Academy and Church, has a proprietary right to truth or is fully or invariably human. Yet I cannot imagine that it is the path of health or sanity for either to desire to conquer, to obviate, or even to do without the other. I can only conceive of the two noble, imperfect human institutions engaging through theology and the other daughters begotten or adopted by Academy in dialogue, in the Common Quest for the relevance of Truth and Humanity to life in the world today.

Finally, it is my very great pleasure to make a matter of public record my deep and lasting indebtedness to others involved with me, some unknowing, some in *agōn* shared and joy, in the Quest: To the myriad members of the scholarly community whose faithfulness allows Academy to function and makes possible such a contribution to dialogue as this: especially to Karl Jaspers, Jacques Barzun, Erich Kahler, Walter Stuermann, David Riesman, Frank Pinner, J. Kenneth Galbraith, Bernard Berelson, and Martin Esslin — most of whom I have not met. To Mrs. Rosemary Shepherd, whose typing gave shape to more than one chapter, and to my mother, Mrs. Anna E. Hall, who added to a lifetime of instruction and encouragement hours of the drudgery which a manuscript inevitably demands.

To Karl Barth, who through four years of intensive direction, through friendship beyond them and through material for a lifetime of study has shown me what theology is about, both in the sense of what it deals with and of what it is doing.

To Reinhold Niebuhr, with whom I never actively studied or worked but whose energetic analysis and consistent personal embodiment demonstrated to me not only what ethics is and the prophets are, but what a Biblical prophet would be today; and to Paul Lehmann, who has blazed the trail for all who would think and live out of the mighty depths of Karl Barth's theology and the potent relevance of Niebuhr's ethic.

To Fred Denbeaux, who through seven years of dialogue has practiced The Art of Theology. Any merit in the discussion of "Theology as an Art" which follows derives from his inspiration. The inartistries are my own.

To my wife, Marcia Brown Hall, who wrote the book — in the sense that no idea, no emotion, no expression found here arises outside the context of our one-flesh relationship.

                                                                                    C. A. M. H.

THE COMMON QUEST

Introduction

The Crisis of Intellect

W E ARE LIVING IN A TIME OF CRISIS!" So runs the theme song of
twentieth-century man, and it has become so much a part
of us that we no longer notice when someone sings it out. To the
extent that we are still children of the nineteenth century, however, we have tacitly hoped and expected that each present crisis,
too, would pass away and leave us somehow commanding vistas of
serenity. In some secret recess of our hearts we have refused to
learn the lessons of the Harding Administration that there is no
Normalcy to go back to, and that as far as the eye can see no new
Normalcy beckons us on to its embrace. Noting all this, George M.
Gibson speaks of " the crisis character of existence," which seems to
represent for modern man the essence of his total experience.

No traditional structure has been immune to the powerful acids
of change, to the " shaking of the foundations." Local, national, and
international politics have experienced revolutionary effects around
a globe on which scarcely an isolated area remains untouched. Industry, commerce, whole ways and standards of living, have suffered the overturning. Inevitably, the life of man's spirit, his entire
existence as a person individually and in relation, has been subjected
to the same crisis. First our artists — painters, sculptors, composers,
poets, novelists, and dramatists — have whispered, sung, and roared
their immediate awareness of " the crisis character of existence."
Again, scientists, who both as architects and as technicians have
gained prodigious triumphs in the process of bringing about our
new age, are among the citizens of that age most aware of its shattering potential. For more than forty years there have also been
theologians who attempt to understand crisis in terms of its original

Greek meaning: *krisis* = judgment. They see the crisis character
of existence as God's judgment decisively falling on the strivings
and products of man's existence, putting an end to old possibilities
and meanings but, at the same time, opening up new directions and
possibilities. Finally, the crisis character of existence is nowhere
more acutely felt than in what Jacques Barzun has called " The
House of Intellect." Precisely because of its deliberate commitment to
the burden and the liberating power of knowledge, intellectual life
in the Western world has been experiencing a fundamental crisis in
man's understanding of himself and of his world. The House of Intellect has become a house divided, divided not so much by ill will
as by uncertainty regarding the permanence and unity of its foundations.

The present effort, because of the title it bears, is inextricably involved both with Christian theology and with the " academic
world " of higher education in the United States. Both are viewed as
existing within the fundamental crisis of our time. This statement
has important implications for our task. Their common experience
of crisis excludes many imaginable directions for a book with the
subtitle of " Theology and the Search for Truth." When we realize
that Christian is shaken by precisely the same crisis as Everyman,
we cannot view the Christian Gospel as merchandise that can be
produced to exacting scientific specifications, packaged attractively,
and sold on the academic market. With some reluctance we must
also reject the option of preparing a " How-to " manual, which
would present university pastors, professors of religion, and zealous
Christian students with formulas and techniques for missionizing
intellectuals. The crisis judging modern Christian thought and life
will not allow us any static view of the Gospel and its implications;
but this does not mean that we are free to invent a Gospel, or wish
to do so. In fact, we must next explicitly reject the idea that the
Christian turns to the academic world hoping to discover a gospel
there. Further, it must be clear that the Christian does not " break
into " this world to raid it, to plunder the " treasure-houses of
Egypt," to enrich his system at the expense of secular learning.

Instead, the Gospel *defines* the Christian by giving him his identity
and providing him with clues to the meaning of his existence. The
cognitive effort by which he attempts to explicate this identity and

to draw out the implications of these clues is called theology. We shall, of course, have much more to say about the nature, tasks, and methods of this cognitive effort, but at this point let it suffice to say that the Christian theologian exists in the academic world as a human being on precisely the same footing as other academicians. He possesses no hidden secret which licenses him either publicly or privately to posture on a high bluff overlooking the teeming world of his scholarly colleagues. On the other hand, he does not come to the Academy as a poor relation admitted — with some embarrassment to secular intellectuals — out of deference to the theological past of the Western academic family. The theologian exists in the academic world as the representative of one of the legitimate academic disciplines. He is an academic man and, like his academic brothers, may also be an intellectual.

At this point we must give our attention to the word " academic," and then attempt to illuminate the nature of the crisis in the Academy. The word " academic " in general usage is a synonym for " dull," just as the word " dogmatic," which theology uses as a synonym for " theological," has come to mean " inflexible and intolerant." " Academic " is generally considered equivalent to " pedantic and impractical " and is often accompanied by such a derogatory companion as " mere." Even within the Academy itself a clear distinction is made between formal " academic " values and profound and sweeping " intellectual " concerns.[1] We hope, however, to discover and use fresh meaning in the word " Academy " and its derivatives.

As to the crisis of the Academy, there are many critical problems in education today which are basically technical or practical in nature. Even though each of these raises questions about one's " philosophy of education," our concern with them is only in their relation to the fundamental crisis of the modern intellect. Two particular phenomena of our times, however, are especially symptomatic of such practical and technical dilemmas which point to the deeper crisis beyond their own scope. The first of these is our American version of the earth's present population explosion. We are continually being told that the flow of postwar babies adds up to a tidal wave that has swept through the outer breakwaters of primary education, is now flooding the harbor of secondary education, and is plunging irresistibly onward, threatening to swamp the port cities of higher education. One response that has contributed to a solution at the outer bastions is a drive to arouse public opinion and enlist financial support for the schools. Campaigns have been organized and set rolling under the banner: " When your child is ready for college, will college be ready for him? " It is hoped that funds will be forthcoming to invest in the education of a larger generation or generations which shall one day more than repay this initial outlay. Unfortunately, there is a strong tendency for those who concentrate on this approach to come to conceive of education as no more than a production process. From this point of view, the current crisis in higher education might be analogous to industry's problem of converting for war production in the early 1940's. The basic need in such a case is to divert resources from conventional consumer-oriented production, first to retooling and then to producing military matériel. The trick is simply to divert enough of your resources, and to do so soon enough. In education this would mean finding in every remote corner of our human and material economy, money, materials, and skills to provide sufficient books, buildings, and teaching machinery soon enough to educate our young wave.

The underlying danger in this approach grows out of the difference between the machines involved in hard-goods production and the human beings involved in education. In industry one need only change the production machinery and reprogram the production routine in order to switch from making automobiles and locomotives to producing tanks and airplanes. In education, however, " retooling " includes creating teachers. At the outer breakwaters and harbor installations of primary and secondary education this problem has been soluble. We have a sizable reserve of college-trained people who can conceivably be persuaded to use thir capabilities in teaching. But no such reserve of present or potential Ph.D.'s exists to help us maintain college and university teaching on a high level of competence.

This crisis in human resources raises anew a whole covey of basic questions. What is the nature of the education we hope is going on in the academic world? Can it be as well or better served by techniques that require fewer instructors? Behind these lie the still deeper questions: Just what is the nature of *homo academicus?* What should the academic man be like if he is to teach the youth involved with him in the learning process? And what indeed do we intend that the " product " of the academic world shall be? If education is fundamentally no more than imparting information and scientific or scholarly techniques, there may well be " production machinery " more efficient than man to do the job. But if education involves more than making a highly polished and efficient thinking machine; if reflection, judgment, understanding, are our aim, if we seek to awaken the venturesome curiosity of a vital human spirit, then machines cannot do it all.

This point was perhaps best made by one of the recent rash of cartoons featuring large and complex computers. One particular computing device of almost human appearance had round gauge faces and dial bands where eyebrows, eyes, and nose should be. From the mouth slot poured a steady stream of white paper tape on which was printed "the answers." At the cartoon moment two white-smocked scientists anxiously attend the computer, one taking readings, the other tabulating at a desk. Looking at the tape, the former announces somewhat incredulously: " It says, ' Cogito, ergo sum '! " This cartoon ludicrously but effectively dramatizes the difference between performing the functions of a brain and cogitating, reflecting, striving for understanding. Precisely this difference marks the distinction between fostering an intellectual human being and mass-producing a thinking machine.

This is why teaching must be done at a college or university largely by instructors who are themselves not only reservoirs of information and distilled wisdom but also sources of learning how information and wisdom are gained. Those who evoke learning must themselves be more than parochial experts. They must possess and be able to communicate some measure of participation in man's intellectual venture. They must understand the distinction between what Kant called " technical reason " and the deeper probings of reality and meaning by man's spirit. They must themselves take part in the dangerous struggle to relate the two if they are to be of any real help to young people who enter the academic world seeking a new dimension of existence.

We would also point to a second pressure factor creating immediate crises in education which carries us still closer to the heart of the fundamental crisis than does our own tidal wave of educable youth. In the middle of the academic year 1957–1958, a new body intruded itself into the earth's atmosphere, and this intrusion raised profound disturbances in the atmosphere of the Western intellectual world. Presidents and deans of liberal arts colleges and universities began to be bombarded with questions and suggestions from news-papermen, politicians, incoming students and their parents, and even prospective instructors. Were they planning to revamp or re-vise their curricula and their whole approach to education because of Sputnik? The Space Age, hard on the heels of the Nuclear Age, had taken its place beside the Age of Anxiety, generated by two World Wars and a depression, and its cousin, the Age of Analysis. New and pressing questions, sometimes reflecting old prejudices and frustrations, welled up and rushed to the fore. Should we not now stop wasting our time and money on things irrelevant to the world of Modern Man? Should we not deemphasize the arts and humani-ties in order to put the stress where it really belongs, on the sci-ences — the sciences pertaining to man's biological existence and health, of course, but primarily the physical sciences, above all, nu-clear physics and whatever was necessary to producing guidance sys-tems and improved rocket propulsion? Fortunately, I think, Ameri-can higher education has turned aside the more dangerous thrusts of these suggestions. Unfortunately, however, in so doing we have al-lowed the initial impact of critical pressures on the American Academy to be dissipated without producing the kind of reevalua-tion of the meaning and goal of education so sorely needed. The Sputnik-crisis-in-education should have been understood as pointing directly to the fundamental crisis of intellect which inevitably in-fluences, for better or worse, the effectiveness of our education in building a civilization *fit* for life in the immediate future. If this crisis is decisively expressed neither in the need for increasing the quantity of education nor in shifting the emphasis from one set of methods and contents to another but lies deeper than both, in what phase or mode of man's intellectual life may we find it? *The funda-mental crisis of the Western Intellect is experienced as acute pressure at the seam which binds knowledge and conviction.*

The knowledge we speak of here is not perfect or ultimate. It is neither that immediate apprehension of Plato's Ideas nor that participation in the Father (and the Son in whom he is revealed) which is eternal life (John 17:3). Such knowledge seems both too high and too intangible for the modern institutions of the intellect. Besides, such an exalted knowledge would subsume conviction within itself and could feel no such tension between them as is evident in the crisis of Intellect. Rather, we speak here of a knowledge that is available to the modern intellectual *qua homo academicus*. It is the product of his scholarly discipline and activity, the use of his technical reason. The modern intellectual is, in many ways, the obverse of the Renaissance man and the Enlightened man and he looks upon them with a mixture of nostalgia, envy, and disdain. Unlike them he does not aspire to universal knowledge. He does not share the "prescientific" Renaissance confidence in the harmony of the macrocosmos and the microcosmos which guarantees the correspondence between the music of the spheres, on the one hand, and the harmonies of nature and of art on the other; he does not share Enlightened faith that his participation in Reason will enable him to traverse Reason's all-encompassing network of highroads and thus become Reality's master. Our intellectual is at once a very unpretentious man and often infinitely self-assured. His humility consists in his very disavowal of omnicompetence, and this disavowal is so often repeated as to become a veritable confession or creed. He is aware that his area of expertise is clearly, strictly delimited by his subject matter and his method. Yet within this area, partly because of the power of his method and partly because of his very exclusion of considerations not directly related to the object of his study, the modern intellectual feels himself more competent than his predecessors in any age. Both his humility and his confidence have, however, increasingly isolated his knowledge from any conviction about the nature and values of his achievements. Paradoxically, his very expertise estranges him from conscious, fruitful relationship with an overarching view of truth and humanity, from that central twin allegiance shared by the parents of Western Intellect, the Christian faith and the Academy.

At this point it is necessary to clarify the primary reference intended here by the term "academic world" or "academic cosmos" for which, from time to time, terms such as "higher education," "university," or "liberal arts college" seem to serve as at least partial synonyms. The modern university and liberal arts college do indeed occupy the focus of our direct concern. The need to understand what they are, however, and what they can become recommends viewing them in historical perspective. We shall attempt to understand the critical state of higher education today through an account of the recurrent histories of the Academy; but first we turn to the more common terminology.

The words " college " and " university," which we employ for institutions of higher learning, achieved this modern usage relatively late in the history of Western Intellect. The Latin *collegium* designated a body of no less than three persons associated by some common function. As late as the Middle Ages this function might unite men for purposes of trade, politics, or ecclesiastical activity. The founding of Merton College, Oxford, in 1264 and Peterhouse, Cambridge, in 1284 mark the decisive identification of the term with educational endeavors. Still, it was not until the Jesuit colleges of the sixteenth century that the shape of something like the modern college began to appear on the European continent.

It is probable that no true university existed before the developments at Bologna at the end of the twelfth century. The universities that began to arise at that time were *student guilds* made necessary by the status of aliens in the medieval cities. The University of Paris came into being as a *university of masters* or teachers sometime between 1150 and 1170, and in 1281 Gregory IX issued the bull *Parens Scientiarum,* which has been called the Magna Carta of the university, giving full recognition to the several faculties of the University of Paris to regulate and modify the constitution of the university. At this time there were four faculties, three designated superior (theology, canon law, and medicine) and one inferior (arts, divided into French, Picard, Norman, and English students' guilds).

It is quite true that in terms of structure and generic descent the universities of Western Europe are the heirs of Paris and Bologna, not of Athens and Alexandria. Therefore, most philosophers and writers concerned with the institutional structures of Western Intellect have placed themselves in the tradition springing from these roots, and have considered " the idea of the university." There remains, however, an institution that is much older, and whose history may prove more instructive with regard to the problems of the modern university than that of the university itself. I refer to the Academy.

Both the actual Academy and its name arose simultaneously, when in about 387 B.C. Plato acquired property, the olive grove of *Academe,* a retreat outside Athens where he began to teach. Legally, the school was a corporate body organized for the worship of the Muses, originally the patron goddesses of poets (and, therefore, of musicians as well) but eventually patronesses of all the liberal arts and sciences. In its first period, the curriculum in Plato's Academy consisted of mathematics, dialectics, natural science, and preparation for statesmanship.

The first academy that fits the modern definition of " a society for the cultivation of literature, science, and art for the pure love of these pursuits, with no interested motive," was the museum of Alexandria founded at the beginning of the third century B.C. by Ptolemy I. All the sciences then known were pursued and the most learned men of Greece and of the East were gathered there to further knowledge. The nucleus of the famous Alexandrian library was also created then. Although the modern Academy was, like that of Plato, born of music and poetry in the floral games of the Troubadours, the prototypes were those of the Renaissance, the greatest of which was the *Accademia Platonica* of Florence, founded by the elder Cosimo de' Medici in 1442. It was here that Ficino and Machiavelli, among others, were active. Another important flowering of the Academy occurred in the France of Louis XIV. When one notes that this develops concurrently with the emergence of the Enlightenment,[2] and brings this fact into connection with the earlier history of the Academy, an interesting pattern begins to suggest itself.

The Academy appears to crystallize as a clear and incisive intellectual force at what might be called " classic moments " for the Western Intellect. It does not arise after an intellectual system has proved itself master of its contemporary culture, to preserve that system from attack and decay. Rather, it arises at the moment when Western Intellect achieves that *consonance of knowledge and conviction* which provides a powerful impetus to the solution of the deepest riddles of man's existence. This is especially clear in the case of Plato's Academy. It was founded during the period of his earlier dialogues during which his doctrine of the forms was being explicated and he was confidently building his philosophic system. His more " critical " later period takes place after the Academy has been established and operating for some years. Similarly, the *Accademia Platonica* emerges at a period when a unified vision of knowledge and conviction were beginning to captivate Western Intellect. It must be granted that modern scholarship has done much to relativize the " uniqueness " of the Renaissance, which arose in Italy and counted Florence as one of its greatest centers; but in its own eyes the Renaissance constituted a rebirth or restoration of proper intellectual conditions, a *reunion of conviction with true and certain knowledge*. Other high points of the Academy also seem to coincide with a sense of wholeness, a unified vision of reality — especially the early French Academies of the Enlightenment.

It may also be significant that when we follow the history of the Academy after each of its high points or " classic moments " we discover certain similar characteristics. At the end of the first historical phase of Plato's Academy a period of dogmatism arose in which attention was concentrated on the direction of reality into various spheres on the basis of a doctrine of numbers. This dogmatism was followed by an antidogmatism in the middle Academy of the third and second centuries B.C. The critical academic spirit was developed in terms of the Academy's *epochē,* " withholding of assent," to the Stoic claims of infallibility for certain sense presentations. In the later phases of the Academy, the triumphant critical spirit, in itself invaluable for purging false tenets from a credulous mentality, led to the breakdown and dispersion of intellectual vitality because it was *incapable of sustaining conviction by itself*. Again, although the rather informal early Renaissance academies comprehended all branches of human knowledge, they were unable to resist the disintegration of the Classical Ideal in the plastic arts. The process of specialization in knowledge which had developed by the mid-sixteenth century led to the replacement of the earlier academies by the elaborately organized institutions of the Mannerist period. Something like this process is also evident in the later academies of the French Enlightenment.

Thus, although we would not attempt a thoroughgoing morphology or philosophy of history for the Academy, it might be well to summarize this brief survey. It appears that the Academy arises at

a " classic moment " in Western thought when knowledge and conviction are creatively related to each other. Its strict attention to reliable knowledge gives rise to a critical mentality, which at first performs the healthy function of attacking conviction divorced from
knowledge. Later, knowledge divorced from conviction may be responsible for the dissolution of the Academy into *cells,* specialized
according to the object of their inquiry, *without any conviction
strong enough to unite them organically.*

If this description of the life of various academies has any real
validity, it may well cast light on the current crisis of the Western Intellect. Any analysis of modern intellectual life reveals, on the one
hand, enormous strides and revolutionary discoveries being made in
many particular fields, especially in the natural sciences. On the
other hand, to borrow a terminology popular in theology, modern
man's sense of alienation or estrangement — reflected in the arts and
the social disciplines, together with the tendencies toward fragmentation even in the sciences — points to the dangers inherent in the
separation of knowledge from conviction in matters of "ultimate
concern." The bearers of Western Intellect among our contemporaries are supremely competent in their own *fields* or *branches* of
learning. They display a fine critical acuteness toward the " phoni-
ness " of traditional dogmatisms (although not always the same
astringent spirit toward newer dogmatisms, notably those surrounding psychiatry, embraced by intellectualism as a whole). Yet the
affirmations which our intellectual is honestly able to make outside
his own immediate competence are often at best minimal and fragmentary. There is an agnostic despair concerning the possibility of
any ultimate meaning, purpose, or even unity of knowledge, which
manifests itself partially as a refusal or inability to arrive at any other
than a purely professional commitment, and partially as a cynical
" realism " regarding life as such.

The Academy, at all periods of its existence, has been devoted to
two values, Truth and Humanity. They have not always been the
exclusive guiding stars in the academic firmament and at some
periods not even the primary ones. Still, no Academy ever existed
which did not centrally affirm them, and probably no third concept
arises to challenge Truth and Humanity as definitive of any modern
academic institution. Yet many specimens of *homo academicus* con-

sider commitment to Truth and Humanity both too imprecise and
too exalted a description to fit their existential posture. To the question, Do you as a teacher and an intellectual feel a primary responsibility to Truth and Humanity? a very common reply would be:
I don't even know what you mean by those two words! This attitude
may well be symptomatic of the state of Western Intellect in our
time. The Academy at present seems far removed from the moment
in its history when knowledge and conviction are united. Instead,
most of the strength of our Academy seems to be spent in a critical
revelation of the weaknesses and naïve frailties of traditional values,
and in pushing ahead along highly specialized channels of investigation. As impressive as these achievements are in themselves, critical
analysis and hyperspecialization seem to be typical characteristics of
the later stages of an Academy. When conviction is corroded at the
foundations and when specialization leads to increasing isolation of
knowledge, the Academy faces the danger of progressive dissolution.

Such an analysis of the fundamental crisis of Intellect leads us to
ask how knowledge and conviction can again be brought into creative relationship. It is as true in academies as in politics that " without a vision the people perish." The academic man surely cannot live
by bread alone, by technical skill and achievement. He cannot survive as an overdeveloped intellect without conviction. But the rebirth
of vital conviction, if indeed it is still a serious possibility for sophisticated Western Man, cannot be conceived and promoted by sleight
of hand. Here the Academy of the free world has the right, and
quite possibly the obligation, to make concrete demands on Christian theology. The Christian Gospel has provided the only base for
conviction on which our intellectual culture has been constructed.
Renaissance and Enlightenment planted noble pagan trees on a
Christian soil which nourished them. Even critical theologies and
the most violent and consistent god-is-dead philosophies have drawn
both structure and vitality from the faith they attacked. Neither
Idealisms purged of Christian insights, nor neutral empiricisms and
pragmatisms, nor returns to primitive apprehensions of natural vitality have ever yet been capable of sustaining the convictions of
Western Intellect. The hunger for conviction in our Academy,
whether overt or manifesting itself in frustration, in boredom, or in
clutching at straws of virtue and value, presents a challenge to Chris-

tian theology. Can theology provide clues which can lead to a revitalization of conviction in the Academy, or is Christian " truth " broken,
empty, dead? Does the Christian theologian actually practice disciplines of sufficient rigor and effectiveness to justify a place for him
in the modern Academy? And if so, how much help, and of what
kind, can he give to today's *homo academicus?*

After years of hoping that a *kairos,* a moment pregnant with
spiritual significance and practical power, awaited Religious Socialism in the twentieth century, Paul Tillich announced that the *kairos*
had been missed, or somehow passed unfulfilled. In its place he announced a " sacred void," a time of watchful preparation. Similarly
in the Academy, no decisive rebirth of conviction appears imminent.
But lest the Academy suffer increasing separation and spiritual dissolution, this hour in the history of Western Intellect should be
looked upon as something like a " sacred void." There are those
who watch for signs of this rebirth and the reunion of conviction and
knowledge, who try to keep open and alive the channels of communication between the sciences and the arts for the conversation out
of which conviction shall arise to take up its role anew. As one of
these, what is the place of the theologian, the communicator of the
Gospel, in the academic world?

I

Theology and Conviction

" What has Athens to do with Jerusalem? "

Tertullian

TO THIS QUESTION, many representatives of the academic world
would answer a resounding " Nothing! " on behalf of Athens.
To this question, many representatives of Christianity would answer a resounding " Nothing! " on behalf of Jerusalem. Both the
history of Western Intellect and the symptomatic current crisis in
conviction in the Academy, however, prevent us as citizens of both
" Athens " and " Jerusalem " from making this reply.

Certainly almost all citizens of Academy today would like to be
free from the control of a Church which " for the sake of its faith "
has often done everything in its power to inhibit the progress of science (one thinks of Galileo, Copernicus, and Darwin) and untrammeled inquiry. Yet the dilemma of such freedom is dramatized
by the contribution to a discussion of *faith and critical thinking* by a
professor whom one would expect to classify religiously as a
" secular " or " cultural " Jew. This academician affirmed the
scholarly techniques of a particular discipline; but when pressed for
a convictional affirmation beyond this, he replied: " My moral code
and behavior are, I suppose, Christian. After all, I am the product of
a Christian society and civilization." Citizens of Jerusalem, however,
are not so quick to take credit (and blame) for the state of that society and civilization, with its glory and its misery. Of Christendom's
glory most knowledgeable Christians might say with Karl Barth:
" The things that are written in Church History are not good." And
to see our civilization's misery we need not look to atheists' atrocities.

It is sufficient sadly to recall Servetus' burning in Calvin's Geneva, and the anti-Semitism of Thomas Aquinas and Martin Luther long before Hitler's entrance on the stage. Each Christian would like to say, " Not my kind of *faith* did these things "; just as each academic man would like to say. " Nor my kind of *thinking*." The life of the Academy and of Christianity are bound so inextricably to each other and to actual existence in our culture, however, that mutual burdens, actions, and responsibilities are inevitable.

Christianity, for its part, is a matter of conviction. Theology is the name for the intellectual expression of this conviction. Time and again, for varying reasons but with something like inevitability, Theology has gravitated to the Academy for the sake of expressing Christian conviction. The story of their life together is — for better or for worse, in sickness and in health, in enmity and in amity — the story of Western Intellectual culture. In seeking to learn how Theology can aid Academy in its current crisis of conviction, then, we must take a brief look at certain crucial points in the history of Theology's dialogue about its convictions with Academy.

How Far to Athens — from Jerusalem?

Theology is the issue of the marriage between a virile Hebraic conviction concerning God, man, and world and the magnificent conceptual equipment of a Hellenic philosophy that outlived the power of its own convictions. In the beginning of theology was conviction. This conviction arose before theology in *independence* of the Academy. The early Christians experienced the presence of the risen Lord and were convinced that God was acting decisively through him. Informal theology arose out of the necessity to explain this conviction and to answer the question: How can you follow an executed criminal rejected by God and man (both Jewish and Roman)? As Oscar Cullmann has shown in *The Theology of the New Testament,* early Christian thinkers were content to answer these questions, which centered on the person and work of Jesus Christ, primarily with the aid of Jewish exegesis of the Old Testament. For this largely *internal dialogue*[1] about its convictions the Church also borrowed language and conceptions piecemeal, as they were needed, from pagan sources, mainly from the popular public vocabulary. Although they were confronted daily with the conflicting claims of the Roman Pantheon, with its mysteries and the various philosophical faiths of the Hellenistic world, at first Christians did little to engage in a formal *external dialogue* with them. This was due to such factors as Christianity's expectations for an early end to history, and its relatively small influence upon learned people across the Roman Empire.

The Greek language, however, became the lingua franca of a Christianity expelled from Judaism and forced to make its way in the pagan world. Greek vocabulary, thought forms, and even content began increasingly to appear, especially where Judeo-Christian conceptions were incomplete. The Apologists, Christian missionaries to the Hellenistic mind, now deliberately engaged in an *external dialogue* in which they set out to show that the Christian Gospel could be couched in philosophical modes. Building on the fact that philosophy, unlike new religions and foreign cults, was tolerated by the state, the Apologists treated Christianity as a philosophy and made the claim that it is, in fact, the only true one. The process of being philosophized, in turn, put Christianity under the influence of the viewpoints, methods, and concepts of Hellenistic thought, particularly of Stoic rationalism. This represented a major step in the development of formal theology.

The next stage in this development is symbolized by the rise of the catechetical school of Alexandria, probably about A.D. 190. Under the leadership of the brilliant intellectual Clement and his still greater successor Origen, theology, the ecclasiastical science and academic discipline, was developed and the Church's affirmation was transformed by the methods of philosophical speculation. Clement presented a clearly recognizable Christian Gnosticism. Like the heretical Gnostics he differentiated between *gnōsis* (the largely esoteric *Christian philosophy* of the Gnostic) and *pistis* (the *faith* held by all Christians, accepted solely on the strength of authority). Unlike them Clement held that the two "kinds of knowledge" are not absolutely contradictory but are necessarily related stages, *pistis* being the prerequisite of *gnōsis*. Clement, then, attempts not only to couch Christian conviction and the Academy's cognition in the same terms but also to relate them in a dialectic movement.

Origen went far beyond this insight of his teacher and eventually

constructed a Christian " science " capable of competing successfully
with the Greek philosophical and religious systems on their own
level. His *Peri archōn* (first principles) is the first system of thought
in the Christian Church. On the one hand, Origen forged a vocabulary for Christian theology in direct dependence on Neo-Platonic
speculation. On the other hand, he made monumental contributions
to the understanding of the Bible, as much in terms of solid literary
analysis as of speculative interpretation.

In Origen we begin to see a new type of relationship between
Theology and the Academy as their *dialogue* gradually passes over
into the *absorption* of one by the other. In spite of the strong Biblical
interest of Apologists like Origen, Tertullian begins to mistrust a
theology that shows signs of being *assimilated* into classical culture
and Academic thinking. In terms of the familiar summary of his
theology, *credo quia absurdam* (" I believe because it is absurd "),
Tertullian gives the first negative reply to his own question: What
has Athens to do with Jerusalem? He insists on the *independence* of
theology from philosophy.

At this point we realize that we have described all of the three
possible relationships between Theology and Academy. We have
moved from *independence* to *dialogue,* first internal then external, to
absorption or assimilation. This movement may prove to be typical
but, though one type of relationship may dominate at a particular
period and these periods may often succeed each other in the order
independence-dialogue-absorption, this movement is clearly not inevitable. The appearance in Tertullian of an apostle of *independence*
at the same time Origen is carrying on *external dialogue* and possibly moving toward *assimilation* is significant. It suggests that more
than one relationship may be important at the same time and, in addition, that a dialectic tension may exist between the relationships
themselves.

This relationship between relationships is dramatized and embodied in the complex and powerful person known as Augustine.
Torn within and pulled from without by a thousand tensions in a
crucial age for both Christianity and classical culture, Augustine,
though he produced no complete system like Origen's, expounded
a coherent view of God and man, of church and state, of time and
eternity, which embraces a multitude of the tensions he knew.

Among the most important of these are the relationships between Theology and Academy. On the one hand, Theology for him must be profoundly Biblical and *independent* of a State, a culture, an Academy which wished to capture its vitality for its own ends. On the other hand, Theology lives not yet in the New Jerusalem but in Athens and in Rome, where relative truth and justice, genuine though corruptible, are achieved here and now. Therefore, Augustine risked the use of Neo-Platonism, a language of the city of man, in both *internal* and *external* dialogue concerning the city of God. The success of Augustine's effort to maintain both *dialogue* and *independence,* together with the richness and practicality of the conception of human life he gained as a result, is attested by the fact that a thousand years of Christian thought and culture lived out of the " Augustinian synthesis." And when the synthesis dissolved, the reconstruction of thought and life within the Church was spearheaded by Luther and Calvin, both as Augustinian in thought as was the former in monastic affiliation.

Augustine's influence on the centuries following his work is immediately evident in both the form and the content of theology. Theologians did not write new and massive systematic theologies after the manner of Origen. This was partly due to the fact that the intellectuals of those times complacently felt that the Christian faith had already received its decisive formulations from the Apostolic Fathers, and especially Augustine. The primary form of theology was the so-called collections of " sentences." These collections were made up of the selections from the Church Fathers considered most typical and trenchant by the various collectors, the greatest of whom was Peter Lombard, an Italian who became bishop of Paris. His *Sententiarum Libri Quatuor* earned him the title of Master of the Sentences. The influence of this collection was so far-reaching and enduring that as late as the sixteenth century the theological education received by the Protestant Reformers was based on them and not on the intervening works of Anselm, Thomas, and other great Scholastics.

The main reason for the relatively static nature of theology in the centuries following Augustine was that the polemic energy of the Church was directed not toward new intellectual challenges from without but toward the creation of a *corpus Christianorum* (a

Christendom) out of the barbarians of Europe. As M. A. Schmidt
has pointed out, this was a period when there was, in a very practical sense, no time for creative intellectual work. This was a period
of migration, when even theology "traveled light." The missionaries going from Italy and England to Germany wished to take
along only the most important bits and pieces. For them, in essence
the *Sentences* represented a "portable Augustine" with some additional fragments from other writers.

This secondhand theologizing persisted largely because pagan
classical culture as a challenging option *independent* of ecclesiastical
selection and control was dead. Academy apart from the Church did
not exist, so that for all practical purposes any learning carried on
can be said to have been accomplished by an Academy *absorbed* by
or *assimilated* into theological interest. The so-called Carolingian
Renaissance represented a conscious effort to enlighten the victorious
but uncultivated Franks of central Europe by contact with the best
of English and Italian thought and the relics of Latin culture. It did
not represent a significant permanent advance, however, even
though it did reinstate the seven liberal arts and brought together
some of the most creative spirits of the age; for with the collapse of
the Carolingian culture, many cathedral and monastic schools came
to an end. The others were too concerned with the struggle for survival to provide any impetus for a spiritual and intellectual renewal.
It was only in the course of the eleventh century, under the pressure of important theological controversies, that a decisive advance
was made in an intellectual dimension. I refer to the appearance
and refinement of the dialectical method which created Scholasticism.

The dialectical concept lies deeply embedded in the roots of the
Academic tradition. Aristotle reports that Zeno of Elea first used it
when he accepted the position of his opponents and then showed
that it leads to contradictory conclusions. The Socrates of Plato's
early *Dialogues* demonstrates the rootage of dialectic in dialogue.
With Socrates, dialectics became the art of eliciting a satisfactory
definition of some term, often ethical, by systematic alternation of
question and answer. Plato himself transformed the method to investigate the forms or ideas. Aristotle distinguished dialectical
reasoning from demonstrative, believing the latter alone yields

knowledge. The basis for the distinction is his tenet that in dialectics the premises are the opinions of the many (*hoi polloi*), or at best of the experts. He held the premises of demonstrative reasoning, on the other hand, to be true and primary. The Stoics took the decisive step of dividing logic into rhetoric and dialectic. From this point until the end of the Middle Ages dialectic was simply identified with logic.

The dialectical method came to the fore in the theological school of Chartres, founded by Fulbert around the beginning of the eleventh century. Berengar carried on in Tours the application to theology of the dialectical method he had learned from Fulbert. It was the consequences of this kind of thinking which provoked the great controversy surrounding the interpretation of the Mass. Though traditionalism prevailed over dialecticism in the immediate issue, the dialectical method had demonstrated an originality and power which orthodoxy soon appropriated for its own.

Genuine Scholasticism decisively appeared first in Anselm of Canterbury. Anselm starts from the Augustinian dictum *credo ut intelligam* (" I believe *so that* I may know "), which begins in the *independence* of Christian conviction and moves into *internal dialogue*. He accepts the faith of the Church and strives to transform it into clear logical knowledge by use of the dialectical method. His ontological proof for the existence of God depends on the necessity of its being thought. This demonstrates the extent of his confidence both in human reason and in its usefulness in *dialogue* with Christian conviction. Further refinement awaited the bold mind of Peter Abelard, who considered dialectics worthy not only to be the handmaiden of theology, but to receive attention for its own sake. His attitude is demonstrated by the reversal of *credo ut intelligam* to *nihil credendum, nisi intellectum* (believing nothing I do not first know). His great work *Sic et non* (*Yes and no*) reflects his faith in the ability of dialectics to *resolve* the contradiction he deliberately sets up. We must focus attention on this resolution to appreciate that he is actually reinstating a kind of *external dialogue* by faith with reason, its equally respected independent partner in learning. While embracing extremes, he wishes to find a logical middle way. In pursuing this desire Abelard sets up a dialectical movement invariably echoed in every Scholastic *articulus*,[2] the fundamental building block of the great *Summae*.

The most highly developed work in this form, Aquinas' *Summa Totius Theologiae*, a veritable masterpiece of literary architectonic, which is successively divided into *Partes, Quaestiones,* and finally into approximately 2,500 *Articuli,* embodies the Scholastic ideal of harmonizing reason and revelation in one system. In it Aquinas creates a kind of *internal dialogue* of conviction, for he combines the rationality of Aristotle with the Platonically colored Catholic Christianity of Augustine and the Neo-Platonic mysticism of Dionysius the Areopagite. It is extremely instructive to contrast Aquinas' *Summa Contra Gentiles* with this masterpiece. The *Summa Theologica* uses the *summa* form of European Christianity, incorporating the debates of Christian thinkers, in addition to Aristotelian logic and Biblical content. But in the *Summa Contra Gentiles* we have an *external dialogue* by which Aquinas hoped to convince the Arab Aristotelians that "philosophy" (Aristotelianism) is more commensurate with Christianity than with Islam. The *summa* form and quotations from Christian authorities, so characteristic of the edifying *internal* dialogue of *Summa Theologica,* are entirely absent from *Contra Gentiles,* which is totally dependent on Biblical sources for its Christian flavor.

Almost as soon as Aquinas and his great Franciscan rivals (especially Duns Scotus) had completed their magnificent intellectual edifices, unmistakable signs appeared throughout the Church that the vast unified cathedrals of medieval culture could not stand forever. And within Scholasticism itself, a new phase marked the end of the magnificent closed intellectual systems of the high period. Late Scholasticism is symbolized by the *via moderna of* William Ockham, an English Franciscan who taught in Paris. Ockham and the "modernists" extended the distinction established between faith and knowledge by Scotus into a clear-cut separation, thus sowing the seeds of a new declaration of *independence* between Theology and Academic reason. Ockham disputed the ability of human reason to attain to a knowledge higher than that available to the senses. Thus he rejected all forms of the Realism advocated by the orthodox theologians of his day with regard to the universals. Instead, he agreed with the Nominalists, who had been judged heretical near the end of the eleventh century, that categorical concepts are mere *nomina,* abstractions of the understanding, and that only the individual things are " real." But Ockham was not so much interested in the agreement itself as in the linguistic study that produced it and in the analytical handling of particular problems.

One such treatment produces what might be called Ockham's empiricist tendency, closely allied to his celebrated " razor " or principle of economy, which slashes away at the presence of unsupported assumptions. Again, he exercises great care in the study and use of language in logic. Related to these, but perhaps more important for us, is his *criticism* of traditional metaphysics, especially as argued on the basis of the demonstrative character of the proofs for God's existence by the speculative philosophers of the thirteenth century. Ockham was aware that a Christian metaphysic is only possible if one *presupposes* the existence of God. The ousting of traditional metaphysics from philosophy meant a real separation of theology and philosophy, as a result of which many of the problems customarily assigned to metaphysics were treated as matters of faith rather than of reason. The *independence* of Christian theology and Academy's philosophy made possible, on the one hand, a thoroughgoing philosophical critique of dogma. But Ockham, unlike successors of later centuries, did not use his critical studies of the linguistics of logic to evacuate meaning from faith. Even while the critical aspects of his work are proclaiming Scholasticism's self-reduction, Ockham demonstrates that power and careful consistency which make Neo-Thomism even today the leading representative of the Rationalist tradition. And by coveting the liberation of God from enclosure in a rigid philosophical system, Ockham himself prepared the way for Martin Luther.

In the spirit of Ockham, the Lutheran Reformation sought freedom for the Gospel from a legalism it called Jewish, just as the Swiss Reformers advocated freedom from pagan syncretism. In his spirit, all celebrated the independence of the Gospel from intellectual absolutism. *Sola scriptura, sola fide* (by Scripture *alone,* by faith *alone*) rang the watchwords of risked certainties, and outrunning Ockham's intent Luther could with bold imprudence condemn Reason as the whore who seduced Christians from the exclusive sway of God's Word received by faith. Though Luther, because of the vagaries of temperament and history, does not produce any consistent system of thought, his view of the relation between Church and Academy might well be understood as part of his separation of the "two kingdoms." Regardless of later refinements that might soften the sharpness of this division, Luther maintained the fundamental distinction between the Kingdom of Christ and the Kingdom of the World established in his early writings. The former is the *inward* kingdom where *Gospel* holds sway *sola fide,* and *Scripture alone* guides the *true Church* in ministering to the *free* Christian man who does *not sin* and *owes* no man anything but *love.* This kingdom must always be maintained as *independent,* and protected from the encroachments of the *outward* kingdom where the *works* of the *Law* govern and proud *Reason* is queen. Here *sin* is powerful and the *Church of Antichrist* (as well as the *state of tyrants*) may oppress. Even when society is *just,* this outward kingdom is always laden with *obligation* to which man is debtor.

Though these kingdoms are *independent* and must be kept distinct, Luther is clear that they coexist, and in his two-edged thesis for *On Christian Liberty* they are even related positively: "A Christian man is (inwardly in faith) a free lord over all things and subject to no one; a Christian man is (outwardly in works) a dutiful servant of all things and subject to everyone." [3] For the sake of the Christian man, inwardly free and immediately related to God by faith through his Word, Evangelical theologians made important strides in exegesis and Biblical theology. For the sake of the outward man, the State, the Academy, and other worldly institutions were perfectly free to cultivate and utilize the traditional rationales developed by *external dialogue,* which Luther considered valid here. Luther himself defended traditional structures on massive fronts of the "outward kingdom," into which Lutheran intellectuals soon reintroduced a thoroughgoing rationalism closely resembling the natural theology Luther had exorcized from the "inward kingdom."

The Swiss Reformers willingly accepted Luther's formal principle, "by Scripture alone," and his material principle that Scripture is to be understood with the key of "justification by faith." They were more centrally interested, however, in the *realization* of the Kingdom of Christ than in preserving its pure and inward character.

This is symbolized by the fact that John Calvin exploited an *internal dialogue* with the Old Testament, in his third (or normative) " use of the Law," precisely because it is the major Biblical source of constructive guidance in social, economic, and political matters. This infuriated the Lutherans, who feared above all else the encroachments of Law from the outer to the inner kingdom, preferring to risk the invasion of rationalism instead. Calvin himself was prone to the blandishments of reason. Like the other Swiss Reformers and Luther's successor, Philip Melanchthon, he was a child of the Northern Renaissance Humanism, less affected by Ockhamist radicalism than Luther, more at home with Augustinian Scholastics such as Bonaventure. So Calvin, though he certainly intended primary stress on his doctrine of the " internal testimony of the Holy Spirit " as the sole guarantor of the Bible's validity, added: " So far as human reason goes, sufficiently firm proofs are at hand to establish the credibility of Scripture." [4] And this was enough to open the door for his successors to begin building systems increasingly dependent on the authority of Reason, the partner of their *exterior dialogue*.

Thus, in the seventeenth and eighteenth centuries Lutheranism and Calvinism both produced an Orthodoxy that has fittingly been called Protestant Scholasticism. The first generation of Reformers had forged a theology based on the naked risk of faith. Orthodoxy, however, theologized on a faith propped up by rationalizations. Uneasy about the rationalist's traditional assertion that faith represents an inferior and uncertain form of cognition, they sought the security of a plausible close-knit logical structure. And indeed they, too, produced theological systems of impressive intellectual stature, systems that revealed a Protestantism moving from the *independence* of Luther, past the *internal dialogue* of Calvin, to the attempt to create a Christian culture (like that of the Catholic Middle Ages) in which Academy would be largely *absorbed* in Theology. In the Lutheran universities, Theology's preeminence was emphatically underlined. All other disciplines were directly related to it. Yet, although the natural sciences were far from complete freedom, it was in these universities that the theories of Copernicus were first advocated. But in the queen of the sciences, dogmatics, Scholastic methodology, and precision — finally even Aristotle himself, the " damned, proud, roguish heathen " despised by Luther — were gradually reinstated.

Protestant Orthodoxy in the final analysis, then, came to differ fundamentally from that of Roman Catholicism only in its choice of the presuppositions for its logical system. The Roman Catholic structures were built on the conception of imperfect nature completed by grace, and of the one, holy, Catholic Church as the embodiment of that grace. Lutheran Scholasticism operated on the premise that the outward dominion of Law was dominated by sin and directed toward death, but that grace brings man in his inmost being justification by faith alone. Calvinist Orthodoxy concentrated on the decrees of men's election by the Divine Sovereign, whose kingdom demands fulfillment in the lives of his servants, the elect.

The Glorious Revolution and the Tolerance Act of William III in the late seventeenth century signaled the end of Europe's religious wars, and the sharp differences within Christian theology became less important to Western Intellect. Leading intellectuals increasingly turned away from fine but often fruitless theological dialectic and began to create a new *independent* view of life and of the world. This is the process the modern Academy has designated Enlightenment, in which the Western thinker has found himself, for the first time during the second millennium of Christianity, living in a spiritual world not unconditionally dominated by the Church.

The most radical effects of the Enlightenment were felt on Roman Catholic soil, in France. There, relatively few of the clergy were won over to the unfettered exercise of Reason, while a great portion of cultured laymen fell under its influence. This led to a critical split between the Church and a culture which rapidly became anticlerical, even anti-Christian, and finally revolutionary. Even though Protestantism learned more easily from the still more profound intellectual revolution in England and Holland, the Enlightenment symbolized a vast spiritual overturning which forced massive mutations on pedantic Protestant Orthodoxy. To this Enlightenment, which culminated in Kant's *Critique of Pure Reason,* all theology had to respond. Roman Catholicism chose not to risk critical attrition and *absorption* in Kant's new Idealism but to return to the old Idealism it had forever *absorbed* into the theology of Thomas Aquinas. For the first time in almost fifteen hundred years, Christian intellection was faced by a massive secular option, and Protestantism was unable to draw this culture into a synthesis it could control. It was torn between risking *external dialogue,* with the threat of *absorption* into the secular culture, and retreating into Pietism's attempt to reestablish the pure *independence* of primitive Christianity. Thus was set the stage for the appearance of the most pivotal theologian since the Reformation: Friedrich Schleiermacher.

Schleiermacher was a man of varied genius, and torn by the tensions between his authentic belonging to Pietism (through his school days with the Moravians), to the Academy (through his philosophical, historical, and psychological studies), and to the burgeoning Romantic culture (through his affinities with its poets and musicians). His first epoch-making work is an *external dialogue,* the very title of which, *Speeches on Religion to Its Cultured Despisers,* reveals Theology addressing an independent and antipathetic spiritual force. Schleiermacher strikes a chord as ancient and authentic as the prophets of Israel and as modern and intense as any Existentialist or apostle of the Absurd when he says: "I appeal to nothing except your contempt." In so doing he cuts himself off from the cumbersome trappings of Orthodoxy, indeed from Theology itself, to lay bare the nerve of Religion in man. He intended thus to correlate the authentic experiences of piety and aesthetics, to unite the lover of beauty with the lover of God. This aspect of the *Speeches* turned out to be more than an *external dialogue* with a current Academic culture, for it gave the impetus to a whole "theology of culture" in which Theology came to be threatened with *absorption.* But Schleiermacher's decision to concentrate on Religion had still more far-reaching ramifications than this for Theology. Christianity was relativized as one concrete form of Religion, and the "history of religions" movement which grew up from this start could never absolutize, that is, recover the uniqueness of Christianity again.

In his *Christian Faith,* perhaps more descriptively "the faith of *a* Christian man," Schleiermacher displayed further revolutionary tendencies. The *internal dialogue* of Christianity was suddenly no longer the debate of the Church with her long history but the meditation of the pious individual upon his own soul. From this beginning sprang both new liberal Christian subjectivisms and the more objective "psychology of religion." Finally, the Romantic philosophy

Schleiermacher developed in the first half of his book as the tool for explicating his Christian faith in the second half helped to shape the "philosophy of religion" movement. When one adds up the useful contributions of these ". . . ies of Religion," which replaced theology in liberal Christianity, it is not hard to understand why "a hundred years of Christian thought lived out of the mind of Schleiermacher."

The appearance of Karl Barth's *Epistle to the Romans* shortly after World War I marked the dawn of a new declaration of the *independence* of theology from culture. Barth attacked *Kulturtheologie,* a theology so closely bound to a culture as to be subservient to its fate, a theology so hungry for intellectual respectability in the Academy that it could no longer free itself from the weaknesses and errors of the Intellectual Establishment. Barth discovered such a theology regnant among the heirs of Schleiermacher. It was dependent on the politics, the social ethics, the Academy, of culture. Therefore Barth proclaimed anew a distinctively Christian theology, dependent solely on the Word of God for its validity, free from the control of philosophy or any other guarantor of Academic truth. This theology acknowledges its human frailty, its lack of susceptibility to a proof which compels assent, yet claims a rightful place among the disciplines of the Academy.

WHICH WAY TO ATHENS — FROM JERUSALEM?

Modern theology has grown up on the ground cleared by this declaration of *independence* for theology and discontinuity with an *assimilated* theology. Some thinkers have absolutized *independence,* others have drifted back toward *assimilation,* and many have attempted to engage in a *dialogue* involving Academy. In previous treatments of these relations we have asked, How far to Athens — from Jerusalem? Sometimes, as from Tertullian, we have heard, You can't get there from here! Sometimes, as from *Kulturtheologie,* we have heard, We're already there. But most of the time we have heard that the distance is finite, and that some people think they know of a negotiable road. For today, then, we are left with a question, namely, Which road? or perhaps, Which *way* to Athens from Jerusalem? We have seen that pure *independence* and complete *absorption* do not put Theology and Academy in communication. We may further recall that the most creative and effective communicators of theology in the Academy — Augustine, Aquinas, the Reformers, and Schleiermacher — have carried on an *internal* or *external dialogue* involving the rest of Academy. As a matter of fact, they tend to have engaged in both, or to have combined *independence* with *interior dialogue* or risked *assimilation* for the sake of *exterior dialogue*. We would expect, therefore, a satisfactory way leading through *internal* or *external* dialogue, and the names of three theologians suggest themselves as we search for a potential guide.

In Reinhold Niebuhr we have perhaps the greatest Christian theologian born an American citizen.[5] His truly prophetic embodiment of an unblinking Realism, both eminently pragmatic and profoundly Christian, has been immeasurably valuable to the Church, the Academy, and American culture in the past forty years. Niebuhr has created an atmosphere in which ethical thinking, especially in the realm of politics, will persist, perhaps for decades to come. But the mantle of the prophet is infinitely more difficult to pass on than the crown of the king, the bishop's hat, or even the robes of wisdom. By nature, Niebuhr's contribution has been more incisive and particular than constructive and systematic. He has created miracles of relevance to the fleeting moment and not a perennial Christian philosophy. And so it is with deep gratitude, and therefore with regret, that we must search elsewhere in the attempt to find a foundation for communicating conviction in the Academy.

In addition to his own contribution, however, Reinhold Niebuhr has given us an intriguing characterization of our other two potential guides. He has said that if Karl Barth is the Tertullian of today — as he has often been considered because of his No to natural theology, and the Wholly Other God of his *independent* theology — Paul Tillich is our Origen.

Tillich's theology has presented several of the aspects in our spectrum of relationships, but Origen-like he is perhaps best understood in the terms of his first autobiographical sketch as a man " on the boundary." The end of World War I found Tillich, like Barth, tremendously disillusioned with the particular *Kulturtheologie* of Imperial Germany. Subsequently, however, while Barth rejected *Kul-*

turtheologie and *assimilation* in all forms, Tillich rejected as irrelevant a Church and a theology from which the Germany of the Weimar Republic became increasingly *independent*. Unlike Barth he did not reject but affirmed the interdependence of theology and culture in general. Thus, already in 1919 we find him presenting a "Religious Philosophy of Culture," and he has tried to establish a conjunction between theology and the intellectual dimensions of culture from his book *The System of the Sciences According to Their Subject-matter and Method* (1923), through *The Religious Situation* (1926), to *The Theology of Culture* (1960).

For years Tillich actively addressed the extra-Academic world of culture in terms of his Religious Socialism, which he developed and presented primarily in the languages and logics of Academy and Theology. The failure to apprehend the expected *kairos* (or pregnant moment) of Religious Socialism, together with his transplantation to America, however, marked the end of his public ethical activity outside of Church and Academy. Still, the knowledgeability and power with which he has used his method of correlation, synthesizing the philosophical questions of culture with theological answers, has won widespread respect and admiration in all sectors of Western thought. In recent years, as we see in the later volumes of his *Systematic Theology*, Tillich has turned increasingly toward a theological *dialogue internal* to the Church. On the other hand, his theological synthesis has engaged such diverse interests as psychology, social theory, art, psychoanalysis, and physics more characteristically and with greater apparent success in an *external dialogue* with Academy.

This success might well lead one to affirm Tillich's method and program as *the* avenue for communicating the Gospel in the academic world. One can only be grateful for the cohesive power with which Tillich combats what Jacques Barzun calls the forces of fragmentation within the house of intellect. Tillich has generated a language in which he can communicate on many subjects with many people within the Academy of America in the atomic-space age. But one must also ask whether Tillich has provided a foundation of conviction on which to combat the more fundamental problem delineated by Barzun; namely, the intellectual's alienation from anti-intellectual culture which has turned Intellect's critical energies into defensiveness toward "outsiders" and annihilatory pronouncements upon creativity and even upon itself.

This question must be analyzed both from the standpoint of the truth of Academy and the truth of the Gospel. Within the Academy, Tillich would no doubt be most willing to have his contribution evaluated in the area of philosophy, and indeed it is precisely here in the realm of ontology that the crucial issue resides. Tillich begins with the ontic apprehensions fundamental to all human thought and expressed in the role of the verb "to be" in human language. He assumes that language correctly and satisfactorily mirrors the nature of reality. This allows him to postulate as necessary a ground of being, or abyss of being, being-itself, and a *meonic,* negational nonbeing, which he describes as beyond, beneath, and above being and beings, sustaining or threatening them.

Once in ancient Greece the psychic health of one man implanted a fundamental flaw in all of philosophical psychology. For Socrates it was no doubt true that to know the good was to do it. This psychic superiority, however, stamping its impression on the structure of Greek psychologies, left the whole philosophical tradition with no mechanism for dealing with the problem of the will. Similarly, Tillich's personal apprehension of being is so immediate, and his skill in articulating it into a coherent ontology is so consummate, that the difficulties others may experience in espousing a doctrine of being are concealed. We are left unaware that Tillich's initial cognitive act, the affirmation of being, is undeniably an act of faith. That Plato, Aristotle, Origen, Augustine, and Aquinas have shared Tillich's certainty does not make it any more or less than a prelogical presupposition found fruitful by man but not susceptible of incontrovertible proof.[6] The acceptance of Tillich's ontology, then, is not different in kind from the acceptance of the Christian Gospel, and in fact there are many who do not affirm the Christian faith but do accept an ontological one. From the side of a non-anti-ontological philosophy, John Herman Randall, Jr., recognizes with Tillich the importance of ontology, but questions whether Tillich's particular ontology is not itself a kind of krypto-theology unacceptable as a legitimate part of philosophy.[7]

Of what significance is this criticism in our quest for an adequate basis on which to place theology among the arts and sciences? First, we are dealing quite literally with the *essential foundation* of Tillich's philosophical theology. It is so central, in fact, that we might almost designate his systematic thinking neither philosophy nor theology but "theontology." Further, his entire attempt to *communicate* the Christian Gospel in the academic world hangs upon the acceptance of his ontology. Presumably it is useful because it provides an indisputably common ground in which theology and all other cognitive endeavors are rooted, so that through this rootage and this ground real communication takes place. The success of this approach is by no means automatic. There was a time in Germany long ago, before Soviet tyranny discredited Marxist communism in the eyes of the Western world, when Tillich hoped that it might be possible to correct communism from within. He erected his Religious Socialism on an ontological foundation and hoped to "slide" this same ontological base underneath Marxism so that the insights of Religious Socialism could be brought over into communism to reform it internally. Tillich soon abandoned this approach. It proved unsuccessful not only because many communist thinkers rejected Tillich's ontology, but also because even granting a common base in being, they proved adamant against any change communicated through the ontological channel.[8]

This extreme example can alert us to the limitations of Tillich's universal ontological foundation for thought. There are many citizens of Academy who are persuaded by Tillich's analysis of modern man, illuminated by his analysis of culture, of art or of history, who are not at all convinced by the theology which is designed to fit into his "neutral" structure and to answer his ontological questions. Some merely stop listening when theological considerations overtly emerge and take over the center of interest; others are actively disappointed; some even feel betrayed when they sense that a Christian theology has been smuggled into their thinking. From the other side, more ingenuous theologians wonder whether Tillich's God of Abraham, Isaac, and Jacob, which, "against Pascal," he holds to be the God of the philosophers,[9] really is the God they know through the Biblical revelation.

These comments do not amount to a repudiation of the Tillichian option for communicating the Gospel in the academic world. Rather, they amount to a suggestion that this option is not exclusively valid and relevant for our time, a suggestion that the present attempt need not strike out on Tillichian lines. If we have failed to choose both Reinhold Niebuhr and Paul Tillich from among our three potential guides, however, have we not burned our bridges, since we are left with only the improbable conductor, " the Tertullian of today," Karl Barth? We must come to this conclusion, if we assume that apologetics (*external dialogue* on the fringes of assimilation) is the only viable posture for Theology in the Academy. The very name of Karl Barth stands for a radical rejection of any conscious apologetic to culture. His *Nein* rings as clear as ever against apologetics, against natural theology, against a general ontology, against " orders of *creation*," or any other " first-article " theology. The door would seem closed for anyone to become a " Barthian apologist " in any sense.

To attack the problem from a different starting point: *which* Karl Barth (if any) has taught us something we might take with us into the American Academy if we wish to communicate the Christian Gospel to its citizens? The young liberal lies buried beneath the rubble of World War I, and the disciple of the Christian Socialists, Kutter and Ragaz, belongs in the same past with Tillich's Religious Socialism. The author of Romans seems at first the least likely candidate among the Barths, for it was he who proclaimed the " infinite qualitative distinction " between God and man, including the man of Academy. But we must remember that this apparently Tertullianesque theology placed all men — theologians, philosophers, scientists, and artists — and all institutional structures of Church and State in and under the same crisis, the same judgment of God. This accomplished two things: it established a kind of common footing for all; and it provided a pungent description of a palpably weak and threatened culture. The long-range result of Barth's liberation of theology from culture *within the Academy* was that it put him in a unique position to initiate the necessary critique of the Hitlerized culture with which traditional State-Church theology, both conservative and liberal, was hopelessly entangled. Still, as Barth himself has long since recognized, it would be a mistake to absolutize such a troubled, atypical time. He now wishes his theology to be remembered, used, and tested not merely in terms of its historical relevance, but first of all as to its internal validity within the living, continuing stream of dogmatics produced by the Christian Church.

With the starting point of our investigation thus fixed within the Gospel and not within some particular Academic tradition or on so-called neutral ground, it is extremely important in what follows in this chapter for us not to expect to proceed on the basis of an "unbiased, presupposition-free" view of man and the world, or on some traditionally accepted common definition of humanism or of cosmology. We must allow this theology to proceed on its own basis, for the present, to an understanding of man and his world — including the Academy. Only when this has been accomplished should the citizen of Academy not committed to the Christian Gospel begin deciding whether Protestant theology has anything to say to him about man, his world, and especially existence in the Academy. It is precisely because we suspect that this critical evaluation will find convictions about intellectual man and his truth needed in Academy that we turn to this Barth of the "theology of the Word of God." for it has become increasingly clear that the word of this theology is *Reconciliation*.

Academy, ever since the Enlightenment, has prided itself on freedom from the Church. The very fact that we find this word of Reconciliation in the theology *of* the Church, *by* the Church, and *for* the Church would seem to discourage any attempt to live in "the world," in the free neutral Academy, on the basis of a theology about Reconciliation. Barth continues to insist that the Church must remain the Church, only the Church, and that the intellectual servant of the Reconciliation can serve it best, and perhaps only by writing, explaining, and perpetuating Church Dogmatics. Yet I would suggest an analogy that may help us use in the Academy this understanding of human life.

In the field of dogmatics, Barth's use of the so-called Christological starting point is revolutionary; no earlier theology so radically finds and maintains its source and center in the Reconciliation. An analogous revolution occurred in the realm of theoretical physics with Einstein's theory of relativity. Einstein's discovery has had literally world-shaking implications, but those who are most intimately acquainted with its inherent possibilities tell us that the surface of its potential has hardly yet been scratched. Until now we have been able to utilize only Einstein's *special* theory of relativity. The almost incomprehensible value of his discovery will only become evident, we are told, when his *general* theory of relativity is fully exploited. It is my belief that the theology of Reconciliation has an analogous potential. Barth has rediscovered in the New Testament a *cosmic* reconciliation, which applies to the whole of reality. What he himself has constructed with relentless consistency and urged his followers to continue is a kind of " special doctrine of Reconciliation," a Church Dogmatics seeking the implications of Reconciliation for the Church, while what awaits execution is a " general doctrine of Reconciliation," built on the same foundation. Perhaps we may begin to be able to discern the shape of " general Reconciliation," and how the Gospel might be communicated in Academy on the basis of it, as we investigate Barth's own discovery.

THE RECONCILIATION AND ITS COMMUNICATOR

A theology about Reconciliation must be rooted in the classical Pauline formulation, II Cor. 5:19: " God was in Christ reconciling the world to himself, . . . and entrusting to us the message of reconciliation." This is the Gospel, the Word of Reconciliation, which is the heart of Christian conviction. The Christian is aware of being determined by the reality it describes. A theology of Reconciliation does not capture and imprison the Word so as to become an imperious Queen of the Sciences dictating to her Academic subjects. Theology is merely the conscious witness to the Word of Reconciliation and, from time to time, other Academic disciplines may unconsciously, in the legitimate pursuit of their own business, bear more effective witness to this Word than does Theology. The Word of Reconciliation is not a theology; it is a vision of reality, a story, a Gospel, the Christian Gospel. It is the Gospel that Christianity would communicate in the Academic world.

The first question that Paul's statement of Reconciliation incites in an inquiring intellect is an epistemological one: Where is God to be found? The answer we receive is that he *was in Christ*. He *is* not decisively revealed in nature (as for all primitivists from the priests of Baal and Dionysus to Rousseau, Picasso, and D. H. Lawrence). Nor *is* he immanent (and transcendent) in rationality (as for all essentialists from the pre-Platonic Pythagoreans through Hegel and Tillich). Nor *is* he within general or special human experience (as for all " psychologists of religion," from the disciples of Augustine's *Confessions* through John Wesley and C. G. Jung). He *was* not merely with, behind, beyond, and under Jesus of Nazareth. He *was*, in a way uniquely decisive for Christian knowledge, *in* Jesus Christ, and only *through* him was and is God redemptively present for man. Therefore, to the related question, *What* is to be found in Christ? the incredible answer is, All (theological) knowledge.

In the God-become-man, Christian theology finds God, the true God and all of God, Creator, Judge, Redeemer. It discovers, with equal force, its particular perspective on man, on all sorts and conditions of men. With its key of the event of Reconciliation, Theology is not simply dependent on an Augustinian dialectic between Original Righteousness and Original Sin. Nor does it blithely affirm either a Renaissance, Enlightened or Romantic optimism, or an ashtray-cartoon brand of original sin that says, " People are no damn good." It claims to see *beyond* optimism and pessimism, or an unresolved tension between the two, and realistically to affirm *there* a New Humanity. It finds *man* in his innocence (at Christmas) and his misery (on Maundy Thursday and Good Friday) and his glory (on Easter and Ascension Day).

The tremendous implications of Reconciliation for the Christian affirmation of Humanity Barth has put in a nutshell in such an essay as *The Humanity of God,* and at length in Volume IV of the *Church Dogmatics,* especially in Book 2. There to illustrate how we receive knowledge of humanity he uses the illuminating figure of the " Royal Man " to carry us into the *activity* of God in Christ. The Royal Man, like the Prodigal Son of Luke, ch. 15, goes into a far country; or, in Pauline terms, he who is equal with God has "emptied himself, taking the form of a servant " (Phil. 2:7). In the active person of the divine servant we see that Reconciliation tacitly includes alienation, estrangement, within itself. In the reconciling act, the life of the Royal Man, *man* sees himself squandering his natural gifts, *wasting* his *substance* in riotous living. It is, then, the Royal Man as the bearer of all Humanity who knows himself estranged from the Father, alienated from the continuing source of all his good. But " alienation " and " estrangement " are not the final decisive realities for man. The Prodigal Son returned to the Father's house, expecting to "work off" his debt in continuing alienation. Instead, he is reconciled, reunited with the Father. In the Royal Man, man as man is (and may know himself as) reconciled beyond estrangement and alienation to the source of good for the whole of empirical reality. This is the basis on which Christianity radically affirms humanity. Of this reconciled man the supposedly Tertullianesque Barth can say that *he* must become the measure of all things.

Though "alienation" and "estrangement" are part of the everyday vocabulary of his self-understanding, paradoxically modern American man, child of the Freudian Ethic, often fails to recognize the metaphor of Reconciliation as one of the most valid symbols remaining in the classical Christian vocabulary. We are aware of subconscious oedipal conflicts and of the enormously complex psychosexual forces that can destroy parental-filial harmony and marital relationship; but though we expect knowledge to exorcize nameless dread and to help us endure these tensions, we stop short of fully acknowledging and affirming the reconciling love that claims to resolve them. The Biblical witness to Reconciliation is rooted in precisely this world which the Freudian Ethic has familiarized for us. The ambivalent relations of father and son are the basis for understanding the history of God and Israel together in Hos., ch. 11: "When Israel was a child, then I loved him. . . . I taught Ephraim . . . to go [walk], taking them by their arms; but they knew not that I healed them. I drew them with cords of a man, with the bands of love. . . . And my people are bent to backsliding from me. . . . How shall I give thee up, Ephraim? How shall I deliver thee, Israel? . . . Mine heart is turned within me, my repentings are kindled together. I will not execute the fierceness of mine anger, I will not return to destroy Ephraim: for I am God, and not man." Here we see the whole pattern of paternal tenderness turned to rage by unresponsiveness, of filial ingratitude which characteristically will not submit to charitable constraint, and of the father's disciplinary love which will restore and not destroy. Nor are the explicitly sexual dimensions of all man's intimate concerns lost on Hosea, whose most frequent metaphor makes of Israel the unfaithful wife promiscuously casting her affections to unworthy para-

mours. Yet beyond all marital tensions, all covert and overt unfaithfulness, beyond all oedipal conflicts, Hosea speaks his decisive word,
the word of Reconciliation: " Therefore, behold, I will allure her,
and bring her into the wilderness, and speak comfortably to her. . . .
And I will betroth . . . [her] unto me for ever. . . . And I will have
mercy upon her that had not obtained mercy; and I will say to them
which were not my people, Thou art my people; and they shall say,
Thou art my God " (ch. 2:14, 19, 23; see ch. 1:10). Already here in
Hosea, the Biblical vision of redemption centers in Reconciliation,
in what Tillich refers to as the reunion of the estranged, in the re-
establishment of vital, integral human wholeness which for the
Biblical mentality can only be rooted in the primal community of
man and wife, father and son.

    In addition to the *in*tensely personal quality of Reconciliation in
Hosea, II Cor. 5:18 f. bears witness to a vast *ex*tensive dimension essential to " Paul's Gospel," found in the daring claim that in Christ,
God reconciled the *world* to himself. What Paul proclaims is not
merely the Reconciliation of the Church to God, but also and equally
the Reconciliation of the extraecclesiastical *kosmos,* the ordered universe outside the Church. Barth suggests that Church and world
can be related to each other graphically as two concentric circles.
Both circles have their real *objective* center in Christ, whose lordship
over all things has been actually and permanently established in
God's reconciling act. The mark that distinguishes between the men
of the two circles — and this alone leads Barth to think of the
Church as the inner of the two — is that the Church by definition
is that organic human reality which acknowledges and proclaims
that *its* center and essence is the Royal Man, the reconciling Christ.
The " world," on the other hand, is defined by its inability or refusal to " cognize " and acknowledge the centrality of its Reconciliation to God, which is also the essence of *its* actual order. This
real *subjective* differentiation between the Church and the other
structures of the cosmos does not lead Barth to undo his earliest
assertion, namely, that man does not control God. God remains free
to reveal himself not through the Church but through the " world "
and, specifically, the State, or the Academy, even at their most
antithetic.

    Barth has always refused to lay down principles or guidelines by which to test whether or not a political party, for example, is bearing witness to the Reconciliation through its program in general. Is it possible, then, that Barth's " universalism " or his " Christological monism " can provide us with a clue for the centripetal movement needed by the divided house of intellect? Does the statement " Christian epistemology is Jesus Christ " shed any light on all knowledge? Does the theology about Reconciliation have anything to do with physics and music after all? Dietrich Bonhoeffer can affirm a world-come-of-age on a Christological foundation, and try to establish a way of speaking to and for a nonreligious Christianity; but for Barth himself the Church in order to be the Church must speak *in the Church for all the world to hear* the word that God has reconciled the *world* to himself. The spelling out of a " general theology of Reconciliation " for the establishment of conviction in the non-ecclesiastical Academy has not been seriously attempted. If Reconciliation is to be used as the foundation for understanding the relation between Theology and the Academy, however, some such " general " scheme will be needed.

The loaded word in this statement, the word that demands immediate clarification is — general! We must ask, From which direction is the *general* Reconciliation to be established? And we must answer, From the same direction as is the *general* resurrection! One is reminded of the convention on philosophy of religion at which, following a paper on the resurrection of Christ, a philosopher rose to his feet and reflectively posed the question: " Let's see now, what would be the general concept of resurrection? " It is precisely Paul's point in I Cor., ch. 15, that the Christian logic of resurrection must be an " inverted " syllogism, contravening conventional logic. There is no general principle of resurrection of which Christ's rising is a particular example, no general class of resurrected men to which Jesus belongs as a particular case. The philosopher's general logic concerning resurrection could only be: Major premise — men do not rise from the dead; minor premise — Jesus Christ was a man; conclusion — Jesus Christ did not rise from the dead! Paul's inverted logic (inducing generality from the scandalously single particularity) runs: Jesus Christ rose from the dead; Jesus Christ was and is full, complete, and representative man; therefore, man shall not be conquered by his last enemy, death (I Cor. 15:26). And the message of Reconciliation moves in the same direction as this inverted syllogism of resurrection.

What would be a *general* Reconciliation of the world to God in Christ? We are immediately tempted to make the " natural " mistake of our philosopher of religion questing for general concepts. Insofar as Theology has considered itself a branch of philosophy it has separated nature and grace and then generated a theism in which it began with a " natural " theology it claimed the " natural " man accepts naturally; it began with a " general " revelation available without grace or faith and then added " special " revelation which demonstrates how grace completes good but imperfect nature. The Academic man not committed to Christianity is supposed to be forced to agree with Christian theism about the nature of man in general; he is supposed to balk, if at all, only after philosophy " becomes Christian " by adding faith and grace, Christology, Trinity, and salvation. This kind of " Christian philosophizing," however ancient, honorable, and majestic it may be, fails to do justice to the revolutionary character of Paul's inverted syllogism. It is not Adam, the natural Everyman, who decisively and permanently defines man in general. The Jesus of the Christian Gospel is not a general repairman, simply undoing the damage incurred through Adam's tumble. Paul's Gospel takes a radical change of direction from the fulcrum point of scandalous particularity in Jesus Christ. He is the man who is the measure of all things. Because of him the destiny of man in general is no longer death but resurrection to *life*. Because of him the cosmos itself is reconciled with God.

Is there not, however, an analogy that corresponds with reconciliation, and is more accessible to experience than is resurrection? If there is, it cannot be an expected recurrent happening, function, or process, but would have to be an unexpected, unique bestowal, like a general amnesty. A general amnesty creates a new category out of its beneficiaries and sets them free to become what they are subsequently, irrespective of their earlier history. This is the fundamental value of using the analogy of the general amnesty for the cosmic Reconciliation. Its limitation is that an amnesty affects only the *status* of men within society and before the law. It does not provide a new being for the amnestied men. The Reconciliation for Paul, however, is a creative power, so that the reconciled cosmos and its living members are new creatures. Still, the amnesty does aid us in viewing the Reconciliation insofar as its beneficiaries are defined by a past event, a fresh eruption of freedom which opens the way for a new reality.

At this point, having tried to suggest in what sense Reconciliation provides a positive base for a general understanding of man, it becomes imperative to face the other question on which our entire study must stand or fall: What has the one total, general Reconciliation to do with *Truth,* specifically, the Truth of Academy? The Reconciliation as we have described it can only mean that Truth is somehow, finally one and not many, unifying and not divisive. This affirmation in ages of optimism seems almost a banal commonplace. At various times confidence in the ubiquitous validity of ideal forms, in the universal permeation of the cosmos by an integral rationality, in the wholeness of the fabric of materiality, in the unbroken chain mail nexus of causality, or in the inexorable intent of Fate or Nature or Providence, was held to guarantee the oneness of Truth. For most sensitive moderns, however, alienation, brokenness, contingency, indeterminacy, and the relativism which atomizes reality destroy all ease and confidence in the unity of Truth. Not only do they not think that Truth is of a piece wherever it is found, they do not even have the slightest confidence that the particular, limited truths we do trust are pointing in anything like the same direction. This is indeed precisely the main manifestation of the crisis of conviction that threatens the life of the modern Academy.

To meet this crisis in which a splintered world presents us with fragments of truth but cannot satisfy its hunger for wholeness, Christianity has only one unique source of strength. This is not found in the unity of the natural order, or even in the hope of a final perfected whole. It is found in the Reconciliation. The Christian, who has experienced God's Reconciliation, can find the vision of Paul the most *universal* of all affirmations: God was in Christ reconciling the cosmos to himself. If this is the fundamental Christian statement about the nature of reality now, it means much more than that the Church has its conscious center in the Reconciler; it means that all truths have the same one ultimate objective foundation and guarantee, regardless of the divergent individual apprehensions of truth.

To be sure, the Christian makes this affirmation of the oneness of the cosmos and then of the oneness of Truth as a human being: finite, limited in time, in space, in apprehension, and certainly also limited in the power of his faith. This means that the Christian is no more able to guarantee the unity of Truth than is any other human being; the mere fact of his Christian affirmation of Reconciliation does not automatically give an intellectual the ability to describe the convergence of truths. What does happen is that the Christian who is a citizen of Academy experiences and participates in the oneness created by the all-embracing Reconciliation. He is now free to begin searching for clues that indicate that every legitimate approach to reality discovers a part of the one Truth essential to his existence, to his self-understanding, to his integrity as the practitioner of an Academic discipline. He is free to do so, and it may well be part of the business of the Christian in Academy to bear witness to the unity of Truth and to help discover its implications.

"God was in Christ reconciling the world to himself . . . and entrusting to *us* the message of reconciliation." In this " Apostolic we " (us), Paul has included the presentation of the message about Reconciliation within God's very act of reconciling. He was doubtless primarily interested here in asserting the legitimacy of his own role. But this " us " also means that the " message of reconciliation " is entrusted to all Christians. In this sense, each Christian communicates the Gospel somehow or other, whether he will or no. Each is a communicator, an ambassador, as Paul says in the next breath (II Cor. 5:20). There are, however, many different " countries " in which Christians serve the same message of the one total Reconciliation. And each " country " has, so to speak, its own language or languages which the ambassadors to it must speak and in which they must communicate the Gospel. The country that concerns us is the Academy, with its own highly developed customs and languages, and with a long history of acquaintance with the Church and its truth. What we are seeking to do is to utilize the implications of the discovery that the world participates in God's Reconciliation in the same objective way as does the Church. Therefore, we must now investigate what it means for a theologian to be an ambassador to this country, for a Christian "communicator" to participate in the life and work of the academic world.

First of all, let it be said that being an ambassador of the Reconciliation does not mean that one can be a foreign body in the *corpus Academicus*. *The Christian's primary citizenship is in the reconciled cosmos, the two concentric circles including Church and Academy.* If he is also qualified for the work of the Academy, he knows himself as belonging in and committed to the academic world in a particular way. We have identified the theologian as a servant of the Word of Reconciliation in a cosmos where the Church imperfectly acknowledges that Reconciliation and the Academy unconsciously, sometimes unwillingly, but often more effectively testifies to it. For the question, Who shall teach theology in the Academy? this ambiguity seems to create more problems than it solves. In the first place, theology has been inseparably woven into the fabric of Western culture. This suggests that everyone, or at least every brand of historian, in Academy should teach theology. And in fact many academicians in the pursuit of their disciplines, which today are usually done *independently* of theology, must understand and give authentic expression to the theological texture of life and thought in the West. It is bad scholarship to assume that Dante and Bunyan and Dostoevsky are either modern " secular humanists " or are inferior insofar as they fall short of this plane our intellectuals have achieved. It is bad scholarship to interpret their attempts to theologize as, for example, so many writhings on the shaft of the Freudian pin which impales them. And when the fundamental nature of science is investigated to its philosophical depths by a Copernicus, a Newton, or a Darwin, the positive as well as the negative effects of his religious convictions must be taken into account.

On a second and more direct level Academy engages Theology when modern intellectuals, who are themselves members of the academic community or else by their creativity provide the vitality that sustains it, essay a dialogue with conviction using theological symbols. A Toynbee may find man's religion the essence of his history; a Jung may discover religion to be a necessity of man's psychic life; an Ingmar Bergman, an Albert Camus, and certain of the dramatists of the Theatre of the Absurd may find the religious questions the most interesting ones to which art can address itself. Their ideas and their works must be evaluated by canons of academic criticism *and* as attempts to theologize; but we are still talking about theology in a secondary and a derived sense.

Overt theology in the Academy, however, obviously arises out of the study of the Bible, its history, its literature, its interpretation, and out of the study of Christianity, of Christians, and of the Church — the faith, the life, the thought. We shall have to ask in later chapters: What right have these *studies* to be in the Academy? What is their role? What is their relationship to other disciplines? Here, however, we ask about the *person* who teaches these disciplines in Academy. To whom or what are his loyalties and responsibilities? Since we are considering the teaching of and learning about the Biblical-Christian reality in the Academy, rather than any form of "indoctrination in Christianity" which might be undertaken in a sectarian seminary or professional Divinity School, we might expect the Academy to produce, train, discipline, and employ its own specialists in Religion committed to its own catholic visions of universal truth and common humanity. Should not the Academy produce its own theologians, just as it produces art historians, botanists, analysts of literature, of government, and of the human psyche? Such theologians would be responsible to their students, their colleagues, to the officers and trustees of the Academy which provides them with bread and with a spiritual nourishment beyond bread. Like their colleagues in all disciplines they would be responsible to their material, to represent it objectively and faithfully.

But when we look at those who do in fact theologize in the Academy we discover just how important *conviction* is for this particular professional concern of the Academy. The majority of those who care to be involved in knowledge of the Biblical-Christian reality are themselves graduates of some ecclesiastical institution of higher learning, and most of them are rabbis, or priests, or ministers of the Church. This in itself seems discouraging to anyone who wishes Academy to sponsor theological disciplines for it suggests empirically that theology even in the Academy is properly the business of the Church. Theology appears pragmatically to be one of those disciplines, and there are many in Academy, which is the legitimate concern only of those who are unable to ignore it. And such people make up the Church or, less frequently, an Anti-church.

But if his is the business of the Church, does the theologian belong in the nonecclesiastical Academy at all? Is he free and able to serve God in the Academy *and* be true to the scholarly values to which *it* is dedicated, whether it be " Christian," " neutral," or " secular "? The Church from its formative moments through its struggle against Hitler has ultimately said about its theology: " We must obey God rather than men." [10] But this is necessary to state in such polemic terms only when " men," in the Jewish *ecclesia* of the first century or the idolatrous German state of the twentieth, declare open war on the humanity of man and on the truth which sets men free. Ordinarily the Academy, true to its own business of serving humanizing truth, presents its Christian and Jewish theologians with the gift of freedom to pursue their vision of Truth and Humanity. In this normal case the theologian can find no conflict between his ultimate loyalty to " God " and his complete commitment to the " men " of the Academy. The theologian in the Academy does not ever appeal, even secretly, to any " special status " or to his relationship to God as his guarantee for " truths," or for " ultimately correct " interpretations of facts!

Does this, then, make him unconditionally responsible to scholarship? Yes, he is responsible to true scholarship at every moment. This is *his* reasonable service, *his* logical duty, the dedication of *his* actual existence to God (Rom. 12:1). Like the *manual* craftsman of Ecclus. 38:34, whose prayer is in the handiwork of his craft, the Judeo-Christian academic man fulfills his reasonable service to God in *his* vocation, the exercise of *reason*. The theologian, like any man of the Academy, must abide by the internal necessities of his own discipline, for nothing else than a strict adherence to his perpective on truth is objective scholarship. He must also, however, be open to the whole truth, to total objectivity, to *all* of the facts and to no fancy. The theological scholar is as fully human as each of his colleagues, constantly in danger of forgetting the strengths and limitations which the nature of his discipline imposes upon him. He must always exercise each of his disciplinary tools as rigorously as possible and follow them loyally and honestly, and as far as they will go. He must trust his scholarship wherever it leads him. This is an essential part of his Christian commitment to the one Truth.

Further, of course, this attitude extends to the academic institution which provides material support of his endeavor. The theolo-

gian is committed to a totally responsible attitude toward his
Academy. He will credit and depend upon the commitment to
Truth and Humanity on the part of Academy. Then and only then
does he have to expect and to command the freedom to understand
Truth and Humanity from his peculiar perspective. This relationship will also determine his attitude toward his students. No more
than his colleagues will he look upon them as simply plastic stuff to
be forced into the mold of his indoctrination, as raw recruits to be
dragged and hounded and pounded through an intellectual obstacle
course. When he demands discipline and exacts standards of precision he does so out of a desire that the students should be growing, developing human beings committed to the search for Truth in
all things and through all human life.

Some of this has a high-sounding theoretical ring that would become hollow if we failed to speak of the inevitable *conflict* between
loyalties to Gospel and to Academy which arise in concrete cases.
One philosopher concerned with theology in the Academy has
said: "The Christian theologian is that intellectual who agrees to
be objective about everything *else*." How do we propose to resolve
the conflict contained in this barb?

The same Paul who provided us with the unified vision of a
reconciled *kosmos* seems in the first chapter of I Corinthians to perceive a fundamental contradiction within *cognition* when he sets
wisdom over against folly. He who, according to Acts, ch. 17, was
judged foolish by Stoic and Epicurean philosophers in Athens itself,
here differentiates between the wisdom of God as Christianity knows
it and the "world's" love of wisdom (Greek philosophy) which rejects God's wisdom as folly. Paul sees God's wisdom and power in
the self-revealing weakness of "the cross," which he proclaims and
the world calls folly.

If this antithesis between two kinds of truth were taken as final,
one might conclude that a Christian could only be a kind of enemy
agent in the Academy, and that Theology is, after all, an illegitimate
pursuit in the Academy both from the standpoint of the wisdom of
God and from the standpoint of the Academy's wisdom of the
world.[11] Yet when we place the whole paradoxical structure of
I Cor., ch. 1, within the context of the central Christian affirmation
of Reconciliation, many things become clear about the relation

between God's wisdom and the wisdom of the world, and also between Theology, the Church, and the Academy. We have represented the whole cosmos by a large circle which has received a radically unifying center in the reconciling act of God in Christ, and the Church by a smaller concentric circle within the cosmic one. The Church is *in* the world by virtue of the one, total Reconciliation, but it is not *of* the world, by virtue of the one fact that the Church speaks about the Reconciler. Paul refers to himself, as we have referred to the theologian, as "entrusted with the message of reconciliation," the "word of the cross" with which he confronts the wisdom of the world. Paul, and with him the theologian in the Academy, clearly *is* the Church in the world. Shall the theologian in Academy, then, produce *Church* dogmatics and only that? Shall he not leave the (academic) world to its wisdom and attempt to be true to the folly of God and only that, even if it is again rejected by the wisdom of the (academic) world?

When "the Church" speaks in the Church it speaks what it affirms and partly understands and imperfectly knows how to express in life, in its own peculiar language, the language of Jerusalem and not of Athens. Within the Church "the Church" proclaims its word primarily in this language, and the inquirer must come and learn this language to "hear" the message entrusted to the Church. In the Church the Church ordains men to proclaim this word in a manner accurate and relevant to the Biblical witness. To train these men the Church maintains its theological seminary. Normally, in this country, this seminary is not a direct and integral part of "the world's" Academy. The seminary is a trade school, a professional school of the Church for the sake of its special trades, professions, occupations. As the law school, the medical school, the technical school, or the business school serve the legal, medical, engineering, and business "trades" or professions, so the theological seminary serves the Church. How should not such a school, concerned with ecclesiastics and Church polity and the art of preaching not speak a "medical jargon," a "legal Latin" all its own? And why should not the Divinity School be the professional judge of the validity and usefulness of any new theological discovery, just as the medical school and medical profession test drugs developed by the chemistry department of Academy? In short, when "the

Church " speaks in the Church it may speak about the folly of God
in a language that is not the language of Athens. The language it
uses may not be, or may no longer be spoken in other corners and
fields of Academy. When " the Church " speaks in the Academy,
however, it must still speak of the folly of God, but it must do so in
one of the languages of the wisdom of the world. If the Gospel is
to be communicated, if Theology is to do business in the country of
Academy, it must deal in the linguistic currency of the land.

Even so, can the academic world, " the world " as Academy, admit
a discipline whose ultimate justification is not the wisdom of the
world, but that " wisdom of God " once judged foolish? Many
things have happened since Plato first met with his like-minded
contemporaries in the first academic grove. Much has transpired
since the wisdom of the Stoics and Epicureans laughed Paul off the
Areopagus. Many gods have died, many wise words have beaten on
the empty air with none to hear, and trembled away into silence.
Many academies have been born to strut in youthful pride, then
been dissolved into fragmentary specializations as the result of some
crisis of conviction. Sometimes the Church has had to protect, to
sustain, and to nurture the Academy and its truth; often the Church
has learned to express its word in the languages of the Academy.
The language of Nicaea had not been the language of Jerusalem,
any more than had the Platonism of Augustine, the Aristotelianism
of Aquinas, or the philosophies used by Protestants in the last two
centuries. For that matter the very language of Jerusalem, the language of Canaan, had itself to be pruned and shaped before it could
be used by Israel, by the Church. " The Church " has always proclaimed the Word of God in borrowed language. This hunger for
new and richer, *living* language of men has repeatedly brought the
Church to the Academy.

The modern Academy, of course, has precise tools with which to
test the use of language, borrowed or freshly coined, in cognitive
work. Is not a self-respecting Academy, willing to stand up for its
rights, its tests of truth, competent to test the validity of theological
language — and find it wanting? How can the wisdom of men now
avoid repeating its rejection of the folly of God? Perhaps we must
begin to answer this question by recognizing that whenever any discipline in Academy seriously asks, What is Man? and What is

Truth? it risks folly. Academy in Paul's day was experiencing a crisis of conviction, yet the philosophical wisdom of men was still sufficiently agreed upon the framework of its own folly with respect to Truth and to Man to refuse the " folly of God " which did not fit the frame. Today, however, no such comprehensive common frame exists, no such folly is generally received by Academy. Scientific wisdom cannot guarantee the existence of Sophia, the philosopher's mistress, at all. Philosophy can only bear witness to its vision of wisdom in philosophical language within the Academy. The Academy can question and challenge the consistency of this language, it can interrogate the philosopher as to what his language "means" and as to how it applies to reality. The Academy with its various perspectives can pragmatically evaluate the humanity, the style of life, that philosophy creates and sustains. But Academy can neither verify nor invalidate philosophy's love of wisdom, its claim to wholeness of seeing or penetration beyond (meta-) physics. Similarly, a behavioral psychologist, or sociologist or anthropologist can devise and operate methods and techniques which again the Academy as a whole with its command of general statistical methodology and scientific reasoning can follow, challenge, and perhaps even verify or falsify. The Academy can also pragmatically evaluate the kind of humanity which Behaviorism describes and creates. But the Academy can neither warrant nor categorically negate the premise that man *is* his behavior.

Similarly, Theology comes to the Academy with its wisdom governed and controlled ultimately only by the folly of God. In the Academy, however, the theologian as "the Church" speaks about God, makes cognitive response to the revelation, the folly, of God in language common to the expressions of the wisdom of men. As in the case of the philosopher or the "behavioral scientist" the cognitive response of the theologian, his theology, can be questioned, challenged, tested by Academy for its consistency as speech in the language of the wisdom of men. Further, the Academy can and should evaluate pragmatically the humanity, the style of living which Theology not only proclaims but also produces. *Understood and defined in this way theo-logy, speech about God, cognitive response to God's revelation, is a legitimate attempt to communicate the Gospel in the Academic world: legitimate from the standpoint of the Church which produces it and from the standpoint of the Academy whose concern is the intellectual quest for Truth and Humanity.*

If we have been able to establish the *legitimacy* of theology as an academic discipline, we have not yet made sufficiently clear its *value* to either the Church or the Academy. Although the details of this task will occupy the rest of the book, it may be well at this point to suggest the areas of theology's usefulness. First, for the Church, Theology in the Academy presents certain responsibilities and certain potentially creative challenges. The Church, in the Church, in its dogmatics, will always reserve the right to test the language of " the Church " in Academy by the criteria of its essence, the folly of God, Jesus Christ. The Church must do this for the sake of its own health and vigor, and for the sake of " the Church " in the Academy.

The Church, however, may also have to pay attention to the theology in the Academy *humbly,* accepting the challenge and judgment. When the Church produces theologians for the Academy, it tacitly confesses that the God who reconciles the cosmos to himself will not limit his concern to the inner circle which acknowledges its awareness of this gracious act. Even when the Church makes its best effort at living on the basis of Reconciliation, it ought always to be aware of the world outside the Church which sometimes more effectively expresses the Reconciliation. This does not relieve the Church of its responsibility to fulfill its service to the Word of Reconciliation. The Church must remember that God's Word, even though it may be forcibly locked up in its bones, becomes a fire not to be contained (Jer. 20:9). And when it looks with candid eye at the citizens of the Academy, the Church will see that in the House of Intellect are many of the ablest sons and daughters of the Church whom the Church by less than its best effort has driven away and estranged from awareness of God's Reconciliation. Should not, then, the Church in the Church be humbly grateful for a theology that can speak about God in language that these best minds understand and respect? Is it not precisely in the Academy itself, in the outer circle of the reconciled world that the Church should create theology to meet honest, demanding "inquirers"? It has been the experience of the present writer, multiplied over and

over, that the most constructive theology — not only the most exciting and sensitively creative but also that which builds humane
lives — in the Academy has come from those first freed by contempt
from the stultified conventionality of the human institution which
calls itself *ecclesia*. The Church should be humbly grateful for these
human beings who become aware of God's Reconciliation outside
its human inner circle. And the Church should also be grateful for
the content of the theology addressed to it from the Academy. In
the first place, the Church is *nourished* by the fresh vitality of the
speech about God in the language of the wisdom of men, even while
the Church *tests* it on the standard of God's folly. And in the
second place, the Church may find itself judged by the speech about
God in language not yet its own. The prophets, all being " the
Church " in the world, all brought into the Church words against
the Church which were true speech about God. It may be that the
Church again today may have to learn to hear language learned in
Academy " against " the Church, when it listens to theology forged
in the citadel of Truth and Humanity.

And in its turn, the Academy: How can and should Theology
serve it? What has the wisdom of men to gain from those who
speak of the folly of God? An answer to this is perhaps suggested
by the fact that Theology in its necessary attention to the folly of
God makes the most daring claims about Man at his extreme limits.
On the one hand, it is insistent on the limitations of man, on his
relativity, his finitude, his being-conditioned. Let behaviorists speak
of social determinism and cultural relativity, let Freudians speak
of a determinism that reaches into the inner life of the mind. Theology will speak of the infinitely free Subject who defines us as objects by his action even while he enables us to respond freely to
him as though he were the object of our finite thought. On the other
hand, let Idealism and Enlightenment speak to alienated men,
chronically at war with others and with themselves, of Man's infinite possibilities; let science unfold its story of man's increasing
knowledge and control in a bewilderingly complex universe; let the
artist speak of the unlimited possibilities of man's developing and
revealing himself in his art. Theology will speak to finite, alienated
man of himself as that part of a reconciled order which God has
chosen as perpetual son and companion.

Such extravagant, even celestial, claims must be redeemable as terrestrial real estate. Such million-pound notes of faith must be convertible into the small change of everyday living for the wise man of the world to concern himself with them — and this shall be the primary business of Chapter IV. Nevertheless, such folly itself challenges all wisdom to reach down to its depths, to push back its limits, to trace its sustaining tap roots to their source, to break out beyond the sound barriers and gravitational fields that too often limit academic disciplines to purely utilitarian considerations never consciously related to the fundamental questions about Truth and Humanity.

What has Athens to do with Jerusalem? We have tried to suggest that each must *be there* for the other. But how shall we get to Athens from Jerusalem? In answer to this question we have proposed an *internal dialogue* of Theology about its own convictions, in Academic language and in Academy. And we have suggested that this *dialogue* may, in the process of internal unfolding, assume *external* dimensions as well. Yet in this chapter we have consistently focused upon the relationship between Theology and Academy from the standpoint of Jerusalem. Now it is time to turn to the Athens in which Theology must find a place to live and do its business. More accurately, we must turn to a place just outside Athens, the grove of Academe, and explore its topography.

II

The Topography of the Academy

*" Seeking truth and the improvement of mankind, the university
aims to stand for man's humanity par excellence.* Humanitas *is part
of its very fiber, no matter how often and how deeply that term has
changed its meaning."*

Karl Jaspers, The Idea of the University, *p. 134.*

*" Truth is forever the product of search. It is forever acquired and
never possessed. . . . But nothing about the nature of truth will
ever be communicated by a cold intellectualism which divorces
knowledge from human experience. If he is to learn about truth, the
student must be present as his teacher struggles to obtain it, and as
his own powers grow, he must begin to join in the battle. . . . I recognize that our students, being products of the training, indoctrination, and instruction to which we have allowed them to be exposed,
are not particularly suited for education as I have tried to define
it. . . . That is why we do not have an academic community today.
This is why students and teachers . . . do not communicate with
one another. . . . This is why there is no common faith. This is why
we are all lonely in the midst of a very large crowd."*

Frank Pinner, in The American College,
ed. by R. Nevitt Sanford; pp. 963 f.

I F JASPERS' ringing affirmation could stand alone, we would be apt
to rest, reassured about the unshakable stability and unchanging
course of higher education. We could remain smugly satisfied with
our stereotypes, preserving a vague glow, a misty nostalgia toward
" the good old college days," whether we had known them in fact
or in fiction and fancy. But beneath the surface of Jaspers' state-

ment there is an ever more difficult struggle to uphold the very things he affirms, and this conflict emerges into the open in the words of Frank Pinner, shattering our stereotypes. Community, a common faith, communication, are all strongly desired but not possessed. They seem all but unobtainable. Becoming aware of this situation demands of us a fresh overview of the territory claimed by Academy, a new survey of each portion of ground for its own sake and in relation to the rest.

THE ACADEMIC GROVE IN A TECHNOLOGICAL WORLD

At the end of the preceding chapter we suggested that the Academy is a *topos,* a place in the cosmos defined by its intellectual activity. What we now propose is to investigate this place, this Academic grove, in a kind of topographical survey which is intended as a fresh beginning, a treatment of Academy as an unknown land. Let us try, then, to disengage ourselves from familiarity, and come to Academy as it now is with freshman-freshness. Perhaps in this way we shall be able to discover something of what life and work are really like in this place, what it is that motivates and unites the rich diversity of its activities, and what draws certain activities into clusters apart from others.

In choosing this approach, we necessarily neglect, or at least relegate to a contributory role, the studies of certain problems which cannot be neglected if higher education is to survive and be of service. For example, if the Academy and the rest of the university grouped around it were treated metaphorically as a modern industrial plant we should have to ask, How is it to be financed and operated (1) productively and (2) efficiently? With nothing but respect for the importance of these problems and admiration for those who contribute to their solution, we are required by our particular task abruptly to leave this complex of questions to them. Again, if we were to treat Academy as an organic continuum, a perpetual growing ground for the fruits of man's intellectual venture in various times and places, the history of this formal setting of human life would prove interesting and instructive. But the Academic grove has suffered too many of the ravages of war, too many forest fires; too much erosion has washed away topsoil for us to expect to find Plato's planting there. Earthquakes have brought such upheavals in convictional substrata that the modern Academy would find too little of sufficient relevance to return to for this to be our primary approach. We will gratefully employ the great archaeological surveys of the uses of this site in the past, but we must concentrate our primary attention on the sprawling complex of buildings and grounds occupying the university campus today.

We shall begin, then, with the American university as it is, a conglomeration of undergraduate departments grouped in " schools " of " liberal arts " or humanities or sciences — partly by accident of Topsy-growth, partly according to roughly similar attitudes or methods and ostensibly related subject matters — together with appended graduate programs often dominating the character of the departments, and professional schools, loosely related and semi-independent, standing on the periphery of the university. Although our primary concern shall be with Academy in the narrow sense, the undergraduate liberal arts and sciences " heart " of the university, to understand this entity we shall, first, briefly have to address ourselves to the reality of the contemporary university as a whole. But when we do, we must focus our attention on what goes on precisely in the teaching-learning process in various subdivisions of this campus. The important relationships to culture, to professional concerns and research for their sake, must be subordinated to an attempt to discover the nature of the Academy which actually confronts us, and how its tasks may be done so as to utilize its real assets and fulfill its true nature. Ours is not the *universitas magistrorum et scholarium* with corporations preeminently of students as in Bologna (the first modern university) and its imitators, or of teachers as in those taking Paris (its great twelfth-century rival) as the model. Ours is also not the later literary-based *universitas litterarum,* capable of fostering such practical professional disciplines as those of medicine, law, and the Church, but never really able to relate to a technology banished to the second-rate status of a technical high(er) school. We are fortunate that our American Academy has developed during the transition into a technological age, and that our characteristically pragmatic and experimental bent of mind has left us with a strong, flexible university capable of growth and adaptation to a changing world without divorce from the riches of the past.

For the American university at its best is, proudly, a genuine " universe of knowledge." We would assert that it is still both possible and desirable to plan for and build universities in which the Academy forms not only the center and foundation for the graduate training of academicians, specialists, and scientists but also the center and foundation for the whole range of professional schools — technological as well as medical, legal, commercial, and theological — together with those for practical and creative arts. Structurally, therefore, the American academic institution is well suited to the ever-increasing complexity of modern life with its ever-changing demands upon Academy. But this very versatility of Academy goes hand in glove with Academy's crisis of conviction, for the activism which does a thousand different jobs efficiently draws the men of Academy farther and farther away from conscious foundations of conviction without allowing leisure for the contemplation and speculation necessary to rediscover them or to find new ones. Therefore, rather than studying the superstructure of Academic architecture — be it ivory tower or factory — it seems necessary for us to delve to the foundations beneath it. We must discuss the actual topography of Academy and attempt to discover something essential about the taproots of conviction which sustain life and work in Academy, and how these convictions function.

When one engages in a topographical study, one asks not only, What peculiar whims of the natural process produced this terrain? but also the more immediately useful question, What properties of the soil and of the microclimate foster any plant or animal life here at all, and then favor just this kind of life in this spot? Therefore, we shall have *first* to ask what our current topography reveals about the " place " called Academy *as a whole,* and come *later* to consider its *parts and their relation* to one another.

To state the first question less symbolically: *What kind* of educational institution is the Academy to be? *Which* of the divergent *tasks* education can set itself is *most appropriate* to the university and, above all, to Academy at its heart? Karl Jaspers has said, correctly I think, that professional training, education of the whole man, and research are the three things required at a university, since the university is simultaneously a professional school, a cultural center, and a research institute.[1] This affirmation rests on his fundamental conviction concerning " the idea of the university," in which these three functions and institutional forms are so indissolubly united that one cannot be cut off from the others without destroying the living whole of the university and also crippling itself. Where this fragmentation occurs it is one manifestation of the crisis of conviction, since each of the functions of intellect or spirit needs the others to help it relate convictions about ultimate reality to concrete existence. Teaching, for example, absolutely requires the substance provided by research while, theoretically at least, the best teacher is he who through sharing his research draws the student into the continuing process of discovery.[2] Within the multiform university as a whole, with graduate and professional schools organically united through the undergraduate Academy, all three functions or activities (teaching, research, and professional training) must be carried out in each of the faculties (the Academy proper, the graduate and the professional schools). Still, one function may be more appropriate to one faculty than to another. Thus, *research* may be most appropriate to the *graduate school, professional training* to the legal, medical, technological, or theological " *school*," and *teaching* as such (or, *learning for its own sake*) most appropriate to the undergraduate *Academy*.

In terms of the central symbol of this chapter, we are principally concerned with the topography (or microtopography) of the Academy, but this must be set in the context, the environment, of the topography (or macrotopography) of the university. Remembering that Plato's " place " took its name from the grove outside Athens to which he and his circle retired from the busy marketplace to worship the Muses and to contemplate the works patronized by these divinities, we have been thinking semiconsciously of the Academy as a kind of grove — perhaps on a hillside outside some modern metropolis — in which, with sufficient leisure and isolation for contemplation but with easy access to the city, one pursues the life of the mind and spirit. And yet the symbol of the grove has become too limited to stand for the modern Academy. The mental and spiritual sustenance provided for culture by Academy is more inclusive than the symbol of the olive grove allows. The diversity demanded of Academy today corresponds to the diversity of modern agriculture itself, so that the symbol of the grove must be extended to include orchards, vineyards, and fields of knowledge and of learning.

Where, then, does one find the graduate schools in this macro-topography? In terms of actual geography, communication between the various faculties of the university is fostered by proximity and a sharing of facilities in which conversation comes easily. Metaphorically speaking, however, the home of pure research would be on the rocky pinnacles far above the city, and the mountaintop astronomical observatory or weather station would be their symbol. Figuratively, they would be farthest removed from direct contact with the life of the city. They are directly connected with the Academic areas by passes and valleys, and their usual commerce with the city runs through the Academy. There are perhaps also valleys running from some of the pinnacles directly to the city, bypassing the Academic preserves; but this must be the exception, for if it becomes the rule, it threatens that separation of teaching and research against which Jaspers warns.

The professional schools would be, of course, " downtown." This is not to say that they *are* the city in the macrotopography of the university. Our topographical map is a highly specialized one, the purpose of which is to show the contours of formally organized *intellectual* life. There is much " real life " in the cities and suburbs in which professional schools are found, just as much " real life " goes on in the groves and on the pinnacles, and this real life serves as more than a subject for study. It is itself the immediate market which the intellectual community of the university is to supply and to serve. The professional schools are most directly involved with the life of the city: the medical school with the health of society, the business and law schools with economics and politics, the divinity school with the Church, the technical school with industry. Therefore, symbolically, they are in the city and the normal circuit of intellectual life consequently flows from the city to the Academic groves and back again in a continuous and mutually enriching process. Thus, this macrotopography of the university suggests that the Academy is situated at the crossroads not only as a necessary way station between general culture and all intellectual culture on the heights but at the crossroads of normal traffic between graduate and professional schools as well.

This topographical silhouette may serve as a partial answer to the question: What kind of educational institution is the Academy to

be?; but the nature of Academy is further revealed by a consideration of *how* Academy is to be cultivated or, without a figure of
speech, *how* learning is to be carried on in Academy. In the course of
its history the university has employed three clearly distinguishable
teaching methods. Jaspers characterizes these as: (1) Scholastic instruction, which is limited to the mere " transmission " of the tradition; (2) apprenticeship, which has the unique value, as well as limitation, of being highly personal, and at its best stresses the needs of
the underling; (3) Socratic dialogue, which places teacher and
student on the same level in a common freedom. The " large lecture–objective exam " course in the university leaves us still familiar
with the first method, while the " star professor–graduate assistant "
relationship may resemble the second, but there is also wide agreement with Jaspers' conclusion: " Education at a university is Socratic
by its very nature." The Socratic method fixes no hard and fast educational system; rather, it imposes " endless questioning and ultimate
ignorance in the face of the absolute." The *method,* of course, carries
within it the Socratic view of reality and of the goals of the process.
Education is a " midwifery, in which the student is helped to give
birth to his abilities and powers." [3] This strong assertion inevitably
involves broad and deep responsibility on the part of the citizens of
Academy as men to and for man.

For Jaspers, this commitment to *humanitas* requires above all the
awakening, quickening, heightening, and deepening of *personal* responsibility, that companion and guarantor of the right to the university's most precious quality: Academic freedom. Socrates assumed
that what was true for himself is true for all men, namely, that if a
man knows the good he will do it. The problem of moral integrity
is thus fundamentally, even exclusively, a problem of the correct
cognitive process. The Hellenistic psychology, as a result, lacks the
Pauline-Augustinian-Protestant insight concerning the perversity,
weakness or bondage of the will, which under certain circumstances
" will " not do the good, even if it " knows " it. Jaspers, himself a
Socrates in the Nazi period, felt as deeply as Einstein and a host of
other Western intellectuals the collapse of the supposed bulwark of
Academic integrity. Here in the very stronghold of the mind, as in
many other areas of life, the Nazi period shows modern man how
puny are his powers to resist the demonic. Precisely in the citadels

in which they are upheld in pristine *theoretical* purity, loyalty to fundamental convictions failed to maintain *operational* effectiveness. The citizens of Academy lost responsibility as men to their own canons of truth, and then willingly yielded, or gave up without a serious struggle, their Academic freedom.[4] Though this is one of the earliest and clearest manifestations of the modern Academy's crisis of conviction it is by no means the last, so that the dramatic collapse of the German academic world may still be instructive to us. Exercised in the depths by this problem and passionately concerned for Academic freedom, Jaspers asserts that in the Socratic dialogue " personal responsibility is carried to its utmost, and nowhere alleviated." It is not the purpose of this book to " preach at " the Academy or the Church, and we shall not fill these pages with moralistic warnings. Let it be said here, however, emphatically, and once for all, that in their common quest to discover the meaning and current implications of Truth and Humanity the quality and character of the men and women of the Church and of the Academy as human beings are always at issue, as they are always at stake, and all the safeguards which each historical institution can provide must always and everywhere be applied.

The second corollary of the presuppositions of Socratic dialogue, as brought out by Jaspers, is one generally ignored, namely, the fact that a dialogue always takes place between two. The rigor of direct, and, insofar as possible, mutual, interrogation is enhanced by concentration on the subject matter and the movement of one other mind, without the distractions of interruption and the mere presence of an observer which tempts the partners in dialogue to compete for his approval. In Jaspers' terminology, two people make up a discussion — the communication of a common search — while three create an atmosphere of debate, since the element of power (over the other or others) is there to be struggled for. Which of us has not seen this element of power drive a dialogue into a destructive and demeaning duel, or else into a polite Alphonse and Gaston act which gets nothing clarified or solved. Jaspers' suggestion may at least serve as a corrective for the almost uncritically accepted American assumption that learning is enhanced and discovery speeded up and improved by expanding the dialogue form from " duologue " to " tetralogue " to " octologue " and more, thus creating that more-the-merrier mentality which prevails from the advocacy of "committee thinking" to that of group therapy to that of the perpetual bull session as a presumed learning device.

A doubt may persist, however, about the *universal* prescription of the Socratic method for higher learning. On the one hand, the mere "transmission" of the tradition called "Scholastic" is indispensable to all disciplines which must first of all teach their "vocabulary" — their grammars and syntax might also be added — before any real thinking can begin. This is perhaps clearest in the case of the sciences, for example, organic chemistry in which a vast program of memorization is relieved only by interesting laboratory work in the first year of study. In the second place, "apprenticeship" may seem an attractive and useful option where a brilliant professor of creative mind — and this is not exclusively found in disciplines directly related to the arts — teaches his students to "get inside his mind," not merely to "see things his way" but really to *think* after him. This has its dark side educationally, however, when the great man *uses* his students to do only the menial portion of his research, and not much more than his mannerisms are actually passed on to generations of his students. Finally, it could be argued that the Socratic method is outmoded in the technological age, and only still applicable to philosophy, theology, literature, history, and the arts, while true sciences require a kind of rigor not produced by such a rambling and haphazard method. In point of fact, when scientists engage in authentic Socratic dialogue it often proves the most useful method of teaching science, particularly on the advanced level.[5]

Actually, genuine dialogue can arise on all levels of work in Academy when all participants are adequately informed. The skillful instructor is able to utilize the contributions born of successive dialogues in fostering a deeper common understanding of the nature of a discipline. Even on the beginning college level, I have experienced the most genuine and valuable learning neither through the lecture nor the unguided free-for-all exchange of the so-called discussion method, but through the use of what I would call laboratory techniques. In such a learning procedure, the students become familiar with the tools of a discipline and their rudimentary use through reading and explanation during early sessions of the course. Then, analogously to the procedure in natural science, they are instructed to repeat for themselves the classic experiments of the discipline. The results achieved by each student, together with the reasons behind them, make up the raw materials of dialogue from which all benefit in class. In the case of Biblical studies, a student becomes acquainted with the mechanisms of literary and form criticism and is then asked to work out some of the classic problems of Pentateuch or Synoptic Gospel research. The discussion of results makes clear why these techniques are valuable, how they work, what are their limitations and, above all, brings the student into an immediate working relationship with the text itself.

The objection to a dialectic method of learning raised in the name of science and the laboratory variation on the Socratic dialogue are together symptomatic of the profound effect which science has had upon modern life and culture in general and on their intellectual dimensions in particular. The attempt to measure the extent and intensity of this effect requires, among other things, a definition of culture, since the discussion of the impact of science has centered around the terms " scientific " or " technological culture." C. P. Snow, with typical Anglo-Saxon directness, defines culture by saying: " Without thinking about it they (scientists, whether conservative or radical, Christian or materialist, aristocrats or proletarians, of rich or poor birth) respond alike. That is what a culture means." [6] Any given culture possesses a common language in which often very sophisticated ideas can be communicated. Thus, Perry Miller finds Jonathan Edwards, whom he looks upon primarily as a writer, rather regrettably producing *theology* simply because that was the language of his culture, whereas a generation later the American Enlightenment represented a culture whose common coin was *political* ideas. Jacques Barzun finds the medieval and modern cultures two of the best examples of the phenomenon of what we might call a common language of culture: " Though (the medieval is) often called a religious culture, it is more exact to call it theological, in the same fashion as ours is scientific. Just as few men were then theologians, so few among us are scientists. Just as the language of theology ended by permeating common thought, so with us the language of science." [7] Barzun, then, calls ours a scientific culture insofar as science is the prevailing influence upon it. His own definition of science, however, as " the body of rules, instruments, theorems, observations and conceptions with the aid of which *man manipulates physical nature* in order to grasp its workings," [8] fits better the term " technological culture " preferred by others.

There is universal agreement that the technological revolution [9] has overturned the cultural patterns, not only material but also intellectual and spiritual, of the past. But there is a widespread disagreement as to where we have been left by the revolution. Do we now have one culture, or two, or three, or many? And what will tomorrow bring: clarification or utter chaos? C. P. Snow brought the debate into focus by announcing that we in the West have two: an older literary culture and the modern scientific one. Living, or having lived, in each, he was profoundly aware of the tension between them, and writing in the Sputnik-filled air of the late 1950's he warned that failure to move posthaste into the era of the engineer could bring disaster.

My own Academic pilgrimage has some similarities to Snow's, and may cast further light on the crisis of conviction which the technological revolution has helped bring upon Academy. At the beginning of my six years of study at a technological institute on a university campus, we teen-aged tyros considered the liberal arts students intellectually inferior playboys — " lounge lizards " was our word — who did not really work at their imprecise disciplines. The students at " East and West Jesus Tech," the two theological seminaries adjoining the engineering schools, were looked upon as hopelessly pallid if not downright futile. Our professors may have been more enlightened than we — but not much. Some of them encouraged us to think that the horrendous developments which had shaken the confidence and easy optimism of our parents and grandparents — the disillusioned Crusade for Democracy, the Great Depression, and the War against Fascism then in progress — were merely products of society's blind refusal to be directed by scientific thinking. If politics were only wrested from the grip of the glamour boys and the lawyers and put into the hands of disinterested scientific thinkers — physicists, chemists, and engineers — modernity, happy and secure, could begin.

The very moment of triumph for technology, however, revealed to us all that man cannot live by technology's "bread" alone. I remember the days before Hiroshima when the inventor of one of the most important instruments in physical chemistry led us through the intricacies of the subject, in between absences for work on a top-secret project. It was he who first brought us the news that "the bomb" had been dropped, and told us that this meant the dawn of a whole new scientific and cultural world beyond the shattered bounds of the "laws" of indestructible matter and energy. One recalls that soon, however, scientists were not repeating pious Morse's "What hath God wrought?" but were recoiling with the anguished whisper, "My God, what have *I* done?" With sudden awareness of the limitations of science these men plainly announced: "What we have created, we cannot control. It is up to somebody else." There was even some talk that this fantastic scientific and technological breakthrough must now be matched by the same kind of crash program of research leading up to a corresponding breakthrough in ethical science, religion, and psychology to enable man to cope — as he had never done with any previous military discovery — with the totally destructive power of the Ultimate Weapon. This awareness that technology alone is not enough to build a culture satisfying to the whole man grew into the conviction that led me to Theology at the chill gray dawn of the cold war. The call for ever *more* technology, then and since the Sputnik crisis, to counteract the dangers posed by a relentlessly technological opponent has only deepened this conviction.

Dissatisfaction with the modern world into which technology has plunged us is all very well; but is there a serious nontechnological option for culture in our day? The split between science and literature, to which Snow has given a name by his "two cultures" terminology, has been evident since the war between Darwinians and Romantic writers in Victorian England. English education has institutionalized the separation by a specialization in either science or literature which dramatizes the split. The question with which this fact leaves Snow is whether there are actually *only* two cultures, to be reflected in Academy, or whether the social scientists are right to demand recognition as a third entity neither so naïvely "uncultured" as the scientist, nor so backward-looking as the pessimistic humanist. Academy may well require this third classification and subdivisions of all three, but Snow refuses to admit more than two cultures at present. Jacques Barzun, on the other hand, would (in

Science, the Glorious Entertainment) join those who say all non-scientific-technological symbols are broken, critically ill, or dead in our time, at least to the extent that there is but one culture that provides modern man with a common language and way of thought.

Out of the apparent disagreement emerges at least this much that is clear for the modern Academy: whether one recognizes one or more cultures, scientific technology now defines the rules of the game. It is to be either "science alone," or " science and . . . ," or " science, but. . . ." There are those who advocate with Snow the pouring of ever more Academic resources into technical training as necessary to survival. Although it is difficult — and certainly undesirable — to argue against survival, others insist with Barzun that science as a set of accomplishments and as an approach to all reality is " unfit for monarchical rule." [10] For him, only when science is recognized as a magnificent treasure hunt carried on with the help of fascinating equipment for the game, in which all acknowledge that it is the seeking not the finding that counts, does the scientific quest become the glorious entertainment in which all intellectuals may and should engage. Otherwise, if one attempts to stamp all Academic disciplines into a rigid mold, which is supposed to be patterned after some physical science, science has, as John Macmurray puts it, stepped "out of bounds." It simply will not do in administering Academy today and planning for its future to say: " Tomorrow is already technological. Let everyone receive a technological education, and let the humanists cram with whatever intellectual baggage they may the last precious crannies of the Academic spacecraft into the future." As Barzun puts it, there are a myriad situations of immediate moment to living beings in which science is irrelevant. At best, for Macmurray, science is but one of three modes of reflection corresponding to one (the technological) of the three typical activities which characterizes modern man's everyday life.

Although science and its technology are not to dominate the shape of Academy, we must still ask how they have affected the values on which Academy rests. If scientific symbols alone are " live," as some hold, in what shall the citizen of Academy believe? Though he may be familiar enough with the rudiments of technology to drive his car skillfully and be able to change a burned-out fuse, the humanistically trained modern who no longer believes in " those fairy tales

about God " often regards scientific technology with either a rever-
ence or a fundamental fear which used to be reserved for the numin-
ous, the *mysterium tremendum*. Respect for technological achievement is not, however, enough to think on or to live by. What needs
to be attended to in the intellectual world is the crisis of conviction
beneath the surface of technological achievement. The words of
Thoreau in his nineteenth-century Walden express the technological
dilemma better than those of modern authors who do not seem to
know them. Upon encountering a workman in his Walden, Thoreau
inquired what he was doing. The man proudly replied that he was
stringing the telegraph wires which would be the first direct and
practically instantaneous link between New England and Texas.
" But what if," Thoreau retorted, " the people in Boston have nothing to say to the people in Texas? "

This " what if " is the start of all the questions about the relation
of scientific truth to the humanity of man which we have hardly
begun to answer. This is why in describing the authentic nature of
Academy we must turn to matters of ultimate reference obscured by
the misunderstanding of science which has put it out of bounds by
pretending it has replaced, or obviated, or gone beyond the classic
questions of conviction and values which made men human and
wise. Jacques Barzun in 1964 echoes the call of Alfred North Whitehead in 1924 for the citizen of Academy to regain the high ground
where man can satisfy through many means all his capacities for
reason and belief. In the same spirit we would seek to drive the thinking of the one culture, or the two, or the many, beyond the utilitarian
operation of Academic disciplines that reflect these cultures to the
underlying continuum of convictions that unite Academy as a universe of knowledge. Needless to say, this kind of talk requires more
precise definition if it is to lead to enlightenment. What Barzun
points to with the term " high ground " and others such as Jaspers
are after when they speak in Idealistic terms of the " idea " of the
university, we refer to when we speak of conviction in Academy.

Conviction, Criteria, and Community

" Conviction," as used here, points to the adherence to certain
ultimate criteria as valid for evaluating the nature and quality of

reality. In this sentence the word " adherence " refers to the subjective dimension of conviction, namely, convincedness, or what Theology would call faith or belief. The words " ultimate criteria " designate convincing symbols, transcending each particular, concrete set of circumstances, by which we attempt to describe ultimate reality. Evaluating points to the power of the ultimate criteria to impress themselves upon our understanding of particular sets of circumstances, and to guide our concrete decisions and courses of action. This terminology, of course, contains many " unsupported assumptions " about reality and man's way of knowing it. At present we attempt to justify it merely by proposing that it describes both Theology's fact of faith and that " ration of dreaming " Academic man " must have " [11] to survive and grow as a whole man and an intellectual. Now we must try to ascertain whether indeed it is useful, not merely for Theology but for Academy as well.

In the last chapter we dealt with theological conviction, with faith in a Reconciliation that overcomes all destructive separation between knowledge and belief as well as between finite, even sinful, man and infinite, righteous God. We discovered that the theology about Reconciliation yields the ultimate criteria of Truth and Humanity for our thinking and living. To be sure, these criteria received there a decisively Christian definition, directly derived from what Christianity understands to be the *true* revelation of authentic *humanity* in the event of Reconciliation. In this chapter we shall seek to discover the content and quality of Academy's conviction concerning its tasks in relation to the nature of reality. This is a task that would have been simple in Idealistic Greece, under the " theological culture " of the Middle Ages, or the puritanical " Protestant Ethic," and also for the Christian humanism of the Renaissance, and for the Enlightened humanism of the eighteenth century. But precisely the technological revolution, which left all these behind through its fantastic advances on the plane of material culture, has created a massive confusion on the level of intellectual-spiritual culture which infinitely complicates our search for ultimate criteria by which to evaluate the work of Academy.

At the beginning of Academy stands Socrates, teacher of its teachers, shaper of the world created by Plato in the grove. And as Campbell Stewart puts it: " Socrates was a metaphysician with an unshakable belief in man, not as the measure of all things, but as the embodiment of a principle of Truth which was in the universe itself." [12] One would expect, then, that the "principle of Truth" would be the indispensable founding value of Academy, that Truth would be the ultimate criterion for evaluating all Academic existence. But the word "metaphysician" is poison in the ear of many citizens of Academy today. The truths science teaches them are, or seem to be, tangible, demonstrable generalizations about cold, hard facts. "Truth," and indeed "ultimacy," has an empty ring. The Academician who today writes across his breast, "I am a Truthseeker," is regarded as a quixotic quester for the Grail, or an Academic alchemist seeking the substance that will transubstantiate all the different stuffs of Academic knowledge into the same purest gold. We say that Truth is too presumptuous a term for us; we will seek more modest, more realistic goals. Some of us seem content with that and spend an academic lifetime in pursuit of ever more modest goals. Many of the rest of us always mean to come back to the question of Truth, beyond the attainment of certainty of method and control of territory within our field, but never quite get around to it. There are, of course, those who wistfully look back to earlier periods of Idealistic temper and say, for example, "Wouldn't it be nice if Cardinal Newman turned out to be right after all?" Many exceedingly earnest and, generally, younger citizens of the Academy would, however, deliberately take their stand with what Kent Bendall has named "a *firmer* agnosticism which would eschew for the present *all* such options (as Christian theism)." [13] Such agnosticism is indeed "firmer" in the sense that it is safer, less risky, less liable to the danger of losing not only "intellectual respectability" but also of losing contact with correct, bounded, precise verifiable language in general.

Interestingly, however, it is the two men usually regarded as the founders of Existentialism, the philosophy rooted in concrete anxiety rather than derived from abstract absolutes, who affirm Truth most profoundly and unconditionally. When Karl Jaspers turns his attention to the nature of Academy he asserts that for the citizen of Academy: "To be permeated by the idea of the university is part of a way of life. It is the will to search and seek without limitation, to allow reason to develop unrestrictedly, to have an open mind, to leave nothing unquestioned, to *maintain truth unconditionally,* yet recognizing the danger of *sapere aude* (dare to know)." [14]

Martin Heidegger, characteristically, probes "Truth" by proceeding etymologically, developing his thought in dialogue with the pre-Socratic philosophers. The word for truth, *alētheia,* derives from *lēthos* (the veil) and *lētheia* (veiledness). With the addition of the alpha privative, then, truth means *un*veiledness, *un*hiddenness, *un*coveredness, *dis*closedness, *un*concealment. For Heidegger, truth is the unveiling and unveiledness of reality created or discovered by *man* as authentic, free, open existence.[15] It is important in this connection to understand that "man does not 'possess' freedom as a property; it is the contrary that is true: freedom, or existent, revelatory *Dasein* (being there) possesses man." Then, "Truth is not the mark of some correct proposition made by a human 'subject' in respect of an 'object' and which then — in precisely what sphere we do not know — counts as 'true'; truth is rather the revelation of what-is, a revelation through which something 'overt' (open) comes into force. All human behavior is an exposition into that 'overtness' (openness)."[16] For Heidegger, then, Truth is an unveiling of reality as a whole, especially a self-revelation of and for the unveiler or discoverer of truth. Truth is the business of man in Academy, through both the exactitude of science and what he believes to be the still greater authentic rigor of poetry and philosophy. Both men would rather risk the loss of the values sought by what Jaspers calls a "thin humanistic education" than risk losing the unconditional dedication to truth.

As a matter of fact, the great American experiments in "general education" programs, designed to produce well-rounded men instead of narrow academic specialists, have come to much the same conclusions. This is especially clear when the University of Chicago's report on the *Idea and Practice of General Education* begins on the note that "the history of American education illustrates . . . that preoccupation with the practical may, in the long run, be dangerously impractical." Still more significantly, the report recognizes that though "the processes of thought for reaching truth about one subject matter differ from the processes required to reach truth in another," the efforts of all disciplines unite to produce one thing: "What is required in general education can best be described by the term 'wisdom.' " [17] This statement is typical of the experience of the three great institutions which initiated the experiments: all stress, if not Truth as some kind of absolute, the truth-seeking activity and ability of Academic man. Where Chicago says " wisdom," Alexander Meiklejohn, of Wisconsin, chooses the term " intelligence." The Columbia report focuses on no single word, but its intent is commensurate with the designation by its subsequent dean of Academy as the house of " intellect." Still, for the American Academy, Truth is rarely truly absolute, that is, it seldom stands permanent and alone. [18]

Thus we see that in terms of Stewart's characterization of Socrates as the believer in man " not as the measure of all things, but as the embodiment of a principle of Truth," the European citizens of Academy today are more faithful disciples of Socrates than are their American cohorts. On the other hand, the American Academy tends to take the more nearly Aristotelian approach that man *is* the measure of all things. Whereas Jaspers makes only a qualified affirmation of humanity as a central value for Academy, [19] the American mentality — even while affirming truth-seeking activities and abilities as basic to Academy — tends to stress these for the sake of enhancing the human person. " Wisdom," " intelligence," being an " intellectual," are advocated in the sources we have quoted for the sake of serving " men in the creation and maintenance of a social order " and " to prepare the student for experience, for coping with . . . the problems of living a full life." Though all this terminology stems from the period in which the general education experiments were Academy's great adventure, these statements still legitimately point to the humanistic quality of the American Academy's primary aim. Looking back on the experience of these experiments and their applicability today, current evaluators see two clearly separate forces at work: " The first is related to the ideal of a civilized and cultivated person, and in different ways the courses worked out in Amherst, Columbia, Chicago, Harvard, St. John's College, Sarah Lawrence, Scripps, Reed College, and in England at the University College of North Staffordshire, have this principle to guide them. . . . The second principle represents a continuation of the notions of adjustment (characteristic of so many arguments about the curriculum at the high school level)." It is the second trend that produces "how to" courses in "family living, the citizen and the state, science and the community . . . in various (American) colleges,"[20] calling forth condemnations of a "thin humanistic education" from Europe.

The key word describing the direction of this second trend is, of course, "adjustment," but the question it raises is: Adjustment to what? Adjustment must be made to some concrete reality, such as an existent culture, or to some ideal, standard, norm, or set of criteria. The "Athens and America" curriculum of the Wisconsin experiment is most illuminating in this regard. In addition to the concrete reality of contemporary American culture, both the ideals of the Athenian state and the Great American Dream — or the vision of the Kingdom of God in America, as H. R. Niebuhr defined it — gave solid points of orientation toward which "adjustment" could still be undertaken. But the confusion of our present culture about itself — is it one, two, or many . . . of what? — and in particular the pressure to conform to a technological culture that is better at providing means than illuminating ends, creates great confusion for the adjustment-oriented Academician. For many even of the most enlightenend citizens of Academy it seems almost axiomatic that society outside the grove is not only collectively impersonal and ignorant but menacing in an almost demonic way. Witness Christian Bay's acrid description of life in our time and culture: "Like rats in the psychologist's maze, most of us are driven through our social labyrinths by our needs and anxieties, physically we walk erect but mentally we are too unsure of ourselves and our steps to stand upright and gain an overview of society and a perspective on life."[21] Sensing the dangers of *assimilation* and *absorption* into this destructively lonely crowd, many forward-looking intellectuals call for a real dimension of *independence* from this culture. The values sought in personal development are differentiation and integration within the person and the mature capacity to wait,[22] not the ability to adapt and make the most of the moment. With Riesman, the "civilized and cultivated person" is now defined as inner-directed, oriented toward norms independently determined and maintained, as opposed to other-directed, conforming to some social pattern for the mass man.

In order that the college may assist the developing student to achieve this, many of the leading thinkers of Academy are suggesting procedures with a surprisingly classic religious ring. If our technological culture can provide no productive and sustaining base for intellectual and spiritual life, if the everyday business of classroom and laboratory is insufficient to create unifying bonds, let us withdraw a bit to form ourselves into a kind of living-learning community peculiar to Academy. "Let us close our gates," says Frank Pinner, "for the academic community needs to be protected from the dictation of the multitude. Let us first be masters within our walls." [23] This is, after all, the monastic ideal. And let it be clear that in selecting such a model strategists of Academy are not choosing a purely selfish, passive, or defensive one. Monasticism, especially in the West, has always advocated retreat not only for the salvation of the monk, but also so that he might gain resources to work for the salvation of the world, through prayer and works of charity and finally even through militant evangelism. There is evidence that early Palestinian monastics retreated to the desert not primarily to flee the evil of the city, but rather, to grapple with the demons on their desolate home grounds before they could attack the urbanites. This monastic ideal appears in unsuspected places and forms in our day. Protestant theological seminaries have been heard to utter the declaration that their own communal life had better exhibit the character of a colony of heaven if God's kingdom is ever to be realized in the city of man. The same spirit was evidenced when Arnold Nash called for an *order* of Christian scholars, men like those of the French SCM, which provided courageous wartime resistance to Hitler, who "cannot give up seeking what God demands of us when he gives us a vocation to be scholars, philosophers and historians." [24]

Yet it is the "secular" Academic institutions themselves that have in the most interesting way appropriated the ideal of the monastic community precisely for their educational purpose. To be sure, it is a religious educator who makes the case for the residential college community as the unique source of Academic values: having distinguished between the *universitas litterarum* as a *unity* of sciences in one integrated whole and the *universitas magistrorum et scholarium* as an independent *community* held together by the ideal of a common search for truth, Elton Trueblood identifies the large modern university as "implying *unity*" with the former, and the college as "implying *community*" with the latter. *The Idea of a College* for him, then, means that the college "exists in order to *provide a situation* of maximum rapid growth in the life of whole persons." [25] Almost more to the point, however, is the fact that the general education programs were often intended for a limited community. At Wisconsin, for example, Alexander Meiklejohn's report suggested that the experimental college work with about thirty-six hundred students and faculty members divided into fifteen or twenty colleges, with the faculty serving, on different levels, both the whole and a particular college or division. [26] Woodrow Wilson had advocated for Princeton, early in the century, an unsuccessful scheme for Princeton quadrangles which would have drawn faculty and students together while short-circuiting the clubs. But it is at Harvard that something closely akin to Meiklejohn's proposal has most nearly achieved fulfillment.

The story of Harvard's "enriched" dormitory, or the "Harvard House System," so excellently told by Christopher Jencks and David Riesman, begins at the same point as Meiklejohn's America half of the Athens and America curriculum, namely, with the *Education of Henry Adams*. In the mid-nineteenth-century Harvard reflected there, "education" shunned the student for the research function, and the students became increasingly bored and often hostile. In the ensuing period (1869-1909) under President Eliot's "experiment in *laissez faire*" or "cafeteria education," more charitably known as the free elective system, this hostility "was abated by the increasing indifference of both (faculty and students) to education." [27] Out of Eliot's policy, which led to the virtually uncontrolled proliferation of courses, came the expansion of Harvard College into the University. The growing separation between student and professor, humanity and academic subject matter, seemed irreversible under the existing and developing institutional conditions.

President Lowell, however, at least symptomatically reversed the trend of institutional development with his proposal of an "honors college" within the university. Though this form of the reversal was not realized, the "house system," which grew out of it and which was inaugurated in the fall of 1930, represents a quantitatively more significant if not more radical departure. The original plan called for seven houses, "each of which represented Harvard in microcosm, affording the students an opportunity that had not existed since the eighteenth century for intimacy with dissimilar students." But with the tutorial, the real purpose of the house system has been to restore communication between teachers and students. For this purpose, along with 250 to 450 students, each house has a master — usually selected from the senior members of the English and history departments, often a former undergraduate, and therefore more apt to identify with the college and sensible of his role in creating a residential community there — and, since 1952, a senior tutor who has acted as the house's dean of students, and about a dozen resident tutors. In addition, each house has had a number of nonresident tutors, who periodically engage in tutorial sessions and mealtime conversation, plus a dozen or more senior associates, leading members of the faculty from various departments who attend various functions within the house.

The entire experiment — after thirty years deemed sufficiently successful not only to continue but to expand — constitutes a response to a commonly recognized failure of the university as an educational production line to provide that fundamental and indispensable activity of Academy: dialogue; for it is essentially the total involvement of human beings in dialogue with the material of learning, and with each other in the process, that has broken down. As learning has become impersonal on the grand scale, teachers have carried on their important dialogues with their material among themselves or more often alone. The students have received intravenous injections of precooked, predigested results, and thus been inoculated against real dialogue with the materials or the teachers of a discipline. This leads to Pinner's complaint that we have no Academic community, no communication, no common faith, but loneliness in the midst of today's very large crowd. Therefore the secular-monastic Academic community has arisen as an answer to such protests, as an attempt to provide living-learning situations on a scale small enough to foster genuine dialogue.

The presence of dialogue is, of course, primarily symptomatic. It is the mechanism of that "midwifery" by which the Socratic Academy brings to birth the student's abilities and powers. Here again the American Academy is far more aggressively humanistic than is the purely Truth-oriented European tradition. Whereas Jaspers' midwifery requires him to " hide in paradoxes " and " make himself inaccessible," the behavioral scientist Robert Knapp calls for the reinstatement of the third historic role of the American college professor, which gave him a " character-developing " function in addition to his research and informational ones. This function, which Knapp wishes to see united with the informational one, makes the professor a guide and counselor for the total person of the student.[28]

Finally, however, we must ask a more penetrating question of the secular-monastic Academic community: Precisely what does it wish itself and the men it makes to be and do? This is partially answered by the strong feeling shared by many who advocate such an Academy and expressed in Pinner's statement that the knowledge fostered and cherished by Academy should be " dissensual " rather than " consensual." This distinction reaches through and beyond Socrates, who was called corrupter of the youth because he led them to question the unexamined beliefs bequeathed them by society, to the Old Testament prophets, who spoke God's word to the people *against* corrupt kings, merchants, and priests. In contemporary terms Pinner defines as " consensual " all those kinds of knowledge with respect to which the general public at a given time tends to have no reservations, while " dissensual " refers to those kinds of knowledge (usually new, yet already tested, and at least temporarily successful in the marketplace of ideas) with respect to which the public has explicit or implicit doubts and which, accordingly, are less likely to be supported by the institutions of society. Within the closed gates Pinner is convinced that the university " must encourage, nurture, defend, and spread those disciplines which are now dissensual." [29] It must do so not only for the sake of its own integrity but also for the very purpose of discharging its responsibility toward the community. For the final directive to Pinner's secular-monastic Academic community is not: " Close the gates! " After a genuine community of men has been created, and those who live the life of the mind are masters within their own walls, then and only then " can we shift from a posture of defense to one of offense, which is our proper posture. For our mission is, after all, to see that the best of human achievements in the realms of truth and beauty come to conquer the world: not only to dominate the lives of our students inside our walls but ultimately those of the multitudes as well." [30]

We have thus discovered in Academy that there is a widespread desire for man in the house of intellect to "regain the high ground where he can satisfy all his capacities for reason and belief." Many desire, with M. Rokeach, a "belief system" because it seems to be constructed to serve both (purposes) at once: "to understand the world insofar as possible, and to defend against it insofar as necessary." [31] An artificial and unconvincing "belief system" fabricated just to satisfy these needs is delusive and self-defeating, but where we find an authentic one we characteristically find its nucleus in one of two criteria which transcend the details of any particular intellectual work. On the one hand, most clearly delineated, and most typically advocated in the European Academy, is the unconditional allegiance to Truth, which enhances a man's humanity and shapes a particular type of personality yet *only* as "a spontaneous by-product, not a conscious goal." [32] On the other hand, less precisely defined, is the more typical adherence of the American Academy to Humanity as its ultimate criterion: what is sought is a high level of development in personality, which is characterized chiefly by complexity and wholeness. For the attainment of such a growth pattern in colleges and in people of college age "rationality is the central objective," though, in the opinion of the editor of *The American College*, it would be too far-reaching for a work considering the goals of college education to hold forth rationality (one of the names for the truth-seeking activity and ability) "as a general philosophy of life." [33]

Thus, Truth and Humanity are too often made to seem competing criteria to be held in tension by opposing factions, say science and the arts, in Academy. This, in fact, cannot and need not be true. Truth, with all our reservations about its reality and its attainability, bears finally upon the work of every discipline in Academy. And Humanity, irrespective of the many disparate and unconvincing definitions given it in various corners of Academy, must remain a central abiding criterion that no discipline can ever ignore. A "thin humanism" that does not adhere to the canons of truth with strict rigor will not produce men and women. And a methodologically impeccable scientism that ignores the truth about *man* can always fall prey to some new Nazism. Truth and Humanity as guiding stars in the firmament of the reality Academy investigates, as transcendent norms for evaluating Academy's life and work, cannot be competing values or divisive directors. They must instead be coordinate, they must form a continuum, the basis for what José Ortega y Gasset means by " synthesis."

Though in many ways a nineteenth-century thinker concerned with the problems of the Western European nation most isolated from modernity, Ortega was profoundly aware of the emptiness of an intellectualism oriented toward conflicting values. He had been strongly influenced by the divisive dualism of Dilthey's distinction between the " historical reason " appropriate to the *Geisteswissenschaften* (literally, spiritual sciences, or humanistic disciplines) and " scientific reason." Sensible of the sharp and apparently incurable rift resulting from Dilthey's dualism, Ortega y Gasset says: " It has led to the elimination of the prime concern: culture." [34] By " culture " Ortega y Gasset means neither of Snow's two nor any third or fourth culture to which the university should train its students to adapt and conform. Rather, when he says the university should put the ordinary man " at the height of the times " this is to be done through " a rational approach to the conflicting value judgments of the cultures of the world," through a fundamental philosophizing that investigates " what it really means to be [for example] a good physician for our times." [35] It is in line with Ortega's " cultural synthesis " that his translator, Howard Lee Nostrand, reports a synthesis seminar, involving faculty of some twenty departments at the University of Washington, which has " explored contradictory notions of human nature " from the partial insights of various disciplines.

This attempt is symptomatic, first, of the need for a search for fundamental motifs within and beneath the individual disciplines of Academy, and also for a common set of ultimate criteria as the basis for the unity of the Academic cosmos. This is why we believe the role of Truth and Humanity is so vital in relation to Academy, and why we postulate that they are not two separate and competing norms but a continuum or constellation of ultimate criteria for Academy. This is why we must choose as definitive for the nature and task of Academy a statement such as that of the Truth-oriented

Jaspers correlating the two, the statement with which we introduced this chapter.

Thus far in this chapter we have set the Academic grove within
a cosmos, a presumably ordered world of reality, and we have just
been trying to describe (in terms of the Academy's own self-understanding) the ultimate criteria: fundamental characteristics of the
reality of this cosmos, which may also be used as standards of description and judgment within the Academy. It must be made clear
again at this point that such criteria are not immediately available
to any extension of the mechanisms for receiving sense impressions,
nor are they identifiable as the distillates of empirical data exacted
under the heat and pressure of any form of logical operation. They
are also not, strictly speaking, simply matters of taste — they are not
as petty and partial as that designation would make them appear.
These criteria are, for those who live under them, articles of faith,
primary presuppositions, fundamental premises — too primal for
formal proof. They can only be tested and affirmed by all of life,
including thought, for their power to create, to describe, and to
judge reality as a whole and the realities within it. The tentative
character of all human apprehension of these criteria, no matter
how ultimate and important they may be in themselves, necessarily
recalls us to the theme of the human knower's humility. As Walter
Stuermann points out, one of the persistent relations between science
and religion is created by their common attitude of humility in the
face of the ultimate. No one of us " possesses " the ultimate criteria,
and at his relatively secure best neither the scientist nor the religious
man permits the pretense that he does.

We have discovered among the attempts of the Academy to express the various facets of its self-understanding two recurrent
themes, designated by various terminologies but reducible to the
terms Truth and Humanity. These are the classic criteria of the
cosmos which the Academy has from the first sought to *know*. They
also turn out to be the same terms as those we have selected as
perfectly adequate expressions of that knowledge of reality called
the Christian faith. This does not mean that at this late stage we
are simply going to identify the understanding of the ultimate
criteria held by Church and Academy, and then use this as an excuse either to subsume the Academy, together with its functions,

under the Church, or the Church, together with its functions, under the Academy. On the contrary, we intend to affirm the discrete and valid identity of two institutions, with fundamentally different functions, techniques, and perhaps even prescriptions for society. That they belong together in a fundamental and enduring way is assured and symbolized, however, by the ultimate criteria they share. Truth and Humanity have the same form for both Church and Academy, and they refer to the identical reality.

At the same time, from the different perspectives of Church and Academy, Truth and Humanity may well have different appearances. To mention two dimensions of dissimilarity, Theology today still bears the imprint of the personal and the particular, while Academic cognition still tends toward the general and the impersonal. This means that for Theology Truth is characteristically tied up with the special revelations of God to which the Bible bears witness, culminating in the earthly historical existence of the *person* whom the Fourth Gospel calls the Truth; Humanity likewise is understood through the Second or Last Man (*'ādām,* in Hebrew) who embodies the new creation, the Reconciliation of the First Man (*'ādām*) alienated from his Father-God. In connection with this single decisive revelation are a multitude of very particular persons and events that reveal special facets of the one Truth and the one Humanity.

On the other hand, the Truth of the Academy has by Academic definition the character of unexceptionable universal validity. Some citizens of Academy will wish to complain that Humanity is not a truly universal or ultimate value, and that only the discredited anthropocentric conceit can still pretend that a cold, impersonal astronomical universe " out there " may not just as well be hostile or destructively indifferent as benevolent to the self-styled " microcosmic " egotist. Nevertheless, both Church and Academy live in, are made up of, and serve a world of earthlings. For the world which concerns them, Humanity (even though it may be a symbol for something larger, such as G. B. Shaw's " Life Force ") must remain an *ultimate* criterion. The God known to Theology does concern himself centrally in the costly business of redeeming the man of this earth, and for all practical purposes the world of concern to the scientist is pretty well enclosed by that inverted Babylonian bowl called the firmament atop an earth which man is called upon to fill and subdue, exerting dominion over all existence within the system thus defined.

Each of the Academic truths is marked by a generality that adequately covers all the possible, or at least known, particulars within a given field. No one particular fact or " truth " can found a new Truth. The greatest power of such a fact is to demonstrate that a wider, more inclusive generalization is needed to replace the old Truth which did not cover all known cases. Humanity, in its turn, has not only a characteristically general but also an impersonal ring in Academic usage. Though there is great stress on the individual in the Franco-revolutionary and the Anglo-Saxon traditions, the individual, with all the peculiar or unique traits that may survive the determinative social and psychological pressures toward conformity, remains an instance of a general type. It does not seem too much to claim that any true and abiding personal uniqueness of the individual ultimately stems from the *Hebraic* emphasis on bodily particularity, which to preserve human identity beyond death can conceive only of a bodily resurrection. Insofar as Academy's view of Humanity arises from its own primary *Hellenic* roots, the *peculiar* trait is nonessential and perishable while the *typical* is essential and immortal. Personal identity is not preserved when the spark of the soul is again caught up in the divine flame, when the drop of human reason dissolves once more in the shoreless sea of Mind that is Divinity. Character development may sound to novitiates in behavioral science like an invention as new as the actuality of space travel, but Aristotelian ethics depends on the unfolding of the *ēthos* (or character) of the general *type* to which the individual in question belongs.

Thus Truth and Humanity are the ultimate criteria of the reality described both by Theology and by Academy, yet neither " possesses " these criteria and each can only bear its own peculiar kind of witness to their validity and usefulness. For Theology, knowledge of these ultimate criteria arises out of the very center of its own subject matter, the heart of its conviction concerning the Reconciliation. The criterial complex of Truth-Humanity thus derived then guides the work of Theology and judges its results in detail and as a whole. For Academy, a sense of the power and relevance of Truth-

Humanity arises out of the work in particular disciplines and in the attempt to see the significance and interrelatedness of all intellectual work as such. Where awareness of these ultimate criteria is vague and fragmentary in Academy's current crisis of conviction, there is often nostalgia for a "belief system" that would unite the forces of Academy and allow them to be focused on the problems of contemporary civilization.

WHOLENESS DEMANDS CLASSIFICATION

This last consideration points in a valid and important direction, for the affirmation of Truth and Humanity by Academy is no mere mystical experience designed to impart some mysterious spiritual quality qualifying the scholarly technician to live in the house of intellect. Truth and Humanity are worthless if they are irrelevant ideals; they are of interest to us only if they perform the same practical function of unification, criticism, and evaluation for Academy as for Theology. The practical value of these criteria becomes evident as soon as we realize that they characteristically appear in Academy as a sense of wholeness, unity, and universality. What the Academy seeks is knowledge which is generally valid for all areas of reality which involve, touch, and surround man. On the lowest level of abstraction, this has led to the growth of the American university in many new directions, until it has become a sprawling complex whose parts are justified and limited by the pragmatic-utilitarian criteria: Does it work? Is it useful? At the very least, on this level the American Academy can lay the quantitative claim to encompass all knowledge. The great general education experiments have built on this reality and have pushed beyond it to attempt to discover the bonds of this universality. Yet it is Jaspers, with his Idea of the University, who expresses the practical meaning of Academy's ultimate criteria with theoretical clarity. Like his American contemporaries, he desires no return to the original seven liberal arts as a cure for our current problems, but points to the actual university of today as a true universe of knowledge, corresponding to all of man's authentic cognition. The mere assertion of universality and faith in the oneness of Truth is, however, not enough, for as he says: "The wholeness of knowledge . . . presents us with the task of classifying all knowledge." [36] And in performing this task, he relies upon a theoretical norm from the past as little as any of the Anglo-Saxon scholars of Academy. Instead, he depends upon the pragmatic validity lent to the modern university by the test of time and upon the relevance of various Academic activities to areas of modern life.

He insists on the term " university," because it relates to the universe as a whole reflected in the Academic " cosmos of knowledge." Within this cosmos he asserts the legitimacy of the three classical higher faculties, which we would call professional schools, saying: " Theology, jurisprudence and medicine cover permanent areas of inquiry; understanding of religious revelation, of statute law, both private and public, and of the nature of man." [37] Since these three no longer " cover the whole of modern existence," however, he advocates the addition of that reflex of Snow's second (or first) culture, technology, long since made an integral part of the American university. There are many questions that could be raised about particular parts of Jaspers' historically justified Academic cosmology, but those most relevant to us concern the one " lower " faculty, which he also affirms in spite of all its shifts in meaning and structure. This lower " artistic " Academy has a largely preparatory preprofessional, or even extraprofessional, character. [38]

We should like to raise the question, however, as to whether this lower faculty adequately serves the general Academic educational purposes vital to the development of human personality. It is true that at these universities the higher faculties often open their lectures to auditors from all faculties, so that anyone sufficiently interested can sit in the presence of quantum mechanics, Michelangelo, or an exegesis of Ezekiel in Hebrew. These courses are almost always carried on in the interests of specialized professional problems or esoteric scholarly research which, as is true of many courses offered in American universities, are *never* related to fundamental intellectual and human concerns. As a result, the student is left with widely separated clots of knowledge with no interconnecting fiber.

It is a fundamental thesis of this book, however, that each discipline, including professional ones, has its place in Academy partly by virtue of its ability to engage in dialogue with other disciplines about its own subject matter and about the bearing of Truth and

Humanity upon it and upon other Academic concerns as well. This is the kind of presupposition that has led to the general education experiments. The architects of these experiments made no attempt to return to some such model of unified cognitive effort as the classical or medieval liberal arts ideal. Instead they began with the existent divisions of arts and science (and often social sciences as a third) and tried to forge a synthesis of human knowledge and knowing. In this attempt they have characteristically discovered that the vital bonds must be sought — even within groups, as we shall show in succeeding chapters — not in similarity of subject matters or of methodology, but in goals, aims, and values which transcend both. In the face of the current crisis of conviction within Academy, we feel that without attempting to impose a " value system " upon Academy we must endeavor to discover *how* those goals, aims, and values which bind together Academic pursuits accomplish their purpose.[39]

In the search for an answer to this How?, the citizen of Academy may well find himself once more in the original grove of Academe, not so much to hear what was discussed there or with what tools as to recall the importance of conviction and how it related to the work of intellect. In Plato's day, when the grove of Academe was dedicated to its abiding symbolic function, there were Absolutes abroad in the land, Ideas, Forms. The most important — or at least the most commonly revered — of these increasingly came to be the Good, the True, and the Beautiful. Plato and his father in dialogue, Socrates, referred to the three with great seriousness and awe but also with unsystematic abandon. Often only one is mentioned, sometimes a different one than we might have expected in the given context. Occasionally one is openly used as a synonym for another. Sometimes two appear together, but there seems to be no consistent coupling of any particular pair. Sometimes one is exalted above the others as the highest, the Idea of Ideas, the Form of Forms. Usually this is the Good, but not even that is consistent. No fixed hierarchy or even conjunction seems to have been formulated by Plato himself. The Platonic triad of the Good, the True, and the Beautiful seems to have been forged as a later work of the Academy. It is, however, so implicitly ingrained in the life of the Academy that Campbell Stewart, in a brief but excellent history of higher education, can say:

" Education was concerned ultimately with right action, right think-ing, and the affirmation of the inner and permanent world of the true, the good and the beautiful." The early Academies could make a claim for this inner world analogous to that for virtue and justice which " were in the mind of man because they were a priori in the mind and purpose of his Creator." [40]

Like the Nephilim, the " giants of old " in Gen., ch. 6, the Abso-lutes have apparently disappeared from the land. In the contem-porary Academy one could win more votes with the slogan, " There are no absolutes " (or, " Everything is relative ") than with the slogan, " Truth is the only absolute " (already a reduction of the original claim by 66.66%). It is my thesis, however, that the Platonic triad has left a discernible imprint upon the Academic landscape; and it is so intimately related to all of the work of Academy that it can be of value in classifying the terrain within the Academic grove. One would be surprised if he were to discover himself the first to entertain a thought of this kind, and I am grateful to ack-nowledge the contribution made by Erich Kahler's lecture, *The True, the Good, and the Beautiful*. To be sure, he has a different conception of their relationship to each other (Truth is the ultimate support of both the good and the beautiful: " It is incontrovertibly the founding value "), and makes quite a different use of the triad than shall we. Two aspects of his work are extremely significant for us, however. First, his expression of a conviction we share: " It was, indeed, the purpose of this lecture to demonstrate that, con-trary to appearances, the true, the good, and the beautiful have not altogether perished from the earth, that, secretly, clandestinely, they are still here."

His second contribution is the creation of the concept and the term " relative absolutes," formally analogous to what we shall call " classifying values." After declaring that twentieth-century experi-ence has shattered our belief in " integral absolutes " or " stable noumena," Kahler continues: " While these firmly established real absolutes have vanished from our intellectual sky, there still subsist for us certain ' relative absolutes ' . . . ' absolutes ' which are not actual absolutes at all, in the literal sense of the word and in the ancient sense of the concept, but which appear always in inextricable conjunction with changing conditions. . . . They are in every respect limited and dynamic absolutes. . . . When I speak of 'the true, the good, and the beautiful,' what I have in mind are such relative absolutes moving along, changing, with the changes and ranges of our human condition." [41]

For me, as for Kahler, "the true, the good, and the beautiful," are limited and dynamic concepts; but I would prefer not to designate them by the misleading term "absolutes" at all. Rather, I consider them to be the *values* of use to Academy in its "task of classifying all knowledge." It remains necessary to discuss what kind of values the good, the true, and the beautiful now are for Academy, and in what sense they can serve a classifying function for Academic disciplines.

Jaspers speaks of a cosmos of reality and gives us a cosmology of the microcosmic university; Macmurray uses the term "geography" to describe the whole world, the world of reflection and the inner world of man; others, like Arnold Nash and Snow, speak of a map of knowledge, or a cultural map. Like Jaspers we have used the term "cosmos" to refer to reality as an ordered whole, and we have identified Truth-Humanity as the complex of ultimate criteria for any meaningful and worthwhile existence possible to man in this cosmos. Thus, Truth and Humanity have an important bearing not only on Academy but also on all areas of our topographical allegory, including professional-industrial, urban culture and life on the esoteric pinnacles of graduate research. Our "classifying values," on the other hand, are to be used in designating and determining the basic divisions in the topography of the Academy itself.

Before utilizing these values to classify, however, one requires additional clarification of the distinction between the ultimate Truth-Humanity criteria and our more proximate and immediately apprehensible classifying values. The good, the true, and the beautiful, on the one hand, are values that characterize separate and distinct divisions of the Academic topography, and are quite terrestrial. Truth and Humanity, on the other hand, are more like stars defining a constellation in the heavens of the cosmos, and they bear upon and are relevant to all meaningful existence. Though they are only known "by faith and not by sight," they are valid for and applicable to all divisions, sectors, tracts, or plots of Academy, as well as outside it. Thus, Truth must never be misunderstood as the exclusive property of those regions or sectors, those disciplines of Academy dedicated to " the true," nor is Humanity excluded from equal relevance to them. Again, Truth is an ultimate criterion bearing significantly on the grove of " the good "; and, further, Truth and Humanity give significance to, and are the goal of, all activity in the fields called " beautiful." It is clear that the *ultimate criteria* are conceived as being shared by and serve to *unite* Academy's endeavors. But how do our *classifying values divide* the fields, the activities, the techniques of husbandry within Academy's grove? Plato's Academe *was* a grove, both literally and symbolically, for though various forms of worship, meditation, and reflection were carried on there, philosophy was the universal intellectual solvent, the sovereign discipline that united *and* categorized all. One could rightly speak of *a* grove of Academe. Today, however, disciplines have grown quantitatively to such an extent that we might prefer to speak symbolically of the *groves* of Academe, were it not for the truly qualitative distinctions between subject matters, methodologies, and directions of inquiry among various *groups* of disciplines. Because of these differences we prefer to represent various *groups* of disciplines in Academy by *grove, orchard, vineyard,* or *field.*

There is little doubt that our contemporary Academy is moving toward a full acceptance of a threefold division within its walls. Alongside of the traditional groups of the humanities (or liberal arts) and the sciences, the social studies are making an ever surer place for themselves. What to call this newer grove or field of Academy is not so simple a problem as one might think. On the one hand, there is a genuine desire among these Academicians to be free of the " inexactness " and pessimism of the humanities. This corresponds to the attempt to prove by methodology and equipment, the use of graphs, computers, and higher mathematics, that these disciplines are true sciences. Yet, this group wishes at least complete autonomy, corresponding to a third culture in Snow's terms, if not ultimately to *lead* the Academy in a sally forth " to conquer the world." [42] Whether Social Sciences (distinguished from Natural ones) as, for example, at Harvard and the University of Chicago, Contemporary Civilization as at Columbia, or the currently popular and lucrative title Behavioral Sciences, no fully satisfactory designation has yet been coined for this vineyard or grove. Of the titles that have been used, Contemporary Civilization seems to have real cogency, partly because it is prejudicial neither toward the arts nor toward the sciences, partly because it emphasizes the fact that these disciplines in their present form are of relatively recent origin, and that many tend to focus on the present and ignore the past. Psychology, for instance, may well place even Freud in the shadowy past with the forgotten " prescientific " classical faculty psychology that reigned from Aristotle through the Neo-Kantians, while sociology characteristically sharpens its tools on the most recent suburban development or housing project. On the other hand, the natural sciences expend even less effort, if possible, on the past, thus earning equal claim to the title " Contemporary."

There is, however, a neglected term of the past that seems to us to have many advantages, above all, that it provides a viable substitute for the overloaded term " behavior." This medieval designation would christen the group of disciplines of which we are speaking, " the arts of conduct." We shall shortly develop these relationships more fully, but already at this point our predilection for this term will reveal to the more perceptive reader the identification of each of our " classifying values " with one particular grove, orchard, or field, with one division or group of disciplines: specifically, " the true " will point to the sciences, " the beautiful " to the arts, " the good " to what we shall provisionally call the arts of conduct.

Next, we must seriously ask ourselves what conceivable good it does to add one more set of symbols to the already complicated terminology of Academic classification. The answer may lie in the consensus of the general education professors who have tried to " think through " the relationships between their own specialities and the most obviously neighboring disciplines. They have agreed that neither methodology nor subject matter gives an adequate key, though some programs such as the magnificently conceived sciences program in the Columbia experiment have a built-in dramatic sweep of high pedagogical value. They usually end up by making the best of traditional ties, or, like Jaspers and Macmurray, attempting to justify continuities in Academic cognition by analogy to continuities in culture. What we are trying to do here is to classify Academic disciplines in terms of the *direction of their inquiry,* or, in the terminology of David Easton, to ask what are the *motivating ques-*

tions of a group or family of disciplines making up a current Academic grove or vineyard, orchard, or field. By this scheme, the sciences are those Academic disciplines which characteristically ask the question, What is the true? in their particular areas of subject matter; the arts characteristically ask, What is the beautiful? in their several areas; and the members of the third group characteristically ask, What is the concrete, practical good? for theirs. Precisely what is connoted by " direction of inquiry " in each of these cases? A " direction of inquiry " includes the specification of subject matter and whatever methodology may be appropriate to its investigation; but the direction of inquiry designated by a specific classifying value points a discipline to its characteristic *attitudes,* to its *goals,* and to its peculiar perspective on the ultimate criteria.

The implications of these three directions of inquiry will become clearer as we attempt to relate Theology to each separately in the next three chapters. A preliminary listing of the probable make-up of these groups may provide some hints, helpful for clarification. This clarification may, further, be assisted by an extension of our topography of the Academy. We have said that a division of Academy, a group of disciplines, shall correspond to a grove or field or vineyard *in* Academy. Now let us suggest that one discipline within a group, say, chemistry within the natural sciences, corresponds to a *region* or *sector* within a field, orchard, or grove of Academy. Finally, a specialization within a discipline, for instance, physical or organic chemistry within chemical science as a whole, shall be designated a *plot* or *tract* within a *region* or *sector* of a *grove* within Academy.

The sciences, then, which ask, What is the true? will include the traditional fact-oriented studies. The range of these is suggested by Columbia's " continuous development " plan of organization which led from the physics of macroscopic phenomena in astronomy through the kinetic theory of matter and electron field physics (electricity and optics) back through the physics of particles (atoms and molecules), including the periodic table and Bohr's model of the atom, through special relativity and related cosmological questions to chemical analysis, chemical reactions, equilibriums and probability, organic chemistry, which — after the traditional somewhat digressive trip to physical chemistry — leads through biochemistry to biological individuals, a path ranging from photosynthesis up to sense organs and nervous systems, then to the problems of origin and development, of biological inheritance and growth. For our purposes the important thing to note is that the common characteristic that marks each of these cognitive endeavors as " sciences " is their primary (though never necessarily their only) value question: What is the true?

The second traditional grouping of disciplines has usually been called the " humanities " or the " arts." The motivating question for these disciplines, What is the beautiful? points us toward the latter designation as more accurate and useful. The primacy of the question about beauty further suggests that the heart of this group is defined by the use and appreciation of the creative power of music, the plastic arts (including architecture), and the tongues (with special emphasis on poetic, prosaic, and dramatic literature). The very distinction between creation and appreciation shows that we are in a more ambiguous field than in the case of the " true sciences." The nature of the creativity necessary to beauty, as we shall see more fully in Chapter V, leads us diametrically away from the *generalizing* " truth " of science, because the " truth " of beauty *particularizes* the arts through the individual realizations of an artistic vision which are the building blocks of the arts. The regions or sectors of the language-literature complex within the field or grove of the arts illustrate the problem perfectly. The problems of language in our day are increasingly treated in terms of logic, so that progressive language study is carried out primarily in a scientific rather than an aesthetic dimension. Language, for Academy, has become (as at certain other periods in history) more of an instrument, a weapon, a tool, than a thing of beauty. Commensurate with this, while the logic of language and the language of logic are international, appropriate to the factuality and generalizing tendency of science, language defined as *tongue* has the connotations of that particularity with respect to place and time characteristic of art. In this context the question about beauty has the same appropriateness for the creations of language that it does for the creations of music or painting, and, therefore, is as appropriate to the vineyard of the arts as are studies centered in those forms of creativity. This brief characterization of the traditional humanities as " arts centered " seems to exclude such " humanities " as philosophy, history, religion, and even mathematics, most of which were joined with the arts in Plato's original grove and among the seven liberal arts, and most of which are — in varying combinations — included in the faculties of arts or humanities today. These four disciplines or sectors of Academy will, however, shortly receive treatment of their own.

The third group of disciplines is identified by the classifying mark of asking particular forms of the motivating questions, What is the good here, or here, or here; for me, for him, for them? and it presents the most complex situation of all. We have tentatively designated the sectors of this Academic grove the " arts of conduct." This designation is appropriate first of all because of the obviously common ethical bond between " the good " and " conduct." Applied to the realms of existence, " the good " points to norms for useful and satisfying individual conduct and also for the just conducting of human affairs in general, or it describes the atmosphere in which these norms may be made effectual. In addition, the singular number implied by " conduct " is more appropriate than collective terms like " social " or " civilization " to the inclusion of psychology, weaned from the sciences, in this group of disciplines. More acutely than the scientific aspects of psychology, however, the mood which calls the study of government " political *science*" and which demands recognition for the " behavioral *sciences*" warns us of the inevitable unpopularity of the term " arts " in the title of this group. And there is a certain justice in this unpopularity, for the purposes of these disciplines are not primarily those of decoration but those of utilization.

Somewhat paradoxically, then, I wish to propose the substitution for " arts " of a term still more probably destined for unpopularity, namely, " crafts." Against such anticipated criticism, I must first protest innocence of frivolous intent in the juxtaposition of the two terms " arts and crafts." Secondly, I must insist on the highly honorable connotations which should be called forth by the term " craftsmanship." Not only cobblers and carpenters are craftsmen, though these people too lend to the term a sense of dignity, skill, and reliability. A craftsman is more than an assembly-line worker endlessly repeating an operation in which he as a person is not really involved. A true craftsman shapes a particular block of material with his special skill and an authentic degree of freedom and imagination into an object that may have beauty and the "truth" of a job well done, but which is primarily characterized by being useful, by being "good" for something. Craftsmanship with its innate qualities of enterprise and competence and pride in the accomplishment of a worthwhile task is necessary to all the work in Academy, to all the tilling of the soil, the planting, the cultivating, the harvesting in its groves and fields. No scientist or artist can do his job effectively if he is not a skilled and thoroughly competent craftsman. This is why leading thinkers of Academy such as Barzun and Jaspers insist upon a thoroughgoing reinstatement of skillful labor in every corner of the Academic groves. Jaspers stresses: "Genius develops only where it is matched by commensurate commitment, will power, application and craftsmanship." [43] As universal as is Academy's need for craftsmanship, the craftsman's peculiar way of shaping intransigent and unpredictable material, suggestive but not exhaustively exact data, for the sake of utility or "good"ness seems most appropriate to the social scientist in the exercise of his craft of conduct.

Therefore, for the purposes of a fresh evaluation of important and rapidly growing disciplines, the group title "crafts of conduct" shall refer here and especially in Chapter IV to the disciplines of psychology, sociology, economy, government, and their near relatives. The term "craft" in this title will point to the fact that these disciplines possess neither the exactness of the natural sciences — otherwise the best government professors would be recognized as the best presidents, prime ministers, queens, and dictators, the economists would be the richest, and the psychologists the most normal of men — nor do they possess the almost arbitrary uniqueness lent to the arts by the individualizing truth of beauty, but have their own integrity, dignity, and peculiar virtues. The term "conduct" shall point to the motivating question which, though it has particular forms for each, unites them all by its general form: What is the good? Thus, psychology shall be understood as carrying out its experiments, its analyses, its theorizing in the light of the question: What is the good for man as a whole, living entity characterized by a psychic structure?; sociology shall always perform its work with reference to the question: What is the good for man in relation to others: individuals, groups, and institutions?; economics shall be directed by the consideration: What is the good for man in relation to the world of goods?; the study of government shall seek to know and to do "the good for man in the world of politics, of states, and of all aggregations of power under human control."

At this point we must ask whether these neat theoretical classifications — true-good-beautiful, science-craft-art — are merely interesting as ideal maps of knowledge no more practicable than those maps of old which showed a direct westward passage from Europe to India. Or, at the opposite extreme, we might well be asked whether we intend them to be used as a practical guide for grouping departments in the actual administration of a college or university. Our primary intention in developing this system of values for classifying is to help the disciplines understand and evaluate what they *are doing,* in terms of the primary intellectual work of the Academy, both separately *and together,* and on the basis of this clarification to assist them in deciding on and developing new directions for individual and common work. As an actual plan of organization, these value-classifications should work as well as any grouping, and better than some — except for certain disciplines which, strictly speaking, "do not belong."

The idyllic perfection of the plan is spoiled by the omission from any group of some of the most important plantings of Academy's groves, of which we shall mention four: philosophy, mathematics, history — and theology. There is a sense in which these "misfits" are border or boundary disciplines and, therefore, their homelessness among the classifications is more of an asset than a liability since they can serve as bridges across which groups can communicate with each other; and, in fact, it is even possible that they — one or all — can provide the centripetal force required to unify the creative energies of the Academy. But in which group should each of the four fall in the college catalog — with all the attached problems of the "distribution requirements" and extradepartmental "work related to the student's major"? To which of the intragroup committee meetings should the delegates from these departments be dispatched?

These questions could always be met on the basis of historical accident, since all these disciplines are venerable. On the other hand, we might possibly construct of these four disciplines a fourth group called " nondescripts " or, with more fitting dignity, " coordinating disciplines " or " departments of wisdom." Cardinal Newman spoke of the map of knowledge as an organic whole, of which each department is a kind of pie slice, the absence of any impoverishing the whole and each of the other parts. His *manner* of speaking about this recalls Paul's metaphorically calling the Church " Christ's body," each member and organ of which is important to the others and to the whole (see especially I Cor. 12:12-31). Though he intends to speak with respect of the other disciplines and not to assign theology a stifling magisterial role, one is never wholly free of the suspicion that for Newman theology is the *head* of the Academic body, the source and guarantor of wholeness, health, and growth (see Eph. 4:15 f.). Theology, in its exegetical, dogmatic, and practical forms, is and should be master in the ecclesiastical seminary, but we here assign it no such role in the Academy. It shall be the concern of each of the next three chapters to work out the relationship between theology and one of the three divisions or groups of disciplines. The succeeding paragraphs must suffice for outlining such relationships for the other three boundary disciplines.

Philosophy was the queen of the sciences in the original grove of Academe; but, like the Greek slaves far more cultivated than the barbarous masters they served as tutors, philosophy did long and arduous service in the schools of Christianity as the *ancilla theologiae,* the handmaid of the Jewish-born Christian queen. Protestantism, with its critical nominalist tendencies and Scriptural exclusivism, dismissed the handmaid from her servitude as a dangerous and competitive influence, incidentally helping philosophy toward a new *independence.* The Enlightenment completed the job of liberation, so that by the nineteenth century philosophy had again arrived at the throne of Academic primacy — represented preeminently by Hegel's all-knowing and therefore all-powerful system which would perfect history through the perfect state and, as a sort of bonus, save theology from intellectual extinction. The loss of self-confidence which has almost universally afflicted the intellectual culture of the twentieth century has, however, been nowhere more severe than in philosophy. The refusal, the inability, or at best halting, fragmentary efforts to write metaphysics is symptomatic of the fact. Philosophy has largely abdicated the task of "creating a cosmos," of "unifying the whole," and, therefore, of being the queen of Academy. In most cases, she is either no longer asked to do so, or not heeded when she tries. Whichever be the case, if Jaspers is correct in saying that to address oneself to the whole is the philosophical point of view, philosophy seems to be pointing away from her very nature.[44] The subject-object separation finalized by Kant seems to have proved fatal to a unified "view of the whole" after all, and all attempts — from Hegel to Heidegger and Tillich — to soar above the chasm or tunnel beneath, to clamber round it or plumb ultimate depths by peering into it, have produced limited results at best. Philosophy is left to live on one edge of the chasm or the other. Existentialists pull the whole world inside the knowing subject, then cognitize it intensely and often emotionally. The objectivists — including linguistic analysts — narrow knowledge to *things* which can be *handled* with the *tools* of logic. The scientific philosophers talk of cosmology, but their philosophizing, though accurate in its up-to-dateness, is partial, and *all* is mirrored as an *imago machinae*. As an auxiliary or ancillary discipline, philosophy, both for its history and for its sense of order, of logic, is still useful — even indispensable — to everyone. Every discipline *must* philosophize about its nature and its task. But philosophy today does not fulfill its ancient role: it does not persuasively provide the decisive clues to the nature of the authentic whole it named Truth.

It is easy to make a case by definition for the statement that philosophy should not belong to *any* one *part* of the Academy, but the opposite seems at first to be true of mathematics. "How dare one call mathematics a misfit?" someone calls out. "Everyone knows that mathematics is a science." Everyone, that is, but mathematicians and scientists. Mathematics in general "applies" to many sciences, in fact, a science is often partly defined by such application but, as Stuermann points out, there are mathematical systems that have no application. The very way in which the beautifully integrated Columbia science program appended mathematics at the end, awkwardly, demonstrates that mathematics is actually one of our misfits. In a sense mathematics was once the mother of philosophy — in a more radical sense, even, than in the *Principia Mathematica* of Whitehead and Russell. Or perhaps it would be more accurate to call mathematics the essence of philosophy, purer and more beautiful. Behind the non-Socratic shoulder of Plato stood Pythagoras, so it is no surprise when we find the shape of the ideal forms to be circular or, quintessentially, triangular.

Stuermann, who as a modern man has lost faith in systems in general, finds " the only systems of thought that delight the mind and heart and do so with simplicity and elegance are mathematical ones." [45] This statement reminds us that mathematics was originally related not only to the authentic Absolute called Truth, but also to that known as Beauty. There is evidence that mathematics may have originated in an aesthetic context: that of music. It is at least clear that the structure of music has always been mathematical. This was certainly true in ancient Greece, which produced the Pythagorean five-tone scale, but it has also been true of other periods. Certain modern composers have made radical new musical inventions on mathematical models. A much more suggestive and far-reaching connection has been postulated, however, involving the mathematical basis for the new harmonic inventions in Venice in the sixteenth century, together with those of contemporary architecture, and also of cosmological theory.

The trend of mathematics in general during the past several centuries, however, has been toward a reduction of philosophical scope, away from a role in metaphysics and toward an identity as a set of techniques or problem-solving tools. Many mathematicians can be heard to say — sometimes with a suggestion of wistfulness — that their discipline is not in reality a science because it has no proper subject matter; instead, they call it a set of tricks to be manipulated and cleverly combined for the solution of puzzles and games. The extreme expression of this tendency was stated by one of my most brilliant professors in engineering school who claimed that except for pure mathematical speculation and theorizing all mathematics above the introductory calculus should be taught by the department applying it to problems in physics, physical chemistry, or one of the branches of engineering. As a matter of fact, modern mathematics, which has undergone very rapid development since Descartes, is, as Stuermann puts it, *an extension of logic.* " It is a logical discipline," he continues, " in which the basic categories are those of number, class membership, class inclusion, figure, continuity, and so on. One of the chief factors in the amazing growth of modern science after the sixteenth century was precisely the development of a logical language that could express quantitative relationships exactly." [46] Stuermann's solution to our problem in placing mathematics is to group it with logic as a formal science in contrast to the factual sciences to which it is applied. One of the chief clarifications gained by this distinction is the disjunction of mathematics, as purely formal, from content and therefore value. Stuermann would go so far in his modern disdain of system as to say that systems of thought are still possible in mathematics and logic precisely because no question of Truth and goodness is involved. " One deals there with abstract ideas and their relations, not with irrevocable facts and recalcitrant persons." [47] This consideration alone should make clear, on the one hand, that mathematics is *sui generis,* a true misfit not to be confused with disciplines concerned with the *stuff* of truth and beauty and, on the other hand, mathematics' very isolation-in-kind — especially from questions of the good — disqualifies it altogether from possible consideration for a magisterial role.

History, however, is a practically universal Academic solvent. Every discipline, including those of science, needs its own history and the historical context which surrounds it. *Methodologically* speaking, in the nineteenth and sometimes in the twentieth century, the historian and not the philosopher has been king in Academy. In making this statement, I refer to the fact that it has been possible to say: " I am not an artist or a political scientist but a historian whose specialty is art or music, or Russian literature, or, for that matter, war, or the economy of Norway, the government of Finland." Historicism, at its crest, could claim to *be* theology, and certain volunteer pallbearers for philosophy have asserted: " There is nothing left for philosophy to do but to write its own history." From a *metaphysical* point of view, on the other hand, as philosophy (or theology) of history, in thinkers like Augustine, Hegel, Spengler, Toynbee, and, above all, Karl Marx, history has claimed the magisterial role sometimes assumed by Theology or Idealistic philosophy. In direct opposition to all such claims, a Karl Barth would say that there is no place for such a thing as an independent historical discipline in his science, theology. The various forms of theology, dogmatic, exegetical, practical, are each responsible for incorporating within themselves and evaluating their own histories, using, of course, critical historical methodology. Historians themselves are torn between an antiteleological relativism and some form (often quite dilute) of the doctrine of progress. They try not to be overwhelmed by the immense diversity of data across their vast rainbow of subject matters and try also not to succumb to the desire to impose some unjustified kind of meaning or premature pattern upon their data. It is partly out of respect for the integrity and industry of the historian that we have introduced the term " craft " into this consideration of the Academy. Respect for both the unmanageable breadth of the historical subject matter, on the one hand, and for the hope kindled by the Hebraic prophets' sense that history — not nature or reason — is *the* bearer of meaning, on the other, militated against strict inclusion among science or crafts or arts, but led us to place the historical discipline among the magnificent misfits of the Academy.

The fourth of these, theology? Its case, as we have said, must yet be tried — and in greater detail. We must see in the following chapters whether it succeeds or fails to fulfill its ancient role, whether it speaks with relevance to the whole of modern life or has been reduced to a useful bag of tricks, whether it is very busy but ultimately indecisive. We must investigate whether or not it bears conviction into the Academy, and whether or not it can communicate its conviction to the other disciplines — whether it can learn *from* and *with* them and also has something to *tell* them and the world outside Academy as well.

III

Theology as a Science

"Theological science proceeds differently [from the secular sciences]. Assuming the existence of revelation, theology clarifies the implications and consequences of this faith. It develops special categories to express the inexpressible.

"Both explanations, the secular and the theological, operate with assumptions. They are not, strictly speaking, mutually exclusive. Both are forms of thought which work with assumptions and see where and how far they will get them. Both remain scientific so long as they acknowledge one another and remember in a self-critical spirit that knowability is but a mode of Being within Being, never Being per se."

Karl Jaspers, The Idea of the University.

IT VERY MUCH NEEDS to be said that most studies of science and theology take a radically wrong approach: they get off on the wrong foot and as a result do not leap very high or very far, and turn out to be " surprisingly " unimpressive. One reads the opening formulation and is suddenly made to feel, at best, like a witness to that exciting but uneven struggle, the bullfight. One hopes that the bull, Theology, will be brave and will charge energetically but rather stupidly, for we are to identify with that tantalizing toreador, Science, and the *bull* must die. At worst, we find ourselves like a jigsaw puzzle addict on a rainy afternoon in some unfamiliar and isolated spot: someone has left us with several pieces from one puzzle, science, and others from another, theology, and we are powerless to put them together. These images arise in response to opening statements which ask, specifically: Can theology be made relevant to a technological age? or, Can theology fulfill the demands of scientific thinking? or even, as on a recent book jacket, " Can anyone be intellectually honest and a Christian at the same time? " All seem to assume that modern man can stand upon some unshakable achievement, which may be very small but has a qualitatively prior status in the realm of knowledge, to which all earlier forms of knowing must submit and conform lest they be consigned to the outer darkness reserved for black magic.

The root of these ludicrous and rather sad misunderstandings is a forked one. To begin with, the very name " science " has been usurped in the popular misconception for one kind of science, called " modern," and all earlier intellectual efforts are dismissed as prescientific. It is assumed that Science is defined by its subject matter, which is natural (or created) reality. All knowledge about art and the relationships of such recalcitrant subjects as persons can be very interesting, but it is condemned to being relatively inexact. Such knowledge at best is a secondhand, second-rate science, an inferior imitation of the real thing. Then when the imagination of popular scientism gets hold of the concept not only of quantitative exactitude but also of " scientific method " it makes a related error. It asserts the infallible and immutable character of scientific truth. It is this which forces a magisterial role upon natural sciences willy-nilly and drives all other forms of cognition to their knees before science in the popular imagination. It becomes immediately necessary, therefore, to define science and to distinguish between kinds of science, not only for the sake of the other forms of knowledge, but, above all, to preserve the intrinsic intensity of its power, and to save modern science from the idolatry which would make it pretend to be what it is not.

WHAT KIND OF SCIENCE IS THEOLOGY?

" What characterizes science then," says Jaspers " is this: We cannot achieve universally valid and cogent knowledge of reality except within a framework of assumptions which we know to be only relatively valid." [1] With this statement we have caught the nature of all valid human thought: it proceeds from assumptions by means of the best logical tools for extracting the proper conclusions from them.

The tentative character, the "relative validity," of the assumptions
varies, depending on the nature of the assumptions and the degree
of their abstraction from our sense data about tangible reality. It is
a seemingly irrevocable limit of the human condition, however, that
no assumption at the base of any form of science, any form of
thought, can be proved finally and absolutely, can be unconditionally and permanently valid. All basic assumptions, whether of
natural science or of natural theology, are of a prelogical character:
no matter how powerful the tools of logic may be, the assumptions
are determined before logic begins to operate. Assumptions may be
modified, rejected, even reversed, as a result of the character of the
conclusions logic draws from them, but there is no such thing,
strictly speaking, as a "logical assumption."

The difference in kind between assumptions leads us to two distinctions between kinds of science. Most simply, we distinguish between a "wider" and a "narrower" kind of science, corresponding
to wider and narrower assumptions defining the range of competence which a given science claims. In the general, more classical,
sense *scientia* refers simply to knowledge, not to a random collection of opinions, but to an ordered fabric of genuine cognition, so
that science in this wider sense includes any clear understanding
obtained through the use of precise conceptualization. I would
further insist concerning "wider" sciences in general, as I shall
insist for Theology in particular, that they give clear understanding *about a clearly defined subject matter* which may have a truly
objective character outside the knower himself. Jaspers, however,
with his experience as psychological scientist and then as philosopher, is primarily concerned that *factual* knowledge has increasingly been weaned away from philosophy by science. Therefore, he
tends to identify general and factual knowledge with "narrower"
modern science, while limiting "wider science" to clarification of
what it is I really mean, want or believe, in short, lucid self-knowl-
edge. He thinks in terms of value as opposed to fact as he continues with the claim that "wider" sciences are at the same time
more and less than "narrower" science. "They are more insofar as
they are a creative way of thinking, one that transforms man. They
are less than science insofar as they do not yield any concrete knowledge." But this "less than science" does not disqualify "wider"

endeavors, which are rendered scientific by their clarity and rigor, a rigor which Heidegger declares in the cases of poetry and philosophy to be greater than that of the narrower sciences.[2]

Modern science, however, has developed a clear stage beyond the classic " wider " definition of science. It has " sacrificed " claims to ultimate or total knowledge, and because it seeks knowledge valid for everyone, everywhere, and at all times it " does not require my total personal commitment." By the development and refinement of certain methodological tools, however, and by assumptions that limit investigation strictly to subject matters appropriate to these tools, it has bought with its sacrifices tangible, quantitative, and in some cases, apparently exhaustive knowledge. These solid achievements have led many to ignore the warnings arising out of the study of scientific logic: " Every scientific statement remains tentative forever. . . . We do not know; we can only guess. And our guesses are guided by the unscientific, the metaphysical (though biologically explicable) faith in laws, in regularities we can uncover. . . . Science is not a system of certain or well-established statements; nor is it a system which steadily advances toward a state of finality." [3] This should be enough to relieve " narrower " science of the burden, imposed mainly from without, of pretense to infallibility and omnicompetence. " But it is not just because science is unfixed, tentative, often backtracking, and always unorganized (the fact is that scientific unity does not last long) that it is unfit for monarchical rule," Barzun reminds us. " Far more disqualifying is its irrelevance in a myriad situations that are of immediate moment to living beings." [4]

It is ironical that the very people who insist most loudly that theology is nothing more than the expression of man's insecurity, are the same ones who, in their insecurity, would force the role of Savior upon unwilling science. Much worse, however, are the " friends " of Theology hypnotized by the impressive successes of " narrower " sciences who would cast Theology in their image. There seemed much good reason when, in the first flush of scientific success, Schleiermacher and his followers in the nineteenth century discarded the stultifyingly rigid doctrinal structures of Orthodoxy for " scientific " histories and psychologies of religion. It was the cause of some consternation, however, when History of Religions, having begun with the assumption that Christianity is one of the genus of human religions, was unable to prove it Absolute or unique. It should have served as a powerful warning when Psychology of Religions, having set out to study the nervous and psychic reflexes actuated in the practice of the Christian religion, found itself powerless to prove that what activated these reflexes in a Christian man was truly and uniquely Divine.

Nevertheless, men like Wobbermin in the German-speaking cultural world and D. C. Macintosh in the English tried to model theology on the " successful " modern sciences. Heinrich Scholz constructed an ascending scale of requirements any discipline must fulfill to be considered scientific, in answer to his question, How can Protestant theology be a science?: (1) freedom from contradiction in all the propositions to be constructed by the so-called science in question (Proposition postulate); (2) the unity in its objective sphere (Coherence postulate); (3) all propositions must be drawn up to be capable of being tested " by any reader or hearer who is sufficiently attentive " (Verifiability postulate); (4) regard must be had to what is physically and biologically impossible (Congruity postulate); (5) freedom from " any sort of prejudice " (Independence postulate); (6) all propositions must be capable of being broken up into axioms and theorems and susceptible of proof on this basis, which Scholz insists is " the supreme claim which can be made on any science." [5]

It would be possible to create a religious science on this basis, in fact, many such sciences have been created, and both the validity and usefulness of psychology, sociology, and history of religion are indeed praiseworthy. One must admire the energy and care required for such a project as Scholz outlines, but neither any one of these sciences nor the sum of them is the science, Theology. We could wish to possess the unfailing " prejudice filter " necessary for Scholz's fifth condition, and we shall affirm coherence as essential to Theology, but we shall find it necessary to attack the other postulates during the course of the present chapter. At this point, let it suffice to say that Scholz's scientific theology would have to dispense with most of the important statements about God in the Bible, together with the Trinity and Christology, on the basis of the Proposition postulate; with faith, on the basis of the Verifiability postulate; with the resurrection and ascension, on the basis of the Congruity postulate; and be reduced to a collection of innocuous platitudes by the postulate making "the supreme claim." Such a travesty of Theology could only be possible if one totally ignored the distinction in kind between the assumptions at the base of the " narrower " sciences and those of the " wider." A thorough consideration of all such attempts as those of Scholz's could only lead us to Jaspers' conclusion: " Theological science proceeds differently."

A second distinction between kinds of sciences is implied in this statement, and Jaspers chooses for it the terminology " theological and secular." It is immediately apparent here that he refers to a difference in the kind of assumptions which define the competence of a science, and in this case especially the level of abstraction of these presuppositions. The distinction may be clarified by terminology analogous to that of I John 4:20, " For he who does not love his brother whom he has seen, cannot love God whom he has not seen." The truth of secular science, particularly of the " narrower " kind, is *sensible,* that is, it is defined by the creature we have seen (apprehended with our *senses*). The truth of theological science, on the other hand, though it by no means ignores the creaturely reality we have seen, is defined not by it but by the Creator, whom we have not seen. We hasten to add, however, that theological science does not apprehend the Creator in the same way that secular science apprehends creaturely reality. Theological science is *insensible,* it has no such faculty, strictly speaking, as the senses by which all men regularly and reliably perceive physical objects. It is only by analogy that Theology can speak of the " eyes " of faith. Theology is in much the same predicament when it comes to expressing its knowledge in language and logic. Secular science speaks about creaturely reality in the language of the creature; but theological science cannot speak about God in the language of God, because it does not know God's language or his logic. Theology must speak of the Creator in the language of the creature; theological science has no choice but to develop special categories within human language with which to attempt " to express the inexpressible."

When we attempt to penetrate more deeply into the distinction between theological and secular science, however, the situation becomes less clear. The assumptions of theological science, so-called might be said to exist on three levels of abstraction. On the first level, Theology is interested in certain creaturely realities: revelation, which Jaspers rightly insists is the subject of Theology, occurs to men *in human history*. On the second level of abstraction, Theology assumes that the creaturely reality in which it is interested is *meaningful*. On the third level of abstraction, which presumably makes theological science unique, Theology assumes that it is the God known to it in revelation who lends meaning to particular creaturely reality.

If one now carries out an analogous investigation for other scientific disciplines in Academy, one begins to wonder about the qualitative uniqueness of theological science. All disciplines share not only the first level of interest in a particular portion of concrete reality, but also the second level of assumptions that what they are interested in is meaningful, is useful, valuable, beautiful. At least some disciplines, however, share the possibility of the third level of abstraction in its assumptions: art history, for example, may be interested in paintings because it finds them beautiful; but beyond this may believe that Beauty exists as the most precious reality of all, imparting itself, let us say, through the media of many particular paintings among many other things. In this sense art history could be a " theological science." Other definitions of art history are quite possible and many art historians would, in fact, vigorously combat this one.

Christian Theology as a science, however, cannot dispense with God. It is not one or many sciences about men, nor does it believe that " God " can be reduced to " Man writ large." It talks about God in anthropomorphic terms only because it knows no better symbolism from the creaturely realm to use in its human speech about God. The distinction between theological and secular science holds, in Jaspers' terms, only and precisely because he means a specific revelation recognized by a human community when he says: " Assuming the existence of revelation, theology clarifies the implications and consequences of this faith."

Theology, then, is a science: specifically, that one of the " wider " sciences which is compelled by its nature to be nonsecular. With this double distinction Theology is a science, but then all legitimate Academic disciplines, secular-narrower, secular-wider, and possibly other "theological"-wider disciplines beside Theology, are sciences too. This chapter, however, was not understood as being about all Academic disciplines but about one group called the sciences, or even natural sciences, in contradistinction to the arts and the crafts of conduct. This group was supposed to be especially concerned with What is the true? as the others asked about the good and the beautiful. We must, therefore, ask about three relationships between Theology and the natural sciences.

First of all, granted that there are several kinds of sciences in Academy, is there not one kind, namely, modern science, natural science, " real " science, which is more scientific than the others? We hope shortly to show that there are various tests of truth, one more appropriate to these " narrower " sciences, one to the arts and one to the crafts of conduct. We could only affirm that physics and zoology are more scientific than the study of government and musicology, if their kind of truth is better than, is prior to, the truth of goodness and the truth of beauty. Since by the very nature of all careful human thought this is not true, we must deny that one kind of science is more scientific than others and apply to all kinds of science what Jaspers says about the two designated in our second distinction: "Both explanations, the secular and the theological, operate with assumptions. They are not, strictly speaking, mutually exclusive. Both are forms of thought which work with assumptions and see where and how far they will get with them. Both remain scientific so long as they acknowledge one another and remember in a self-critical spirit that knowability is but a mode of Being within Being, never Being per se." This statement puts Theology as a science on precisely the same footing as physics, zoology, economics, and musicology. All as valid forms of human thought begin with assumptions, presuppositions, and " see where and how far they will get with them." This " where and how far " is governed by the kind of logic used in unfolding what is contained in the assumptions, and by how well the logic is used. The validity of this " where and how far " is examined by one or more of the three tests of truth. When these conditions have been met, only one more remains to be fulfilled for a discipline to be scientific. It is the humility of which Stuermann speaks, and which Barth has called modesty. " Both [secular sciences, " narrower," " wider," and theological] remain scientific so long as they acknowledge one another and remember in a self-critical spirit that knowability is but," and here we substitute a simpler, more generally acknowledged statement, "a part of reality, not reality as such," for Jaspers' ontologically loaded final phrase. Thus for natural sciences to remain scientific, botany, chemistry, and the rest must not only stay "within bounds" as defined by their assumptions and validly use inductive reasoning and the rest of scientific logic, but they must also acknowledge that the disciplines "without the bounds" of natural science are equally scientific if they fulfill the same conditions and none pretends that any of man's knowledge is omnipotence. Man's knowledge is power, but limited power, "tentative forever."

This being, we repeat, a chapter not primarily about all knowledge but about the natural sciences, we turn to our second relationship, that between Theology and the content of the natural sciences. We shall, as a matter of fact, have much less to say about the relationship between Theology and the *content* of other disciplines here than in the next two chapters, for the primary issue which natural science raises in Academy is the *methodological* one. From the negative point of view, this relationship must be discussed with reference to Scholz's Congruity postulate, which demands "regard" for "what is physically and biologically impossible." Theology as a truly humble science must relinquish any claims it might think it possesses by virtue of its subject matter, revelation, to instruct biologists about biology and physical scientists about scientific cosmology. It must acknowledge that Cardinal Newman was on the wrong track when he asserted that geological scientists should be grateful to the Bible for telling them about the earth-covering flood of which they had no other information. Theology has no such content or conviction to communicate to sciences, apart from certain historical data about Israel and the early Christian Church which, used critically, are the most candid and reliable we possess. Rather, Theology, in the example Newman chose, has to learn from geology that there is almost no likelihood that such a flood occurred, and from the historical science of comparative religions that many primitive river dwellers exaggerated their local flood experiences into cosmic myths or legends of religious import. In addition, Theology must listen to what natural sciences have to say about Biblical accounts of the metal axhead that floats on water with unthinkably high surface tension (II Kings 6:6), of the temporary reversal of the direction of rotation of the earth around its axis at Joshua's command (Josh. 10:12-14), the virgin birth, and the resurrection. Of these, the resurrection would appear to be the crucial case. Axheads, floods, and sun-stoppings must be considered unprecedented, contrary to all rational expectation, and of doubtful validity in the realms of physical science. We can only ask, and in fact it is the question Theology should have been asking all along, about the role such physical fictions play in the intention behind the Biblical narrative. Again, the medical significance of virgin birth is far outweighed by its symbolic significance in terms of the New Testament attempt to explain that decisive phenomenon of experience: Jesus of Nazareth. The New Testament, however, goes out of its way repeatedly to assert that in the Resurrection we are not dealing with some form of resuscitation, trickery, or illusion. What it talks about is a continuation of authentic human existence beyond real death in spite of contrary experience and expectation. Nor was the early Church consciously dredging up a memory of a loved one, nor otherwise " bringing him to life " by the power of imagination. For better or worse, the New Testament is not speaking of a Hellenic immortality of the soul, but is making the bald Hebraic assertion of a resurrection of the body. Possessing no clinical record of a cessation of respiration and blood circulation, lowering of body temperature below the supposed critical level, and decomposition (mentioned by the Fourth Gospel not in the case of Jesus, but of Lazarus), all prolonged over a period of days and followed by fully authenticated biological existence, medical science finds itself incapable of affirming the resurrection. Neither physics nor biology provides us any clue to how he lives, or in what form, or where he " sitteth on the right hand of God," but the perdurance of the *human* existence of this *man* is so central to Christian faith rooted in the Biblical witness that the failure of physics and biology to offer it " possibility " does not free Theology from wrestling ever afresh with the problem and the significance for us of the resurrection.

On the positive side of the relationship between Theology and the natural sciences, we must affirm that Theology is interested in the same nature, the same creation, as are they. Their first job is to ascertain the facts about natural reality and to explain them in terms of structure and natural causality. From this point of view Theology can only be instructed by them. The natural sciences, however, are not freed by the urgency and difficulty of this task from concern with the nature of order in tangible reality, its beginning, its process, and its goal. Theology, too, is concerned with these questions about the significance of the facts concerning natural reality, and should be prepared to risk dialogue with natural science in such areas as the origin of life, the nature of human life, the destiny of the human environment, the possibility and the quality of life lived elsewhere than on the earth, and the balance of power between man and the rest of creation.

We have said, however, that the primary issues raised for other sciences by natural science are methodological. Consonant with this, the bulk of this chapter will deal with this third relationship between Theology and the questions raised by natural sciences. These methodological considerations involve all three elements of disciplined human thought: presuppositions, logic, and conclusions. We shall deal in some detail with the identity and the sources of theological presuppositions when we come to the question, How does Theology proceed as a Science? Then we shall ask, What is the Logic of Theology? But we shall begin evaluating Theology as a science by discussing which test of truth is most appropriate for evaluating its conclusions.

How Do Men Know What Is True?

" What is truth? " said Pontius Pilate when confronting the claim of the truth-oriented Jesus of the Fourth Gospel that "every one who is of the truth hears my voice." Francis Bacon calls him " jesting Pilate " and charges that he did not stay for an answer. But whether Pilate was insincere or cynical, a noble Stoic of great but futile vision or a small-minded bureaucrat frustrated by his job, he has left us with the best formulation of the central methodological problem in Academy. On the highest level, on which perhaps Pilate as well as Jesus was speaking, the question is more than methodological. Both the Christianity of the Fourth Gospel and philosophical Idealism found and find Truth ultimate or absolute. In assigning the name "Truth" to one of the focuses in our constellation of ultimate criteria for both Academy and Theology we have preserved this "more than methodological" dimension. It does little good, however, to bear witness to, to affirm, to remain steadfastly loyal to, Truth unless we have some way of knowing what is true and what is not. Therefore, philosophy has developed various techniques and mechanisms, which break down into three principal tests of what is true. Initially, each of these tests was intended to characterize all disciplines, all sciences in Academy, but increasingly they have proved to be most helpful in clarifying the methodological questions on which the natural sciences have trained the attention of the whole modern Academy. Recalling that these narrower "sciences par excellence" are defined and differentiated primarily by their various and specific answers to the classifying question, What is the true? we gratefully turn to consider truth as correspondence, as coherence, and by the pragmatic test, as utility or relevance to life.

The first view of truth in the Academy is the classic and persistent one that it *corresponds* to reality. Depending on what we mean by reality, a set of quite concrete and particular data, on the one hand, or a particular metaphysic or *Weltanschauung,* on the other, and how literally we take the word "corresponds," the "correspondence theory of truth" may claim either to give us precise understanding of the material of exact science or to bring us close to the secrets of being itself.

More precisely stated, the historic formulation of the correspondence theory runs: "*veritas est adaequatio rei et intellectus.*" Theoretically, this adequacy (or approximation) of intellect and of object (or thing) can work either of two obverse ways. Objectively, from the standpoint of Idealism, truth is the likeness, agreement, or correspondence (*homoiōsis*) of a given thing (*pragma*) to the original *logos* or *Idea.* Therefore, "*veritas est adaequatio rei ad intellectum*": truth is the agreement of a thing to its perfect Idea or Form contained in image in the intellect. The modern Academy, however, usually restricts the sentence to its empirical, inductive form, emphasizing the limitation of the knowing subject, "*veritas est adaequatio intellectus ad rem.*" This means practically that truth is the agreement of a *statement* (*logos*) to *pragmata,* the facts. As

Heidegger, to whom we are indebted for these formulations of "correspondence," [6] points out, both forms of the theory conceive truth as "rightness." A still more instructive designation of the truth defined as "the conformity of a statement with a fact" is *correctness*, preferred, for example, by Kahler.[7]

This second formulation has such a solid commonsense appearance that it is easy to see why "correspondence" has survived, with what Kent Bendall calls a nagging appeal, all criticisms of the first understanding that a perception was true if the image in the mind was an accurate replica of the object existing outside the mind and copied by the perception. There may be no eternal forms or primary qualities to put us in possession of the Truth about reality; and, ever since Kant, serious thought has been convinced that no knower possesses "the thing itself," but only phenomena, appearances, sense perceptions, for which there is no guarantee of correspondence with the object of knowledge. Since perfect *adaequatio* between intellect and its object is exactly what we cannot assure, correspondence is no absolute test of truth. Still, though we may never be able to tie down what correspondence really is, even with the concept of mathematical "isomorphism" between systems, we apparently shall always be convinced that some facts somehow correspond to some statements about them. This second, relative formulation of correspondence as correctness is the basis for the method of the modern natural sciences. Without the ability to observe, measure, and report data with reasonable reproducibility in propositions (statements) on whose definitions we decide to agree, no "narrower" science of any kind is possible. Defined by this kind of relative or phenomenal correspondence, all "narrower" sciences might with equal justification be called "behavioral sciences," for no modern or "narrower" science is a description of what things *are*. Instead, they all describe how various concrete objects — stars, plants, people, governments, economic systems — *appear* to us to *behave* under certain conditions. When the question "Why?" presses us farther and deeper, beyond and beneath, the description of behavior toward some more nearly ultimate correspondence, we realize that we must utilize theories, symbols, models which are "tentative forever" and that the correspondence test cannot discover Truth. At the same time, however, the second formulation of correspondence as *correctness* of a statement about a fact, designed to salvage something valid from the ashes of an attractive theory, does offer a limited but valuable test of truth. Truth as correctness is *the truth of the true,* the kind of truth most appropriate to science in the "narrower" sense.

Deprived of absolute correspondence and unsatisfied with limited or relative correspondence, but anxious to possess the Truth, philosophers devised the "coherence theory of truth." According to this theory, a system or account of reality should be so constructed that any thought, belief, or proposition implies the others in the system and they imply it. In Kahler's simplest, syllogistic example: A mammal is an animal that gives birth to living young and nourishes them with milk. A whale is and does these things. Therefore it is a mammal. Coherence is valid within a self-contained system; it is harmonious, balanced, beautiful. However, Truth is all truth; it must satisfy the philosopher's thirst for a unified vision of the whole, and more and more complex problems bring in increasingly non-homogeneous elements and stretch the coherence theory thin. This is clear, for example, when one tries to construct a unified view of natural sciences. And when one tries to deal with higher levels of abstraction the questions arise: Whence did "the rest of the system" come? How does our initial fund of beliefs get generated and related to reality in a nonarbitrary, rational way? As Bendall points out, further, the coherence theory demands the *correspondence* of reality to logical necessity: "For the coherence theory seems to suggest that 'reality' must be . . . what the only possible fully coherent account of anything would be an account of." [8] Thus, the coherence theory is condemned to a deterministic rigidity that must inevitably fail to embrace all reality and therefore reality as a whole.

But while coherence is inappropriate to a totally comprehensive Truth, absolute and universal, coherence is supremely appropriate to the truth of a limited harmonious system not necessarily nonarbitrary and nonparticular. This is to say that coherence is appropriate to the truth which characterizes beauty. Just as we have said that some kind of *correspondence* is necessary for the existence of any kind of science, so we may say that some kind of *coherence* is necessary for the existence of any kind of art. Just as we have said that over the limited range of their concerns relative *correspondence* defines for sciences the truth of the true, so we may say that over the limited range of their concerns limited coherence defines for arts the truth of the beautiful.

Such talk about " some kind of " and limited or relative absolutes increasingly led Anglo-Saxon realists along the line of thinking that since neither absolute correspondence nor absolute coherence can produce perfectly reliable truth, it is time to ask: Why rely on half-absolutes? Why not become honest relativists about truth? This produced a range of views usually covered under the title, " the pragmatic conception of truth." In some circles this takes the less personal form of an instrumental or utilitarian view, as when Bendall suggests that in the pragmatic tests, " truth and falsity are possible properties of a conceptual scheme . . . which is designed to function as an *instrument* in coping with our environment." [9] Various pragmatists would give their own versions of the conception that results are the reality which defines truth, but none more trenchant than that of Oliver Wendell Holmes, for whom "the best test of truth " is its ability to win acceptance in the marketplace of ideas. With this more personal form of the pragmatic test we are approaching the existentialist version of it. Kahler complains that all other modern forms of truth have shrunk to purely formal relationships. Only authenticity or genuineness, *conformity* of the appearance of an object, an utterance, a being, with its origin reaches beyond this. The criterion of authenticity applies most clearly when we refer it to the human being. Here truth, says Kahler, " takes on a substantive, existential significance. It becomes a quality and a value." [10] He means by this to give intensity to the pragmatic test and version of truth, but there is no question of making pragmatic truth absolute or universal in its extent. Rejecting from the start the very concept of universal truth, pragmatism seeks to define the truth of a statement, a system of thought, or an institution by its relevance to the life of man. The pragmatic character, then, is patently appropriate to the disciplines we have called the crafts of conduct, for the pragmatic test of truth attempts to discover the truth of the good, the relevance of relationships, systems, and institutions to particular needs, desires, and aspirations of man, in and for all the personal and social aspects of his life.

Our investigation of the three principal definitions of truth and the tests which correspond to them has shown that no single conception leads us reliably to all truth, to Truth itself, and that no single conception is comprehensive enough to cover all the needs of Academy. We have discovered, however, that each of the conceptions has a limited validity and that each form and test of truth is appropriate to a different group of disciplines. The situation is analogous to that of acid-base chemical indicators. There are several chemical compounds, including those known as phenolphthalein, methyl orange, and methyl red, which are color sensitive to a certain band of the pH (acid-base) range. No one indicator is useful over the whole pH range, but if several sensitive to different portions of the range are used, fairly good coverage can be obtained. Similarly, we would suggest that although correspondence, coherence, and pragmatic relevance do not make Truth accessible to Academy, correspondence (or correctness) is most appropriate to the sciences as the truth of the true, coherence is most appropriate to the arts as the truth of the beautiful, and the pragmatic concept of truth is most appropriate to the crafts of conduct as the truth of the good. We have also spoken of Theology as a science, and claimed both status and rigor for it. We have not, however, demonstrated any of this rigor, nor shown cause for the inclusions of Theology in a chapter centering in the " narrower " or natural sciences. To be sure, we have claimed that the greatest contribution of these sciences to Academy is methodological, to a clarification of the nature and content of the fundamental presuppositions which define a discipline, to an illumination of the logic used by Academy, and above all to consideration of the validity of Academic work, of the conceptions and tests of truth. In this chapter we must subject Theology to scrutiny in all these areas, but it is immediately imperative to examine more strictly the kind of truth by which Theology claims to be defined, and thus whether it belongs fundamentally, in the methodological sense, among the sciences of correspondence, the coherent arts, or the pragmatic crafts of conduct.

To begin with the apparently most inclusive theory and test of truth, Theology says with audacious humility that its truth *corresponds* to reality. In saying this, it looks at empirical reality as a whole and in its manifold concrete parts, but it claims to look through these realities to their significance, to their relationship with ultimate reality. The developments of modern empirical sciences have helped Theology by forcing theology to recognize that these " deeper " levels are in fact the only ones with which it is conceivably equipped to deal in any adequate or unique way. We have spoken of specific instances in which this lesson has had to be learned, but we come now to the classic case concerning the Biblical doctrine of creation and the advances made in experimental and theoretical biology, beginning with Darwin. Revelation, in this case, proved not to be a " science " and, in fact, inferior to " science within its own bounds." More instructive than the fascinating circus of the Scopes monkey trial is the so-called Babel-Bibel controversy in Giessen, a university town in Germany, around the turn of the century. Under the influence of the discovery that Gen., ch. 1, was probably dependent for its " natural science " on Babylonian thinkers of the sixth century B.C., the town was divided into "warring" factions upholding the Babylonian or the Biblical origins of the doctrine of creation. Then as now, those who would uphold ancient Oriental cosmology against the implications of twentieth-century astronomy, biology, and geology within the groves of Academe, condemn themselves to failure, if not to open ridicule. The statements of modern science simply correspond more closely than any yet devised to the empirical facts we know. Yet Theology continues to assert that whether the mechanisms of generation and development are best described for the time being by firmaments and fiats or by astral explosions and condensations succeeded by a long process of evolution, the creative force and direction originates with the God it knows in the reality of Reconciliation. This state of affairs clearly indicates that, on the one hand, Theology cannot dispense with the correctness of statements about facts provided by the natural sciences, but that, on the other hand, the assumptions which define Theology are of little use in dealing with the facts about mechanics, electricity and magnetism, the nature of matter, and wave motion.

We must still ask, however, whether Theology as a science is defined by the correctness or correspondence of its statements with the facts about religion. As the *Journal for the Scientific Study of Religion* sensibly puts its case in answering, What do you mean " Scientific "?: " The scientific study of religion . . . is the effort to discover as many facts about religion as possible, to organize these facts into as fruitful generalizations as possible, and to challenge these generalizations with as keen and sensitive insights as possible." This statement does define one or many religious sciences, as does Scholz's set of criteria. Theology, however, ultimately treats psychology, sociology, and history of religion and scientific church finance qualitatively in the same way as it treats biology, chemistry, and geology, although the former set may quantitatively be of greater use to Theology. Yet Theology is not one of the sciences of religion; instead it uses those disciplines in the same way the arts use their art-sciences and the crafts of conduct use the legitimate "more narrowly" scientific statements of the behavioral sciences. We shall go into the details of these relationships in Chapters IV and V, but at this point we must assert that the assumptions which define Theology do not allow it to be judged primarily on the basis of the correctness of its statements about any empirical data. Is it then to be defined primarily as a craft of conduct which uses the statements of behavioral science but is itself responsible to a particular form of the question: What is the good? Or is it like an art that uses the statements of fact made by an art-science but is itself responsible to the question: What is the beautiful?

The test of truth as coherence seems to many to offer Theology the surest possibility of being established as a science in Academy. To be sure, it is futile to try to fit Theology with jigsaw puzzle precision in the space left by, say, philosophy, literature, and history — in the way that chemistry fits in the space surrounded by astronomy, physics, and biology — and claim that the collage represents a coherent view of all knowledge. At the same time, however, Theology continues to assert that its tenets and ideas have an inner coherence, that peculiar mutual appropriateness we have spoken of as the truth of beauty. Yet what kind of logical criteria can be used to establish and measure this coherence? This is the problem that persistently plagues those who would carve out a place for Theology in an isolated corner of Academy by asserting that it is used consistently and critically, and so understood by its own practitioners. The phrase "by its own practitioners" militates against such a theology's being tested "by any reader or hearer who is sufficiently attentive," those open-minded intellectuals whom apologetics believes to be lurking on the sidelines of Theology, waiting to be convinced. On these terms,

Theology would seem to be either too whimsical and arbitrary an art to be taken seriously as a truth-oriented science, or else to be an esoteric hyperspecialized study, the centrifugal drive of which helps separate rather than unite the disciplines. In either event, the attempt to define Theology as a science by the coherence conception of truth leaves it at best as " true for us theologians only " in a way which also does not " let God be God " and does not do justice to the universal dimension of the Reconciliation of all men, all things to him.

This leaves us then with the pragmatic test for theological truth, which provides a criterion honored both in ancient and modern thought. Common sense instinctively turns to it, especially in the area of morals, as the crucial test which will determine whether we can dispense with Theology or not. Moderns from Maugham to Camus have searched for a moral structure that would stand up without God for a prop, while Christian thinkers turn almost automatically to morals as that aspect of life from which religious belief can be " read off." Jesus himself, in a direct line with the prophets of the Old Testament, has given the classic formulation to the pragmatic test of the truth or falsity of prophecy: " By their fruits ye shall know them " (Matt. 7:20). The most rigorous form of the pragmatist's test of truth is formulated in the inference: " If the concept of God is true, then it is useful." As Stuermann points out,[11] this statement has two forms, the negative or critical one being: the concept of God is not useful, therefore it is not true. This question of usefulness is the question about the good for man which we have called most appropriate to the crafts of conduct. Therefore, we shall discuss in detail in the next chapter the complicated, relative, and difficult process of formulating and evaluating a theological ethic to be tested pragmatically. To make this process the primary test of the truth of Theology, however, would be to make the Word of God depend for its validity on a Gallup poll of the opinions of men. The positive formulation, " True, therefore useful," on the other hand, assumes a prior establishment of the truth of Theology before it can produce pragmatically valid conclusions. In this case we are cast back upon the test of truth which we have called the truth of science, the truth of the true. This means that before it is coherent as an *art* and before it is relevant as a *craft of conduct* Theology believes itself to be a *science, consistent with reality.*

This may indeed seem strange, since Theology has appeared least compatible, in the whole spectrum of disciplines, with the assumption of natural science that true statements correspond to *empirical facts which correspond to reality*. The very statement which we have heretofore assumed as the definition of Theology as a " wider, non-secular " science now forms the basis for our claim that methodologically speaking Theology is defined as a science by depending on *correspondence,* the test of the truth of the true, for its validity. " Assuming the existence of revelation, theology clarifies the implications and consequences of this faith." *Revelation* provides, in fact is itself, the data to which the statements of Theology must conform. Theology assumes that reality is not limited to its appearance to our senses but that revelation is the unveiling, the unconcealment, *of reality*. Revelation, from the side of the Revealer, reveals Truth, that ultimate criterion of Academy and of the Church, and Theology is a science because it is a human effort after the truth of the true as a classifying value, because its statements must be measured for their correspondence with revelation. This methodological identification of Theology as a science creates great problems for all scientific thinkers of Academy who are used to assuming that all the reality we can *know* comes to us through our sensual apprehension of its appearance. Therefore we must ask now in detail how revelation is received, by whom, and how reliably; how can anyone who is " sufficiently attentive " identify and understand the presuppositions of Theology so that it will be possible for Theology to communicate its convictions, and for Academy to follow and criticize the logical unfolding of them and the conclusions that are derived?

THEOLOGY AS THE SCIENCE OF REVELATION

Theology begins as a science, we have said, because it makes presuppositions which it assumes correspond to reality. Then, since the form and content of these presuppositions is revelation, is the Word of God, Theology must " develop special categories to express the inexpressible." Finally, in fulfilling the requirements of the nature of science, Theology must " clarify the implications and consequences of this faith " — " through rational and conceptual means." The word that is most likely to irritate the average citizen of Academy in

this proposed definition of a science is " faith." Even to many sophisticated intellectuals " to have faith " means to accept something that
isn't true, the very opposite of everything science stands for. Yet faith
plays an indispensable role in all scientific Academic thinking. All
rational thinking begins with prerational assumptions, so that faith
in the sense of an acceptance of premises unsupported by rationalizations is necessarily shared by all disciplines. In this sense, faith and
logic are not contradictory, but are consecutive human operations in
the cognitive process. Faith comes first to establish the identity of the
materials with which logic is then to work.

Theology, however, is dealing with religious faith and Academy
suspects that this is qualitatively different from the faith she uses,
and is irrational, arbitrary, emotional, uncontrolled. Theology claims
that faith is its channel of cognition, connecting it with its scientific
subject matter, revelation. Since revelation is, by definition, God's
disclosure of his Word to man, faith is a two-ended or two-sided
channel. With almost embarrassing naïveté Theology explains that
from God's side faith is the knowledge given *and* the channel of its
giving to men; from man's side, faith is openness to receive knowledge from God *and* is the content of that reception. For the Synoptic
Gospels faith creates the atmosphere for healing and is the channel of
the power to move mountains; for John and The Acts it receives the
Risen Lord and is directly connected with the coming of the Spirit;
for the Pauline corpus it is the gift of right relationship with God
which man's morality and rationality and correct divine service cannot produce; for Hebrews faith is the substance (assurance) of what
we hope for, the evidence (conviction) of things not perceived by
sense. Faith is not irrationality, not antiknowledge; it is cognition,
knowledge of God.

Karl Barth has expressed this Christian claim that faith is knowledge in terms of four changes rung on the German verb *kennen* (to
know) or the noun, *Kenntnis* (knowledge). On the first level,
Kenntnis itself designates the knowledge of personal acquaintance
which is the most fundamental kind of human knowledge. The Biblical concept of knowledge is clearly determined by a form of personal acquaintance both intimate and powerful. The Old Testament
use of "knowledge" for the most intimate and profound human
contact, sexual relationship between husband and wife, is most

clearly symptomatic. Knowledge of God is equally profound, personal, and total: "knowledge" is the expression used to signify relationship with God in its fullest sense. The Fourth Gospel, for which Life is a reality of the highest importance, can say: "And this is eternal life, that they *know* thee the only true God, and Jesus Christ whom thou hast sent" (John 17:3, italics added). This passage, which understands knowledge in line with such Hebraic expressions as "My people are destroyed for lack of knowledge" (Hos. 4:6), allows "knowledge" to be used of no incidental informedness, or even of an infinitely sophisticated, complex, and difficult "knowing about." Knowledge in its central Biblical usage is that personal relationship which has life and death significance. This is the form of knowledge that is the deepest level of faith, and it is *not* identical with Theology. Theology, as we said in Chapter I, is the Church's speech about God. It is not direct and immediate knowledge of God, but a human intellectual effort. Faith does not give Theology a superrational faculty or tool, by virtue of which it can dispense with reason or carry on along the same line when reason runs out. Faith (*Kenntnis*) is God's gift of knowledge of himself to man, and Christians walk by faith and not by sight. Nevertheless, their walk in the light, as both John and Paul might put it, does not provide them effortlessly with truths, such as tables of French verbs and techniques of integrating differential equations, or, more to the point, with Truth, the will of God, that wisdom for living so hard won by the rest of humanity. Their walk in the light is simply a style of living, under God, which here and now provides a perspective, the basis for reflecting upon the same realities in which all men live. This reflection on the realities which we encounter from the standpoint of God's self-revelation is Theology. Thus it should be clear that though Theology is not identical with faith as *Kenntnis,* it requires faith for its creation and, humanly speaking, for the final judgment of its correctness. This does not mean that a theology cannot be read, worked through, and perhaps, even taught without overt, conscious faith, and that both sympathetic and unsystematic critics "outside the faith" do not provide very valuable criticism and correction. In fact, God seems almost characteristically to lead a stubborn Church, slow to learn, through the advances of others more receptive to truth. Still, faith is necessary to Theology, and faith seems somehow indissolubly bound to the Church.

This is immediately seen in the second form of faith, that as *Bekenntnis,* which means confession as *acknowledgment* or affirmation. Barth's insistence on this form of faith grows out of his experience with the Church Struggle against Hitler when those who refused to compromise their faith were known as the *bekennende Kirche,* the confessing Church. The title is almost redundant since the Church, by definition, is that portion of Reconciled humanity which affirms or confesses the Reconciliation. Since this *Bekenntnis,* then, is a form of knowledge (*Kenntnis*) involving the Church, it is a form of Theology, for it is part of the Church's speech about God. But *Bekenntnis* is not Theology *as a science* [12] because it does not necessarily utilize " rational and conceptual means " to " clarify the implications and consequences of its faith." It simply testifies to its faith regardless of the cost.

The same is true of *Anerkenntnis,* acknowledgment of God. This form of faith, or knowledge, is as worship a kind of Theology, because it is the Church's speech about God. Some Christian traditions, notably the Anglican and the Orthodox, would claim that this is the primary form of Theology, and Macmurray considers it *the* mode of reflection appropriate to religion as distinguished from rationality as appropriate to science. But it is as a science that we are interested in Theology in Academy, and like *Bekenntnis* and for the same reasons, *Anerkenntnis* is not a science.

There is a fourth form of faith as *Kenntnis* (knowledge), however, namely, *Erkenntnis.* This form is connected with its derivative, *Anerkenntnis,* by the concept of " recognition "; but where the longer word designates a ceremonial act, *Erkenntnis* points to an intellectual re-cognition. It is that reflection upon the immediate knowledge of faith (*Kenntnis*) which we have spoken of in distinguishing *Kenntnis* from Theology as a science. *Erkenntnis* is that form of faith appropriate to Theology as a science. It attempts to put the knowledge of faith into rational and conceptual form. Its knowledge is the human cognitive [13] response to God's revelation.

We have said that faith is the channel through which God's self-revelation occurs to men. We have denied, however, that faith is itself, or can be connected with, any anthropological faculty or center. Faith is not a property of the eyes or ears, or mind or heart, but describes the whole man. We have said that in the event of revelation faith has two sides: Man's and God's. There is a concept in Theology appropriate to knowledge which refers both to God and to the whole being of men of faith, namely, *spirit,* as when Paul, speaking of positive assurance, says " the Spirit itself beareth witness with our spirit." The very term " spirit," however, is a dangerous one in the modern world and most of us feel a sense of estrangement in its presence. In Academy it often connotes imprecision, and raises suspicion of a desire to escape critical scrutiny by appeal to an inscrutable supposed " transcendent "; even to our everyday ears it has a spurious ring, and its religious synonym " ghost " literally conjures up the phony, or at least the ludicrously absurd. The German word *Geist,* to which our " ghost " is cousin, is pronounced with solemnity in the German University, but Anglo-Saxons rather blushingly translate *Geistesgeschichte,* intellectual history, as though " intellect " exhausts the range and creative power of the human spirit.

All this embarrassment stems from a twin root embedded in the very heartland of the nineteenth century. On the one hand, all of us, " religious " and " secular " priests of knowledge and of this technological culture, are willy-nilly heirs of the moralistic piety of revivalist America and Victorian England. These sources would teach us: (1) that " spirit " is superior to " mind " (that religious sentiment is better than " mere " thought) and (2) that " spirit " is superior to " flesh " (that asceticism is better than " yielding to the tempting blandishments of nature "). On the other hand, the Romantic or Transcendentalist vanguard of the nineteenth century was drunk with spirit, and we have not yet recovered from the resultant hangover. It was that master of subtle and complex systematic construction, that Apostle of Optimism, W. G. F. Hegel, who declared that All is the self-unfolding of the Absolute Spirit. The established power that organized the nineteenth century believed him to the hilt, although the disgruntled disestablished in Europe already lent a sympathetic ear to the pronouncement of his reactionary pupil, Karl Marx, who said that All is the self-unfolding of the Exclusively Material. So it came to pass that the catastrophic disappointments of the twentieth century became disillusionments with the doctrine of progress, and with the promised self-fulfillment of Spirit. The doctrine that Spirit is the monistic force that explains all became so distasteful that a Karl Barth, reacting against Schleiermacher — perhaps the highest meeting point of the philosophical Spirit with that of piety — can consign " spirit " to terminological retirement, an exhausted concept perhaps to be refurbished in the twenty-first century.

Neither the Pietistic nor the Idealistic Spirit, however, really caught the Hebraic essence of the Biblical spirit which indispensably animates what both Protestant and Roman Catholic theology desire to, in fact must, say about revelation. Both Pietistism and the Idealistism proceed down dualistic paths of thought, and conceive of spirit antimaterialistically, thus denying the goodness of creaturely reality. For them the material, the creaturely, the bodily, is inherently evil. Spirit is identified as mind, primally as Divine Mind, but then as participation in divine rationality. The Hebraic contrast between spirit and flesh, however, is not the inherent dualism of (good) mind and (evil) matter; instead, " spirit " refers to the reality of the Creator and his power, while " flesh " refers to the derivative creaturely reality in its weakness. This is nowhere better illustrated than in the poetic parallelism of Isa. 31:3. The synonymous members read:

> " The Egyptians are men, and not God;
>   and their horses are flesh, and not spirit."

Creaturely assistance, flesh (the Egyptians and their horses), is not to be depended upon because it is weakness not might, God, spirit. In a certain sense, man as animated by the *Rūah 'elōhīm,* the breath or Spirit of God, has spirit that can be called his own, as long as man lives, i.e., God chooses to let his spirit abide with flesh (Gen. 6:3). The New Testament preserves the primary Hebraic understanding of flesh and spirit when John 1:13 contrasts flesh, man, with God; and when Paul contrasts men who are flesh and men who are spirit (Rom. 8:2-16). Paul can speak of bodily existence already as good as dead because of sin, and contrast this fleshliness with spirit as living humanity (Rom. 8:10). Immediately after, however, God's Spirit gives life to mortal, i.e., dying, bodies so that they can no longer be considered flesh in the evil sense. From this and many other passages, especially in Paul, it is clear that man as flesh means man, mind and body, under the *dominion* of sin and death, while man as spirit means man, mind and body, under the *dominion* of God.

There are, however, a pair of very interesting passages in which

God the Spirit and the spirit of man are distinguished and set over against each other. In the first (Rom. 8:16), Paul says that when we who are God's call God *Abbā,* Father, " it is the Spirit himself bearing witness with our spirit that we are children of God." Here, man's spirit would appear to be used in the general anthropological sense current in the Hellenistic world of Paul's day.

Something more specific seems intended in I Cor. 2:11: " For what person knows a man's thoughts except the spirit of the man which is in him ? So also no one comprehends the thoughts of God except the Spirit of God." The important thing that has happened here is that to the Old Testament conception of the Spirit of God as denoting might has been added the conception of the Spirit of God as denoting cognition. This brings us into direct contact with the conception of spirit developed by the Fourth Gospel.

Truth and its relation to what is true is a central concern of the Gospel of John. This is of great importance to the definition of Theology as a science. In John, the Reconciliation, which is the significance of " God was in Christ " (in Paul's terms) or " the Logos was made flesh " (in its own terms for the same reality), means Truth as well as Grace, true Light identical with authentic, abundant eternal Life. On the empirical level, the Fourth Gospel has a concern for *veracity,* that something should be true or correct rather than false or wrong. It makes a significant difference that Jesus " tells the truth " about himself (ch. 8:46), that the Samaritan woman speaks truly and does not lie when she says, " I have no husband " (ch. 4:17 f.), that Peter does not tell the truth when thrice given the dangerous opportunity to affirm his relationship with Jesus. In each case " truth telling " may indicate the quality of a relationship to the Truth of the Gospel — Jesus' effectiveness, Peter's ineffectiveness, and the woman's new openness to the Truth which liberates — but in each case the " indicator " is an active, audible human undertaking in the face of human auditors who may disapprove of the truth-telling act.

The adjective " true " provides the bridge between empirical veracity in John and the *authenticity* underlying it. The Logos of the Prologue is the *true* light of all men (ch. 1:9, which refers back to v. 4), Jesus is the *true* bread from heaven (ch. 6:32) and the *true* vine cared for by the Father (ch. 15:1), the one *true* God who has sent him (ch. 17:3). " True " here refers to the genuine character of what it designates. On this level it is not contrasted with a state of uncertainty or absence of truth. Rather, what is *true* contrasts with the counterfeit, with the actively malicious and misleading. The *true* is Light which darkness struggles against but fails to overcome (ch. 1:5); it is Life against which death and even murder are prevarication (ch. 8:31-47). This last sentence takes us to the deepest level of Truth, where as Life, *vitality,* Truth is the content of the Gospel, of Reconciliation. The Word which was where and when God alone could be, in the beginning, was made flesh. In this incarnation of the Logos, God was in Christ reconciling; he who was one with the Father is also now one with man, so that men beholding this his "glory" are in the presence not only of reconciling Grace but of the Truth that is *alētheia,* God's self-revelation. The Truth is the act of God's speaking his humanity: the Truth in the incarnate Word is the unique way the Father has been "made known" through the only Son. This paraphrase of the climax to the Prologue (ch. 1:14-18) illuminates another key statement of the Gospel (ch. 8:31 f.), which says that he who continues in the *logos* of Jesus will know the Truth which liberates man. This is a passage which the apologists of the ages have used to assure the Academy that Christianity, too, worships Truth. Unlike some who say that the Truth of the Fourth Gospel has nothing to do with the Truth of Academy, I do not wish to disparage the power of truth on any level and in any form to liberate man. However, such a carte blanche for "all kinds of truth" is not what John 8:32 gives us. It asserts that those who by faith remain in the logos of Jesus, the Logos made flesh, will know the Truth which sets men free from the bondage of darkness and death into the liberty of Light and *vitality.*

The *veracity, authenticity,* and *vitality* of the Truth proclaimed in John, however, are not available to man as spirit without God's Spirit of Truth. The intimate connection between the Spirit and the Truth is already suggested by Jesus' statement to the Samaritan woman that God is spirit, and the true (authentic) worshipers of God shall not worship him *at* Jerusalem or *at* Samaria but *in* spirit and *in* truth. Worship in the spirit is, in terms of this parallelism, worship in the Truth John is concerned to proclaim. After identifying Jesus Christ with Truth (ch. 14:6), the author of John emphasizes repeatedly that it is the Spirit of Truth then residing in this

Jesus which shall soon be with the believers (v. 17). The truth-imparting task of the Spirit, whom the Father will send in Jesus' name, is to teach them "all things" (chs. 14:26; 16:13). "All" does not mean that the Spirit gratuitously implants in the heads of believers the answers to a mathematics exam or even the principal parts of a Hebrew verb. The Spirit's truth is the Truth which sets men free (chs. 14:6; 8:32). As *vitality* it is not equal to the sum of all facts, but as definitive Truth no *authentic veracity* is irrelevant to it. Finally, and of the greatest practical importance, this Spirit of Truth is not an indefinitely postponed gift, promise, or "reality" which never seems to arrive in our concrete existence in its historical time. In the Fourth Gospel (ch. 20:22) the Risen Lord says to the seeing-believing disciples: "Receive the Holy Spirit," none other than this Spirit of Truth.

The New Testament, then, insists that the Spirit brings Truth into human existence, into the human spirit, into the human cognitive process. We must repeat that this Truth is *not* Theology. It is, however, *revelation,* the subject matter Theology presupposes. We have said that it is through the channel of faith that Theology receives the assumptions about revelation which define it as a science. And we should like to know how the spirit of man identifies revelation, the action of the Spirit of Truth. Therefore, we must now concentrate on the question: In what aspect of human existence does the Spirit give this Truth? There are three classic answers which, though they overlap, are quite distinct and sometimes even conflicting. They claim that revelation occurs, that the Spirit gives Truth: *in religious experience, in the Church,* or *in the book.* We are all aware of oversimplifications of each of these claims which, in the desire to imprison God and distribute him for human consumption, endanger the legitimacy of the claims. We all know the Christian who volunteers to name the place, the hour, the day of the Spirit's revelation to him and who, like Eliphaz, Job's miserable comforter (Job 4:12-21), demands that we recognize his consequent authority to speak the Truth. We are familiar with the Protestant who taps his coat where it contains a pocket Testament and says with a knowing wink, "I've got the Word of God — right here." We have seen the newspaper caption: "The above photograph shows the bishop of X bestowing the Holy Spirit upon the priest whom he is ordaining." We should not allow these corruptions, however, to close our minds to the possibility that experience, Scripture, or Church may be the locus for the discovery of Truth. Instead, we should be reminded that the Spirit is like its cognate, wind, in that it " blows where it wills, and you hear the sound of it, but you do not know whence it comes or whither it goes " (John 3:8).

The Old Testament repeatedly connects the Spirit with powerful human action, usually religious, often ecstatic. The judges, who resemble frontier marshals embodying the power and sometimes the wisdom of justice more than they do congressmen or law professors, only " judge " when the Spirit of Yahweh " comes upon them." A Samson only creates justice by his mighty deeds when that Divine Wind blows through his being. Saul, a normally phlegmatic man, is designated as God's when the Spirit comes mightily upon him and he joins a band of wandering prophets in their ecstatic display (I Sam. 10:10). The prophets, too, characteristically make pronouncements on individual, social, economic, and political ethics under an influence of the Spirit so powerful that it sometimes spills over into physical effect. (This is not in the least strange in the ancient world, which considered epilepsy the holy affliction, for which Julius Caesar is said to have envied Alexander the Great with an intensity producing emulation. No wonder epilectic Dostoevsky, himself something of a modern prophet, can identify the prophets as epileptics and create the Christlike epileptic idiot, Prince Myshkin.)

The New Testament makes a single suggestion that Jesus himself, precisely at the beginning of his public ministry following the Descent of the Spirit-Dove upon him at his baptism, knew such ecstasy: " And when his friends [those who had known him before the start of his ministry] heard it [that by the Spirit he drove out demons], they went out to seize him, for they said, ' He is beside himself ' " (Mark 3:21 and parallels). According to the earliest Church History, The Acts of the Apostles, the effects on the believers at Jerusalem on the first Christian Pentecost were such that onlookers required Peter's reassurance that this intoxication resulted from being full of the Holy Spirit (Acts 2:15 ff.). Paul, who could boast of a similar, in fact, a surpassing, ecstatic gift (I Cor. 14:18), is thankful for it and desires all believers to have similar religious experiences, because this gift is a clear — and at that time normal — sign of the Spirit (I Cor. 12:10, 28, 30; 13:8; 14:1-9).

Although Enthusiasts of all ages, including the left wing of the sixteenth-century Reformation, the camp meeting and other revivalists of our own country, Pentecostals of many types, and even otherwise sober and conservative members of a Yale student group, attest to the validity of this experiential gift of the Spirit, we would *deny* that it, or any milder form of religious experience, *characterizes the Spirit of God as the Spirit of Truth*. Genuine and salutary these experiences may conceivably be. Some "religious leaders" have approved their cultivation as an at least "harmless" and at most "happy" outlet for energies that might otherwise burst out in Bacchanalian excess. Their legitimate place in the Academy otherwise, however, is *limited* to the fact that they, like all other forms of human experience, are raw material for scientific study. The phenomena of religious experience may indeed ultimately be caused by the Holy Spirit. Psychology, for instance, cannot prove that they are not — any more than it can prove that they are. It can only show that the same psychological mechanisms and effects can be produced and reproduced by other proximate causes — such as the epilepsy, insanity, and drunkenness of which the prophets, Jesus, and the apostles were accused — some salubrious, others destructive. The experiential effects of the Spirit become interesting to Theology as a science *only* when they are brought in conjunction with the effects of the Spirit of Truth through Scripture or the Church.

This was already true for the apostle Paul as I Cor. 14:5 pointedly asserts: "Now I want you all to speak in tongues, but even more to prophesy. He who prophesies is greater than he who speaks in tongues, unless some one interprets, so that the Church may be edified." The Spirit of Truth is, in point of time, first of all the Spirit in the Church. Earlier we said that the Church is the locus or community of faith, and precisely as such it is the locus or community in which the Spirit of Truth is operative. The promise of the coming of the Spirit is in Acts, ch. 1, as well as in John, to individuals and it is upon "these men [who] are not drunk, as you suppose" that the Spirit falls to make them witnesses to the Truth (Acts 2:15, 32). Witnesses they are (this is the purpose of their collective identity, ch. 1:8) in the double sense of having seen together all Jesus' ministry from Baptism to Resurrection, and of *bearing witness* to the *Risen* Lord (chs. 1:21 f.; 2:32). It is this twofold witness peculiar to them which constitutes them apostles (ch. 1:26), the first Christian targets, victims, or beneficiaries of the Spirit's Pentecostal attack on their normal psychic functioning. Others who are convinced by their witness repent, are baptized, receive the Spirit, and are added to the apostles in a makeshift, emergency community, unlike communities organized by the Red Cross following a disaster only in that their common mood is hope and joy instead of sadness and despair.

The acts of the Spirit in the Church are reminiscent of many activities attributed in ancient Israel to Yahweh or to his Spirit. In addition to the ecstatic speaking already mentioned, various people in the Church are said to be " filled with joy and with the Holy Spirit " (Acts 13:5); " full of the Spirit and of *wisdom* " (ch. 6:3, 10, italics added). At this point we see that the Spirit at work in Christians is not only the spirit of power and ecstasy; but as the producer of faith and wisdom he is the Spirit of Truth as well. Some cases that at first appear to be sheer displays of power are more properly seen as part of the victorious struggle of light against darkness, of Truth against falsehood, proclaimed in John 1:5. Particularly prominent in this category is the struggle of Paul against the "false prophet" Bar-Jesus before the Roman proconsul Sergius Paulus. Paul, full of the Spirit, correctly announces that the "hand" of the Lord will blind Bar-Jesus for a while, and Sergius Paulus is impressed not simply by the power but is "astonished at the teaching of the Lord" (Acts 13:4-12). On the one hand, this is reminiscent of the situation in which the validity (truth) of Jesus' proclamation of the Kingdom of God is disputed by the Pharisees, and he replies: " But if it is by the Spirit of God that I cast out demons, then the kingdom of God has come upon you " (Matt. 12:28). It is precisely the Spirit who produces and validates the kingdom among men. On the other hand, Paul's encounter with Bar-Jesus reminds us of the struggles of the prophets, especially Jeremiah, against the false prophets. In those disputes, the true prophets, the prophets of the Truth, are known to the people (by criteria we shall discuss more fully in Chapter IV) as those who can say with *veracity* and power: " Thus says the Lord." Interestingly, in The Acts an *authentic* prophet can declare: "Thus says the Holy Spirit" (ch. 21:11).

This turn of phrase immediately brings us to the third locus of revelation in human existence by reminding us that God is spirit and also that the Spirit is God in his action (including the use of language) in human history. It also makes clear that in the terminology of The Acts it is the Spirit who speaks by the prophets. This is made explicit in several passages declaring that it is the Spirit who spoke and speaks in those decisive written witnesses to God's redemptive acts in Israel, the prophetic words of Scripture. Thus, "The Holy Spirit spoke . . . by the mouth of David" (ch. 1:16); and "The Holy Spirit was right in saying . . . through Isaiah the prophet" (ch. 28:25). These passages go along with occasional strong indications of the importance of the Old Testament for the Truth of the Christian Gospel. The Jesus of the Fourth Gospel says to the proper, pious adherents of the Old Testament: "You search the scriptures, because you think that in them you have eternal life; and it is they that bear witness to me." To "search the scriptures" is indubitably praiseworthy and "eternal life" is for this writing the highest value for which man can search. It is to John what the Kingdom of God, the pearl of great price worth whatever the search for it may cost, is to the Synoptics and justification-sanctification, life in Christ or in the Spirit, is for Paul. For John 5:39, however, the important question is whether this eternal life is "in them," in the Scriptures themselves, or whether they are witnesses to this Life made man in Jesus Christ.

Pharisaic and some of rabbinic Judaism, which invented verbal inspiration of the Bible, Protestant Orthodoxy, which took over the theory, and modern Biblicism, all would insist that Holy Scripture is the source from which Life as such flows. In extreme forms of this position, such as the so-called English system of apologetics developed by the Plymouth Brethren, even the existence of God and salvation through Christ are made to depend upon the authority of the infallible book. The mainstream of Christian Theology, on the other hand, has insisted that the Scriptures are the *decisive human witnesses* to the eternal Life given to men in the Christ event. Since this decisive human witness to the Truth of revelation is given by men of the Church, the question of how Theology learns about revelation must inevitably be discussed in terms of the *interaction* between the Spirit in the Bible and the Spirit in the Church. We have, then, the New Testament acknowledging the Spirit at work in the Church, and the Church acknowledging the work of the Spirit also in the Scriptures which still speak. Both in the New Testament account of what was happening in the early Church and in the creation of the Old Testament literature by men of Israel, however, any sober observer from his vantage point in Academy might say: " It may be all well and good for you Christians to talk about an invisible ' spirit ' behind it all, but the plain empirical fact is that the Church produces Scripture." Roman Catholic theology must immediately reply to such a " neutral ": " You are right (except for your inability to ascertain the operation of the Spirit in the actions of the Church). Those Protestants are wrong who set the Bible *against* the one-holy-catholic-apostolic Church. The Church has produced and preserved the Bible, has always been and remains today the one infallible interpreter of the Bible to men — and that precisely because the inspiring Spirit is at work in the Church."

Protestant theology (and this book can only ultimately represent its own indebtedness to the Reformation) would then insist on a distinction between the Spirit in the Church priestly and in the Church prophetic. From a very realistic point of view, Church history, beginning with the decisive formation of Israel's religious heritage and extending to the present day, can be understood as a continuing dialogue between the priestly and the prophetic elements of faith and life under God.

The priestly element can be characterized as the constructive and conservative institutional aspect of the Judeo-Christian heritage. It is concerned with the maintenance of the Church, worshiping Israel, in continuity with past practice and with an organizational solidity promising some measure of security in the present and future. Laws and liturgy, rites and rules, belong primarily to it. The prophetic element, on the other hand, strives to keep alive the critical function of faith, speaking afresh the primal Truth of God in the political, economic, social, and religious situation of the day. There can be no doubt that prophecy and priesthood are overlapping functions and may even be united in the same Biblical book or figure. For example, the figure of Samuel arises ambiguously out of the primeval mists of Israel's Palestinian literature and history to join Ezekiel, the priestly prophet by or about whom the book of that name is written; and, of course, the legendary Moses is as surely prophetic for the Deuteronomists as he is priestly for the priests. In a kind of New Testament anticipation of the three-office theory of the work of Christ, developed through the Middle Ages and formulated by Calvin, Hebrews adds the picture of Christ as heavenly High Priest to the Synoptics' prophetic Jesus of Nazareth.

Fundamentally, however, clear parallel lines of *opposing* tendency can be drawn pitting Amos and even regal Isaiah against the established religion of their day; Jesus and Paul with the Pharisees against the cultural theology and religion of the Sadducees; Jesus and Paul against the pharisaical mind which hangs back from and hampers the kingdom or Judaizes Gentile converts; the Reformers (Francis and the various monastic leaders of reform as well as the Protestants) against the papacy and ecclesiastical decadence; Puritans and Wesley as well as Unitarianism against various forms of ecclesiastical establishment. The priestly element characteristically says, " Let us come together apart from the nations (or the world) to form a holy people unto the Lord." The typical prophetic voice proclaims, " Hear the word of God against the nations, or the world, or against *his* Israel, his unfaithful spouse, against the Church, which should be Christ's unspotted bride."

This is not to say that in the dialogue between prophet and priest all truth, humanly speaking, is on one side or the other. The priestly responsibility to God the Spirit provides and protects the institution that produces the prophet and many of the raw materials of his prophetic vision and, practically speaking, tends to offer him what protection he has in his proclamation against established power. The prophet who tends to stand with Yahweh's poor, the have-nots (Amos 2:6, where " righteous " equals " needy "; Luke 6:20, " Blessed are you poor, for yours is the kingdom of God "; I Cor. 1:26 ff., " Consider your call, brethren; not many of you were wise according to worldly standards, not many were powerful, not many were of noble birth; but God chose what is foolish in the world . . . , God chose what is weak in the world . . . , God chose what is low and despised in the world "), often shares their lack of a sense of responsibility to the existent structures of politics, religion, society, and economic life.

One important fact must be noted, however. In spite of many severe persecutions of Israel and Christianity by world empires, Assyrian, Babylonian, Hellenistic, and Roman, it is not they "who kill the prophets." Not Athens nor any Rome but *religiously orthodox Jerusalem* kills the prophets (Matt. 23:37; Luke 13:34), kills Jesus, the prophet without honor in his own land, kills Stephen when he reminds it of the typical prophetic plaint: "You stiff-necked people, uncircumcised in heart and ears, you always resist the Holy Spirit. As your father's did, so do you. Which of the prophets did not your fathers persecute?" (Acts 7:51 f.; see also Ex. 33:3, 5, and Jer. 9:26). The true prophet seems always to require the priestly institution to produce him and people whose consciences are attuned to the justice of his critique, to afford him some measure of hearing and protection, but then characteristically it rejects him, only later (usually posthumously) to recognize him as the true theological interpreter of his time. This is the true history of the Bible.

Such a statement as this last assumes that the Bible is prophetic, and is itself *against* the priestly institution, the Church. It ignores many facts about the Bible: principally that it contains the starting point and heart of all Jewish and Christian laws and liturgy, and in Chronicles even a history of Israel interpreted by priestly theology — albeit a pale imitation of the more nearly prophetic histories of Samuel-Kings. (Aside from Hebrews and the Pastoral Epistles, the New Testament contains surprisingly little priestly material or priestly thinking.) It is altogether symptomatic that the Bible almost always gives us *only* the distorted "minority reports" on history produced by the prophets. We never hear in the Bible sympathetic or even unbiased reports of how priests and people felt and thought in the eighth century when Amos, Hosea, and Isaiah told them that their elaborate religion with its conspicuous consumption was hated by God and should be abandoned in favor of fair business practices; or how the many decent priests felt when in the sixth century the Deuteronomic reform threw them out of work and forced the people to travel to Jerusalem if they retained sufficient interest in religious rites; or how the faithful Jews of the first century felt when Jesus and Paul repeatedly provoked the Romans and endangered the *licit* status of sound and moral Judaism. There are no contrary Biblical examples to balance the figures of Jeremiah and Paul, who moved away from their priestly heritages into prophecy.

It can be no surprise, then, that for Protestantism the Spirit which speaks in the Bible is the spirit of prophecy. In Calvin's classic formulation, the Bible is the prophetic word inspired by the Holy Spirit, and to have effect in us it must be confirmed by the "internal testimony" of the *same* Spirit (not by the Church, which is itself grounded upon Scripture, Eph. 2:20).[14] According to this view. the prophetic spirit is prior to the priestly as promise (justification by grace through faith) is prior to Law (Gal. 3:17). Though the priestly function of the Church is absolutely necessary, neither its progenitorship and nourishment of the prophets nor its eventual canonization of their statements is the decisive factor in the reality of faith. That vital force is the prophetic Spirit, the Living Word of God.

Where is this living Word to be heard today? The Protestant position holds that the prophetic voice of the Spirit is most apt to be heard when men of faith who long to hear the Word spoken to them and their contemporaries listen to the decisive witness to revelation, the Scripture. This is why Christians apply every available tool of interpretation to the Bible to learn what the Bible claims God once said to men, and through this means attempt to discover what God might be saying to them now. Roman Catholic theology is more apt to contend that if we would hear the Word of God, we should go to the *locus classicus* of revelation, to the priestly institution ordained to receive and transmit revelation, the Church.

The important thing common to both Protestant and Roman Catholic theology is that both Bible and Church are considered witnesses to the decisive revelation of God, to the Reconciliation effected in the Christ event. Whether with the Reformers we extend to include the New Testament that word of the Johannine Christ about the Scriptures, "They are they which testify of me," and claim that through them the Spirit leads into all truth concerning Christ, or with Roman Catholic tradition claims that the Church is the continuation of the incarnation of the Word in flesh, Christian faith affirms first its object, revelation, and then a decisive witness to or guardian and interpreter of this object. Roman Catholicism may claim that the Church has been given the Spirit, and thus she is the infallible interpreter of Scripture, however erroneously an individual Roman Catholic may interpret it. Protestant theology may insist that the Spirit who freely inspired certain witnesses to revelation, and thus created their truth, continues to speak about that revelation and to create faith where those Biblical witnesses are read and heard. In either case, however, we have the elements that define the science of Theology. In the perspective of history *Theology* may well be *a continuing dialogue between Bible and Church, between priestly and prophetic elements of the faith in revelation.* Although this statement may be a correct theoretical description, practically we must live under Paul's awareness that the gifts of the selfsame Spirit are diverse. The genius of Roman Catholicism is not primarily prophetic but priestly, as that of Protestantism is the reverse. Roman Catholic theology, though increasingly concerned with Biblical studies, characteristically assumes that it finds revelation through the organism of Holy Mother Church, understood as the continuation of the Incarnation of the Word. Protestant theology characteristically assumes that it finds revelation in the living prophetic Word of the Bible. Protestant theology may, therefore, be more apt to carry on its scientific work in dialogue with the Academy not committed to the Church, for Academy may itself well be the bearer of prophetic critique. This, however, does not undercut the statement, established in Chapter I, that all Theology, including that forged in dialogue with Academy, is the Church's speech about God, and that the Church is Theology's final human judge.

Evangelical or Protestant Theology as the *science of revelation,* then, cannot be church history — " scientific " or " spiritual " — nor can it be a philosophizing about Being Itself or even about God. As our practice throughout the book has illustrated, Evangelical Theology must essentially be exegesis, a humble, attentive response to the Biblical witness to revelation. Theology as a science, however, is not identical with what is called scientific exegesis. Just as Theology is not a " scientific history " of the Church, nor a sociology of a religious institution, so it is not an accurate political, economic, social, or religious history of the situations described in the Bible; it is not a form-critical or a source-critical analysis of Biblical literature, nor is it the sum of these. All are legitimate cognitive understandings of distinct usefulness to the theologian, but none are Theology, the science of revelation of the Word of God to living men. Does this mean that Protestant theology is being asked to relinquish all the fruits of the labors of the last one hundred fifty years by which it hoped to become " more objective " and remain intellectually respectable in a world increasingly filled with what Schleiermacher called "cultured despisers"? On the contrary, Theology must be grateful to all sciences that cast light on its subject matter, and most especially for the contribution of scientific exegesis, which applies the principles of literary criticism to the Bible with perhaps greater rigor than does the Academic study of any other portion of the literature of mankind. So thorough has this study been that one sometimes hears the claim: " There is today a general consensus on the meaning of most of the Bible." Must such solid achievement be sacrificed if we appeal to the classic claim that the business of Theology is revelation, and that the Spirit who inspired the Biblical witness is indispensable to the truth of Theology?

Already in the 1530's John Calvin was clear that the business of Protestant theology is the Bible. Even his most systematic work, his *Institutes of the Christian Religion,* still the most widely acclaimed Protestant work qua " system of thought," claims to be neither more nor less than an introduction to or summary of the teaching of the Bible. Calvin and the other Reformers faced the charge that their " right of private interpretation " made of the Bible a putty nose to be modeled according to senseless whim. They saw and attempted to cut themselves off from the unpredictable excesses of the spiritualistic enthusiasts of the Reformation's left wing. They would have been suspicious even of the quietistic " inner light " of the Spirit because of its liberty to dispense with the Biblical witness and eventually with the decisive revelation attested there. Under " private interpretation," Luther subsumed all his own years of Biblical study and teaching in the highest tradition of learning of the Church. And Calvin's training in Christian Humanism led him through the study of Greek and Hebrew, of ancient history and the history of interpretation, to bring all the fruits of learning to the authenticating " internal testimony of the Holy Spirit " to the Truth of Scripture.

It is in their spirit that Christians from the Enlightenment to the present day have used the tools of philology, history, and philosophy to produce scientific hypotheses helpful in discovering what it was that the original author of a given book or passage, verse, or phrase intended to say. And let it be clear that this is the aim of scientific Biblical exegesis, and that it is on this level that the " scholarly consensus " has been achieved. The primary objective goal of scholarly analysis of literature or of any other work of art is the "intent " of the artist, author, or composer. This would seem to be an indispensable foundation or at least starting point for determining what a given work " says."

As we shall show in more detail in Chapter V, an art historian, musicologist, and especially a literary critic, then sometimes attempts to move from or build upon this to postulate what the work of art "means " for " us " or for " man as man." At its best this attempt constitutes a rethinking or reliving or re-creation of the work which makes it "come alive." The attempt always involves some view of " man as man " or of " us " as well as a view of what the beautiful is and of how art works aesthetically. These necessarily extrinsic factors may often be more dangerous than helpful in *ex*egeting, reading the message *out* from within the work. Beyond this the theologian has forced upon him the immeasurably more complex situation created by the claim that he has not only the voices of people and ideas, times and places, to hear and echo, but that here God has spoken and speaks his Living Word. In the face of these difficulties, we must ask whether the theologian can hope to define his epistemology and method of exposition. Can he control or predict or validate the logic by which he " unfolds the implications of his subject matter, revelation "?

WHAT IS THE LOGIC OF THEOLOGY?

We have discussed the tests of truth by which the conclusions of a discipline are to be evaluated, and decided that methodologically Theology must be a science, since before the tests of coherence or pragmatic relevance may be applied its statements must satisfy the test of consistency with the subject matter defined by its assumptions. We have further seen that the subject matter of Theology is revelation, the Word of God to which Theology attempts to listen faithfully, attentively, openly, as it is spoken through the Bible which participates in a continuing dialogue with the Church. Now we must turn to the third methodological area to ask about the nature of the mechanism for moving from the assumptions of Theology to the conclusions about them. We must ask whether there is any particular logic proper to Theology or whether Theology is a self-willed outlaw to logic and on this count really no science after all. A reader of Augustine might insist that Theology's logic is that of Platonic thought, a Thomist might insist that Theology uses Aristotelian syllogisms (just as Orthodox Protestant thinkers speak of propositional revelation). One could in fact find theological representatives of forms of logic down to that of " process philosophy " and the linguistic analysts who, in their simplest formulation, might say that Christian Theology is the common language of Christians about truly personal relations. This very pluralism in logics, however, seems on the one hand to lead us back to the " putty nose " charge against Theology instead of onward toward theological light perpetual. On the other hand, this pluralism of logics reminds us that no single kind of logic is a necessity of thought, and that ostensibly *universal* formal logic itself is simply " a way of thinking inherited from the Greeks and their *special* experience of ' Being.' " [15]

According to all that we have said so far, it may be most fruitful to look more closely at the very nature of logic from the standpoint of Theology's desire for an orderly unfolding of its scientific subject matter. This would seem especially in order since modern logic has been developed almost exclusively in terms of scientific discovery in the " narrower " sense, and is so firmly tied to the propositional relationship connecting empirical facts. The sometimes unfortunate, sometimes minimal, results obtained by applying this logic to sciences, arts, and crafts of conduct not dealing solely with empirical data have led to a mutual frustration of these disciplines and of logicians themselves. Among the thinkers who have been driven by this frustration to attempt to get behind natural scientific logic by historical and philosophical means, perhaps the most thoroughgoing is Martin Heidegger. He has used the tools of philology in investigating the roots of logic beyond Aristotle in the pre-Socratic language of poetry and philosophy. These studies may provide a healthy starting point from which we may apprehend the logic of Theology at the point at which the New Testament consciously begins to express the Hebraic insights of the Judeo-Christian witness to revelation in the language of the Greeks.

Heidegger's philosophy, which he prefers to name Phenomenology, is one of the clear demonstrations in the history of philosophy that modern linguistic analysis is not a radically new invention, but simply raises once again to primary importance the classic philosophical task of using words precisely, predictably, and with clarity. Existentialism, in Heidegger's brand of it, uses the very linguistic tools that its harshest critics employ to denounce it as lacking in philosophical objectivity. This is especially demonstrable in the case of Heidegger's treatment of logic, to which he devotes one third of his *Introduction to Metaphysics*. He begins by describing the commonly accepted understanding of logic and its magisterial role in all thinking. "Logic is the science of thinking," he says, "the doctrine of the rules of thinking and the forms of thought." [16] "Furthermore logic passes as a secure and reliable science," neutral among the *Weltanschauungen,* everywhere, for everyone for the last two thousand years: essentially the same. Yet, Heidegger would ask, "What does 'logic' mean?" It is, he answers, an abbreviation for *epistēmē logikē,* the science of the *logos.* How, he further inquires, did the science of thinking become the science of *statement,* for that is what *logos* means here?

Delving behind and beneath the "where we are" to the "where we should be," Heidegger gets at the "where we went wrong" from the "historical, i.e., the essential origins" of first the unity and then the separation of *logos* and being, or as he terms it *physis* and *logos.* The word *physis,* which is usually rendered "nature," he translates "being" in an almost more primal sense than derivatives of *einai,* the verb "to be." Being in the sense of *physis* is for him "the power that emerges." Similarly, Heidegger presses back behind all of the layers of meaning for *logos* as "word" or "speech" and claims to find in both Heraclitus and Parmenides, pre-Socratic philosophical poets, the concept of gathering or collecting. The *logos* is the power of collecting which discloses itself most obviously by transforming phonetic sound into the words of coherent speech. At the culmination of his discussion of the primal significance of these terms, Heidegger attempts to show the inner relationship between *physis* and *logos* in his formula, *physis = logos anthrōpon echōn.* Heidegger's formulation, as he understands its Greek components, translates: Being requires the gathering which "has" man; or, more precisely, "Being, overpowering appearance, necessitates the gathering which pervades and grounds being-human."[17]

He then traces the degeneration of this lofty understanding from the point at which *physis* is "veiled and misinterpreted" by Plato and Aristotle as "idea," that which is seen in the visible, thus freeing *logos* to break loose from being, declare its independence, and eventually assert in formal logic its domination over being. The most dramatic and important symptom of the degeneration is evident when we trace what happens to truth in the process. "Initially," says Heidegger, "the *logos* as gathering *is* the event of unconcealment (*alētheia*, truth), grounded in unconcealment and serving it. Now [in Plato] *logos* as statement becomes the abode of truth in the sense of correctness . . . and this process culminates in Aristotle's proposition to the effect that *logos* as statement is that which can be true or false. Truth, that was originally unconcealment (*alētheia*), a happening of the dominant essent itself (*physis*), governed by gathering, now becomes an attribute of the *logos*."[18]

The situation has changed little in logic to the present day, though Heidegger traces some further mischief done by Christian theological distortions of *logos,* and misuse of Heraclitus. I would like to suggest, however, that Heidegger himself has in one sense failed to point out just how scandalously and cavalierly Theology has abused sacred Hellenic principles in the bold Johannine Prologue, and also perhaps how this very distortion accomplishes something quite like the aims of these same "decisive" Greek poets who make the ultimate so immediate for Heidegger. In spite of his early training toward the Roman Catholic priesthood, Heidegger's own heart beats to the Greco-Germanic rhythms of Being and the pulse of his mind and pen follow. From the standpoints of both form and pathos Heidegger must ascribe to Being the place and role in thought which Theology can only assign to God. For example, as the prophets say to men, "Hear the word of the Lord," Heidegger speaks of man "addressed by the voice of Being."[19] It is no surprise, then, that Heidegger says: "*Logos* in the New Testament does not, as in Heroclitus, mean the being of the essent, and gathering together of the conflicting; it means one particular essent [thing that is], namely the Son of God."[20]

Rudolf Bultmann, Heidegger's long-time cohort and one of the most eminent New Testament scholars of our time, does not believe that the *logos* of John is to be understood as derivative.[21] The *logos* of which we read in John, ch. 1, is truly primal. It is with God, "before the foundation of the *kosmos*" (John 17:24). The *logos*, moreover, is no mere intermediary being (or prior creature) as in Philo and the Neo-Platonists. The same *logos* which is with God *is* God, say the translations, but the Greek, as Bultmann points out, is still stronger: it says, literally, "God was the *Logos*." That is, there can be only one *God*. If " one " is " a " God, he is *this* God. This *logos* who is really God is identified as the creator, the agent, and the action: God creating the cosmos. Nothing is prior to God, not even the " isness " that identifies God and *logos*. Philosophy inveterately places Being at the beginning, with God then related to, understood through, defined by, his relation to Being, even where a Christian philosopher attempts with Tillich to make God the ground or abyss of Being, Being itself, or the God beyond god. Being need not be prior to all, including God, except where the Greek experience of being is allowed to define the rules of reality and thought. Theology rooted in Biblical revelation defines Goodness, Truth, and Beauty *solely* by what God has done, is doing now, and shall do. Theology has no knowledge of them which can conflict with God's *Logos,* his Spirit, his self-revealing action. Theology corrects its knowledge of personal relations, of fatherhood and sonship, of conjugal love, of brotherhood and neighborliness, even of enmity and warfare (see Matt. 5:43-48; Eph. 6:12-18) by what it learns through the actions of God. Similarly, what Theology must say about being it learns through God's self-revealing action. God gives and defines isness, he lends Being or essence or nature to being, as to substance, subsistence, to the essent, to being-there, to existence, to what-is or stands in or participates in being. And precisely for the Prologue to John, it is God the *Logos* with God through whom all other reality is " made " (ch. 1:3) and ordered into a *kosmos* (v. 10). All of this, it would seem to me, fulfills all conceivable dimensions of what is implied in Heidegger's *logos* in his formula: " Being [ultimate nature, *physis*] necessitates the gathering or collecting [*logos*] which *has* man." The Biblical *Logos* is not *a* mere essent derivative of Being (as Heidegger says) but is the God prior to Being itself. This *Logos* fulfills the role assigned to the Heraclitus-Parmenides-Heidegger *logos* in a quite different way, but to my eye and ear and spirit, fulfills it to overflowing.

Thus Heidegger's protest against the scope of the *Logos* itself in John 1:1-3 is unjustified, but there is a philosophical scandal, a flagrant heresy against which Heidegger's protest is far too mild. And this is that this *Logos* of the Prologue prior to the Being of being is wasted, demeaned, degraded, profligately poured by God into an essent, mankind, and worse, not into mankind as such at creation but into a particular essent in the middle of history, Jesus of Nazareth (ch. 1:14). It is here that Christianity claims to know the eternal *Logos* decisively, in fact, at all. It is in the cross of Jesus of Nazareth that the *Logos* reveals itself as the Word of Life, as grace and Truth (vs. 14, 17). Thus, characteristically it is in the redeeming or reconciling act that God speaks his self-revealing Word, the Truth, and his people, including the authors of the New Testament, know the Truth through faith, their obedient hearing of that Word. This means that the lively *Logos* which redeems, controls the Biblical *logoi* (statements) as well. For example, all extensive New Testament discourse about the creation or genesis of nature is relatively late (John 1:1-10; Heb. 1:1-3; and even Col. 1:15-20), well after the Church's decisive wrestling with the redemptive significance of the Christ event, which John comes to understand in terms of the Incarnate *Logos*. In these three " creation " passages the thought implicitly runs: " We now know that he through whom we have experienced redemption is he through whom the *kosmos* was made, has light and life (John 1:4), is upheld by God's *Logos* of power (Heb. 1:3), and that in him all things hold together (Col. 1:17)." [22]

What we have now asserted about the *Logos* is that, in the first place, the God who " was the *Logos*" spoken and heard uniquely in the Christ event is the source and sustaining power of all other reality; that implicitly, in the second place, this self-revealing *Logos* is Truth, the unveiling of what really is; and finally, that this Divine *Logos* controls the other Biblical *logoi* by imparting to them and requiring of them correspondence with its own character. This summary reveals that we have accomplished something quite important for Theology as a science, precisely with respect to the position some draw from Tertullian's, " What has Athens to do with Jerusalem? "

namely, that " Theology has nothing to do with logic." That conclusion, which seeks to preserve the purity of faith by retreating into
some traditional language not explicitly or formally logical, is *denied*
to Christians by the very nature of God's choice of self-revelation by
Logos, by the *logoi* of speech, the coherent structure and power of
which is assured by the fact that this utterance is God himself in
action. Any language of faith that is not to be incoherent babbling
must conform to God's own utterance with *its* interior logic. In
short, any language of faith that is true must obey a logic, a science
of statement and thought. In saying this we are departing from an
explicit denunciation of formal logic, such as that of Heidegger,
which seems to suggest it be banished from the deepest levels of
cognition for its crimes against the primal gathering *logos.* Our position, however, drives us farther to the question whether the *Logos*
that *denies* Theology the right to il-logic *prescribes* any particular
logic for it. We should like to suggest at least a point of attack on
this question in the form: What is the true logic of Theology, the
" theo-logic "? No obvious, no perpetually valid, answer offers itself
to Protestant Christian theology, so our next step can only be in the
nature of a humble *approach* to the question.

Our approach begins with a repetition of the observation that a scientific logic must be appropriate to or correspondent with its subject
matter. For most sciences today the criterion of correspondence has
shrunk to the limited but secure concept of correctness. It must for
Theology be at least that: correctness in terms of a language that corresponds to the data. This has, in fact, already been dealt with in a
preliminary way in the statement that the data of Theology are the
data of revelation and that the language of Evangelical theology must
correspond to the content — but by no means to the *verba ipsissima,*
the identical syllables of the book — of Biblical revelation if its
logic is to be correct. The inner connection of the *Logos* with the
content of revelation, on the one hand, and with the logical nature
of speech, on the other, guarantees this.

In the first place, then, the *Logos* is identical with the subject matter of Theology as a science, God's self-unveiling. This is, in terms of
Christian faith, that primal identity of *Logos* with ultimate reality
from which, we are told, the whole Greek understanding began and
formal logic developed. This identity also means that any logic that

truly, correctly, corresponds to this *Logos* shall indeed do justice to the subject matter of Theology. It is indispensable to note the priority and control of this primal *Logos* over its logic, and not vice versa. Not even the principle of contradiction, so dear to formal logic, is sacred, as is already clear from the fact that the logic of the language about the basic nature of the *Logos* is contradictory: we have gone about blithely repeating the formula that the *Logos* was *with* God (which means, at least, distinguishable from God) and that at the same time the *Logos* was (and is) God, as though these statements were not contradictory. And if the fact of distinction rather than separation between God and his *Logos* exempts these statements from contradiction, no such excuse could be made for the problem of the relations between goodness, power, and the fact of evil which we shall discuss more fully below. Again, no complete set of statements about what Karl Barth has called " the general event of human existence in its insoluble dialectic " could obey the prohibitions against contradiction. We must, of course, be very careful to distinguish genuine contradiction from paradox, but this flouting of the contradiction principle by " theo-logic " demonstrates the fact that in Theology the subject matter (the data of revelation) alone ultimately controls its logic.

In this context, let us attempt to distinguish the questions: What is logic? and What is a logic? In saying that logic is the science or doctrine of thinking, I mean to stress that logic is the method, literally, the " path or way around " obstacles to thought, of moving from presuppositions or other data to their implications or conclusions. This clearly indicates that a logic as here understood is a tool, to be admired and employed to the limits of its usefulness, neither to be deprecated and ignored nor idolatrously regarded as an end in itself. This view of logic implies a plurality of logics, of tools each with real but limited value. Some formal logic, finally, remains in every case the best tool for expressing content in a clear and meaningful way and, thus, for communicating conviction. This seems to point to the idea that different logics are appropriate to different subject matters. In a certain sense I believe that this is true, in spite of its apparent contradiction of the general agreement that logic is the most unchanging and therefore most reliable of disciplines.

Today's living logic has concentrated on two problems: science and language. The logic of scientific discovery and technology has tended to stress the validity of a certain kind of logic, thus at the same time crystallizing logic in one particular form and implicitly criticizing all other kinds of logic. Linguistic logic has reminded us of the consistent structures of language, but for many this result is of secondary importance to the discovery of the unique integrity of each separate language. This discovery, however, leaves us to ask how the coherence and critical power of an individual language is to be guaranteed and controlled. What we have said about the relation between the *Logos* of Theology and the *logoi* about it points to an objectivity in the subject matter of Theology as a science that provides this guarantee and control. This claim to objectivity moves on a quite different level of validity than does that social relativism which demands " lingui-logical " independence for each group of people interested in the same thing, be they poets or peasants, biologists or beatniks, chemists or Christians.

The logic of Theology, then, is the logic that bears *true* witness to, consistent with, the *Logos* of God. It is the logic that effectively communicates Christian conviction, and as such it is necessary for the valid pursuit of Theology in the Academy. The *Logos* has a kind of holy, in fact, quite magnificent, monotony: Jesus Christ, the same yesterday, and today, and forever. This tempts us to seek for a perennial " theo-logic." Such a quest for the Holy Grail of " theo-logic " would be vain, I think, because Theology is written by men in the language of men, regardless of claims that the Spirit does or does not speak through their speech, does or does not make *logos,* language, out of the *phōnē,* the sound of their voices. The ages of man have different languages, as do their times and places, and each time and place and age has one or more correspondingly valid logics to unfold its convictions *into understanding.*

Theology, therefore, must always learn to use new languages, new logics with which to speak effectively of the *Logos* which lights every man who comes into the world (John 1:9) to men of ever new ages and times and places. Theology in the Biblical mold has been, humanly speaking, the most inveterate borrower among the sciences of the Academy. In Biblical times it borrowed and *forged into the instrument of the* Logos *of God,* the language as well as the agricultural skill of Canaan, the liturgical poems as well as the architecture of Phoenicia, the religious myths as well as the science of Babylon, Egypt, and Persia, and the religious and philosophical vocabulary of the Hellenistic East with its talk of Wisdom, *Logos,* and Savior.

In the time of the Christian Apologists and mighty Augustine, forms of Plato's language provided the logic of Theology. In the period of wrestling with " the whole Aristotle " Aquinas' synthesis of the methods of " the Philosopher " with traditional Christian thinking gave Theology its logic. Nominalism and perhaps even such a philosophy as Neo-Kantianism have had their usefulness in supplying language and logic for Theology. Must we say in each of these cases, then, that a different way of thinking provided Theology the logic it used as a science? I must reply: I think *so.* Each of the successfully borrowed languages and logics was in its own day not only familiar but also associated with a cognitive effort convincing at that time. They would not have been useful to Theology if they had not previously proved their consistency and their worth in some other context, but such proof is not what establishes the validity of Theology couched in the terms of one of them. This would be true if Theology were made a science by the immutability of its logic; but Theology is still made a science by its *Logos* which must find a logic consistent with it, and effective in unfolding its significance for concrete human existence.

" Has not this been done, once for all? " say various groups of modern Christians. In *Aeterni patris* of August 4, 1879, the system of Aquinas was declared normative by a Roman Catholicism that thus turned its back not only on Kant and his successors but on all the earlier competitors of Aquinas. Most of rationalistic Protestant orthodoxy would follow in declaring that the permanently valid " theo-logic " is that of the baptized Aristotle. Others would make the sixteenth-century Lutheran formulas or such Reformed documents as the Westminster Confession normative for *form* as well as content. Still others would make the religious experience of a Francis or a young Luther, or a John Wesley, the parameter for Christian thought as well as life, while many — especially in British and Scandinavian circles — would take the act and the formulas of worship as definitive for the form of all Christian language. It must be pointed out that worship is a living and therefore a growing and changing thing, and the credal formulations of the Reformation were the products of contested argumentation and compromise, many of them quite openly intended to be valid " until further notice." Even, or perhaps most conspicuously, Nicaea represents long and bitter struggle in which the issue was still in doubt for decades, even centuries, after its formulation. And in each case the language and therefore its particular logic may no longer be adequate to " the general event of human existence in its insoluble dialectic." In the first place, the current state of our knowledge about existence may enable us to falsify a language and logic that formerly appeared valid. Further, we may be in a position exegetically to see that the logic of the borrowed language is, after all, not consistent with the logic of the *Logos,* the content of the Gospel. No, Theology in the flux of human history has not found a permanently adequate linguistic logic to call its own. Theology's theme must, perhaps always, remain that verse of " O Sacred Head, Now Wounded ": " What language shall I borrow To thank Thee, dearest Friend, for this thy dying sorrow, thy pity without end? " Theology's language, its logic, must be adequate to bring " my thanks " to God's incarnate *Logos* for that redemptive act which is decisive for me. And the language is, characteristically, borrowed — from somewhere.

Scrupulously honest theologians today can be heard to say in the Academy: " We have no language." This should be no surprise in the light of Theology's history of borrowing; but it has in it the pathos of faith's cry: " *What* language shall I borrow, right now? " Present Theology tends to borrow a bit of modern science — as much psychic science as possible, the discoveries of sociology and its related disciplines — an apparently shrinking bit of Existentialism, and a lot of literature and drama, from Shakespeare to Sartre and Eliot to Edward Albee. Put together, it adds up to *phōnē* not *logos,* more sound and fury than sense. " Why not borrow one language, one logic, the logic of modern science and have done with it, so that ' real ' sciences will have some respect for Theology? After all, that is the language and logic of modern culture." Why not, indeed? Is Theology not up to the task? Or is not " the logic of modern science "? As we have earlier suggested with respect to Scholz's postulary requirements for Theology to be an empirical-inductive science, and as Barzun has strongly insisted about the relation between science and a myriad situations . . . of immediate moment to Western man wishing to be a "natural and moral philosopher,"[23] there is a dangerous incongruence between the logic of science and what Theology is *required* to say. I suspect that science, in its *exclusive* attention to empirical data and assumptions about them, has trained our imagination to kinds of symbolism of limited appropriateness for Theology. Scientific symbols may be much richer than I suspect, and I would be grateful for the demonstration of this on the edifying and practical exposition of the topics of Theology: God, man, Christology, creation, sin, reconciliation, and final redemption. At present, however, the logic of the "narrower" kind of science does not appear to make its language rich enough for Theology to borrow — and depend upon.

What, then, is the language that Theology shall borrow today? There is none. The very crisis in the Academy, the crisis of conviction, is symbolized by the fact that there is no common understanding of sufficient power to create a coherent language in which modern Western man can assert his right to be "a natural and moral philosopher." Theology, then, to communicate its conviction must apparently forge its borrowed language out of many pieces, a chain of many links of logic, each persuasive in its own way to some people in one area, and the whole must carry its conviction. But how is the chain, the language, to be forged? What is the intellectual tool? To repeat our earlier formulation, How does the *Logos* exercise control over "theo-logic"? The answer, it would seem, is implicit in the question. A distinction between two *kinds* of logic, both of which are needed in Theology, has been emerging from the preceding discussion. There is a *logic of language* that must be coherent and expressive if Theology is to make persuasive sense; and there is a *logic of the content* of Theology to which the logic of a particular borrowed language must be appropriate if that language is to correspond to revelation, is to be useful to Theology as a science. Theology does not have a *modern* language fully corresponding to its content, any more than modern culture and Academy have such a language for the heights of aspiration and the depths of ultimacy. What we do hope to begin to develop here, however, is a logic of the content, a logic of the *Logos* of Theology, by means of which that *Logos* can critically direct the forging of the *logoi,* the links in the chain of a modern theological language.

Christian Theology, from the Evangelical or Protestant point of view, must ever be fresh, relevant exegesis of the Biblical witness. But who shall be the creaturely interpreter, responsible for this freshness and relevance? The Church, of course, the community of *faith,* created by the witness of the Holy Spirit inside the hearts and minds and bodies of men. It is true that " we have this treasure in earthen vessels," that the Word of God becomes speech and writing through frail, fallible, human subjectivity, but we must avoid introducing this subjective element one step too soon. Our formulation, so far, is still not sufficiently " objective," that is, it does not pay quite enough attention to the scientific subject matter itself. The missing reality is that designated by the formula: *scriptura magister scripturae est,* which signifies that the Bible is its own best interpreter. This formula points in general to the unity of the Biblical witness, in spite of the extensive diversity of its witnesses. It specifically implies some central vantage point of interpretation from which the whole is to be viewed. For Christian faith this can only be the decisive act of God's revelation, the reconciliation effected in Christ. If the *Logos* is to control the statements of Theology, how else is it to do so than through its own imprint on the Biblical source of Theology?

Karl Barth has suggested the *methodological link* between the content of revelation and the content of exegesis when, in the first volume of the *Church Dogmatics* he claims that Revelation, identical with Jesus Christ, and Holy Scripture are two forms of the Word of God, and that they are strictly, theologically, related to each other and to the third form, Proclamation, as are the three persons of the Trinity. In other words, written as an equation, this hypothesis would read: Revelation: Holy Scripture: Proclamation = Father: Son: Spirit. At those moments which occur again and again when the Word of God is really spoken to men through the Bible or through proclamation of the Gospel, the content of this speech is revelation, the *Logos* incarnate in Jesus Christ. This identity of the incarnate *Logos* and the Biblical witness to him at the moments when Truth breaks into human reflection suggests to me a formal analogy. This instantaneous equivalence of the content of revelation in Jesus Christ and in Holy Scripture implies that if we have an accurate formal description of one of these forms of the Word of God, there should be a strictly analogous formal description of the other, and, though we do not make use of it here, of the third form of the Word of God as well. Let us use this as a working hypothesis, and attempt to suggest some implications of assuming that the central content of Scripture also governs its interpretation.

The primary implication of this suggestion is that the approach of the theological interpreter to the Bible must be rooted in something analogous to what is known as the doctrine of the two natures of Jesus Christ. The classical formulation of this key Christian conviction is that Jesus Christ is true God and true man, two natures or substances in one person, distinct but related, neither mixed nor sharply divided. The insistence, first, that he is God, true, perfect, and entire, guards against the views of Ebionites and other Adoptionists, and all forms of Arianism. In each case the formula asserts that God the Son or *Logos* is God, in every sense "before" all else. With respect to him, "in the beginning," means before any form of creation or emanation, certainly before Jesus of Nazareth grew "in favor with God," and the Spirit descended upon him at his Baptism (Luke 2:52; 3:22). The insistence, second, that he is man, true, perfect, and entire, militates against every form of the earliest and most persistent of Christian heresies, the Docetic. The Greek verb at the root of the word "docetic" is *dokein* (to seem or appear, but *not* to be). Thus for the Docetics of all ages some God appeared to be human in Jesus of Nazareth, but really was not. He did not really sweat, and grow angry, as we do; the indivisible God did not really suffer, God did not submit to death, more bluntly: God did not die.

At this point in the argument we have come quite close to the issues dealt with in Chalcedon's words about the one Jesus Christ in two natures "neither mixed nor sharply divided." It was Eutyches who declared Jesus Christ to be monophysite (of one nature), and Leo the Great who extended Augustine's view to say that though Jesus Christ is one person of the same substance with the Father he is dyophysite (of two natures), which must not be mixed or confused as though God and man were really ultimately the same. Chalcedon also insisted that these two natures were not sharply divided, rejecting Nestorianism, which implied that Theology has to do with two Christs united only by a common attitude. In its decision, Chalcedon failed to answer the vital question, Precisely *how* are the two natures united in one person? This question has also not been resolved more satisfactorily by subsequent thought. We are left, in the most central area of Christian cognition, at Chalcedon. Each theological generation must test anew Chalcedon's conformity with, and effectiveness in, expressing the Biblical answers to Who is this Word of Life "which was from the beginning," which the apostles have heard, have seen, looked upon, and touched with their hands (I John 1:1)? And each generation is set the task of trying to push beyond Chalcedon to a more adequate expression of that Biblical witness for its people in their time, in short, to wrestle with this unresolved " how."

What Chalcedon did accomplish was to provide really important qualifications which show how we may *not* answer the " how." In teaching us that we cannot get around the chasm of the Christological paradox to the holy Zion of God's Truth via Alexandria on the south or Antioch and Constantinople to the north, Chalcedon teaches us that we must face the paradox itself and, if we cannot *resolve* it, we must affirm its clear statement. When we propose, therefore, to take our best knowledge about the key to Christian faith as the key to exegesis and through this source as the key to Theology, we are proposing something very dangerous and difficult to deal with. We are taking the most irresoluble of the Biblical paradoxes and proposing to make it the key to all " theo-logic," to the whole process of Christian cognition. We appear to be condemning ourselves to logical failure, and yet the tangible, historical reason the Council of Chalcedon, A.D. 451, has been remembered while the one-sided Robber Council of 449 had remained a historical curio is that the formula of Chalcedon *has proved useful* not only for practical problems like those we shall consider in the next chapter but in problems of thought as well. Let us attempt to discover, then, what the decisions of Chalcedon might mean for Biblical interpretation if Holy Scripture and the Jesus Christ described by Chalcedon are two forms of the same living Word of God.

To begin with, we must beware of the Eutychian idea that the body of Jesus looked like a human body but was not, or that in some Docetic way his humanity was only partial or illusionary. This would correspond to the idea that the Bible itself, while appearing to be made up of genuine words of man is really not. Accordingly, the Bible would be so exclusively the Word of God that the study of the *logoi* of the Bible as human literature would be irrelevant. In some forms actually taken by such a view of the Bible, the human scribe is a mere amanuensis taking the dictation of the Holy Spirit. It would, of course, be futile to waste effort on investigating the mind of the human author if the thoughts expressed in the Bible are in no sense conditioned by that mind, which is absorbed into the divine mind not limited by partiality or historical contingency. This states an extreme form of the position, but every theologian is tempted at certain sticking points to shun the painful concreteness not only of the suffering Jew on the cross in the first form of the Word incarnate but also those of the mysteries of the human author's struggle with words and ideas in the second form.

In the opposing tendency, one is tempted to be an Adoptionist or Arian. After all, scientific Biblical criticism can tell us so much about the history and literature of the Bible. Why can we not be satisfied with the supremely good man and with a very, very good book? Why can we not simply say that the true God is the true man writ large, and that the Word of God is simply the words of men writ surpassing well? Of course we may stop with the historical Jesus and " scientific " exegesis, if we think no *Logos* became flesh in the former and none informs the *logoi* to be understood through the latter. One *may* do so, for on earth there are only the Church and the Book to say him nay.

For most theologians, however, these two extremes do not offer the most appealing temptations. These pitfalls are reserved for the various forms of Nestorianism. The dangerous error of Nestorian Christology occurred when real concern for the *two distinct* natures became so overriding that the *connection* between them was neglected and the natures *became* separate. In a very real sense, the history of Biblical interpretation has been plagued by this tendency. Even great Origen, whose method of interpretation has so long been considered normative for Catholic Christianity, is not free of the Nestorian tendency. Origen speaks of *separate* levels of interpretation, and of comprehension, which he develops in analogy to a trichotomous view of man as body, soul, and spirit. He speaks of *literal, moral,* and *mystic* (by which he means an allegorical understanding available to the Gnostics, knowers) corresponding to the three parts of man. The most perplexing problem for a trichotomic view of man in the Church is, of course, the person of Jesus Christ. Origen absorbs the sinless, because immaterial, soul in spirit (*Logos*), which then takes on a human body. Yet even though he coins the term " Godman " (*theanthrōpos*), which should serve to guarantee humanity in Jesus Christ, Origen's Neo-Platonism triumphs and makes bodily existence at least a lower if not a directly reprehensible aspect in Christ. Correspondingly, the "literal" interpretation of Scripture done first is left below on Origen's higher flights of " spirit."

This has set a tempting pattern for Protestant theologians as well. Even such a brilliant exegete as Bultmann, equipped with all the tools of modern scientific research and hypothetical extension, tends to use these empirical methods (the tools of " literal " interpretation) first and *then* to turn to a reading with the eyes of faith (through Existentialist spectacles) possibly corresponding to the higher Gnosis of Origen. Perceptive theologians would warn us that *any* attempt to analyze the Bible as the words of men *separate* from the Word of God *must* leave us with a pseudo-Christological interpretation, even where one has the best intention of considering the Bible also, but *separately,* as the Word of God. This criticism is a valid warning, but the fact that the method criticized is based on a bad or weak Christology (namely, a Nestorian one) should not rule out as pseudo-Christological all attempts to relate the solutions of the problem " Word made flesh " to the problems of relating Bible as Word of God to Bible as word of man.

How, then, may we proceed to a *correctly* Christological interpretation of Scripture? We must first of all remember that the " how " of relating the two natures of Christ is usefully restricted and qualified but *not* formulated with *positive* rigor, so that we can expect *no more* rigorously positive formulation of a principle of Biblical interpretation: *one person, two complete and perfect natures, unmixed and undivided.* This would seem to imply, first, that the *Logos* of God and the *logos* of man are *one* for faith when the Spirit authenticates a Biblical " word " to faith. That Biblical *logos* is *at the same time* both perfectly authentic human literature and completely (not partially) divine self-revelation. Just as it was a hopelessly irretrievable error when the Antiochenes said, " This act was done by Jesus of Nazareth and that by God the Son," so we must never allow ourselves to say, " This Biblical saying is God's Word about himself and that is man's word about God." Insofar as the Bible is canonical, a measuring rod for faith, we possess no tool that will enable us to *separate* the Word of God from the words of men. We can say that this Biblical statement offends formal logic's demands for noncontradiction; we can say that a given "miracle" is impossible within the natural order accurately surveyed by modern science; that certain key points of Daniel's narrative are historically inaccurate, contradicting correct evidence within the Bible itself; we can claim that a given saying of Jesus in the Synoptic tradition is *more probably* an authentic statement of the historical Nazarene than another statement in John — though this is a quantitative likelihood on a much lower level of certainty than the other cases cited.

These results of research may give us a more accurate grasp of the human history of Israel, of Jesus Christ, of the Church. They do not, however, allow us to identify the Word of God from among the words of men, as though accurate historical statements alone — sometimes or always — were the Word of God. Similarly, no dogmatic test — neither Luther's " my spirit just won't enter " the apocalyptic literature, especially Revelation, nor even his " Hebrews does not do business with Christ " because it doesn't mention justification by faith — gives a Geiger-counter indication of Divine radioactivity and allows a surgical separation of the Word of God from the words of men. The theologian who would attempt to understand the Word made flesh by Christo-logic and write Theology, contemporary speech about God, must listen in the Biblical witness for revelation, the authentic Word of God and authentic words of men at the same time.

Practically speaking, then, how is exegesis, Theology as a science, to proceed? We have indicated that Christology has to proceed along the path, " both . . . and . . . at the same time." It may begin with the outline, " conceived by the Holy Ghost, born . . . suffered . . . crucified, dead and buried, descended . . . ascended . . . shall come." It must in every age test these dogmas of the Church against the best of its knowledge of what the Bible has said and is saying about Jesus Christ. The crucial factor in this activity is that the man of faith who is trying to learn what it means that the Word became flesh must always attempt to hold himself open to see and hear how the one whole person Jesus Christ, true and complete

God, true and complete man, unseparated and unmixed, is at work. Exegesis can never be satisfied, on the one hand, to say either, " The man Jesus said and did so and so about 1,935 years ago," or " The men of the early Church thought he was God the Son "; nor, on the other hand, can exegesis be satisfied to say, " God speaks to me when I read the story of Christ and the Church in the Book." All this may well be true, and can seriously and justifiably be said, yet Theology as a science must at the same time wrestle with both the decisive past words of witness about the past incarnation of the Word within our time and space, and what the whole of that Living Word says to us today.

Theology as a science must always look and listen at the same time for *both* the what and how of the authentic words of men long dead and what and how God is speaking to us through them today. We can say, then, that the eyes and ears of faith are completely human eyes and ears; and if the ears and eyes are to receive the Word of God by faith they must be binaural and stereoptic. Exegesis is never complete, in fact, at no moment is it truly itself, until it also asks: Does God speak *now* through this study of these words, and if so, how? This reminder by no means signifies that Protestant theology as a science is more than Biblical exegesis. It does mean that exegesis itself demands not only a knowledge of humanity in its literary, political, economic, social dimensions in particular periods of past history; exegesis also includes knowledge of, and concern for, humanity in all its dimensions today. In short, exegesis is not a restrictive, *ex*clusive discipline, it is *in*clusive in the most profound and demanding sense.

We are left with one vital question about Theology as the genuine and rigorous science of revelation. This has to do with the controlling position of the reconciling *Logos* within and over the logic of Theology, the how and what of the *in*clusive exegesis defined here. The reason we were free to suggest that Christology might be a formal key to exegesis is that the content of Scripture's normative quality for Christian faith is its central concern with the significance of the incarnate Word. When we affirmed the formula, " Scripture is *the* interpreter of Scripture," we meant that the answer to the question Who is he? provides the key to validate Christian exegesis now — and within the logic of our definition there is no other conceivably valid *exegesis* except the exegesis of the Old Testament by Jewish faith. This hypothesis, of course, implicitly assumes that the content of Theology finds and determines a form appropriate to it. Only if this is true can we legitimately expect that the *Logos* will control the *logoi*, the statements about it. Let us now put this hypothesis to a test, by asking what light this understanding of Theology as a science sheds upon one of the most perplexing of all theological problems: the relation between the God known in and through the Bible and the reality of evil.

How Does the "Logos" of Theology Control Its "Logoi"?

Walter Stuermann, in his book *Logic and Faith*, has raised this problem in a quite provocative way. Using the structure and power of scientific logic to uncover the root presuppositions of the solution usually attempted, he suggests a reexamination of these presuppositions with an eye to fresh possibilities. As he defines the problem, we are dealing with the factors of God's goodness and power and assume (against the Idealist tradition which tends to claim that evil has no reality, but is merely an absence of good) that evil is a reality that we must deal with in considering God's goodness and power. Defining his symbols as p, omnipotence, unlimited power or control over all that is; p', limited power; g, unlimited goodness; g', limited goodness, he notes that there are four possible combinations which could confront and deal with the problem of evil: gp, $g'p$, gp', $g'p'$. Though he briefly deals with only the new solution he advocates, we shall make at least a few comments on each.

Taking them in the reverse order, we find that $g'p'$ symbolizes the situation in which God is limited in both goodness and power. This, of course, offends highly developed creedal statements with their insistence upon a kind of Hellenic perfection of attributes in God. But Stuermann has the courage and sound theological sense to deal primarily with the Biblical roots of Christian Theology and to criticize a creedal statement when it appears to conflict with them. The logical possibility $g'p'$ seems to offer least advantages as a completely adequate symbol for the Biblical God, but it does point up certain aspects of the Bible's representation of God. With respect to goodness, the Old Testament has long been charged with depicting an immoral God, and New Testament figures such as Ananias and Sapphira in Acts, ch. 5, not to mention Jesus himself, receive harsh treatment *from* God. On the other hand, the collective-complaint psalms, which ask why God does not destroy the enemies of faith but allows them to torment " good " men, serve as one starting point for speculations about a God *not powerful enough* to deal with evil even in the supposedly sacred Biblical history. The classical case in which the $g'p'$ hypothesis would seem to offer help is the crucial history of Jesus Christ, precisely because we are not allowed to exempt his true deity from any aspect of his unipersonal reality. His *limited power* is self-evident in his human weakness, above all, in his susceptibility to death, and the unblemished *goodness* of one who drives businessmen from their stands, speaks to holy Pharisees as Matthew's Jesus does, and destroys a harmless fig tree would seem to be suspect. Yet it must be objected that none of these limitations is *inherent* in God; all are voluntarily accepted in the incarnation. Further, in terms of the entire sweep of Biblical concern, a God limited both in goodness and in power not only falls short of the Biblical representation of creation and ultimate justice, but would lack the *goodness* to justify the unjust (Rom. 3:26) and the *power* to deliver from the house of bondage (Ex. 20:2, *passim*), and to conquer the mighty enemy (Luke 11:22 and parallels).

The option gp' seems designed to agree with the doggerel complaint: if God is good he is *not* God. It attempts to preserve God's goodness unsullied by the corrupting touch of power, assuming that purity alone ensures divinity. This would seem to be a high form of Greek mythology and tragedy. In Hellenic thinking the gods may be very agreeable, even lovable fellows, but they are ultimately as powerless in the face of fate as man himself. Gp' would seem to scrub every fleck from the Olympian visage but still leave God ultimately impotent where power counts. This God would not be weak, he would simply not be strong enough.[24] The appeal of gp' is that our God remains unsoiled. He is above all sordid, material existence, free to be himself, Absolute, unfettered, perhaps even impassive. He is, in short, uninvolved. He does not allow himself to be compromised by anything approaching a contact with evil. He may, in fact, be in full control in any area not touched by evil — if indeed there be such. But this God hardly seems a distant relative of the

Biblical God who gets himself *involved* with an enslaved class of Semites who then become a stubborn, ungrateful people. And the ultimate scandal of the God of the Bible is that he, really he, becomes flesh, the weak and corruptible blot of existence called *a* man. It may in a distant realm express an option *nobler* than the Biblical God, but the picture of deity symbolized by gp' does not represent the God of the Old and New Testaments.

Stuermann himself speculates in the direction designated by $g'p$, a God of limitless power, limited in goodness. This is the God Calvin's enemies attacked when they said, " His God is a devil." Calvin was quite properly horrified, for he did not intend to damage God's goodness when he asserted God's power to *use* evil for his own ends. His opponents were probably ultimately correct, however, for the naked power of Calvin's God was Calvin's " front-door error " concerning the problem of evil. To clarify this point we must attempt a more exact definition of evil. Evil is the opposite of all that God wills and does. What God wills and does is creative, preservative, constructive, renewing. Evil is, then, destructive of all life, relation, and meaning, the frustration of all redemptive efforts to re-create and restore the lost and broken. Calvin's God masters evil and uses it to punish the wicked men, and most of them he punishes not redemptively but destructively. Calvin buys omni-omni-omni-potence for his God at the price of using some of all power *for Evil's ends*.

There is, nonetheless, a majesty and grandeur about Calvin's glorious deity that dwarfs lesser conceptions. He may be inhumane, but this is partly because he is not limited by the human. Stuermann points out the kind of concern for the vast extrahuman creation which Calvin showed in his view of the creation as a mighty mirror of God's glory. And Stuermann extends this in suggesting the appropriateness of $g'p$ for expressing modern science's appreciation of a huge cosmos beyond man, also plagued by evil, or destruction. He faces more openly than Calvin the charge that if God is God, he is not good. Stuermann is willing to accept the idea that " God is himself incomplete or has evil as a part of his nature." [25] This idea is, of course, obnoxious to the entire Hellenistic tradition of Christian Theology with its insistence on a flawless God. That, however, is irrelevant, if it is consistent with and expresses the actions of the God who " brought . . . [us] . . . out of the house of bondage," and

who " was in Christ reconciling the world to himself." Such a position could only finally be maintained if the Bible could be shown to
misinterpret its own history. It is the Gnostic demiurge who imparts
the evil of his own nature to creation, not he who looks at the works
of his Word and pronounces them good. The Holy One of Israel is
called righteous altogether, and by his own faithfulness to the covenant commands his prophets to demand justice of men. The Incarnate Son of God is he who on his own account knew no sin, but became sin for us that we might be God's righteousness in him (II
Cor. 5:21). Stuermann's thesis is daring in its logic and courageous
in its intent. It has much to teach us, but ultimately fails to do justice to the central Christian claim that " God so loved the world that
he gave . . ." *all* to oppose the destruction of the good for man.

In each of the first three cases, $g'p'$, gp', and $g'p$, the logic of the
position is inadequate to the *Logos* which must control the *logoi* of
Theology and their logic. Thus, we are left to wrestle with the classic solution, the target of centuries of richly varied criticism. It is
both inconsistent with our experience of reality and self-contradic-
tory, we are told, to claim that God is both all-powerful and unal-
terably opposed to evil, yet evil exists. It seems a fatal weakness that
the traditional option symbolized by gp is the only one that fails to
give any room for the ultimate origin of evil. $G'p$ allows God to
"make" evil, and gp' lets it arise outside his control or ken, while
$g'p'$ gives evil unlimited possibilities. But gp simply cannot say how
evil really began to exist. At best, Augustine can say that God must
have foreseen *more* good to come if evil were allowed. Gp has made
much of the concept of freedom. Some have thought that the problem would be solved if God allowed man or the rest of creation the
freedom to serve or to rebel. This transmission of responsibility to
the creature, however, is ultimately Pelagian, a robbery or derelic-
tion prejudicial to God's power.

Our only defense of or attempt to understand gp must begin and
end with our Christological key. And the first step of our exposition discloses and admits a metaphysical deficiency. Just as the doctrine of one person–two natures may give us no ostensible direct
access to the periodic table of the chemical elements, it may also not
supply answers to all the questions philosophy can ask. The Christology of the *Logos* or of God the Son does not appear to offer light

on the problem of the *origin* of evil. This is rooted in the fact that Biblical thinking, especially in the New Testament, moves from the redemptive experience and its explanation to the problems of origin and preservation. The *only* source of knowledge peculiar to Christianity and therefore its *only* possible unique contribution to man's knowledge of, or perspective on, reality is God's revelation of himself as Redeemer in Jesus Christ. It would be self-delusion, as well as misleading to others, were Christian Theology to claim any other service to human cognition than to attempt to learn what this one source and perspective implies for man's total understanding of reality. The witness to God's redemptive act does include a fresh perspective on the origin of the cosmos (the ordered universe): "All things were made through him, and without him was not anything made that was made" (John 1:3; see also Col. 1:15-20; Heb. 1:2). We have, however, no real clue, even in these affirmations concerning the cosmos, of the origin of evil.[26]

Although we learn little from it about the *origin* of evil, the witness to the reconciling *Logos* tells us much about the *nature* of evil. The *Logos* is the source of light, life, truth, and reconciliation beyond all alienation, estrangement, or separation between God and his creation. Evil is darkness that tries to overcome the light (John 1:5); it is destruction and threat to life (as captor of man in disease and other forms of demonic possession in the many accounts of exorcisms, and as murderer in ch. 8:44): it is the lie that enslaves (vs. 32, 44). Finally, we may well infer a further characteristic of evil from its opposition to the cosmos-creating *Logos* and in connection with its nature as lie: evil is antilogos, disorder, chaos in opposition to cosmos. We should never allow ourselves, in pointing out the limitations upon the adequacy of all human logic to express the *Logos,* to forget that *Logos* is the root of all logic, and affirms our human logic wherever it is capable of establishing correctness or coherence, wherever it is capable of excluding error. *Logos* as speech affirms the logic of language and negates all sound and fury signifying nothing. For evil is not only chaos that frustrates life and obscures light, it is also the chaos that destroys sense and meaning and the power of language and logic to convey them.

In addition to giving us special insight into the nature of evil, however, cognition of the person and work of Jesus Christ also gives us a particular perspective on both power and goodness. God's power is not simply naked might to bend all to the divine will. Were this so, we might postulate that evil would never have existed. God's unique and unsuspected power, in the light of Incarnation and Reconciliation, is to convey not only life through birth but his own eternal, abundant, and true Life to man. The Biblical mind, in contrast to the religious philosophies of the world around it, was careful to make a separation between Creator and creature so clear that it has been called an " infinite qualitative distinction." The terms " spirit " and " flesh " denote Creator as might and creature as weakness. Precisely the last thing desired or expected by the prophets of the Old Testament was that the Messiah, a creature, should *be* God himself, the Creator. The witness of the New Testament surprises us, then, when it says that God has used the last power we would have expected, the power to lay down, to empty himself (Phil. 2:7) of infinity and omnipresence which were invariably included in man's picture of him. He used the power to put himself under the power of evil, and become obedient to death (v. 8). This power was used to create the power for God to communicate himself redemptively to man, in what Luther called " the great exchange," taking what was ours so that we could receive what was his (II Cor. 5:21). This remains today the power we find most difficult to accept and to conceive. We no longer are astonished at the thought of a power that can transform species, and the incredible forces involved in the release of nuclear energy are for us a demonstrable commonplace. But God's power to communicate his own goodness through the humanity of one man, bound to his time and place, to humanity everywhere and always, remains the most difficult power to comprehend. Yet it is precisely this power to which Christian Theology refers when it speaks of God's *omni*potence from the standpoint of the *Logos*. This power is conceived not as separate from, or in competition with, the powers of which physics, biology, and astronomy speak, for God's redemptive power — not merely his creative power — includes these. It is one of Stuermann's great services in his discussion of this problem to have reminded us that God's redemptive overcoming of evil involves the whole of the *kosmos,* not just its human fragment. In Rom. 8:22, Paul speaks of the whole creation (*ktisis,* what is made, rather than *kosmos*) groaning under bondage to evil (corruption) awaiting the final redemption which shall justify God's designation of the creation: good.

In our discussion of the way in which the concept of the redemptive Logos illuminates our thinking of God's power, we have already inevitably begun to consider what God's goodness means. Much of the New Testament, both in the sayings of Jesus and in Paul's theologizing, is concerned with the problem: How can God be just and the justifier of the unjust? (see Rom., ch. 3, especially vs. 25 f.). From the standpoint of the common faith of New Testament Christianity, God's righteousness — his goodness and his justice — have been brought to light apart from law. This means that God's goodness cannot be measured by any *fixed* standard. Rather, his good acts in a certain historical setting establish moral or ethical standards which are valid for men in that setting. How and what these standards have been and now may be is the problem of the next chapter, when we shall ask, What is the good in various areas of present human existence?

God's goodness, then, creates justice apart from the law which can only condemn evil to be punished by power. This goodness frustrates evil by imparting itself to the creature, which longs for and needs goodness but which, oppressed by evil, does not possess it. The question that always burns in the mind of that longing creature is, *How* does this happen? Just as, when we spoke of God's power from the standpoint of God's Reconciliation in Christ, we could not avoid mention of his goodness, so now in speaking of his goodness, we must refer to his power. God *has power to do good* to his creation by virtue of the incredible decision and action of binding himself to man, through one particular man but to mankind, *a living continuum in time and space*. God's goodness justifies unjust men at all times and everywhere by means of the power of God to bind the creation together in a continuum that does not die, and to bind this creation integrally to himself. God's redemptive goodness frustrates the power of evil to make men God's enemies (Rom. 5:10), and to use even God's sometime standard of goodness for men, the law, " which held us captive " (ch. 7:6), to keep man estranged. Evil, which was an elusive foreign force until the *Logos* became flesh susceptible to it, was overcome by God's goodness which then was able to absorb evil into itself. Again metaphor is required for illustration, though none is perfectly adequate. Paul in Rom., chs. 6 and 7, suggests that Christian Baptism represents the *death* of our enmity against God and of the power of law to condemn us (ch. 7:6), as well as the *arising* of our new and eternal life (ch. 6:4 f.). It is as though the Incarnation bound evil to the *Logos* through the creation of which he became a part; the death of Jesus Christ, symbolized by the "drowning" of Baptism, "drowns" the evil he drags with him beneath death's waters; the *life* of the *Logos*, which survives death itself *revitalizes* the creation inexorably connected with him and now cleansed from *lifeless* evil. Thus the reconciling act of God gives us a really fresh and independent view of his goodness and power precisely because it is in it that God has dealt decisively with evil.

It is important to note that this solution we have offered to the dilemma inherent in *gp* conforms to the *content* of Christo-logic. It is only by being wholly true God and wholly true man at the same time and thence forever, that evil is dealt with and God's goodness and power are revealed. Further, this Christological discussion has demonstrated that the other three options, *gp′*, *g′p*, and *g′p′*, are only related to Christian Theology as partial descriptions of *preliminary* stages of the relationship between God and his world. They are not and cannot be adequate to the decisive Christological root of Reconciliation. To deal with evil in the way Christian Theology *must*, and thus to deal with God's power and goodness as Christian Theology in correspondence with its subject matter should, any of the three must pass over into the paradoxical problematic of *gp*. This illustrative treatment of the problem of evil has been intended to demonstrate how the *Logos* controls the *logoi*, the statements of Theology and their logical interconnection.

Returning to the terms of that opening statement by Karl Jaspers which we have used to define Theology's integrity within Academy, we have attempted first to fix the source of the assumptions that define Theology as a science (a legitimate Academic discipline), and then to show that the test of truth which is most appropriate to Theology is that of *correspondence* which marks Theology as a science (before it may be an art or a craft of conduct). Finally, our search for the most satisfactory logic for Theology to use in unfolding its apprehension of *revelation* has uncovered no linguistic logic equal to the task. Instead, we have tried to develop a Christo-logic, a logic of the *Logos,* with which Theology may critically create and judge a linguistic logic. Now we have attempted to test this Christo-logic, to see " where and how far " we may get with it in reference to the problem of evil.

We have attempted in this complex but orderly process to establish Theology as a science in Academy in terms of the methodological stipulations peculiar to sciences. At this point let us remind ourselves of Professor Jaspers' clause, " Both [theological science and secular science] remain scientific so long as they acknowledge one another." First of all, we must be clear that nothing said here represents a derogation of " science within bounds " or a desire to exclude the critical power of any historical, literary, or natural scientific knowledge or tool of knowledge which may be useful to Theology in performing its scientific task or in a critical evaluation of its results. Secondly, we must be clear that we do not expect that this chapter will make Theology " intellectually respectable " to any citizen of Academy psychically indisposed to entertain, even as a working hypothesis, the subject matter of Theology and the logic it demands for its unfolding. Theology as a science cannot dispose of " Word of God " or " Holy Spirit," as though they could be reduced to the words of man and the human spirit. In this sense, Theology as a science is not an apologetic, for it *cannot* be validated outside " the theological circle," by any other material or formal science. Theology as a science has simply, humbly, and as accurately and clearly as possible to define itself within the hearing of the whole Academy, and ask for the kind of hearing on its own terms which can communicate its content and lead to faith. Even though carrying on Theology as a science within the Academy may not lead to wholesale conversion or reconversion of intellectuals to Christianity, it is valuable to the Church, which alone can declare Theology untrue to faith, to have its Theology directly confront all other knowledge and other faiths; and it is valuable to the Academy, which otherwise would be impoverished by the lack of a science not only representing a challenging and influential response to human experience but also representing an ultimate faith constantly driving other sciences to their own roots of presupposition about the nature of reality.

Theology as a science has a great deal of business in the Academy. As a science, it does not, however, possess the same degree of accessibility we shall encounter in the next two chapters. In the second of these, Theology must face the test of its ability to produce a response to beauty in the human spirit. But first it must directly face the challenge we have thrown out to all those disciplines we call the crafts of conduct: Answer concretely, here and here and here and now: What is the good? And as you answer, remember that the truth of your answers shall be tested in the court of common human experience by the simple question: Does your answer work?

IV

Theology as a Craft of Conduct

*"I owe no obligation to forum, campus, or senate. I stay awake
for no public function, I make no effort to monopolize the platform,
I pay no heed to any administrative duty, I shun the voters' booth,
the juryman's bench. . . . I serve neither as magistrate nor soldier.
I have withdrawn from the life of secular society. . . . My only
concern is for myself, careful of nothing except that I should have
no care. . . . No man is born for another who is destined to die for
himself."*

Tertullian, De Pallio, 5.

IT IS ALL RIGHT, I suppose, for the best trained minds dedicated to
the Christian faith to amuse themselves with intellectual fun and
games called 'theology and the way-out fringes of knowledge,'"
said an esteemed citizen of Academy estranged from traditional religion, "but I should think you would always wish to get back to
your real business, to what really counts. As an intellectual I don't
care whether theology has anything to learn from or to teach or to
do with cybernetics, or whether a theologian peers through a metal
cylinder full of glass and solemnly pronounces that microbiology is
safe to believe in or has 'interesting implications' for 'Christian
knowledge.' What I do want to know is whether or not you are
there when the going gets a bit sticky, whether you really have anything to say to me when I covet my neighbor's wife, or become a
social disgrace or a financial bust — or when my child dies. After
all, that is your real business."

Theology as a science is necessary to the Church. It also has quite
a bit to do with whether the Christian who lives the life of the

mind, and is thus a citizen of the Academy, " is there " for others to
turn to for words and empathy, or simply as a steady resistance
against which they may whet and test the convictions that might
uphold them in a given hour. Theology as a science ought to be a
source for and a test of the words the Church now says about wanting another man's wife, or bankruptcy, or the death of a child. Yet
theology as a science may seem not to speak those words. It may
speak in a language that expresses its convictions to the man of
faith but is not the language commonly accepted by others. It
speaks the truth of science, *consistency* with the facts of its subject
matter. Yet this is not to submit to what Oliver Wendell Holmes
called the *best* test of truth, the pragmatic one defined by the question, Does it work?

This apparent conflict recalls us to the classifications of Academic
disciplines postulated in Chapters I and II, the validity of which is
now to be tested in the arena of practical problems in the life of
man. It is our thesis that in this present chapter we are not *primarily* concerned with the classifying value appropriate to the sciences, namely, " the true," tested by correctness or consistency with
the data, but that in the field or grove of Academe whose sectors are
to be called crafts of conduct we are *primarily* concerned with the
motivating question, What is the good for man? tested precisely by
Holmes's " best test," relevance to life *here and now*. Admitting, in
fact asserting, that it has real business in everyday affairs, theology
as a cognitive response to revelation has with quiet consistency, and
from time to time with dramatic power, submitted its *concrete*
judgments about *contemporary* man to the test of relevance. This
test may well not have the same ultimacy for theology as the scientific test of conformity-with-revelation. And yet, when theology risks
its utterances in the arena of history where men of all faiths enter,
watch, participate, it dares the pragmatic test the prophets chose
when they declared, " Hear the word of the Lord in the marketplace"; the pragmatic test the apostles risked when they replied to
the threat of force, " We must obey God rather than men." Theology stands before the same *ultimate* authority when it says, "I am a
Christian because the Christian Gospel gives me more truth about
actual man than any other key," as when it says, " Hitler cannot
dictate what the Church must say, because Jesus Christ is Lord."

Theology as a science attempts to operate as a witness to the self-unfolding of the Logos of God, *there and then,* and from that point through time and space throughout creation with a scientific trueness that sometimes seems incomprehensible and irrelevant to men outside this faith. Theology as a craft of conduct attempts to operate as a witness to the self-unfolding of the same Logos of God *here and now,* in time and space before the very eyes and ears of men who place real trust in the empirical data of their senses and in their ability to interpret them. The *ultimate* judgment on theology in either case is the same, and a supremely humbling one it is, for it is made by the same Lord of history on the words of his human witnesses; but theology as a craft of conduct *also* does not shrink from the immediate test of truth which men outside Christian faith may feel more able to trust and more qualified to make: their own evaluation of results in the tangible world of the present.

In the course of this chapter it will be necessary to develop in diverse contexts the relationship between theology and the group of Academy's disciplines that also deal with man's here and now. Already at this point, however, it is appropriate to assess in brief compass the degree and kind of responsibility which theology can and should assume within the circle of social studies oriented by questions concerning concrete and contemporary " goods." What we are dealing with is, of course, the perpetual dilemma of Christian ethics. Theology as the science of revelation asks questions about the true, while ethics asks questions about the good. How, then, shall a theological ethic dealing with contemporary problems proceed? One answer, very popular in the United States and in liberal circles generally, is to make ethics an independent discipline, separate from theology. Such an approach submits Christian ethics unreservedly to the pragmatic test of relevance and makes of it unconditionally a craft of conduct. We, however, must consider Christian ethics a part of theology, the life of the Christian in concrete existence here and now. As a part of theology it depends upon the source and center of theology and is ultimately judged by it. Justification (a reality of theology) is the source of (ethical) justice; Reconciliation is the source of reconciliations in everyday existence. If ethics is to be the craft or science of the good, a Christian ethic must be defined by a Christian definition of the good, just as a Jewish, Buddhist, or

Marxist ethic will be defined by a Jewish, Buddhist, or Marxist definition of the good.

There are several Biblical statements about the good which seem
to establish a meaningful context within which this question can
be handled. From the standpoint of the Old Testament, there are
two classic statements that must be taken together if we are to receive a balanced and therefore accurate impression. First of all, there
are the repeated statements in the first, or Priestly, account of creation that the Creator observing and judging his handiwork finds of
light (Gen. 1:4), of earth and seas (v. 10), of vegetation (v. 12), of
the astral bearers of light (v. 18), of aquatic and aerial animal life
(v. 21), land-traveling animals (v. 25), and, after the creation of
man, of everything that he had made (v. 31), that it was (very)
good. This remains true and fundamental throughout the Old Testament and extends into the New Testament, which asserts that
even though the creation has been subjected during the present age
to bondage and decay it shall be liberated in connection with man's
total redemption to the fulfillment of its own goodness (Rom.
8:19-23). During that present age, however, there is a concrete
" good " for man which has immediate relevance to his entire conscious, willing existence. The prophetic demands upon Israel are
always particular time-bound statements defining the good in a current historical-geographical context. The classic summary of a multitude of prophetic particularities is given in Micah, ch. 6. Here, in
hypothetical statement, Israel asks how in his present distress he can
please God; asks what sacrificial gift will please him now. The prophetic reply asserts that past experience indicates the present definition of the good in terms of appropriate attitude and action toward
other men and toward God: " He has showed you, O man, what is
good; and what does the Lord require of you but to do justice, and
to love *Hesed*,[1] and to walk humbly with your God? "

For the New Testament, in addition to the restoration of creation and the fulfillment of its intended goodness, the good is defined by Jesus' summary of the Law in the two commandments to
love God unreservedly and to love the neighbor as the self. Paul re-
duces this to the still simpler formulation, " For he who loves his
neighbor has fulfilled the law " (Rom. 13:8, 9 f.). This does not
contradict Jesus' statement: " Why do you call me good? No one is

good but God alone" (Mark 10:18; Luke 18:19). Paul's statement is rather in the spirit of I John 4:20: " For he who does not love his brother whom he has seen, cannot love God whom he has not seen." Calvin's excellent formulation of the relation between the two dimensions of love puts it with his typical pragmatism: " Why does Scripture sometimes mention only the Second Table [of the Law, that concerned with love of *neighbor*]? . . . Almost every time the prophets exhort men to repentance they omit the First Table [love of *God*], and urge faith, judgment, mercy, and equity. In this way they do not overlook the fear of God, but *they demand* through signs *real evidence of it*." [2] Thus we see running through the heart of the Biblical ethic an insistence that the ultimate good, the right relation of man and the entire created order to the Creator, must find its practical expression at all points of historical existence. Theology to be true to its own nature and heritage, precisely as part of its task as the science of revelation, must contradict Tertullian by entering and participating in the circle of disciplines that face the pragmatic test of their ability to identify the good in concrete areas of present human life.

What Is a Craft of Conduct?

In outlining the topography of Academy, we suggested and tentatively gave our reasons for choosing the title " crafts of conduct " for the group of disciplines known as social studies or sciences, in preference to the title "behavioral sciences," which has in recent years been canonized in certain circles. Here we must give a somewhat fuller justification of our choice and attempt to define the shape of the grouping we now propose.

We have offered the motivating question, What is the good? as the fundamental key to this grove of Academe. Each discipline or sector in the grove will have to ask this motivating question in several forms, but it is important first to attempt a general definition of the classifying value, the good, for the entire grove. The good for practical living has historically been defined in terms of obedience to some perfect ideal, law, or norm; or else, in terms of the fulfillment of nature or character. The good has been sought in pleasing some (higher, deeper, or more powerful) Other reality, or in seeking pleasure and avoiding pain for the self. The definition of the good which seems to us most generally useful in Academy, however, was already implicit in our discussion of evil in Chapter III.[3] Evil was not simply identified with man's sinning, with transgression, or with immorality. Evil is of greater scope and is not so necessarily personal as are those concepts. Evil, we said, is destructive of all things and all order, especially destructive of all life, relation, and meaning, the frustration of all efforts to re-create and restore the lost and the broken. The good, then, is creative, preservative, constructive, renewing. This definition is sufficient to all efforts in the group of disciplines we call crafts of conduct; for example, where the behavioral approach to evolution says: " ' Correct ' behavior in a natural sense is correct precisely because it favors survival and reproduction, hence it is by definition adaptive. ' Incorrect ' behavior, in the same sense, if widespread and persistent, can only lead to extinction." [4]

At this point, however, we must make explicit one important qualification. In the labors of the Academic vineyard made up of the crafts of conduct we are not really concerned with ideal or perfect good, or with the good of plants and stars for their own sake, or even the good for life as such: we are interested in the good for man. And man is himself both good and evil, creative and destructive. Empirical man is caught, say the theologians, between original righteousness and original sin, between glory and misery. Karl Barth speaks of " human existence in its insoluble dialectic," while the drama critic Martin Esslin speaks of the " irreducible ambiguities " that are essential to the meaning of such a play, such a telling mirror of man, as *Hamlet*. This understanding of man as a far more complex and recalcitrant subject matter for inquiry than any other dealt with by the nontheological sciences of Academy is at the heart of our choice of " crafts of conduct " as the title for our present group of disciplines.

We prefer the term " conduct " to " behavior," in the first place, because of the limited perspective on man which the latter necessitates. The term " behavior " achieved great importance in the Academy with the approach to psychology known as behaviorism, and although behaviorism is no longer generally considered an adequate key to the description of the human psyche, it is still important in

American educational psychology and has left us with the conception of the social studies as behavioral sciences.[5] The keystone of behaviorism, which has always lent it the mystique of a science analogous to the natural sciences, is its rejection of subjectivity in every form and its unqualified espousal of objective observation in studying what was traditionally considered man's *in*most life. Behaviorism denied itself access to *intro*spection and indeed to all inner experience gathered either by self-observation or by analogies drawn from the experience of other organisms. All this was suspect of unreliability. In its place was offered one kind of data, that concerning modes of conduct which could be observed and established by external and therefore neutral observers. Human behavior could be observed as accurately and "scientifically" as the behavior of Newton's apple or the white rats which were to become the best and most faithful followers of the mechanical behaviorist model. Behaviorism was thus inevitably driven to consider the psyche as part of, or at least fully reflected in, human physiology; and it is no surprise that the stimulus-response mechanism becomes a key for behavioral psychology. Watson, the chief spokesman for American behaviorism, for example, thought that personality, as far as it was a useful conception, consisted merely in the sum of one's habits and reflexes, native or conditioned.

As a type, behavioral psychology does not represent so radical a departure from traditional thought patterns as might at first appear. Beginning with Descartes in the seventeenth century and continuing through such thinkers as Lemettrie, Condillac, Helvétius, and Cabanis, we find attempts to reconstruct the human organism on the pattern of the mechanical apparatuses which were increasingly impressing men with their power.[6] In this tradition, then, behaviorism and the mentality associated with it looks upon man's "mind" as a set of responses, including actions and thoughts, sometimes regarded as uncompleted speech, to external stimuli by the human organism centered in the nervous system and the brain. These responses, in fact all that can be known about the human " soul," can be tested and measured by the external observer. Thus, the whole atmosphere of behavioral sciences is clinical and " objective " in the same way as both physical and biological sciences. One learns in a laboratory in controlled experiments; one measures with the tools of psychometrics and describes quantitatively with the help of statistics and other higher mathematical tools of evaluation such as complex variable analysis; one deals with mechanisms, and with predictable, even predetermined, patterns of behavior. One does not deal with what a man might be, with a hypothetical, intangible, " free " soul; one does not ask, " What person knows a man's thoughts except the spirit of the man which is in him? " (I Cor. 2:11). One may not answer " ultimate questions," which may or may not be worth something after all, but one does deal accurately and disinterestedly with what can be known about the inner workings of the human mechanism from without.

It is interesting to note that early in the development of behaviorism the term " conduct " was applied to the set of attitudes and responses described here, but the term " behavior " soon became dominant, though " conduct " was widely employed by John Dewey and is still used by some of his heirs. The contrast between the two terms is instructive. As we have suggested, the term " behavior " in its modern usage in psychology evokes the mechanical model. The machine or organism characteristically has its responses stimulated, its behavior determined, by outside forces and by the laws of its interior functioning. All attempts to objectify social studies through the use of statistics and higher mathematics contribute to the impression that man is to be known and dealt with in the same way the physicist knows and deals with atoms, the chemist with molecules, the biologist with cells, the electrical engineer with electrons, the mechanical engineer with steam or internal combustion engines. One seeks to understand the *mechanism* of change, and the natural chain of causal forces that *determine* behavior. The " behavioral sciences " have ostensibly offered what a modern science normally and legitimately offers: reliability, reproducibility, quantitative accuracy, and probability within well-defined limits.

It is the question of these very limits which raises doubts as to the usefulness and adequacy of the behavioral approach to man. There can be no doubt that it is correct in stressing the oneness of psychic and somatic existence. The whole trend of what we have learned about man in the last one hundred fifty years has destroyed confidence in the old Hellenistic mind-matter dualism, and has taught theology in particular that it was ultimately unwise to desert the

Hebraic unitary view of man in favor of it. It is, however, one thing to affirm a psychosomatic continuum or to call man a multidimensional unity, and quite another to say that "mind" is fully explained by the electrochemistry of the brain and that for all practical purposes man can be reduced to a series of biological mechanisms. Within the field of psychology itself, two of the alternative theories both as old and as new as behaviorism, *depth* psychology and *ganzheit* or wholeness (often referred to by the related name of gestalt psychology), suggest the crucial critique of behaviorism: it tends to be too partial, failing to deal with man in depth and in wholeness. On the other hand, as Gregory Zilboorg puts it, " We must admit that humanism in its true sense is served poorly or not at all when the individual becomes but a psychobiological adaptive molecule of society, when the individual seems to be looked upon as having been born to serve society, instead of society having been developed to serve man." [7] On the other hand, there are very real dangers in splitting man into many men, analyzing each fraction, each role, each aspect of his behavior, though tending to leave out man himself as his articulate consciousness, and then reconstructing man as the sum of his roles. One may well wonder with Barzun whether in such reconstructions, which claim that man is, for example, six kinds of selves (physiological, psychological, logical, metaphysical, moral, and sociopolitical) fused into a single being: will the glue hold? [8]

Such criticism does not attach to the term " behavior " *necessarily;* it does so because of the history of its usage. Therefore, I would like to suggest the term " conduct " to characterize our second group of disciplines and to emphasize certain aspects of human nature and behavior which have not received sufficient attention, and which might afford a fresh starting point from which to break through the dead ends commonly associated with behavioral and positivistic thinking in general. On the one hand, the very fact that the term " conduct " was used in certain early stages of the development of behavioral thinking indicates that it can be used to convey the insights achieved by behaviorism. It is possible for the " external, objective, disinterested scientific observer " to observe, classify, correlate, and evaluate the data of human conduct. On the other hand, however, the free agency of man and his responsibility for his acts seems more effectively expressible in terms of "conduct" than in terms of "behavior"—not necessarily but historically. From its etymology the word "conduct" seems better able to preserve the connotation of conscious, active, responsible *willing* than does "behavior," and this is particularly true in the verbal modes. Even in ordinary language it sounds almost trivial to say, "How did he behave last night?" and relatively impressive to ask, "How does he conduct his business and social relations?"

This becomes especially clear in view of the classifying questions for different groves of Academe. We have suggested that questions about the true define the sciences, and give them the task of describing and predicting. In this sense, a behavioral science — to the extent that it is an adequate science — might well be adequate to describe and predict human behavior. It is our thesis and contention, however, that the group of fields in the Academic grove with which we are now dealing must perform as its ultimate function and self-justification a further task, the prescriptive one. These fields are not useful if they do not finally ask: "What is the good for man in my particular field of concern?" This question, it seems to me, is best formulated in terms of conduct: "How should man *conduct* himself and his affairs . . . 'as a conscious historical being' . . . 'related to others in society' . . . 'in economic and political reality' . . . as well as 'to God (or Ultimate Reality) in religion'?"

The attempt to explain our choice of the word "conduct" has thus spilled over into an explanation of the replacement of the term "science" by the rather curious and controversial designation "craft" for this group of disciplines. "Craft" has been chosen on the basis of a classifying question, but at this point it should be made clear that the classifying questions and the denominations "science," "art," or "craft" are not absolutely exclusive. I would insist, however, that the classifying questions point to fundamental differences between types of disciplines. Specifically here, the disciplines have a fundamentally ethical drive that seeks to use descriptive and predictive information *prescriptively*. In other words, I would hold that social studies fail to fulfill their own nature and mandates if they fail to face the question about the good for man in their own particular areas and to put their answers to the pragmatic test of truth. Specifically, they should ask: "What good is the study of history if

there are no real uses of the past which at least some historians dare
to suggest for the present?" "Why attempt to understand society if
we do not use the understanding to improve it?" "Of what use is
economic knowledge if it does not help us prevent and cure depression and also help us deal effectively with inflation?" "Why learn
about the structure of states and their operation unless citizenship
helps make human life more human?" "Why study man's mind
or soul or spirit and the theory and practice of their education unless education enhances and fulfills those dimensions of humanity?" Finally, "What good is theology (or philosophy) if it cannot
develop an ethic which helps me (and us) to live here and now?"
Such formulations of the pragmatic test of truth seem more fundamental for these disciplines than are questions of scientific correctness.[9]

Though many of these disciplines have always attempted to make
it their professional concern to deal with such questions, and many
have a renewed sense of this responsibility in recent years, none can
be reminded too often or too incisively of it. Too frequently historians, philosophers, political " scientists," and even religious " scientists " claim that they have completed their tasks with description of
the past, or of the present situation, and feel it unscholarly to chance
prescription. As Berelson puts it, " When a current professional like
Riesman or Mills does write about such broad subjects as ' the lonely
crowd ' or ' the power elite,' he often comes under criticism from
the professional fraternity for disregarding the elementary principles of scientific procedures and, in addition, for getting rather farther out into the seas of values than behavioral scientists in their
professional capacity like to sail." [10]

On the one hand, I would insist that such criticism represents a
fundamental misunderstanding of the nature and responsibility of
their disciplines; but, on the other hand, I would venture to suggest
that it points to a basic difference between the character of their
subject matters and that typical of the " narrower " sciences. One
symptom of this is the pseudoscientific trappings sometimes associated with and produced by the social disciplines. I am not here referring to the coining of ever-new and more complicated terms in
the technical jargon, though in some social fields the supply of such
terms seems to exceed the demand for them by the data. I am think-

ing rather of the many graphs and charts that purport to express trends or developments in some aspect of social or economic science, but which fail to indicate the kind or number of units involved in either abscissa or ordinate. This failure to define the units of measure with rigorous precision and to treat the data with unambiguously quantitative accuracy disqualifies such graphs from serious scientific consideration. More ludicrous but equally serious is the fabrication of meaningless units, as in the claim that certain people in a given study "showed a higher happiness index" than others.[11] Though such cases may indicate that a sociologist or economist is straining too hard to attain standing as a scientist, it does not and should not indicate that any mathematics more complicated than counting and the most elemental use of analytical geometry is forever beyond the reach of social studies. "Craft" as it is used in this book intends no derogation of the social disciplines, as though the scholar in these fields were some kind of sub- or proto-scientist on a level below the scientist on the only useful scale of knowledge. The term "craft," in addition to implying that the disciplines so designated have a goal different from that of the sciences, refers to the belief that the social studies actually deal with more complex and inaccessible reality than do the pure sciences. *The whole man, who is the fundamental object of concern for psychology, history, ethics, economics, sociology, and government, will always remain a more complex and intractable object of study than the subatomic particles and stars between which he stands — even more troublesome, glorious, and mysterious than the secret of the primal living cell itself.*

This is not to minimize the contribution that various sciences have made to our understanding of man — they have been and will increasingly be invaluable; but it is also *not* to suggest that these scientific fragments will someday merge — the gaps between them having been closed by new sciences — into a superscience of humanity. The current definition of science on the model of, say, physics is not comprehensive or powerful enough for that.[12] When we suggest that the psychologist, economist, and sociologist are more properly craftsmen than scientists we are placing them, methodologically, in the same position as the engineer. He, more often than the pure scientist who taught him the fundamental tools of his trade, deals with situations too complex for precise mathematical treatment. Often he does not know all the variables affecting the behavior of his particular energy-matter system, and is quite well satisfied if he can deal with those variables which affect his data in a mathematically significant way, and ignore the others. An engineer is quite normally forced to proceed by making some measurements of whose precision he is reasonably confident and then plotting them against each other, two or preferably three at a time, and hoping that some recognizable pattern will arise. He hopes that he will be able to connect the points he has plotted into some sort of curve which he will then be able to approximate by plotting an equation that he has devised, usually not by rigorous theoretical derivation but by a trial-and-error process of developing a mathematical relationship between what he considers the significant variables in his system. His sole criterion is the pragmatic test of truth: Does it work? But with all his uncomprehended complexity, the engineer is dealing with a qualitatively more simple situation than is the tender of the social disciplines within the groves of Academe. Insofar as he wishes to avail himself of whatever assistance scientific methodology affords, the social scholar or scientist must abide by the same kind of procedures as the engineer.

In our technological school course on economics we engineers, already having the background of calculus, were taught by a mathematical theorist. He devised or reiterated equations that attempted to deal with the so-called economic cycles in terms of multiple derivatives of one variable — supply, demand, cost, profit, for example — with respect to two of the others. Such a procedure is both valid and useful, if we recognize what it is and what are its limitations. The use of calculus implies to those who are accustomed to its use with mathematical rigor that the variables are precisely definable and can be related with perfect ideality. If the variables are highly complex, and if our ability to fix their value is inherently inexact, this ought to be made clear. Further, the arbitrary and risky process of " curve fitting," analogous to that of the engineer, should be understood by all who are guided by mathematically treated social science data. Finally, the scholar in the social disciplines who uses scientific methods of obtaining, evaluating, and presenting the facts about his subject matter has the same responsibility as the en-

gineer to proceed *quantitatively,* to define measurable units of the
various properties of his subject matter which he intends to deal
with, to measure in the defined units *how much* of those properties
are actually present under certain strictly defined conditions, and
then to treat his data with statistical and other mathematical tools.
Where these things are not done, a social discipline may be rendered a disservice by calling it a science within the terms of reference current in our technological culture.

In essence, what we have said so far is that our term " craft "
claims both less and more for the social studies than what is claimed
by the term " science." As a claim to quantitative precision, " craft "
is more modest than " science " and therefore more accurately describes social studies, perhaps partly because of the present level of
discovery in these fields but certainly also because of the inherent
ambiguity, or mystery if you like, of the human subject. On the
other hand, when a craft of conduct asks, How ought man to conduct himself? it goes qualitatively beyond the strict limits of a science that asks precisely what man's behavior has been, is, *and will
be.* Our insistence on the word " craft," then, does not claim anything different for the social disciplines than does the man who
calls himself a behavioral scientist *and* says, for example: " There is
some danger that the neuropsychologically oriented behavioral scientist may lose himself in the wealth of data and the free-ranging
speculations that are now possible to him. But this danger is coun-
terbalanced by the promise of a fresh view of man by man," [13] or,
" . . . the result [of the scientific study of human behavior] may be
taken as an important chapter in man's age-old search to find out
who he is and where and how he fits into the larger scheme of
things." [14] I agree with the content. These goals are exactly what the
crafts of conduct should strive for; but I insist that it is methodologically misleading, if not indeed wrong, to set these goals for behavioral science.

At best, " behavioral science " includes *both the secular-narrower
sciences* of the behavior of the human organism *and the " theological"-wider sciences* which alone speculate and " guide the guesses "
of scientists " by the unscientific, the metaphysical (though biologically explicable) faith in laws, in regularities which we can uncover," [15] and which alone can promise " a fresh view of man by

man," of "who he is and where and how he fits into the larger
scheme of things." At worst, "behavioral science" is an unjustifi-
able pretense that *secular-narrower sciences* can do both jobs. It is
more accurate, more honest, more scientific, to say that psychology,
sociology, economics, and the study of government are crafts of conduct that use the methods and results of behavioral sciences in attempting to answer the appropriate forms of: What is the good for
man?

The term "craft," to be sure, has negative connotations that appear at first glance to make "craftsman" an unlikely candidate for
the replacement of "scientist" as the social scholar's chosen self-
designation. There is the connotation of inexactitude and outmoded
inefficiency in the picture of the handcraftsman from the prescientific, pretechnical era. There are, however, some very positive asso-
ciations with craft and craftsmanship. To begin with, we recall that
personal integrity, care, skill, and fruitful labor are all involved in
the type of the medieval craftsman. In contrast to the modern
assembly-line machine operator who acutely feels the lack of these
things, the medieval craftsman felt none of the frustrations involved
in the repetitive reduplication of impersonal, interchangeable products. The workman true to his craft could feel more directly responsible for his creature, could feel more personally involved in its
production, and more easily take pride in its individuality even if it
were "only" a good shoe or chair and not a great work of artistic
genius. This spirit of the craftsman has fled, however, not only from
the man who stands beside the conveyor belt but also from the of-
fice worker, and even from many a modern executive and from the
citizen of Academy. The statements of thinkers such as Jaspers and
Barzun advocating the reinstatement of labor and craftsmanship as
values in Academy point both to the importance of these qualities
and their too frequent absence. Craftsmanship is equally indispensable for the artist who produces what others designate a work of
creative genius, and for the scientist who "comes up with" the
ingenious invention or discovers the point for "technological breakthrough." But craftsmanship is not identical in kind with drudgery.
It grows out of a familiar, conscious regard for a thing, a subject
matter, a vision, an idea, a field, certain raw materials and, ultimately, what can be made out of them.

This last phrase points to one final aspect of craftsmanship, illustrated by the model of the medieval craftsman, which makes it particularly appropriate for the kind of thinking and decision-making advocated in this chapter. The craftsman often would have a kind of adaptability bordering on originality thrust upon him by the particular kinds of things he might be called upon to make with the material at hand. The criterion of his success as a craftsman would not be its exact conformity with predetermined measurements, not the beauty of what he made, though that might well be a by-product, but whether or not the product of his labor was " good " for the purpose of its manufacture. The only test to which he finally could be accountable was the pragmatic one: Is it useful? Does it work? So, too, the economist or sociologist or Christian theologian may give an entertaining and enlightening discourse about a current problem; but he has not fulfilled his task unless he at least suggests some directions for a solution, and willingly submits them to the test, not simply of discussion by his peers but at the judgment bar of history. All in all, the champion of the social disciplines might feel cheated at being deprived of the title " scientist," but he should not feel dishonored by having his task defined by fruitful labor upon material to which he is personally related and the products of which are evaluated by the " good " they are to people here and now.

Thus, we have brought together, as crafts of conduct in Academy, theology, in its inherent ethical concern, and the group of disciplines that share this interest in questions about the good for man. It is time, therefore, to be more specific about the principal regions in this grove of Academe, to consider just what it is, after all, that these disciplines actually have to do with the questions about the good.

PSYCHOLOGY AS A CRAFT OF CONDUCT

In turning first to psychology, we are attempting to lay hold on the keystone of this arch of disciplines, the view of man more or less common to the group. The Germanic tradition within Academe uses the term *Anthropologie* in its etymological sense of a doctrine or science about man, and consequently the department of anthropology might seem the logical place for us to begin. As the term and the discipline it designates are used in English, however, anthropology is primarily the science of the human *organism,* of physical character and environment, and only in the second line social and cultural achievements and problems. Though one speaks of a comeback for humanistic anthropology and finds anthropology in Britain branching over into other social studies such as comparative jurisprudence and political society, what Cora DuBois calls a " theoretical indeterminism " [16] hobbles American anthropology. This is especially true in terms of the contemporary relevance of the discipline, since scientific anthropology so frequently concentrates on archaeology, and on primitive man and his society with its mores or customs. For these reasons, we turn to psychology as the key area within the social fields, the discipline that attempts to understand and deal with man as man.

This was the hope and intent with which great Aristotle embarked on a concentrated, careful, and rigorous study of psychology. All his hopes and highest efforts as a man and a philosopher are summed up in the opening statement of *Peri psychēs* (known as *De Anima* in Latin), the crown of his manifold achievements: " If we consider knowledge in general as something which has value and dignity, there is one kind of knowledge which distinguishes itself from others, on the one hand by the degree of its certainty, and on the other hand by the fact that it has a more worthy and more interesting subject matter. For the sake of these two merits we must put the investigation of the soul in a primary position. The knowledge of the soul contributes much to the progress of every sort of inquiry, but especially to the understanding of nature. The soul is something like the principle of all life, but, . . . to achieve an accurate conception of the nature of the soul is among the most difficult of all undertakings."

As promising as is the prize set before the explorer in the realm of the soul, psychology has appeared to many, even of its own best modern spirits and thinkers, to lose itself more and more in the forest of " among the most difficult of all undertakings," while the value, dignity, and certainty of psychological knowledge has seemed an ever-receding set of goals. With the rise of " objective modern science " as the bearer of the promise of better, surer, more reliable knowledge, psychology has passed more and more out of the hands of philosophers and into the hands of scientists and technicians. There are those who would claim that this development was always implicit, or even began to unfold, in the thinking of Aristotle himself. They would stress the immanence of Aristotle's thinking in contrast to the transcendence of Plato's. Further, they would emphasize the tendency toward what we usually designate inductive as opposed to the formal deductive syllogism that commonly passes as synonymous with Aristotelian logic. Others would point to the contributions of the English philosopher John Locke as basic to scientific psychology. It was he whose emphasis on the reliability and objectivity of sense impressions decisively turned the attention of modern man to its new focus in the problem of the observer, the subject, the receptor of the object through those impressions or, if Kant is correct and there is no *ding an sich* available to the observer, to the phenomena or appearances of the thing known. Still others would insist that the serious beginnings of truly scientific study of man had to wait until the latter part of the nineteenth century and the British origins of anthropology in Tyler, Maine, and Frazer, the first experimental laboratories in psychology set up by Wundt in Germany and William James in the United States, and the early efforts at sociological investigation growing out of the social reform movements attendant upon the growth of cities and of industry.

The scientific status of psychology and its continuing relationship with philosophy remain a subject of considerable fluidity, the uncertainty of which continues to provide fruitful ground for debate. The perpetually controversial legacy of Sigmund Freud offers us a case in point. There are many, on the one hand, who emphasize Freud the scientist and the vast amount of clinical evidence which lay at the foundation of all his theories, and which continues to pile up (ostensibly at least) in support of them. Others, however, insist that Freud's genius and his contribution lay in the courage he displayed in exercising philosophical freedom, in breaking away from philosophical (not just religious) presuppositions held as incontrovertibly self-evident and positing new ones in their place. The dialectic of rigorous scientific technique and philosophical freedom evident in Freud could well serve as a model for the continuing roles of both in the further development of psychology. The tension expressed by this dialectic recalls the frustration Aristotle warns us of in this task "among the most difficult of all." The perpetual dilemma of scientific psychology has often been expressed by the research worker: "We know more and more and more about the brain, but where is the *mind,* much less the *soul,* the psychologist is supposed to study?" This frustration, born of wrestling with man's soul for its secret, breaks out from time to time, even in the greatest spirits in the field, as when William James, writing his publisher after twelve years of work on the manuscript for *Principles of Psychology,* says: "Nasty little subject. All one cares to know lies outside."

At the end of the shortened version of the book which actually appeared two years later, James wrote: "This is still no science, but only the hope of a science." Today, most experts in the field, aside from orthodox and doctrinaire Freudians, believe psychology has not yet experienced the *necessary* breakthrough, the Copernican revolution, and still *await* psychology's Galileo, or Newton, or even Darwin. It is the contention of this book and this chapter, however, that the strictly limiting demands of scientific techniques do not alone offer the access to what we are looking for. Just as God's revelation is the only true subject matter of theology, and this requires that the theologian must go through-but-beyond the linguistic, historical, and literary sciences, so psychology may well see its relation to the psychological sciences. This is nowhere more obvious than in such a definition of psychology as: "Psychology is the science of the behavior of man and animals in their environment." This is the indispensable starting point for modern psychology, but psychology should lead the way for all the crafts of conduct to recognize that behavioral sciences *as such* play a partial and contributory role in sociology, economics, and the study of government. Behavioral sciences provide the most accurate facts and reliable generalizations about certain limited aspects of man's life that can be obtained about any aspects of it, and the crafts of conduct must use these in their real business, dealing with values, decisions, prescriptions of the good for man. Psychology must stick to the "nasty little subject" and turn its back not on the *still limited* scientific approach, but on Nietzsche's fear that this all-consuming concern "is a vice." In doing so, it must also turn its back on the alluring security of a dogmatic, speculative, faculty psychology, whether it be Aristotelian, Thomist, or Kantian. It must not forget, however, that its ultimate goal was set when Aristotle accorded it the first place among the departments of man's knowledge, because of the dignity and worth (and, he would insist, certainty) of its subject matter.

If man is in any serious sense the measure of all things, psychology and its allied discipline anthropology, must *play* the key role among the crafts of conduct, for they must ultimately know about man as man. The other disciplines can describe for us how men have acted in the past, what man does now in various phases of his existence, and even predict how man will behave in the near future. Only indirectly, however, do they tell us what man is; what he can, and, perhaps, even what he should become. That task, among the crafts of conduct, ultimately falls to the psychologist and under this severe burden are defined his responsibilities to psychology as a biological and behavioral science, and his responsibilities beyond them. In this connection it may be well to note a comment on Freud's sense of the proper relationship of psychology to other disciplines. Reflecting upon Freud's role in doing " more than anyone else in the history of psychopathology to make psychology a biological discipline," Gregory Zilboorg points to a passage expressing Freud's feeling " that medical psychology was perhaps closer to philosophy than to natural science." [17] In saying this he reminds us that while modern psychology cannot desert or neglect the scientific study of concrete existent organisms, mechanisms, and behavior in favor of a speculation on the ideal nature of man irrelevant to observable reality, philosophy's fundamental concern for wholeness constantly challenges psychology to remember that it is questing for an understanding of what is essential to man as man; it cannot ultimately be satisfied with anything less. It is encouraging for psychology that Karl Pribham can say: " The American neuropsychological contributions to behavioral science point to a resurgence of the dignity of man as a scientific as well as a political and humanistic tenet "; [18] but the impression given is not strictly correct, for the dignity of man is not discovered or proved by any behavioral science or all together, and it is false to claim that it is. The dignity of man is a prelogical and extrascientific assumption which the behavioral scientist *as natural and moral philosopher* may hold and which his accurate data and reliable generalizations may partially support. Zilboorg is much nearer the mark, however, in insisting on a profound humanism pervading the work of the psychologist. In a very real sense, the psychologist has the right and the mandate to be the humanist par excellence within the Academy, and to suggest directions in which the crafts of conduct may seek the good for man.

SOCIOLOGY AS A CRAFT OF CONDUCT

If psychology finds itself *uncomfortably stretched* between the frustrating small certainties of empirical science and the glowing generalizations of speculative philosophy, sociology has truly been torn by this tension in the Western world. This is less true of American sociology than of its continental European counterparts, for it was born of the concerns of the Social Gospel, then liberated from the confines of these presuppositions by the " objective " or " disinterested " methods of empiricism. At present it is related in one direction to psychology and the concern for the individual man, while in the other direction, being the " science " of man in association with others, sociology represents a common basis for the study of all such relations, economic, political, religious, artistic. Entering the library of a sociologist, one may receive the impression that here at last is someone concerned with *all the products* of man's living, so that for many the sociologist plays the synthetic and magisterial role among the social studies which the systematic theologian claims for himself among the theological disciplines.

Earl S. Johnson, professor of the social sciences at the University of Chicago, formulates this position with unambiguous clarity: " The political, economic, and cultural problems of our time fit into no watertight compartments. No bulkheads separate man's social experience. I take what I trust is pardonable pride in the belief that sociology, of all the social science disciplines, is uniquely fitted to approach these ' synthetic problems.' " [19] Thus the American sociologist displays formal similarities to the philosopher's concern with *all* and with *the whole*. He is, in this respect, far more fortunate than his European colleague, especially the German, who is still suffering from the less fortunate beginnings of his discipline and their severely restricting consequences. The American sociologist has problems getting his results and his advice accepted as he wishes, a fact partly reflecting the rapidity with which his discipline has grown, but also partly reflecting the inevitable resistance to the importance his missionizing zeal sometimes leads him to think his advice deserves. In Germany, on the other hand, the sociologist is perpetually concerned to reiterate: " Sociology wants to be a science, a positive (empirical) science and nothing else. We are not selling, and we will not allow ourselves to be controlled by, any *Weltanschauung* or ideology." We are tempted to dismiss the plight of German sociology with a sigh of sympathy for the undeveloped state of such a discipline, but I would submit that a closer examination of it would be instructive for us, not only with respect to the nature of sociology in particular, but with direct application to our thesis that all the crafts of conduct are, and should be content to be, under a constant tension between rigorous scientific concerns and values defined by philosophic or theological considerations as " goods " for man.

Rene König, editor of the *Fischer Lexikon* volume on sociology, opens the introductory article with the blunt statement: " In this book ' sociology ' is understood as an independent empirical science." He announces that the book will proceed via a series of separations from many " disciplines, systems of thought, and doctrines," and that all these will work together so that " at the end, a sociology will emerge *which is nothing else than sociology,* namely, a systematic scientific treatment of the general structures of social life, the laws of their movement and development, their relation to the natural environment, to culture in general and to the separate areas of life, and finally to the social-cultural person of man." [20] This last statement provides an admirable summary for all sociological science, and is an adequate definition of the work of our (American) behavioral sciences as such; but at the same time the very vehemence with which the lines of definition are drawn calls our attention directly to the painful experiences of German sociology even in recent years. The principal adversary is identified in the statement: " All philosophically determined approaches are immediately eliminated from sociology understood in this way, especially the ' *philosophy of history and society.*'" This primordial exclusion is made partly for methodological reasons and partly on historical grounds. The latter category is divided into historical misunderstandings of the relation between sociology and philosophy, and historical perversions of it. The disastrous consequences of these misunderstandings and perversions have made the methodological distinction crucial, so that König calls not only for exclusion of metaphysics and teleology from sociology but its " separation from all practical disciplines, . . . a clear division from social ethics, social reform, and from ' social politics ' as a comprehensive system of social practice." [21]

The root of the difficulty lies in the related origins of sociology and socialism, especially since one of the pioneers in this area, Claude Henri de Saint-Simon, a co-worker of Comte, fostered both together. Comte split with Saint-Simon, whom he accused of putting the cart before the horse by building a practical doctrine before the scientific system was complete. Many nineteenth-century workers in the social field felt that it was possible to make a gradual transition from sociological theory, which König characterizes as dealing with clearly delimited specific problems and building upon reliable knowledge already attained, to the " philosophy of history and society," which is only interested in the interpretation of the totality of social existence. Practically, however, this meant that one was supposed to ground the propositions of sociology as an empirical science on the highest axioms of the " philosophy of history and society." At the first meeting of the German society of sociologists in 1910, Ferdinand Tönnies declared: " Sociology is primarily a philosophical discipline." From this point the " unanalyzed empirical deposits within philosophical sociology," as König calls them, were relegated completely into the background of a philosophical system based on specific ethical decisions concerning the " right " society unassailably prior to scientific investigation.

The vicious outgrowth of this was that increasingly, from the 1920's on and even in the present *Kulturkritik,* there have been warring left- and right-wing movements, each with some form of " right social order " ostensibly based on scientific empirical research as the basis for their " theory of society " or " philosophy of history and society." Therefore, sociology as an empirical science in Germany has had to cut itself off both from the kind of social Hegelianism the Nazis could use and also from Marxism, thus from "philosophy," "ethics," "reforms," and "values" as such. As a result, German sociology warily insists on complete independence of the sociological concept of culture from the concept of culture in "philosophies of history and society" such as those of Spengler and Toynbee. All of this can serve as a specific warning to Anglo-Saxon sociologists when we remember that in the theory of George H. Mead we find the sociological counterpart of the nineteenth-century Utopia of Progress. It is no accident that Reinhold Niebuhr's invective against naïve and unrealistic (irrelevant) utopianism falls equally upon the liberal Protestant Social Gospel, which gave such an impetus to American sociology, and the Marxist dream of a "classless society." The history of German sociology warns us against any surrender of scientific achievement to some fuzzy but doctrinaire "idealism," including perversions of our thesis that sociology is ultimately concerned with the good for man in all his relationships. We ourselves must guard against creating a "Christian sociology" or "Christian economics" which would be as perverse as Marxist and Nazi "philosophies of history and society" with their dogmatic shackling of scientific procedures and as ludicrous as an Anglican algebra or Roman Catholic calculus would be. And it is precisely the pragmatic test of truth that will protect us from the perverse creation of a *beautiful* and *logically* airtight a priori system that misshapes empirical data.

American empirical sociology, though it may put less emphasis on the favorite German model of the person-society-culture triangle, can live with König's definition of sociology which, after all, represents largely the record of its own achievements. These achievements are indeed impressive. To become aware of this, one needs simply to look at the way in which our understanding has advanced beyond the commonsense level through the careful study of: (1) groups, from the small group that links the individual person to society, to the social classes and publics; (2) institutions, those "established, determinate forms in accordance with which men enter into relations with one another"; (3) social structures, patterns of social interactions and relationships.[22] These achievements are linked with the development of methodological tools to handle social problems in a systematic, scientific way. Sociology has been so much concerned with this aspect that it was once caricatured by a French mathematician who called it the science with the most methods and the least results. As Samuel A. Stouffer has pointed out, sociology today is typically concerned with: " advances in measurements; development of survey methodology; the design of experiments; and some contributions to the analysis of complex social and personal data involving many variables simultaneously." [23] Many American behavioral scientists join König in his caution, warning against " disregarding the elementary principles of scientific procedures " and also against " getting rather farther out into the seas of values than behavioral scientists in their professional capacities like to sail." [24]

There are many others, however, who feel not simply a right but a deep responsibility to relate their scientific findings to the solution of ethical problems. In some cases one is aware that these men are still motivated by the kind of basically religious concern which informed the Social Gospel and the Christian Realism surrounding Reinhold Niebuhr; in other cases one senses that these men are so enthused with the " gospel " and the mission of their discipline that they see it as that central discipline of Academy, that new " queen of the sciences," which can provide the basis for the coordination and communication of all. Either motive, it would seem to me, is a valid expression of the thesis that sociology and all the rest of the crafts of conduct have to do not only with the question of the true, in the sense of the scientifically correct, but also and *primarily* with questions about the good. Specifically, some make very modest statements such as: " We may look on all social behavior as an exchange of goods," [25] which is illustrated by the example of two coworkers of equal social status exchanging helpful advice for esteem, or a parent exchanging the implements and mechanisms of security for the gratitude and affection of the child. In view of the extensive application of the results of behavioral scientific analysis to practical problems, another investigator reminds us that the power of knowledge lends itself to use for either good purposes or evil. He points out the danger that if behavioral science eschews values it " will join in the attempt to substitute science for ethics and aesthetics, to displace humanism with scientism." " The thinking behavioral scientist," he insists, " recognizes that his science is not and never can be a substitute for poetry. . . . Moreover, behavioral scientists can and sometimes do learn from their humanist colleagues about the values that make the life of man more than the life of other animals and so direct part of their inquiries, at least, to subjects that, in the end, really matter." [26]

Their zeal leads other social scientists to be less modest. Impatient with the pessimism concerning man's future among the traditional " humanists " of literature and the arts, these sociologists seem eager to take up the fallen lamp of humanism from the failing hands of those they now regard as the enemies of social science, " the newer humanism." Nevitt Sanford, in summarizing the social science study *The American College,* defines the major functions of social science as *" research, consultation,* and *reform* or initiation of changes by means of special understanding and special techniques. . . . When the social scientist is acting in the role of reformer or initiator of change, he himself is concerned about objectives, and, obviously, he is guided by values of his own. It is this role, naturally, that is most in need of clarification; and it is this role that seems to stimulate the most vociferous antagonism to social science." [27] Aside from the question of antagonism within and especially outside the Academy, we must register our emphatic agreement that social science has a reforming role, a prophetic function, and declare that one of the most important by-products of this chapter should be to help illuminate " this role . . . that is most in need of clarification."

Though he deplores the failure of the humanistic disciplines to accept the leadership of the social sciences, Sanford denies that social sciences will be hampered in their efforts: " They will be able to take care of themselves, in any struggle with the humanistic disciplines. Our real concern is that the humanistic critics of social science will give aid and comfort to the real enemies of contemporary man, which are anti-intellectualism and despair. . . To be ourselves, we must think well, while accepting the guidance of our human feelings. To alter our situation, we must use all the knowledge and intelligence that can be found. Social science has no monopoly on these objectives, nor, in seeking them, any inclination to go it alone. It should, indeed, expect to find natural allies in its humanistic critics. Wrong-headed as they often are, their hearts are in the right place." [28]

Traditionally, the grove of Academe we prefer to call the arts has also been called the humanities. Especially in France, where the great poets and writers have long led social and political reform, art has meant humanism-in-action and has been expected to be in the forefront of ethical concern. Today, however, the social sciences have the tools of description and prediction. If they achieve conviction, perhaps precisely in dialogue with the sensitivity of the artist and the resources for belief of theological and philosophical thinking, they are ideally situated to do the prescriptive task as well. Sciences, arts, and crafts of conduct are not exclusively related to the true, the beautiful, and the good, respectively; but our classifying scheme seems to fit well the contemporary situation in which humanism-in-action is not represented by the traditional artistic humanists but by the so-called scientists of behavior.

Earl S. Johnson, with his allegiance to the ideals of the liberalism given classical expression by writers like John Dewey in the democratic image of men as " persons of goodness and wisdom," and in the role of education to realize this dominating image of " democratic character," is quite clear that the role of the social sciences is centrally and primarily involved with the questions about the good for man. " Human conduct is social," he says, " in that it has consequences for others in terms of better or worse, right or wrong, good or bad. In this sense the social *is* the moral, since moral distinctions are exactly those of better or worse, good or bad. . . . If we should disregard the values or goals to which our social acts take us, we would miss the significance of many, if not all, of the facts involved. Each of the social sciences focuses in one way or another and immediately or remotely on the order which men constitute. This is a social order. In the terms of the foregoing, it is also a moral order." [29]

The social order, thus conceived, is part of a continuum, a cosmos of interrelated orders, comprehending all existent reality, to which corresponds a cosmos of academic disciplines or activities. The pivotal role of the social studies in this cosmos becomes explicit in Johnson's diagram relating the *humane, social,* and *natural* studies. Since *social processes* are those means through which the resources of physical things and processes are utilized to attain " goal values " or humanistic oughts, the *social studies* play the role of indispensable mediator between the *humane* and *physical* studies, and are thus effectively the operating center of Academy.

We have now sketched the range of self-understanding among sociologists: from the extreme behavioral point of view which would insist upon a compartmentalized extrinsic certitude and eschew to sail too far beyond the shallows on " the sea of values," to a point of view which understands sociology as not only necessarily involved in decisions about the good for man in every concrete relationship of his life but also as occupying the magisterial, or at least the reformer's, role among the groves of Academe — a role abdicated or modestly declined by its other traditional and potential fulfillers. Our view of the role of sociology among the crafts of conduct can briefly be stated by referring sociology to the question: What is the good for man *in association,* in all forms of relationship to others, both individuals and collectivities? In the definition given by this question it is clear that behavioral science can perform part of the function of the sociologist better than any other set of techniques we have ever had. Behavioral science is indispensable to sociology in the same way that literary and historical sciences are indispensable to Biblical exegesis. Behavioral science alone, however, falls short of fulfilling the task of sociology when it cuts itself off from values, from ethics or morals, from the question of the good. On the other hand, sociology claims too much if it claims the role of creator and ultimate arbiter of concrete goods. In the first place, its responsibility is primarily related to the social structure of economic, political, and religious aspects of society, and when it asks questions about the good for an economic-social class or a political-social organization it asks about the *quality of personal and collective relationships* and not about the economic or political content (the problems and solutions) as such. On a deeper level, even though sociology may clarify, classify, and measure the strength of human values and may make practical suggestions about the way in which social processes and structures can be operated to serve these values, sociology does not itself create or produce these values and it too can in the end only serve them.

Economics as a Craft of Conduct

Economics occupies an ambiguous place within this family of disciplines, unique but symptomatic for the whole. It is most obviously susceptible to mathematical treatment, and therefore " scientific "; it is also the subject of more moral prescriptions than almost any area of life, not only in the theological past but in the technological present, for, as J. K. Galbraith has indicated: " Man cannot live without an economic theology — without some rationalization of the abstract and seemingly inchoate arrangements which provide him with his livelihood." [30] The supreme paradox of economics, its human glory and misery, is that the concept most dear to traditional American economics has been called the most *impersonal* of all social relationships and at the same time is widely proclaimed as the most powerful motivation in every activity and institution affecting the personal, from marriage and the family to international power struggles including war.

The key term in this paradox is that sacred cow of free enterprise: " competition." Competition's virtues have been extolled by generations which have regarded it as the most free, most fair, most conducive to growth and development of all the relationships devised by man to regulate his collective conduct. Competition, free and untrammeled, was taken as the guarantor of economic justice, Deuteronomic (retributive) to be sure, but impartial and absolute: the diligent were rewarded, the lazy punished. In addition, there was nothing like competition, in business, study, or sport, so deliberately calculated " to make a man " of one. Modern sociological analysis, however, has developed another frame of reference in which competition comes off far less favorably: the spectrum of social relationships runs from *competition* through *conflict* and *accommodation* to *assimilation*. [31] Mutual definition within this context must be carefully drawn and adhered to, since some words intended to have a high positive value may have a negative connotation in other connections, and vice versa. *Assimilation,* for example, connotes primarily " belonging," which involves deliberate choice, even love, rather than a slavish chameleon quality, while *accommodation* connotes adaptation as distinguished from unqualified acceptance. On this scale, *competition* receives a more negative rating than open *conflict* because it is less personal, although one might normally think of conflict as more destructive than competition. This latter supposition is certainly true in the extreme case of mortal combat, but much of modern art, especially literature and drama, illustrates the validity of the sociological schema. One comes to realize in the course of Edward Albee's *Zoo Story,* for example, that a man's hatred flagrantly shared with an ugly bare-fanged dog is for him a more rewarding personal *contact* than years passed in the anonymous competition, the wordless jockeying for position among the eight million place-fillers of a modern city.

The very impersonality of competition has its advantages. In a rather cynical sense, competition offers the competitor (which, in the vegetable model of pure competition, is the wholly impersonal plant taking all available forms of nutriment for itself without " regard " for its " neighbors ") freedom from feelings of guilt concerning the consequences of his triumph for the unsuccessful rival. The somewhat less cynical scientific virtue of competition is that precisely the exclusion of the personal makes economics in the competitive mold more amenable to mathematical treatment, more comfortably scientific. It is from this point of view that economics quite legitimately assimilates higher mathematical models and more extensive and sophisticated statistical methodology than any other of the " social " disciplines. This is why we earlier illustrated the use of a suggested kind of engineering logic with its application to economic theory. At the same time, however, we must keep in mind the inaccuracy of the claim that in such an *impersonal* member of the family of disciplines involving persons as economics, all but two or three of the variables can be considered constant in any given situation. As Heinrich Rittershausen remarks about a specific use of mathematical models in economics: " The difficulty with using models in general is that in reality there exist dozens, in fact usually hundreds of factors whose presence or absence or change is significant for the desired result. In his description the author enumerates three to seven, and assumes with respect to the others that the reader thinks exactly as he does — which naturally is by no means the case." [32]

The use of models, especially mathematical ones, and the limitations on this use highlights the problem of defining the discipline.

Models belong to the systematic approach in widespread current use in contrast to the classic historical approach. The fact that the historical approach will be employed more extensively in our presentation of economic problems is not to be construed as though we would subordinate the systematic approach and scientific methodology to it, nor does it indicate that the current trend does not fit our concerns in classifying economics as a craft of conduct. The systematic approach earned its victory in what is known as the conflict of methods (*Methodenstreit*) fought out in economics about the turn of the century. The historical method, unchecked by systematic scientific considerations, can subserve the specific presuppositions of a philosophy of history that rides roughshod over empirical economic reality.

Another, perhaps more common, definition of the *Methodenstreit* is the conflict between inductive and deductive approaches. What was called the inductive method in European economics grew out of the historical approach which had dominated the field. Its methodological key was to derive generalizations from a mass of concrete particulars. The deductive method starts from specific assumptions — sometimes value-laden ideologies, sometimes hypotheses relatively value-free — which then are applied to and explicated within specific economic contexts. Any success enjoyed by this method rests exclusively upon the correctness of the initial assumptions. Though we tend to think of deductive logic as a largely prescientific intellectual procedure, economic reality is surprisingly amenable to rigorous and formal mathematical treatment, so that the economist is tempted to it not only by the austere perfection of such formulations but also by their applicability. Therefore the deductive method persists today, and, in fact, the methods most modern in appearance — work with models including the so-called " variation method " which employs computers — belong in type to the deductive school. Actually, both sides in the methodological controversy have long since come to recognize that both methods must be used together: the fundamental presuppositions of the deductive process grow out of " inductive " observations and, on the other hand, the generalizations or judgments of whatever derivation must be " deductively " applied and pragmatically (empirically, or even " inductively ") verified.

This combination of inductive and deductive approaches has been designated the "reductive" method, a term perhaps more fully descriptive of the total process than "empirical." The basic outline of the procedure begins with the logical reduction of particular data to theories, which then are fitted into larger theoretical contexts of hypotheses and theories. A second reduction operation takes place in verification when hypotheses or subhypotheses of theories can be checked against properly gathered and analyzed reports, statistics, and financial statements.[33]

The importance of the distinction between inductive and deductive approaches to economics is emphasized by the competition between the two great systems theoretically in life and death conflict in their pure forms today: capitalism and communism. On the one hand, both are "economic theologies" in Galbraith's sense, so indispensable in the modern world that "inductive" economics abstracted from their existence would be unrealistic and irrelevant. They are, therefore, models that define divergent deductive approaches; but, on the other hand, the claim of both to be scientific is nonsense in the absence of continuing "inductive" criticisms. This situation is elucidated by Heinrich Rittershausen when he says that the two systems of order "under general public discussion are *competition,* which Karl Marx called 'the blind rule of the law of supply and demand,' and second, the steering of the economy by a *central* total plan. . . . Both systems provide for an active direction of all partial economic functions from above business management. Both take seriously the need for a sensible guidance of the total economic process. Both systems perceive the goal of the economy as the satisfaction of demand. They differ only with respect to the method of guidance. While the followers of a competitive economy strive for a mechanism through which each individual business is influenced by the consumers immediately, i.e., without the intervention of the government or any authority, the supporters of centrally planned economy advocate a solution by which the government evaluates the assumed need of the consumer, plans in advance, and through central directives mobilizes each individual business in the planned provision for the total consumption."[34] Whether or not one is, or ever becomes, ready to draw from the statement, "They differ only with respect to the method of guidance," the conclusion that neither the methods of pure competition nor those of total planning are sacred, we must recognize that all forms of both systems deal with the same economic factors of capital, production, supply, demand, markets, price, money, and efficiency, under whatever local guise. And whether or not we are persuaded that the solution to the dilemma or the two opposing economic ideologies rests in some synthesis or mixture, we must recognize the power of *economic* forces to shape cultures and nations regardless of their *political* structure.

By this point in the discussion we have ample opportunity to recognize that the most impersonal of the social sciences is, after all, a most personal craft of conduct, so that Galbraith can say: " Like theology, and unlike mathematics, economics deals with matters which men consider very close to their lives." [35] Man is very personally involved in whatever theoretical and operative system of economics provides the answers to the basic defining question: How (by *whom* and through *what* means) is what provided for *whom?* Man may not, as Deuteronomy and Jesus are so eager to tell us, *ultimately* live by bread alone, men may indeed have fought duels in the streets of twelfth-century Paris over the nature and the reality of universals, but it would be hard to persuade many a realist that the acquisition or preservation of goods and possessions is not the prime motivation determining human behavior. Is not the very perdurance, the capacity for adaptation and growth of frankly materialistic Marxism, which claims to be fundamentally nothing more than economic science, proof enough of that?

Others, impressed by the power of economic reality but wishing to employ examples more congenial to Western democracy, could claim for economics a wide range of real and symbolic power over the lives of men. Not only do we decide on food and clothing, residential neighborhood, vacation, and retirement, even political party, religious affiliation, and vocation partly or largely out of economic consideration; but also much of our inmost intellectual or spiritual life is shot through with economic symbols. This is true not only informally, when " our kind of people " is defined economically, but formally when small-group research, one of the newest branches of sociology, models its terminology on economic theory — intimate social " transactions " are " exchanges " of " goods " or " values " — and when ancient religious texts express the most important relation-

ships in economic metaphors. The Bible, for example, chooses for
its motivating center the metaphor of redemption, the buying back
or payment of ransom for the release of a captive. The redeemed
is usually the disinherited or the financially distressed: the Hebrews
in Egypt, Yahweh's poor in the era of the prophets as well as those
to whom belongs the kingdom Jesus proclaims, not to mention the
low and despised, the soldiers, women, slaves whom Paul addresses
as the chosen of God in I Cor. 1:28. The power of economic forces is
attested in the most detailed prohibition among the Ten Commandments, that against covetousness.[36] It is the love of money which is
"the root of all evil," and while our sins are the debts that mark our
poverty before God (Matt. 6:12), it is the rich man for whom it will
be hard to enter the kingdom (ch. 19:23 f. and parallels). All of this
betrays the fact that economic considerations, in addition to wearing
the impersonal masks of competition, reach down into the depths of
personal existence to touch the nerve of profound emotion.

It is, therefore, a fruitful tautology that economics in its constant
concern with goods is really always asking ethical questions, questions about the good for man in relation to those goods. Put still
more bluntly, I would conceive of the ultimate justification for economics as expressed in the question: What are goods good for? or
simply, What good are goods? In a somewhat more sophisticated
formulation of the ethical cornerstone of economics I would suggest
we should ask *how economic forces are to be controlled, directed,
and utilized so as to serve the ends which are good for man.*

Theoretically, at least, all problems of Academic economics can be
solved satisfactorily, and in practice economies reach equilibrium, so
that we may well become satisfied that economic resources are available to resolve all foreseeable economic dilemmas. After all this is
achieved, however, important problems remain, and precisely these
reveal the fundamental nature of economics and its place within the
whole pattern of life. It was an economist who wrote in response to
the question, How far is life rational?: " Not very far; the scientific
view of life is a limited and partial view; life is at bottom an ex-
ploration in the field of values, an attempt to discover values, rather
than on the basis of knowledge of them to produce and enjoy them
to the greatest possible extent. We strive to ' know ourselves,' to find
out our real wants, more than to get what we want." [37] This is not a

statement imposed by "ethics" on "economics," it is a statement about scientific economics which reveals that economics' own fundamental questions are ethical. It is one way of stating the place of economics among the crafts of conduct. Our characterization of economics, indeed of the whole social science group, as a craft of conduct shares the awareness of Paul Samuelson that economics is that "discipline suspended halfway between art and science." Thus from the point of view of the conflict of methods and of motivating questions and classifying values, we do not see economics in Academy trying to sit on two stools or bestride two unharnessed horses, but believe that it has a separate integrity in the primary ethical drive which defines it through the question about the specific goods. Our question, What good are goods? implicitly contradicts the traditional conviction of economists that anything which denies the community additional goods or services is the greatest of sins. The traditional economist, as Galbraith points out, is "excessively preoccupied with goods qua goods" and "in his preoccupation with goods he has not paused to reflect on the relative unimportance of the goods with which he is preoccupied." [38] Such an attitude reflects the carry-over "of the mentality of nineteenth-century poverty to the analysis of twentieth-century opulence."

The alleviation of crying need is, of course, the first responsibility of an economy, and the initial warmth of the popular response to President Johnson's war on poverty testifies to the abiding awareness of this priority. The island of poverty, large and piteous though it may be, within the sea of American opulence does not, however, justify the classical assumption that all of the *scarce* resources of our economy must be poured into some form of poor relief. The problems of poverty today are rather problems of health, education, and geographical location. When Galbraith and others question the adequacy of the "goods qua goods" foundation for an economic theory and ethic, however, much more far-reaching problems begin to arise out of Opulence Ocean. The question, *What* goods shall be produced? comes into view, and not simply in the classic "guns versus butter" form. After defense and general standard of living have been appropriately attended to and more of the resources too scarce for Utopia remain, how shall they be used in a world whose inventiveness produces ever more ways of using them? Shall we devote these resources to alleviating world hunger and improving the world standard of living, hoping thereby to win (as distinguished from buy) new friends or at least blunt the aggressiveness of a hungry enemy? Shall we utilize the "beyond scarcity" resources of time and money to enrich our own spiritual lives? Shall we devote them to "pure" research in all Academic fields with ultimately humanistic intent, thus investing in the remote future? Or shall we simply pile luxury on luxury to satiety? This complex of problems has increasingly become, for us in an affluent society, more and more dominant in economics; and the emergence of these concrete yet fundamental questions about the good for man within the economic sector dramatically reveals both the ultimate nature of economics and the continuing relevance of the Christian faith to it. These particular problems demonstrate why the area of economics does seem to surround a nerve canal leading to the depths of humanity. To answer them economics must discover or decide or at least discuss the ways in which men should conduct themselves, and toward what ends. At this point Christian theology, contrary to Tertullian's "I owe no obligation," has the same concerns and high stake, and should both learn from and contribute to these discussions, discoveries, and decisions.

The persistent question about the good use of goods implies that economic forces can serve evil or destructive ends, and I would add that this power of economic systems for evil is not solely due to the evil intentions of men nor is it merely proportional to them. Economic systems have what thinkers like Tillich and Niebuhr would technically refer to as the "demonic" power to create evil, or — if one prefers the terminology — they can create evil spontaneously. This is not a property of economic systems alone; they share it with all social structures. Beyond the level of evil or "possessed" men or cliques or oligarchies, one can speak of a demonic state in the political realm, whose dramatic symbol is the beast of Rev., ch. 13. Reinhold Niebuhr has taught Academy to distinguish "immoral society" from "moral man," and, if I may be permitted to coin a phrase, that "demonic residual" of society's immorality exists in excess of the sum of evil intentions and acts of moral men. Though economics, as the foregoing implies, holds no monopoly on the problem of evil, at this point in history it may *be most appropriate for economics to ask whether either capitalism or communism has solved the problem of producing good and not evil through the production, distribution, and consumption of economic goods.*

This problem, of course, is nothing new — especially for theology in the Biblical-Christian tradition. We have already cited many of the Biblical warnings against the power of economic drives to corrupt man's goodness. An almost stronger testimony to the capacity for evil inherent in economic drives is the fact that the static feudal society of the Middle Ages was conceived precisely with a view to controlling greed, also checking that *appetitus divitiarum infinitus* which R. H. Tawney translates "the unbridled indulgence of the acquisitive appetite," and directing economic drives into morally acceptable channels.

We should mistrust our impulse to condemn the economic aspects of medieval feudalism out of hand, or to write it off as simply inferior, in the way that animal-drawn carts with solid wooden wheels are inferior to jet transports; or as simply unenlightened in comparison with our "free democratic" recognition of the infinite possibilities of the private individual for wisdom, righteousness, and prosperity. It was this system which knew how to harness the wild horses of economic appetite. With the history of the Greco-Roman economic experiment behind it, medieval Christendom deliberately turned its back upon that past and chose certain strict controls upon the power of economic forces to shape life. Interest charges were considered immoral because of their quite possibly crippling effect on the poor. The responsibility for property and its power was taken quite seriously: it mattered into whose hands it fell. The rich were responsible to uphold, defend, and operate the orders of society. Luther, the pioneer of a *spiritual* revolution, was so tied to this ideal that his most effective document of reform, while announcing the right of any individual Christian to call an ecumenical council of the Church, was addressed "To the German Nobility" because of their status, power, and responsibility within the legitimate existing hierarchy. Even Calvin, who, with his followers, espoused more of the new economic, social, and political forces than did the Lutheran Reformation, insisted that even when the most unjust and anti-Christian tyranny oppressed the people it was to be overthrown only at the instigation of the estates, the established or-

ders of society. The economic counterpart of the distinction in social
and political power was at least as clearly stratified as were they;
but any inequality (injustice would seem to them too strong a
word) was both temporary and secondary in importance when
viewed from the perspective of eternity. The next world was the all-
important one, the kingdom in whose glory all shared. Since it
profited nothing " to gain the whole world and lose one's own soul,"
it was a long-term asset not to have to contend with the economic
baggage which made it so hard to enter the kingdom. The present
Christian world was a divinely ordained hierarchical order in which
each assisted all to attain the everlasting goal. The model of the
early Church as a "communism of consumption" society waiting
for the return of the risen Lord to consummate history was never
completely lost. The poor man was *necessary* to the rich so that in
obtaining eternal life he would have someone to whom he could
give his alms when he heeded the call to " sell all (*sic!*) that he had
and give it to the poor."

We must, in short, not underestimate in any area of life the power
of the medieval synthesis replaced by the Renaissance and Reformation architects of protomodernity. The hierarchical structure of
medieval Christendom represented a titanic collective effort to impose order upon chaos, and thus create a Noah's ark for the sake of
the salvation of all. Scholasticism tried to control evil by incorporating it philosophically and in the popular mythological arts on the
lower, i.e., negative, levels of the scale of the good. Monarchy and
aristocracy represented political order in contrast to the chaos of
democracy (literally, mob rule). Similarly, feudal economy was designed deliberately to hold back the swamping waters imploding
through rifts in the hull of the ark, rifts caused by " free enterprise "
and " private property," credit and commerce. And when the medieval cultural fortress crumbled, when the ship had to be abandoned
and " Roman Catholic " culture became a flotilla of lifeboats on a
largely alien sea, the mourners numbered not only the Fathers of
Trent, but even such as the Martin Luther who vehemently fought
that economic upheaval called the Peasants' Revolt.

In spite of the fact that even those who led the Exodus out of one
gate of the walled city of Medieval culture on to a road leading toward modernity threw all of their weight against other gates to

keep them closed against other men longing for similar dangers and freedoms on other roads, all gates — political, social, spiritual, and economic — flew open one by one, their hinges forever sprung, and the very walls of the fortresslike synthesis came crashing down. Though many individuals, peoples, nations, strove to remain faithful to the Roman Catholic ideal, that ideal of a synthesis in which all forces were held in balance by an order benevolently imposed from above had become a memory and a hope — against hope — for Western civilization. In the political sphere, the various forms of order in which Christendom's loyalties had been more catholic than local gave way to rising nationalism. In the religious sphere, the divergent forces always before held within bounds by loyalty to a holy hierarchy culminating in the bishop of Rome gave way to religious autonomy for state or regional churches, for like-minded Calvinists, Enthusiasts, and Free Churchmen, for the "gathered" Church, Unitarians, the "Enlightened," the "Free Thinkers," and finally the frankly secular. Socially, the old distinctions gradually gave way, usually to be replaced by new ones established along religious or economic lines, but in any case without the old rigidity.

Of all the arenas of life, however, the economic became perhaps the most dynamic. First, commerce and trade extended the market from its localized attachment to manor or town, so that the economy of Christendom was left less at the mercy of local control and local conditions. The mechanisms of credit extended the flexibility of economic power not only over space but also through time. Next, the gradually swelling tide of manufacture burst into the flood tide of Industrial Revolution, which swept aside forever the tyranny of agricultural life over man's fulfillment of the whole range of his wants and needs. This was done, let it be stressed again, over the strong objection of "modernists" so-called, now the Encyclopedist architects of French society and Americans of the stripe of Jefferson and Franklin, all of whom were physiocrats, literally, believers in the "right of Nature to govern" the lives of men — friends of the agricultural countryside *against* the city uprooted from the soil. This opposition, however, coming some two and a half centuries after the religious Reformation, is in the long run no more than a symptom of a rearguard attempt to tame the unbridled economic appetite. This implicit witness to the power of economic forces over the quality of man's life rapidly became explicit in France's bourgeois, or middle-class, revolution. In it the economic forces, set free by the collapse of the feudal economy, organized and erupted to overturn the aristocratic social order supporting an ecclesiastical superstructure which added its oppressive weight upon the lower strata of society. Beyond the obvious fact that medieval Christendom had also been economically and socially "buried," however, the real question remained: What shall replace it? What *more* does the Revolution mean? Does that Revolution, or structures analogous to it, contain synthetic powers as significant as its powers to overturn and destroy, so that Revolution can establish a permanent economic, social, cultural, spiritual order of its own? Or is this Revolution a mere way station on the road to still more sweeping change? These questions are seminal for the development of all aspects of modernity, but above all, for the nature of modern economics.

Although the French Revolution was unable to establish any stable *political* structure, there are many who would uphold the view that in representing the apotheosis of the middle-class man and his "freedom to become" it represents economic normality. Disciples of the Weber thesis, those whom Tawney calls the epigoni who take in his washing, would make the Protestant Ethic primarily, if not exclusively, an economic one and connect it in content, as well as in chronology with the "rise" and "spirit" of capitalism.

Modern economic reality is further illuminated, however, by the insistence of others that the French Revolution was a job half finished or barely begun. Radically democratic theorists (socialists and Marxists) recognize that the French Revolution truncated the medieval social and economic pyramid by lopping off the aristocracy of Church and State; but the same power that had ground the poor at the bottom of the pyramid devolved upon the bourgeois entrepreneurs who now occupied the top layer of the residual hierarchy. Purveyors of the Protestant Ethic and wholehearted supporters of Free Enterprise for Private Owners implicitly recognize that the economic power liberated from the medieval synthesis by bourgeois capitalism is of such intensity and personal impingement that its misuse can injure; but they advocate Free Enterprise as the perpetual answer to the problem of providing the greatest good for the greatest number. This they do partly because they are convinced of the rightness of the institution of private property with its individual liberty, partly because they are convinced of the power of the puritan virtues to channel economic power for good, and partly because they are impressed by the almost magical mechanisms of self-adjustment through market pricing, etc., built into the classical capitalist model. Various limpings, wheezings, and total breakdowns in the machinery of capitalist economies and the distress of associated societies have led even avowed friends of Free Enterprise to solemn prophecies that private capitalism could only survive with the acceptance of severe modifications and controls.

The Marxists, together with those socialists associated with them, are by no means modest in proclaiming the whole structure of bourgeois capitalism a fundamental error, a fallacious freezing of a transitional stage in the proper development of economy from a tyrannical to a truly democratic form. Since Marxist ideology takes the economic aspect of life for the decisive one, its desire to control the misuse of economic resources is even stronger than that of any Christian theology. For Marxism the institution of private property, the appropriation by the few of the goods and means of production needed for the sustenance and satisfaction of all, is the *source of all evil* — really *all*, in a far more literal and radical sense than that intended by the analogous New Testament proverb. Private property plays the role assigned in Christian theology to that historical corrupter of all social and personal existence: original sin. It makes little difference to this ideology whether property is held in the private hands of a few kings and aristocrats or in the private hands of the bourgeois many. Nor are the fumbling attempts of middle-class morality to assuage its guilty conscience by the practice of a few milksop virtues sufficient to atone for the evils of privation of the public's rights to all economic resources. No less radical solution to the problems created for the masses, the proletariat, by the institution of private property will suffice: public confiscation of all goods and means of production and distribution must be followed by the construction of a fully planned economy operated at first by a caretaker administration but eventually directly by the people and for the people without coercion of any kind needed to curb the forms of inhumanity generated by private ownership. To achieve control of a political party, of a country, and then of a bloc of nations, to confiscate all private property and to administer it, has cost Marxism a vast struggle, many sacrifices and victims, significant operational failures, and certain real but unexpected evils from within the system, all of which have inevitably brought basic revisions in Marxist theory, and some disillusionment. To achieve success Marxist economies have had to adopt some capitalist structures and techniques, so that as wistfully labeled " Communist " countries enter the competitive world market they bring, in effect, state capitalist economies into the fray.

On the other hand, the classical capitalist countries and their modern allies enter the arena wearing faces surprisingly not dissimilar to those of the communists, for they have had to correct weaknesses in their systems by state planning. Thus economic history shows us neither a pure and moral capitalist Great Society nor a communism advancing along the road to Utopia, each against its polemic cartoon version of the other. What it reveals is the continuing struggle of man to regulate the production, distribution, and utilization of goods for the attainment of the good as defined by his variously conditioned ethical standards.

Since it is easy to delude ourselves in an era of warlessness and affluence that the capitalist system has indeed solved these problems, has been able to harness the economic forces that can become evil, it is important to remind ourselves that there have been very real and quite frightening crises in the operation of competitive capitalism in the recent past. Many scholars regard the effects of Germany's 1920–1923 inflation and the Great Depression, at least in America, as far more devastating psychologically than World Wars I or II. Exhaustion of resources and bad decisions in specific cases may well have been contributing factors, but those concerned began increasingly to ask whether it might not be that there were inherent inefficiencies in the private free enterprise system and also inherent insufficiencies in dealing with the moral problems traditionally associated with economic power. If in the dark days of war — both hot and cold — there is a tendency to assert that democracy is too inefficient to compete against totalitarianism, there has been a far stronger tendency to desert unaided private enterprise in the face of our economic traumas and to turn to larger nonprivate participation in the economy. In the Anglo-Saxon, especially American, economic world the timely theories of J. M. Keynes, so relevant to the problems of depression, convinced many that a modification of private enterprise with government planning offered not only a straw for a drowning man, but a continuing buoyancy-and-ballast mechanism for the economic vessel. The essence of the Keynesian formula, as Galbraith formulates it, " consists in leaving private decisions over production, including those involving prices and wages, to the men who now make them. . . . Centralized decision is brought to bear only on the *climate* in which those decisions are made. . . . Thus, in times of depression, increased government expenditures or decreased taxation will cause or allow an increase in demand." Conversely, in times when uncontrolled decisions would be in the direction of increasing prices and wages, they " will be reshaped by higher taxes and lower government expenditures." [39]

Purists would decry such procedures as destructive of private free enterprise, by definition, because the government not only interferes with the price mechanism but even enters the market as so powerful a competitor for raw materials and labor as to constitute a monopoly force wreaking still further havoc with the price mechanism. Others, however, would welcome the evolution of the so-called mixed-enterprise system. Paul Samuelson refers to it as the neoclassical synthesis for which he predicts: " By means of appropriately reinforcing monetary and fiscal policies, our mixed-enterprise system can avoid the excesses of boom and slump and can look forward to healthy progressive growth." [40] In spite of this sanguine statement on behalf of ostensibly economic factors, however, the key to the operation of either the theoretical model and practical system of capitalism or of communism lies outside economics. Galbraith has shown this in his discussion of the need for something like " countervailing " consumer power, and in view of the nonsymmetrical character of the Keynesian formula (i.e., its vulnerability to inflation), he is painfully aware that the inevitable controls destroy the freedom of the sacred price-market mechanism altogether. In the case of wartime inflation, as an example of a situation in which demand cannot be controlled and production must be maximized, he concludes: " The only alternative to open inflation is to remove to central authority the power of decision over prices and wages," as was actually done for this reason in 1950 at the outbreak of the Korean war.[41]

In the classical Anglo-Saxon model, "There could be no misuse of private power because no one had power to misuse," while in the Marxist version of the planned economy the same was true but, in addition, the very root of one man's power over another had been torn up and left to wither within the provisional skeleton of the atrophying political institution. But apart from both oversimplifications and the illusions they became, power has persisted and the power of power to corrupt is neither noticeably diminished nor noticeably further removed from the economic realm. In spite of all attempts to say that some adjustment — either in the direction of greater intervention and planning or of less — will make the economic system produce not only goods but the good — justice, satisfaction, and peace of mind — the unsolved problem of economic power is a demonstrable symptom that neither in communism nor in capitalism nor in any combination of them have the unleashed and infinite forces of the economic appetite been harnessed again. Power must indeed be dealt with. This very recognition, however, shows us that economics is not concerned with watertight compartments of life, for the element brought into focus by this discussion — power — is the very stuff of political reality, the subject matter of political science, of the study of government.

Politics — Neither Art nor Science

The study of government occupies a rather peculiar place among the crafts of conduct in their relation to the "modern," the behavioral scientific approach. On the one hand, the "anatomy" of the "body politic" does not lend itself to the kind of partial but precise measurement that yields significant results in physiological psychology. On the other hand, the functions of this body do not lend themselves to simulation by theoretical models of great beauty and usefulness, as do those of economics. It is not to mark political science as a backward discipline if we say that its reality has not yet given itself to political behaviorists on a plane much above that of the pollsters with their immediate concerns, and that both the history and the philosophy of government bulk larger today than do their counterparts in other fields of social study. The much-advertised slogan of President Johnson that politics had been raised from " the art . . ." to " the science of the possible " does not really herald the kind of breakthrough in the study of government which with Roger Bacon, Copernicus, and Newton transformed natural philosophy into physical science. This fact is used by traditional students of government to brand " the political behavior approach " as " psychologizing," on the one hand, and as " mere statistics " on the other. In reply, while the political behaviorists admit that their approach understands political action in terms of " motivations and attitudes " of people, and that whenever and wherever possible it employs quantitative and statistical methods, they insist that " psychological concepts and statistical devices are tools of analysis which must not be confused with objectives." [42]

On its side, political behaviorism as late as 1956 was still deploring the fact that neither empirically oriented theory nor sophisticated research methodology were characteristic of political research as an Academic discipline. For example, in the field of political theory, tradition was accused of partisanship unrelated to empirical consideration of the present. It is extremely interesting, however, that " *political* science," unlike some of its sister disciplines, arose not only out of an interest in increased accuracy and greater technical effectiveness but equally from a concern for the *humanity* which had been squeezed out of the study of government by a concentration on abstraction and on analysis of impersonal structures. Not traditionalists but " behaviorists " recognized that it is more patently impossible to formulate a political policy for dealing with, say, Asiatic or African men and nations without reference to a philosophical view of *man* than, for example, an economic one.

Thus political behaviorism dates itself — somewhat anachronistically — from Graham Wallas' 1908 statement: " The thinkers of the past, from Plato to Bentham and Mill, had each his own view of human nature, and they made those views the basis of their speculations on government. . . . [Today] in most cases one cannot even discover whether the writer is conscious of possessing any conception of human nature at all." [43] Insofar as this charge of ahumanism is just, it may well serve as a warning to all in Academy that intoxication with one's ability to handle a certain portion of subject mat-

ter, to solve intricate but minor or irrelevant problems, is a perpetual threat to any discipline or approach, just as it is to any theology that becomes too crystalline or too entrenched. There is hardly
one of us among the citizens of Academy who is sufficiently innocent of the sin of making marionettes of our human guinea pigs to
cast the first stone charging " mechanical automata " at another. Yet
the charge applies to all of us so universally that it is chronically forgotten in our self-deception and must not " go without saying." Let
us see, then, how political behaviorism in its pursuit of Truth as
" consistency with the facts " upholds its concern for Humanity.

By 1925, when Behaviorism was flourishing as a psychology, and
sociology was also striving to emulate the physical sciences, Charles
Edward Merriam was saying: " Politics, in short, faces the common
problem of passing from rule of thumb to more precise measurement, from the art to the science, and, as in other fields, this process
involves a struggle of the most strenuous nature along a way strewn
with many failures. But anthropometry, biometry, psychometry all
give signs of hope that genuine advance may be made toward discovery of scientific relations in the domain of political phenomena.
Possibly the door of human nature is closed by some decree of nature against the scientist, but it is also possible that we have not
found the key that will unlock it." [44] Dr. Zilboorg sees the *initiation*
of more scientific procedure in clinical psychiatry as a " recently acquired humanism," but he professes to see a recession in humanism
as a result of *further* scientism: " We don't live with one another
anymore . . . ; we ' communicate ' instead. We don't talk to one another; we ' communicate.' We no longer establish relationships to
and with people; we ' relate ' instead. . . . We don't adjust ourselves to this or that situation; we merely adjust. . . . We don't
identify ourselves with this or that person; we omit the word ourselves and we plainly ' identify ' — quite intransitively." [45] Describing this problem in the specific form that faces the political scientist,
David Easton points out that in fact classical political thinking may
have sparked interest in the investigation of human nature rather
than vice versa, and in some way therefore may have been closer to
it than were other related " social " disciplines. Therefore, as the
others one by one split off from philosophy to become separate sciences, political thinking remained tied to philosophy. It was only

when humanity suffered in political science — as indeed it did in philosophy — from what he calls "the enchantment with reason" and from a decline into sterile historicism that a political science separate from philosophy was proposed as an alternative to dehumanization. The risk of what Easton calls "hyperfactualisms" seemed preferable to an outright flight from reason.

The editors of *Political Behavior* declare that in common with all social-scientific inquiry, "three essential elements are at the center of the analysis of political behavior: systematic theory — more or less developed, an empirical approach, and an interdisciplinary focus." The implications of these "essential elements" are spelled out somewhat more clearly in what they call "the most important characteristics of the political behavior approach": "1. It specifies as the unit or object of both theoretical and empirical analysis the behavior of persons and social groups rather than events, structures, institutions, or ideologies. . . . 2. It seeks to place political theory and research in a frame of reference common to that of social psychology, sociology, and cultural anthropology. . . . 3. It stresses the mutual interdependence of theory and research. 4. It tries to develop rigorous research design and to apply precise methods of analysis to political behavior problems." [46] Let us attempt to demonstrate both the strengths of the behavioral approach and the risk of "hyperfactualism" by discussing, first, one of the humane aspects of behavioral advance and, then, the problem of systematic theory.

Bernard Berelson's "Democratic Theory and Public Opinion" demonstrates the way in which political science can be both empirical and humanistic. It utilizes all the objectivity that pollsters can muster and seeks to enhance *human values* thereby. He concludes that the political theory of democracy "requires that the electorate possess appropriate personality structures, that it be interested in public affairs, that it be informed, that it be principled, that it correctly perceive political realities, that it engage in discussion, that it judge rationally, and that it consider the community interest." With regard to personality structure, Berelson enumerates "among the characteristics required . . . self-control and self-restraint as reins upon the gross operation of self-interest; . . . (and) a healthy and critical attitude toward authority." His truly impressive list could have been drawn from many different sources, including the exegesis of Biblical texts having political relevance; but here, it was presumably derived with reference to appropriately empirical political data. In any case it preserves in exemplary fashion the ethical values with which we are concerned in " political science " as a craft of conduct. " The second component required of decisions," says Berelson, " is the possession of *principle;* the electorate is required to possess a body of stable political principle or moral standards, in contrast with fluctuating impulses or whims, to which topical questions can be referred for evaluation and decision. . . . Just what they are for different parts of the population is difficult to say. . . . At this time, however, it would seem at least likely that the *same* avowed principles underlie political positions at every point on the continuum from left to right. . . . Now this is not so empty as it sounds. Democratic theorists have pointed out what is often overlooked because too visible, namely, that an effective democracy must rest upon a body of political and moral consensus . . . a seeming consensus which is accepted at its face value is far better than no consensus — and a seeming consensus is sometimes reflected in loyalty to the same symbols even though they carry different meanings." [47] This statement is especially valuable, not so much for its overt and explicit affirmation of morality as for its willingness to face empirical data, analyze it critically, conclude with " Now this is not so empty as it sounds," and then explicate that conclusion. To what extent, though, does " political behavior " maintain this level of excellence in the realm of systematic theory?

The very statement of the *first* of the three essentials of political behaviorism as " systematic theory — more or less developed " suggests that there are real problems here. Is it *possible* to generate systematic theory out of the analysis of current political behavior without reference to classic political speculation? Classical political thought — especially when it was part of an entire philosophical system in the manner of Plato, Aristotle, and Hegel — was systematic theory, *more* not less developed. Its usefulness was guaranteed by what was considered to be the perpetual relevance of its analysis of man's nature and his political association. This analysis did indeed involve empirical observation of conditions by the philosopher in his own time. When " political behavior " criticizes the practice of operating political study as a sort of museum of the great systematic theories of the past it does so partly on the basis that these empirical observations were not made and treated sufficiently " scientifically," and partly because the conditions of the " simple " past are not considered sufficiently relevant to the complex political situations of the present.

Modern political science intends to build its own systematic theory on currently observed political reality, and to check it against still more empirical data. This latter function is evident in David Easton's statement that general theory provides a set of criteria for the evaluation and guidance of empirical research.[48] How this is to be done, however, presents a real and abiding problem for political behaviorism. The business of constructing systematic or general theory in political science remains a philosophical one. As is well known to philosophers of science, scientific logic can falsify but cannot absolutely or finally verify and establish theory. Thus, if political theory is to maintain a view of human nature and consistent ethical criteria, these must still be derived from sources outside the science of politics itself and then submitted for falsification, or utility, or at most probability, to the pragmatic test of truth. This means that in fleeing from hyperfactualism, " political behavior " cannot afford to become what Easton calls a premature policy science. All its theories must be submitted to the test of relevance to available data, and if as a result systematic theory must remain *less* rather than more complete, then be that as it must. But the grandeur of political thinking has resided in great systematic theories, each in its own time. It is in this area, then, that political science probably can still learn most from its own past. " Political behavior " may well discover more about how systematic political theory is constructed and how it works from the likes of Aristotle, Locke, and Hobbes than from all the treatises on modern modes of logic.

What is it, however, that distinguishes systematic *political* theory from theory in related sectors? Even if the purpose of political thought and practice is to make human life human, we have found a doctrine of man and the question concerning the good for him centrally involved in each of the crafts of conduct. But it is the problem of *power* which marks the peculiarly political concern with man and his good. It is no accident that Rom. 13:1-7, the classical focus of Christian political thinking, centers attention on " the *pow-*

ers that be." Similarly, institutional power is the issue when Aristotle, Thomas, and Calvin, in discussing the advantages and dangers of the various forms of government, ask: Is it more dangerous to risk mob rule (literal translation of democracy) or the tyranny that an absolute despot might impose? It was the awareness of "universal sinfulness" in thinkers touched by Puritanism which led in the eighteenth century to the development of formulas for the division and balance of powers between various branches of government.

Yet the problem of institutional power is, if anything, more serious today, a fact that is reflected in the thinking of the social scientists. We have seen that Galbraith considers a new rationalization of economic power one of the imperatives of highest priority in his discipline. The entire tendency to introduce central planning into economics, even if only for safety's sake, reflects the feeling that power and control are ultimately the responsibility of government. Such a prophetic analysis as the magnificent set of sermonic essays by Reinhold Niebuhr, *Beyond Tragedy,* illustrate this point. Written on the brink of that struggle for the survival of civilization, World War II, they warn that following victory we must get back to the really serious business of harnessing economic power within political control. And today, in defining the true business of political science, Gablentz and Fraenkel declare: "The element of power cannot be eliminated from politics. Politics is the struggle for power." [49] This statement is symptomatic for a school of modern political theory that approaches the whole from the perspective of power. Some scholars see dangers in this approach, fearing that *in practice* power means inevitably not only coercion but also potential destruction, and also fearing disastrous distortion *for the discipline* when the "power school" assumes that systematic theory can or should be a general theory of power alone.

David Easton is highly critical of the "power alone" approach, and in his own definition of political science combines the conceptions of power and value. "Political science," he says, "is the study of the authoritative allocation of values as it is influenced by the distribution and use of power." [50] But let us sample the flavor of the mutual elucidation of power and of political reality in the work of Harold Lasswell, one of the thinkers most commonly associated with the " power approach." [51] " When we arrive at a basic analysis of the interplay of personality and power," he says, " a further step is the consideration of how to put what we have learned in the service of human dignity. . . . Power is an interpersonal situation; those who hold power are empowered. They depend upon and continue only so long as there is a continuing stream of empowering responses . . . even a casual inspection of human relations will convince any competent observer that power is not a brick that can be lugged from place to place, but a process that vanishes when the supporting responses cease." [52] The foundation for Lasswell's analysis is clear from his skeletal representation that in the social process, *Man* pursues *values* through *institutions* (constructed) on resources. The key terms for political analysis are " value " and " institution." After listing a series of value-institution pairs he concludes that any of the other values may serve as the base of power, and power as a base can lead to tyranny, where power is intended to compensate for deprivation of the other values. Good, just, useful holders and wielders of power integrate it with many of the other values. The conception of power which has been asserting itself here is not only more obviously related to modern psychological categories than to mass, muscle, and mallet but, further, is not unlike the power which Paul speaks of in the New Testament as the power of God. He speaks of the cross (I Cor. 1:17) and the resurrection (Rom. 1:4) and the Gospel (v. 16) of Jesus Christ as possessing power, which produces man's righteousness and effects his sanctification and redemption (I Cor. 1:30) in opposition to all conventional standards of economic, social, educational, and hereditary power which God refuses to " empower " by responding to their claims.

Power, then, is in every sense an ethical problem central to political reality. Solely in terms of the power of the political institution, our times demand continual clarification on questions concerning the sources, the legitimacy, and, perhaps most important, the uses of power. Concretely: in what way and to what extent is it " good " for the state to control the life of the individual by legally depriving him of income through taxation, and by coercing him into unrestricted contacts with other people in the business area while restricting his liberty to establish contacts in the area of sexual activity? How much of what kind of its " sovereign power " should a

Western European nation give up to the Common Market, NATO, the UN? How may a powerful nation, ethically speaking, use its power — economic, diplomatic, military — to influence weaker nations? In all these areas " power " bristles with ethical problems so central to the nature of both political science and theology that neither can responsibly ignore them. In the days when the American political system was given the decisive direction of its greatness, our brief theocratic heritage was creatively reformed by a generation whose *language* was as clearly and informedly *political* as that of both the Middle Ages and the Pilgrim Fathers had been *theological* and as that of modernity is in some respects technological. At every new moment of American greatness theological and political thinking have converged in some pivotal figure. Our own moment in history calls for a new convergence of this kind; a dialogue between the Academic forces of political theory and theology concerning power offers the prospect for a practical contribution of vital significance.

Thus, as in the case of psychology, sociology, and economics, we have asserted that political science is a fundamentally ethical discipline and that its problems have been and are of vital interest to Christian ethics as well. Modern social sciences, however, are empirical in their treatment of man's life in modern society, and must inevitably submit their findings and prescriptions to the pragmatic test of truth: Do they work? We have said that as a science Christian theology is not compelled to submit its statements to the pragmatic test of truth, but it must submit them to the test of consistency with its subject matter, the Word of God, and only that test of truth is necessary to it. We have said further, however, that Christian theology also attempts to follow in the footsteps of the Biblical witness which has risked relevance to the political, economic, social, and psychological, to the *human* conditions of its time. Thus, theology also submits its statements in these areas to the pragmatic test of truth.

The question now arises, however, whether or not modern man is seriously interested in the results of this test of theology's truth. Does God care and dare to speak to modern man who possesses science? Has Christianity anything specific to say to modern man, anything to do other than to create an atmosphere of sanctity and security as an island to which he can return, in the same way that modern Japanese executives retreat from scientific and industrial success, pursued in Western garb, into tradition, in the garb of ancient Japanese religion? Or is Christianity with all its words simply consigned with all other "prescientific" words to mere antiquarian interest? Can we simply leave ethics in the Academy to whichever social science is appropriate to each particular ethical question? If not, what conceivable "good" can Christian theology do and be in the areas defined by specific forms of the question: What is the good for these men, precisely here and just now? These are not intended as rhetorical questions, to be brushed aside summarily in the midst of a foggy feeling that "eternal verities" will continue indefinitely to hover over us in a vaguely helpful way, but questions that challenge theology to a fresh, honest reevaluation.

Perhaps theology really should stop pretending to ultimate knowledge relevant to the here and now and abdicate its traditional claim to ethical truth. Perhaps even Jesuit moralists should admit that the relative merits of the decisions of Thomas and Suárez on a hopelessly prescientific problem are of no real pragmatic interest even to themselves. Would a Protestant thinker who became interested in the ethical aspects of psychology not do better to become a disciple of Erich Fromm and promulgate "the art of loving" as the basis for "the sane society" in which "man" would really act not against but "for himself"? Should not a theologian interested in social ethics simply line up behind David Riesman and seek to discern, collect, and try to mold *faces* in the lonely crowd? What after all is wrong if a theology concerned about economic problems frankly admits that Keynes has replaced not only Say and Adam Smith but also Amos and Jesus, so that the best we can do is follow Galbraith and try to find ways of passing the needle's eye around the camel members of the affluent society? Why worry about whether Pius XII or the German Lutheran Church should have fought the Church Struggle against Hitler more offensively, and whether Reinhold Niebuhr really did teach America anything useful about itself, and simply turn political ethics over to Arthur Schlesinger, Harold Lasswell, and Hans Morgenthau? In short, does Christian ethics possess an independent character that will enable it to stand the test of living today, that pragmatic "best test of truth"? Or has the prophetic mantle of Elijah passed once for all to Elishas whose access to the spirit of the Lord does not depend on prophetic ecstasy, prayer, or even faith, but on scientific data-handling methodology?

Prophetic Relevance

This increasingly recurrent reference to the prophetic mode suggests that we answer these questions in terms of a revitalized understanding of Biblical prophecy. We have noted in Chapter III that the entire history of the Biblical people, of Judaism and Christianity, can be understood in terms of a dialogue between priestly and prophetic modes of thought and action. Both the priestly institution and the prophetic voice have an ethical structure and keynote. The priestly institution upholds tradition; conserves ethical values in law and in the Deuteronomic principle of perfectly balanced retribution: automatic reward for obedience to divine commands, automatic punishment for disobedience. To speak in a metaphor of the pragmatic test of truth: when such legalism is judged at the bar of history, the hurricane winds of change find this priestly ethic too inflexible, and, like a tree deeply rooted in the earth but too rigid to bend, it can splinter and break. At the opposite extreme, the Biblical world knows the ethic of the soothsayers, the men who will accommodate their proclamation to any change of weather and, to please the powerful, cry, " Peace, peace," when there is no peace. Before the storms of history this soothsaying ethic bends to avoid the trunk-tearing force of the blast, but its hold on the earth is so shallow that it is soon uprooted and overturned. The prophetic ethic, however, is made for the storm; in fact, it is often called into being by distress, though that is certainly not its only precondition, for the centuries of dark despair between the exile and the coming of John the Baptizer were an empty epoch when " the voice of the prophet had died out in the land."

For the first several decades of modern Biblical study, the prophets were the darlings of a liberalism that attacked religious institutionalism and socioeconomic privilege. At the same time, however, conservatism was unwilling to hand the prophets over to " the radicals " and agreed with Calvin that the prophets were simply interpreters of the law of Moses (though Moses is mentioned only four times in the entire prophetic corpus). Recent criticism has taken two opposite approaches in proclaiming that prophetism has been over-rated. On the one hand, it is claimed that the prophetic ethic is re-actionary, or, in terms of our hurricane metaphor, "too deeply rooted in the past." This school of criticism insists that prophecy is not really progressive at all, in fact, that it retreats from evolving complex and sophisticated society and calls for a return to the simple-minded "good old days" or the nomadic existence in the desert (Jer. 2:2 f.; Amos 5:25; and, above all, Hos. 2:14-20). The other line of attack is that of certain modern political analysts who say of Reinhold Niebuhr's respected record of political judgments: "What can he say about politics and history with his doctrine of original sin that I can't say without it?" Applied to the prophets, this assertion reads: "They are neither more nor less than good so-cial analysts. Their pious theology is unconnected with their correct economic and political pronouncements." Such criticism would con-sider the prophets pure relativists, adapting their messages to the pressures of the particular time they understood so well.

This tendency might not be so obvious in a prophet who exercised a brief ministry, but when one considers a longer career such as that of Isaiah or Jeremiah one finds the prophet changing his pol-icy on the same issue most markedly. Jeremiah came from a family of village priests of the type attacked by the Deuteronomic Reform; but after settling in Jerusalem which benefits by its measures he espouses the Reform and becomes a propagandist for it. Once it is put into effect and attains status, he vehemently attacks it, except that he still employs its terminology and its logic in his critique. Similarly, there seems on the surface of it to be neither rhyme nor reason in Isaiah's attitude toward Assyria. He begins by charging King Ahaz not to call on Assyria for help; then he identifies Assyria as "the rod of . . . [Yahweh's] anger" to punish rebellious Israel and the unfaithful of Judah. Next he counsels submission to Assyria and warns against calling on Egypt for help against that occupying power, then chides the king for paying tribute to Assyria and prom-ises that God will drive off the Assyrian army, but finally warns that God will bring it back if Jerusalem does not repent. In view of con-temporary criticism we must ask: Does prophetism simply vacillate between reaction and relativism, sinking either into a pious obscurantism or into a chameleon opportunism? Or, Does the prophetic ethic combine strength with flexibility so that it not only survives the hurricanes of history but gives shelter, stability, and direction for the development of present and future living? Let us turn first to a brief consideration of the nature of prophecy and the pragmatic test of its truth in the career of Jeremiah, and then to the "how" of prophetic logic as used by Isaiah.

Jeremiah's life demonstrates the tenuous and charismatic character of prophecy, the impossibility of guaranteeing that a prophet will arise to meet a crisis that requires critical and creative redirection. Connected with this is the poverty of professional tools and resources available to the prophet: he really has only words. Though the early prophet was an ecstatic, sometimes perhaps like Alexander and Dostoevsky the "fortunate" victim of the holy sickness, epilepsy, though he may have symbolic objects and relationships — Jeremiah's iron and wooden yoke, Isaiah's wife and children with their symbolic names, Hosea's broken marriage — all these psychological states point to and all these symbols are dramatic substitutions for: "Hear the *word* of the Lord." The prophet has no professional vestments, and as prophet he offers no sacrifices and leads no cult. In a thousand different ways he repeats the motto: "To obey [God's word] is better than sacrifice." Throughout the scene in Jer., ch. 26, following the Temple sermon (perhaps more fully given in ch. 7), we are aware of the conflict between Jeremiah, on the one hand, and the Deuteronomic priests and prophets on the other. Yet it becomes clear that Jeremiah does not stand alone, he retains the support of some of the royal party, he is recognized by some as an authentic prophet like those of the past. Though the prophetic proclamation is generally unpopular (because antipopular during a time of national sickness), the people can be restrained by a protector of the prophet (Jer. 26:24) and will eventually recognize the value of the prophet's words — which is no mere posthumous expression of guilt for mistreating an irascible genius. It is a recognition that the "true" prophet so correctly interpreted his time that his thinking has become a canon, a measuring rod, for understanding the past and the present as well.

Still, canonization is a matter for the ages and "the operation of the Spirit in the Church." How are *contemporaries* to distinguish

and evaluate the true and the false prophet? Jeremiah's great dia-
tribe of ch. 23 advances several criteria. Reinhold Niebuhr has
pointed out in a sermonic essay on this chapter in *Beyond Tragedy*
that the mark of the false prophet is his offer of false security, while
the marks of the true prophet are that his message undercuts that
cry of " peace " when there is no peace, and that he himself also
stands under the judgment of his message.[53] In chs. 27 and 28, however, Jeremiah clashes head on with Hananiah, who claims that he,
not Jeremiah, rightly proclaims, " Thus saith the Lord," and a new
criterion is needed for designating the true prophet. To Hananiah,
who insists that the Lord will break Nebuchadnezzar's yoke from
off the neck of Judah, Jeremiah retorts: " The prophets who pre-
ceded you and me from ancient times prophesied war, famine, and
pestilence against many countries and great kingdoms. As for the
prophet who prophesies peace, when the word of that prophet comes
to pass, then it will be *known that the Lord has truly sent the
prophet*" (ch. 28:8 f., italics added). The true prophet submits his
case against the false prophet to the pragmatic test of truth, to the
judgment of history. He stakes his whole reputation not on some
remote judgment of posterity as to the beauty or fitness of their
work but to swift confirmation. This is the ethical test of truth, to
which the political, economic, social, and psychological analyst must
ultimately submit his work.

In suggesting the appropriateness of the pragmatic test to the prophetic ethic, however, we have opened the door to the question: Is
not the prophet, then, *merely* a good political, social, or economic
analyst? Without the word " merely " we could simply answer af-
firmatively and be satisfied to describe how the prophet arrived at
his analysis. " Merely " suggests that we must still face the questions
concerning the validity of *Christian* pronouncements about current
ethical problems and exactly what may be the unique role of theology in the ethical realm. All these purposes are served, I think, by a
brief analysis of Isaiah's political pronouncements. Isaiah deals with
the usual prophetic themes of social and economic justice, and religious and moral probity, but the thoroughness with which he handles the political area is characteristic and may argue that he was a
responsible member of the court at Jerusalem rather than a religious
official. We have pointed out above that Isaiah's assertions about As-

syria at different historical moments seem mutually contradictory. We could analyze and evaluate the rationale and its potential for continuity at any of several points. Crucial, however, is the period between the fall of Samaria (the capital of Israel, the north) and the deliverance of Jerusalem (the capital of Judah, the south). Isaiah's awareness that this period is overshadowed by Assyria's crushing weight and that God's people are ripe for judgment is decisively formulated in the great "Assyria, rod of my [Yahweh's] anger" passage in Isa., ch. 10. Here Isaiah lays the foundation for that self-critical element in the prophetic understanding of history which finds expression in Jeremiah's designation of Nebuchadnezzar as Yahweh's servant (Jer. 25:9; 27:6 *passim*) and allows the Deutero-Isaiah to call Cyrus of Persia Yahweh's messiah (anointed Isa. 45:1). Though Nebuchadnezzar and Cyrus are also not aware of their relationship to Yahweh, the complete gamut of possibilities is best spelled out by Isaiah for the Assyrian. He asserts that Assyria is the instrument of Yahweh's punishment of Israel, and in some measure, of Judah; far from recognizing this, the Assyrian monarch defiantly believes that he is destroying Yahweh with his worshipers (Isa. 10:7-11); but when Yahweh has finished using Assyria for his purpose, the instrument which would tyrannize over its user will be discarded, perhaps broken or burned (vs. 12-19).

Though Judah did survive the presence of overwhelming Assyrian armies in the land for most of the last third of the eighth century, the greatest danger was reserved for the closing years of the century when most of the Judean cities were overwhelmed, and Jerusalem itself was besieged in 701. The military odds were overwhelming against the city withstanding the siege, yet the siege was soon (and from within the city, apparently miraculously) lifted and Jerusalem remained intact for another century. Isaiah apparently never predicted the fall of Jerusalem to Sennacherib as directly and unambiguously as did his younger contemporary Micah (ch. 3:12), but Isa. 1:27 f. contains the prediction of the deliverance of a repentant Jerusalem (Zion). Regardless of critical doubts about other passages, it is clear that in Isa., ch. 31, the prophet delivers a genuine oracle-before-the-fact which satisfies Jeremiah's later pragmatic test. In the first three verses of ch. 31, Isaiah repeats his often-stated mistrust of the power and willingness of Egypt to help Judah against Assyria, but in vs. 4 f. he clearly states that Yahweh will protect Jerusalem, and in the remaining verses foretells the punishment of mighty Assyria. The key event is the unexpected deliverance of Jerusalem and Isaiah's correct prediction of it. How did Isaiah know, what enabled him to keep intact his long record of correct counsel on the foreign policy of Judah, especially as it related to Assyria?[54] This question requires us to elucidate the theological presuppositions of his political analysis, and this effort may help clarify the nature of " mere " good political (or social, or economic) analysis.

It is considered axiomatic today that for Christianity, for the Bible, for the prophets, God is the Lord of History, but precisely what this means is usually not spelled out. For Isaiah, the meaning of such a statement is nowhere clearer than in the passage that calls Assyria the rod of his wrath. On the one hand, Yahweh is mightier than "all earthly powers." Yahweh is not like the Ethiopians (or Assyrians) and their horses, which are flesh (weakness); he is spirit, which is power. On the other hand, Yahweh is characterized by will or purpose and when this is combined with his might the Assyrians become, as we have seen, instruments of his purpose. Isaiah shares with Amos (ch. 3:1 f.) the conception of Israel's election to a covenant relationship with Yahweh, whom he knows characteristically as " the Holy One of Israel." Yahweh's is the *mighty* hand and arm that wields the rod, the staff, the ax, the saw (Isa. 10:15): Assyria. Yahweh's is the holy hand and arm that by this instrument purify his Israel (his covenant people) by punishment, and throughout the punishment — no matter how severe — Yahweh will not lose his purpose in Israel. Isaiah has a living reminder of God's ultimate purpose in the name and person of his son, Shear-jashub, the incarnation of his prophecy that beyond destruction *a remnant shall return* (cf. chs. 7:3; 10:20-23) to a Jerusalem built upon justice and righteousness.

Thus it can be cogently argued that Isaiah possessed not only an acute sense of the value of political facts but also a coherent theological framework: the *Holy* One of *Israel* working his will through the nations which have military, political, and economic power over Israel for the unshakable ultimate purpose of purifying Israel as the center of the peaceable kingdom which shall include the

whole family of man. It is our thesis that, together, this sense for
the historically concrete and this coherent theological framework
account for the diversity of his pronouncements concerning Assyria
and give them a final unity. Modern historiography tends to see no
necessary pattern in such a series of differing contexts as those to
which Isaiah spoke. Does the pattern we profess to find in Isaiah's
pronouncements really exist, and if so, is it accidental, or imposed
by us, or does it result from what we have called Isaiah's coherent
theological framework? If so, *how* does an Isaiah *combine* his
"merely good political analysis" with his "coherent theological
framework"?

We have spoken of trees in a hurricane, those which are deep-
rooted but inflexible and therefore break before the storm, those
which are flexible but so shallowly based that they are uprooted by
the blast, and those which combine the flexibility of the second with
the firm rootage of the first and so survive as useful growing organisms. Let us now designate the first group of trees as examples
of an *absolutist* ethic, the second as examples of *relativist* ethics, the
third of what we will call a *criterial* ethic. The *absolutist* is the ethic
of strength and inflexibility, willing to risk becoming merely reactionary by clinging tenaciously to the values of a particular context
of the past. It maintains these values as law (and is then called legalism), as a social structure (institutionalism, "classism," nationalism, racism), or as a system of thought (for example, Neo-Platonism, Biblicism, Neo-Thomism, Marxism, or any other ideology
that crystallizes the creative power of a comprehensive idea into a
rigid monument). The *relativist* ethic, of course, holds that there
are no absolutes, and that a great deal of truth resides in the cliché:
everything is relative. To the question, Relative to what? it replies,
Relative to the immediate historical context, or Relative to a culture,
or a society and its customs. A pure relativism rejects any *value* that
transcends the immediate time and place. It allows itself to be guided
strictly by the climate of opinion that prevails, without regard to
any *other* standard of right and wrong or of enduring worth.

How does Isaiah's theopolitical ethic differ from an absolutist or
a relativist one? Since it might seem to contain elements of both,
what might he have said had he been an absolutist or a relativist?
From one point of view, we must note that certain absolutist and

certain relativist rationales end up in much the same concrete decisions. For example, had Isaiah been an absolute nationalist *or* a relativist soothsayer simply seeking profit and approval from the royal
court he would have held the consistent attitude that Judah, or at
least Jerusalem, would survive, in fact could not fall. In either case
he would clearly be absolutizing a relative or at best a partial value,
namely, the prosperity of a nation whose covenant blessing was actually considered by the prophets to be *contingent upon* its faithfulness or obedience to Yahweh. In spite of this apparent similarity,
however, the relativist position of the false prophet whose operative
" theology " is based on his own unthreatened security, not " the
will [or Word] of the Lord," remains the best Biblical example of a
relativist ethic, because it yields to the pressures of its situation. On
the other hand, an absolute pacifism, or an absolute retributive ethic,
or an absolute defend-the-honor-of-Israel ethic, each in its own way
clearly differs from the cultural relativism of the soothsayers. An
absolute pacifism would not only have said with Isaiah, " Do not
ask Assyria for help against the Syro-Ephraimite alliance," and,
" Do not ask Egypt for support against Assyria," but would also
say, " Do not defend yourselves against the Northern League," and,
" Yield Jerusalem without siege to Sennacherib." We have, however, described only two clearly separable opposites, the *absolutist*
and the *relativist* ethics. What of our so-called third way, our *criterial* ethic? It is attractive and also painlessly easy to say, " I advocate an ethic that combines the strength of the absolutist and the
flexibility of the relativist, and eliminates the weaknesses of both ";
but is there really a third way, or does a " criterial ethic " represent
a synthetic ideal shimmering like a mirage between two imperfect
opposites? The definition of the *criterial* ethic is best provided, I
think, by the classical metaphor of celestial navigation.

The navigator in an ocean voyage has a port of departure and a
port of destination, and it is his responsibility to chart a course
from one to the other, to know the whereabouts of his ship at all
times, to know the hazards that stand between him and his goal,
and to decide the optimal course for the present and the immediate
future. To anticipate the dangers, he has weather reports and charts
that warn of adverse currents and hidden hazards of the waters in
which his vessel is sailing. To give him his bearings at any minute

and in relation to his goal, he has the resources of dead reckoning and certain modern navigational aids. Beyond these lies the navigator's ancient ally, however, the remote but predictable celestial cosmos, which transcends the currents and storms surrounding him and provides him with a constant reference that enables him to fix and to evaluate his present situation. The "absolutist" navigator knows where he is because of his fixed stars, but he ignores the situations, the contexts, the waters in which he sails and which lie ahead; like the master of the *Titanic* he takes the position which might be expressed as "Damn the icebergs, full speed ahead." The "relativist" navigator, on the other hand, is so aware of the conditions around him that he may give secondary consideration to ends and destinations: he may ignore the goal and steer by shifting points of reference. The "criterial" navigator, however, is quite aware of the transcendent criteria, his fixed stars, and his position relative to them; but he also takes into account the conditions of the waters in which he moves, and combining both elements of his knowledge he steers a safe course through or around the dangers to his destination.

To translate the metaphor back into the language of concrete ethical thinking, the *criterial* ethic attempts to make decisions *relevant* to really existent conditions in the light of certain transcendent *criteria*. Whereas the absolutist might say, "The same laws apply to all situations in the same way," and the relativist might insist that no law applies to all situations, the criterial thinker asserts: "The *same* transcendent criteria *bear upon* different situations in *different* ways."⁵⁵ "Bear upon" is intended to give a flavor to the criterial ethic quite distinct from that of the absolutist. On the one hand, the term "absolute" literally denotes inflexible standards formulated in total disregard of present conditions. On the other hand, the term "absolute" implies an ironclad imposition of predetermined standards upon a particular present situation. "Bear upon," on the one hand, indicates that though the criteria are themselves "fixed stars," they may appear different from different perspectives. "Bear upon," on the other hand, points to the fact that these criteria really do weigh upon and affect decisions in actual concrete situations. Essentially, then, the term "criterial ethic" describes a style of living and a way of making concrete decisions with flexibility and strength.

Two major gray areas still remain in the consideration of the *criteria*. In the first place, there can be different criterial ethics depending upon the particular criteria to which a given ethic attempts to be faithful. Like " absolutist " and " relativist " the term " criterial " as such has primary reference not to a specific content, but to *formal* and *methodological* questions. The value of " criterial " thinking in forming an ethic that is both flexible and strong is that it combines two distinct ways of thinking: one " scientific " and *analytical* with respect to the context in question, the other *evaluative* and *convictional* with regard to criteria that transcend that context. Secondly, we must attempt to clarify *how* the analysis of a situation and the transcendent though relevant criteria are *related* or *combined*. How do these criteria " bear upon " a situation? Is scientific analysis to dictate what criteria may be used and when? Do the criteria dominate the analysis in a quasi-absolutist manner that distorts the scientific character of the analysis? If neither of these, then what is the solvent, what is the gear, what is the force or instrumentality which *couples* criteria and context? These questions *cannot* be answered *with logical rigor* by the Biblical prophet, by the post-Biblical theologian — or by the behavioral scientist. *These questions are* unanswerable *if we assume that the test of ethical truth is either scientific consistency* or *inner artistic coherence.*

Social " sciences " as science cannot tell what is good or right for man by any mathematical analysis no matter how well programmed. On the other hand, social disciplines are not primarily artistic: they do not produce " ethical truth " by the creative elaboration of a beautiful vision. This is why we have designated these disciplines *crafts of conduct* and insisted that for them there is a uniquely appropriate test of their truth, the *pragmatic* one. To those who would claim the test of workability for science, let it be said that a qualitative distinction is here intended between experimental verification and the pragmatic test of truth. This distinction returns to the belief that man as a whole remains far more complex than any other whole object of the exact sciences. It is because of this fact that social scientists insist that scientific testing breaks down in ethics, for which there is no test.[56] Experimental verification means repeating the kind of experiments whose analysis produced a general formula, and devising special experiments and conditions that will test the limits of its validity. The pragmatic test of a truth, however, always involves the whole of living and not any partial experience of controlled experiment under carefully limited conditions, and the pragmata, the results, of that living are " measured " by the satisfaction achieved through a given style of living.

Even what we have just said, however, is directed less at the question of how a criterial ethic is constructed than how it is tested, and this again demonstrates the clumsiness with which we must describe the interrelation of facts and values when neither element dominates the other. Perhaps, though, the term " craftsman " does indeed best describe the way in which a criterial ethic combines analysis with the relevance of norms and produces concrete decisions that may be tested with the pragmatic litmus paper. If we had logical tools of sufficient power to reduce facts and criteria to a common denominator and then combine them, we would be *scientists* of criterial ethics; if our job were to juxtapose, intermingle, and order various facts and values into a coherent, pleasing arrangement, we would be artists of criterial ethics; but when we attempt to enunciate a criterial ethic we most resemble *craftsmen* who survey the materials at hand, consider their qualities, their condition, their susceptibility to shaping with the available tools, and study certain patterns that have proved useful in the production of the desired article, and then shape the materials to the pattern as well as possible to make an article that will answer the intended purpose. In our metaphor, the materials at hand are the results of scientific investigation and the patterns are the criteria known to a community of conviction. *Like craftsmen* we try to fit together material and pattern, with all the knowledge and skill we possess. With this statement we have neither given a manual of scientific procedure which defines the crafts of conduct as social sciences, nor have we explained how one produces the Word of God at any given moment. We have attempted simply to describe the total human struggle involved in a concrete ethical decision beyond the relativist and the absolutist.

In the process it has clearly emerged that in addition to the scientific work of situational analysis and the craftsmanlike fitting of analysis and criteria, it is tremendously important that political, social, and personal ethics have available convincing and relevant criteria that transcend any given time and local situation. And precisely this makes clear that theology has an important role to play, now and in the foreseeable future, in the development of ethical structures for modern living. This role involves the development, preservation, refinement, and use of ethical values derived from transcendent Christian criteria. Thus, in answer to the earlier question as to whether theology should abdicate all claims in the ethical realms to specific social sciences better equipped to analyze the facts about these areas, we must reply: No. Values do not arise in a vacuum, nor do they appear by chance. When a Fromm advocates love; a Riesman, shared living; a Lasswell, the responsible use of power, they do not invent these values, nor do values simply arise out of a proper analysis of statistics. These values are related to, and usually ultimately derived from, some set of criteria embedded in a fundamental conviction, and some form of community keeps these convictions and values alive and growing. This function for Christian convictions and values is performed by the Church and its theology.

Thus, it may well be that one job of Christian theology in the modern world will be to help produce Christian thinkers who will be good economists, sociologists, psychologists or psychiatrists, and political scientists. Even if this is true, however, Christian theology will continue to exist as something separate and integral over against them and their fellow social scientists. Certainly there should be a dialogue between Christian theology and those social scientists who believe that Christian conviction is or can be relevant and constructive for real life today. Christian theology has much to learn from social sciences about particular facts and structures and the patterns in which they are coordinated. In performing an ethical function theology can no more afford to ignore such valuable information than it can ignore the methods and results of historical and literary research in performing its function of Biblical exegesis. On the other side of the dialogue it is the role of theology to define and uphold conviction, to sharpen criteria and values related to them, to suggest specific values and criteria that may be relevant to specific ethical problems, and finally, to criticize and seek to improve the ways in which criteria and values are currently used in ethical decisions.

We have spoken much about criteria and values in a general way without specifying how they relate to the good for man in particular cases. We have also said that there are several possible sets of criteria and values, without yet attempting a precision of Christian values or criteria. This is the task to which we now must turn. We summarized Isaiah's "coherent theological framework" in terms of: "the Holy One of Israel working his will through the nations which have military, political, and economic power over Israel for the unshakable ultimate purpose of purifying Israel as the center of the peaceable kingdom which shall include the whole family of man." [57] As to the statement of the Christian transcendent criteria, we have devoted a large portion of Chapter I to the attempt to clarify the content of the Gospel, the decisive and joyful description of reality, by an unfolding of Paul's compact formulation in II Cor. 5:19: "God was in Christ reconciling the world to himself." This is the source of our central understanding of man as he really is in his happiness and his frustration and in his well-founded hope. This is man, continuing and changing, with his limitations and his powers for development. This is the man we see in contemporary political, social, economic, and personal situations. This man's failures never surprise us, but we never despair of his ultimate future.

The Christian Gospel, the vision of Truth and Humanity which guides theology in the quest it shares with Academy, is, then, the Christian set of criteria that bear upon concrete situations in actual living. In terms of our navigational metaphor, it is a correct and useful map of the heavens with their myriad stars. The celestial navigator is not an astronomer, however, and just as the theologian concerned with one set of concrete ethical problems is not at that moment responsible for explicating the whole range of theological problems, so the celestial navigator at a given moment and location may need to consult only one star or one constellation as the basis for his navigational decision. Therefore, when he considers a given ethical problem the Christian thinker may concentrate on one ethical *value within the entire solar system of criteria,* or in considering the problems of an entire ethical (social science) discipline the theologian may find one constellation of values more directly relevant than any other. The Pole Star which hovers above the acres of Academe worked by the social sciences, or above the seas they sail, is the value of the good, or the question: What is the good for man? That Pole Star is related to different specific constellations (or individual stars) as seen from different seas. For example, a different value (constellation) would be indicated in answer to the question, What is the good for man in economics? from that suggested as a key to the question, What is the good for man in the personal area? One might call the constellation most appropriate to the personal area " love," to the social area " justice," to the economic area " goods," and to the political area " power." Each of these constellations of ethical or " goodness " values would be defined in relation to the whole universe of criteria, to the Gospel of Reconciliation. Thus *power* of the kind described in Isa., ch. 10, and Amos 9:7 is to be understood theologically in relation to Rom. 1:4, 16, or Col. 1:11, 16, 17, 20; the *justice* proclaimed in Amos 5:21-24 is deepened upon a Christological foundation in, for example, Rom. 3:26.[58]

How Theology Works as a Craft of Conduct: Love and Personal Existence

Space forbids us to attempt four demonstrations: of how *power* so understood is relevant to the problem complex of political power; of how this *justice* may be useful in solving problems of social (now, especially of racial) justice; of how spiritual *goods* relate to the question, What good are economic goods?; and of how this *love* meets the central problems of personal-social existence. One of these brief studies must suffice, perhaps best that set of problems involving love and personal existence with which our chapter began. Let us then attempt to illumine crucial contemporary dilemmas of sex, marriage, and family from the perspective of the Christian experience of love.

We have seriously suggested the critical importance of two particular sets of Biblical insights. In the first instance, we have Gen. 2:24, which the Biblical heritage, including the Synoptic Jesus (Mark 10:7 and parallels) and the Pauline tradition (Eph. 5:31), accept as a normative understanding of marriage. At first glance, Gen. 2:24, coming at the end of the story of Adam's rib, looks like a myth (perhaps an etiology of sexual attraction). Man recognizes in Woman the life companion meet [59] for him: " This at last [after the inventory of all nonhuman living things] is bone of my bones and flesh of my flesh." Out of an original unity of *anthrōpos,* man, God has created a differentiation within humanity through sexual polarity. "There-fore," Gen. 2:24 begins, "a man leaves his father and his mother and cleaves to his wife, and they become one flesh." In this sentence we do indeed have an etiology of sexual attraction, especially in the last ten words, but we have much more as well. It is as if a perma-nent magnet were cut in half and the halves separated. A new north magnetic pole and its corresponding opposite are thus created and they exert an attraction upon each other, a pull to restore the union.

So now sexually differentiated humanity longs for reunion, and this reunion takes place sexually, and creates a new unity — both Ephesians and the Synoptics use the arithmetical " two become one " — which is *one flesh*. Thus in Genesis, in the second account of crea-tion as in the first, the Hebraic mind affirms the goodness of the creaturely world, and here specifically affirms that the sexual drive it-self partakes of that goodness. The human creative drive *erōs* — a creaturely love far broader and more inclusive than what we call eroticism — though not called by that name in Gen., ch. 2, could be affirmed there *with* the ancient Greeks and *against* Neo-Platonism, ascetic Christianity and the Nygren who wrote *Agape and Eros*. Though Paul recognizes the inherent power of the sexual act to create the communal life of " one flesh," [60] the Bible is never so sim-plistic as to represent man as no more than a bar magnet swung this way and that, dragged hither and yon, by a bar magnet of equal but opposite intensity. Limitations are placed upon, or rather a fruitful and constructive context is provided for, the exercise of sexuality. First of all, the strongly heterosexual Biblical world stresses the oppositeness of sexual polarity.[61] Secondly, incest is carefully defined and explicitly forbidden in the Old Testament,[62] and bestiality is a capital crime (Ex. 22:19; Lev. 18:23; 21:15 f.). It is, however, the heterosexual relation among human beings not disqualified by familial proximity which presents not only the possibility of fulfill-ing the nature of man but also the most persistent problems of sexual behavior. The (ostensibly) least serious of these is what we now call premarital intercourse, which was formerly known as fornication (but is covered by the innocuous term " immorality " in the RSV). Although there is some capricious treatment of the subject in the Old Testament, breach of contract and the shotgun wedding are pro-vided for in the legal codes of Israel (see, for example, Ex. 21:7-11;

22:16 f.; Deut. 22:13-19, 28 f.). The Old Testament law and prophets condemn sacred prostitution practiced by pagan religions surrounding Yahweh's people (Lev. 19:29; Deut. 23:17 f.; I Kings 14:24; II Kings 23:7; Hos. 4:13; Amos 2:7), although the metaphor of sexual misconduct is often used to indicate Israel's unfaithfulness to Yahweh's covenant. Adultery is not simply a catchall term embracing the gamut of prohibitions; it refers specifically to damaging the marriage relationship itself. Regardless of its proper etymology, the best translation of the Biblical concept of adultery is the German: *Ehebruch*. *Ehebruch* denotes marriage-breaking, a rupturing of the magnificent one-flesh organic union which the exercise of sexuality has the inherent power to create. To commit adultery is to damage the one-flesh relationship, the " I-plural " that is more intimate than " we," by forming a competing bond that saps the strength of the marital union. This entire conceptual picture is the dramatic opposite of the " each one teach one " manuals of erotic loving from Ovid through Erich Fromm. It is not simply that adultery marks the failure to achieve and maintain the one-flesh norm of overt sexual activity, the norm itself is seriously imperiled by marriage-breaking.

Even with this explanation, however, " thou shalt nots " — whether sanctioned by the Old Testament or the New, or the laws of city, state, and nation — are simply not sufficient moral justification of conduct for modern Western man. Nourished by an enlightened view of individual liberty, with pregnancy made more preventable by developments in birth-control medicine, and the fear of punishment by man or God increasingly remote, modern man tends to agree when Kinseyism infers: if sexual behavior and the laws governing it conflict, liberalize the laws! What we require is a more positive understanding of how the good gift of sexual power is to be utilized than " thou shalt not." The starting point we choose is the very center of the Christian Gospel of God's reconciling love, namely, the incarnation. In saying this we do not refer to disputes about the virginity of Mary, or *how* Jesus Christ was " conceived by the Holy Ghost." It is not that we believe these to be " empty symbols," but rather, that they are secondary and derivative expressions of how the *man* Christ Jesus is the " image of the invisible God " in whom " all the fulness of God was pleased to dwell " (Col. 1:15, 19; I Tim. 2:5). We turn, therefore to the primary expression of his nature, namely, the incarnation of the Word ("the Word became flesh," John 1:14). We search the Prologue to the Gospel of John in vain for a reference to sexuality; but "flesh," most powerfully illumined in the incarnation, comprehends the sexual axis which, as modern psychology has reminded us, runs through the very center of humanity.

We have already discussed the meaning of John 1:1-18 in Chapter III, and from that earlier account we would like now to emphasize the following elements: "Word" symbolizes the whole Biblical conception that ours is the God who speaks (Calvin translated *logos* as "speech"); "flesh means man, not inherently corrupt or evil but the crown of God's good creation, limited in wisdom, strength, and longevity though he may be. That God the Word became man (perfect but real, tangible man) underlines what we might have come to expect from Moses, the prophets, Jesus of Nazareth, and Paul: *man, true man* in the image of God, is creation's speaker par excellence. That the Word became flesh means primarily that God became man; but that this God, who has and is Word, became true man tells us something about what man really is. Man, too, is a speaker and in the long history of the Biblical God and Biblical man together we are confronted with and asked to listen to, to participate in, a continuing dialogue. God and man are not equal partners in dialogue or debate: the word of man is always somehow fragile and featherweight, while God's word is heavy and strong. Even when, Joblike, man for long seasons cries out in his hunger for the word of the living God and does not hear it, God's word still occupies the focus of our attention. In the Garden, precisely when Man has sinned he hides himself and ceases to speak, so that God calls out, "Where are you?" and expects, more, desires, man to answer. It is the story of the Bible that God's word resounds and then God expects from the one being he has made for the purpose — an answer, a response in speech.

It is my thesis that this very response-ability in man is the foundation of his responsibility — to God, to others, to himself. The German equivalent of "responsible" is based on *Antwort:* answer. The man who is responsible is *verantwortlich;* he is answerable for his actions, his speech, his life. These wordplays are not intended as mere playing with words but are meant to fit into the whole modern awareness running the full philosophical spectrum from the Oxford (analytical, common language) philosophers to Martin Heidegger and expressed in the words of some of the former by the slogan: "The ways of language are the ways of living." The "something more than bread" by which man lives is a word out of the mouth of God (Deut. 8:3; Matt. 4:4), to which he then answers or responds in words of his own. This is his nature and his task, to face the question: Who are you? or, What do you have to say for yourself? Man is the answerer who is both responsible *to* respond and answerable *for what* he replies. As such man is man, man is flesh.

The Word became flesh and dwelt among us: God the Son became Jesus of Nazareth to obey the voice of God by speaking the things he had heard from the Father (John 8:38; 12:49, 50; 14:24; etc.). The term "responsible," of course, is extended from the area of speech to cover the entire life of man. In common terminology, man's response to a command, a challenge, a situation, a person, a relationship, an institution, is man "answering for himself," assuming responsibility for what he does and says, for his whole existence. And for each man, as for Jesus, his particular givenness, his time and place, his talents, his relation to family and society, help to define the ways in which he is responsible. Response-ability too is an axis that runs through the very center of his being.

The terminology and form of this last statement parallels that of our statement about human sexuality. Our final hypothesis is that this sexual polarity axis and this response-responsibility axis both are central to man and *mutually condition each other*. In the first place, this suggests that sexuality conditions all responsible human acts and relationships. This, of course, is something that Freudian psychology has gradually inculcated into the Anglo-Saxon mind, progressively overcoming resistance and displacing earlier Victorian attitudes. Man is flesh, animated clay, a thinking, passionate, sentient being, who touches and hears and sees other human beings, as well as thinks. There is no reason two friends should not like each other as men; there is no reason that a mother should pretend she is not a woman, or a son pretend not to be a man. To come to another person as less than a man or woman, whose whole way of being human is involved in that sexual distinction, is to play a less than fully human part in the ensuing relationship. Man is flesh and, paradoxical though it may seem, his spiritual life is apt to suffer too if he denies his bodily reality.

In the second place, *mutual conditioning* implies that the active exercise of sexual powers is the supremely responsible human function. It is at the point of overt sexual activity that the sexuality axis and the responsibility axis intersect in the center of man's existence. There are many other human acts that involve heavy responsibility, but none more so than the sexual act, and it is on this positive basis that I would make a case for today for sexual intercourse within the marital bond, and against sexual activity outside it. The possibility of conception occurring as a result of healthy heterosexual relations is the abiding symptom of the connection between sexuality and responsibility, in spite of the possibility that birth control methods may become foolproof. This statement does not necessarily imply the traditional Roman Catholic view that the sole and necessary good from sexual activity is the procreation of the race; a coequal value is the establishment of the one-flesh bond, fulfilling the mutual need of the two halves of sexually severed humanity. However, the fact that " being responsible for " bringing into the world through an act of sexual intercourse a being incapable of " being responsible for itself " lends that act an aura of responsibility.

It is not, however, merely for the prospective offspring that the sexually active person undertakes responsibility. Modern psychological experience tends to confirm the Biblical view that the forming of a one-flesh bond is a power inherent in the sexual act. Yet, paradoxically, those modern sexologists most concerned to emphasize that sexual potency is the most natural and essential of human appetites and drives which must be expressed, not crushed, if man is to be healthy, turn out to be those moderns who most underrate the importance of sex. They tend to take the position that frustrated sexual aggressiveness (characteristically masculine) often becomes violently destructive, while frustrated sexual receptiveness (characteristically feminine) can turn to masochism. To prevent these disasters those drives must have an outlet. One psychologist has even suggested the purchase of dime-store bric-a-brac which at the needed moment can be hurled into the fireplace to purge or vent " aggressions." Others insist that there is no satisfactory substitute for overt sexual release and that unless some form of this is practiced regularly it is as dangerous for the psychosomatic makeup of man as lack of nourishment, exercise, or sleep, or a stoppage of other eliminatory functions of the body. This might be defensible if man were *only* an animal, driven by sexual instinct to perform the sexual act. But the human sexual apparatus is not dime-store bric-a-brac, and its exercise is not equivalent to taking out aggressions by throwing away something cheap. In fact, our insistence that humanity is partially but centrally defined by sexual polarity does *not* entail the Freudianistic dogma that energy intended for sexual intercourse is the primal form of energy and any inhibition or sublimation is somehow harmful. For us, sexual energy is human energy defined and individualized.

That the *exercise* of sexual power is intended to be the supremely responsible human act is demonstrated in a way so unique as to make all other overt expressions of sexual power seem pale and trivial by comparison. I refer to monogamous marriage. Here as in no other relationship both the power of sexual natures and the responsibility which accompanies it are fully and completely harmonized. As for power, a new organic unity, " one flesh," comes into being, in which man becomes most fully his masculine self and woman her feminine one. As for responsibility, we have already taken the creation of a new life as a symptom of the binding character of sexuality, for emotionally normal men and women take particular responsibility for the helpless newborn babe — and often young parents discover the reality and the nature of human responsibility for the first time then. Secondly, sexual intercourse within its one-flesh mode fosters a sense of responsibility for the *self* in its new wholeness. In the third place, a family should be a living, growing organism and someone entering into a one-flesh relationship with one member of it can in a real sense be grafted into the system of mutual responsibility. One of the first generation of Freudian analysts has remarked on his growing conviction that every sexual act directly involves four people. Presumably he refers to psychological participation by the oedipal parents of the couple involved in the physical act. Without arguing the validity of this specific thesis, it suggests the broader truth that sexuality brings with it a whole wide range of responsibility for others. And these responsibilities are what one or both parties to the modern motel romance are pretending do not exist in one of the most dangerous unrealisms of our time.[63]

Finally, the most abiding sense of personal responsibility is that connected with the other who shares the one-flesh unity. The sexual act which constitutes marriage says: " I assume complete responsibility — to the limit of my capacity, and as I do for myself — for this other person, now." Trite tradition spells it out, " for better for worse, for richer for poorer, in sickness and in health, . . . till death us do part," but this relationship need not be trite or dull but can and should be the strongest, most meaningful, and growing one in life. It often is not, as is abundantly clear in our day. We have almost been taught to expect that one day we would awake to behold an unattractive stranger with whom we are supposed to " go on living " somehow. This is *not* a fate inherent in monogamous marriage, any more than it is the fate of a fruit tree to produce atrophied and bitter fruit, as it will if it is not planted in proper soil and climate, nourished, cared for, and pruned. A marriage, fruitful in joy and satisfaction for all involved, is not more of an accident, no less of a miracle. Few marriages succeed to the full without great care and effort being spent on them by both parties to the one-flesh union. This " care " is of many kinds. It is assumed by many young lovers that the affection which surrounds the sexual consummation of marriage is enough. The conjunction of sexuality and responsibility suggests that continued sharing of sexuality is essential to the health of the marriage, and is part of the mutual dependence and responsibility; but this *alone* is not enough. The one-flesh entity which is a marriage is a living, growing organism, both threatened and influenced for good by a thousand factors in its external *and* its internal environment. It is as important for both partners to maintain a healthy and adaptable relationship to each other and to the whole as it is for every organ of the human body to do the same. Marriage demands such deep participation that its long success is never to be taken for granted. Rather, the *norm is* so great *a miracle* that it might be well for partners to find some way of saying each day: *I choose you today.*

Miracle it may be, but the demanding, challenging norm remains monogamous marriage, in which human sexuality and responsibility are together fulfilled. And it is the thesis here stated and defended that deviations from this norm for the sake of sexual gratification fundamentally involve failure to accept the responsibility which *is* human — either through unwillingness or inability to do so.

It must be made clear that an ethical norm is distinct from an inflexible principle or law. An ethical norm enunciates a standard, attempts to describe the answer to the question, What is the good for man? in a particular area. An ethical norm, by inference from what it is not, also describes deviations from or failures to meet the norm, but it does not carry within it judgment or punishment for them. Thus, modes of sexual behavior other than monogamous marriage are here considered deviations from the one-flesh norm, and are not to be substituted for it as norm. On the other hand, none of them is the unforgivable sin, and though an individual instance should be corrected wherever possible, the *person* involved is *not* to be condemned. Fear should not lead us to destroy, for example, the person who becomes involved in homosexuality.[64] God's forgiveness and his tolerance — the *tolerantia crucis,* Christ's bearing of the cross for *our* sakes — leave the Christian no choice but forgiveness and the same kind of tolerance for the infirmities of others. When these infirmities are curable disorders, as homosexuality often is, however, a Christian ethic must not be misled by a flabby tolerance that inhibits pressing for the cure.

A much more devastating example, more far-reaching in its effect, is presented by what the Bible calls adultery or marriage-breaking. It is unfaithfulness in some decisive form: it is tantamount to the reality of divorce. In our usage, adultery implies divorce already begun, just as divorce means the killing and the abandonment of the one-flesh relationship — the very language we used to define adultery. These statements may have the stiff crackle of legalistic absolutism devoid of any sense of the ambiguities of experience, but the details of the ensuing discussion should prove we are still dealing with a strong but flexible norm.

One common reaction to such statements takes the line: " Come now, don't take yourselves so seriously. ' Boy will be boys ' [though it may be a bit different if ' girls ' try ' to be girls ']; a little affair now and then spices up any marriage, and never hurt anybody." One particularly dull-witted statement of this kind, served up with an I-really-opened-his-eyes relish, was made by an aging but still handsome Don Juan: " I told my boy it was all those other women that made my marriage with his mother work." The dashing Don seemed unaware of the vast fortitude with which his wife shook off his "harmless" acts of insult and held together the home for a son who would never know how to trust anyone fully. In spite of extreme and obvious cases, however, the basic issue of heterosexual monogamy is not a simple one to decide. The man or woman who feels the need for "a little spice in marriage" either chose badly in the marriage partner or has not given what is necessary to the growth and continuing interest of the marriage. A limited experiment in polygamy may sometimes drive the experimenter back into the arms of the spouse, and in any case should meet with genuine forgiveness, but in more cases adultery is a symptom of serious trouble not limited to the unfaithful partner, and adultery becomes divorce already begun. Just as the one-flesh organism involves responsibility to the self and the other but also to others, so adultery and divorce mean a failure — be it flagrant or unwilling — in that responsibility, a failure especially destructive to children.

This does *not* mean that divorce is always the *worst* alternative offered to people unhappily joined by law, social pressure, and all the ties inherent in one-fleshness. There are too many badly contracted marriages, too many instances in which one or both partners has been unwilling or unable to grow and adapt and thus preserve the miracle of true marriage, for that to be true. But divorce itself, in our society and under our law, is often as complicated and painful as "staying together." Our adversary system of judicial procedure demands a plaintiff and a defendant, and declares when judgment is given that there is a guilty and an injured, innocent party to the divorce. While it may be true that one person is relatively "more to blame" than the other, there is no such thing as an innocent party to a divorce — unless it be the children. Almost inevitably each person has failed some portion of his responsibility to the other and the others involved in his marriage. More often than not, it is the fruits of neglect that damage the healthy one-flesh organism rather than the results of abuse. *Sometimes* this damage is so great that it is less destructive to sever the bonds of the one-flesh union, even though the two people involved in the surgery that removes half of their being from them may suffer greater pain and require longer psychic convalescence than is associated with the death of a beloved husband or wife. *More often,* however, divorce is not really necessary and people who become aware of their danger can usually do something about changing attitudes and practices that have harmed their marriage, can even change themselves and help each other to change. Even though in our mobile society we seem to get farther away from family and lifelong friends than we were in an age of greater social stability, the religious counselor remains and has even better training and equipment to help than in an earlier day; and in addition to the lawyer and the physician who often play helpful roles, we have social and psychiatric personnel, often gathered at a local family clinic, to play their role in the most redemptive of human experiences: *reconciliation*.

We began our discussion of theology by saying that the Christian Gospel is the story of reconciliation, that just as the loving father accepts the prodigal son with open arms and Hosea draws his unfaithful wife back to him, so God's purpose and reality is the reconciliation of us all to himself. Now we point back to the Gospel of reconciliation and assert that it finds its most typical fulfillment on the practical level in the establishment and revitalization of the one-flesh relationship in which sexuality and responsibility mutually condition each other and fulfill humanity.

This is the Christian truth we offer to modern man in the Academy and beyond to put to the pragmatic test. We have not here offered case studies and shown how our diagnosis and prescription cured the complaint of John Smith or Mary Jones. We have attacked but one problem-setting in one of the areas studied by the social disciplines. But we have tried to show what the criterial ethic is, what the criteria are and how they are related to actual modern situations. It remains for this rationale and these prescriptions to be put to the test of living by modern men and women. For in no other way can we discover whether the Gospel, theology, the Church — which may all be very true in their own scientific terms of consistency with God's revelation *there and then* — are really " there " *here and now* for actual human beings who ask, What is the good for man? and demand that the answers be measured with the pragmatic test of truth by which *all* ethical decisions are tried.

V

Theology as an Art

The painter listened long and patiently to the discourse by the theologian on the ultimate significance of modern art, a monologue that inevitably concluded: " Now, what do you think? " " I have one observation and one piece of advice," replied the painter. " The observation is that you have a great deal of information and an ingenious mind. The piece of advice is: ' Shoemaker, stick to your last! ' "

THE TWO central problems of this chapter emerge from the above conversation. On the one hand, it illustrates the *dilemma of the relationship between creative art and the scientifically oriented modern Academy*. On the other hand, it points to *the problematic but fruitful artistic dimension of Theology*.

ART IN THE ACADEMY

Almost every contact between the creators and the interpreters of art, between art and the Academy, reveals that the Academy both needs the vitality of art, and fears its freedom. What results is too often either an obsequious courting of the artist by the academician or a battle royal in which the critic strives to master the artist and to use his creations as grist for some academic mill. The former case is too sterile — except, perhaps, insofar as the artist receives some psychological and economic wherewithal to continue producing works of art — to deserve further discussion. The latter case is too common and too perverse a relationship to be ignored.

I recall a broadcast — too fleetingly and partially caught on a sum-

mer night abroad for proper documentation — in which an author
was characterizing the artist's predicament.[1] He described a writer's
conference convened around his works by a publisher in some peace-
ful sylvan setting. It was not long before the academic critics had
made it plain that he existed *only* to produce raw material for them
to criticize. He further illustrated the domineering attitude too often
assumed by Academy through the example of the academic book discussion. " Have you ever gone to a discussion of *Moby Dick,*" he
asked, " having read the book but none of the commentaries upon it?
Then you remember how inferior you were made to feel to those
who had read one or more commentators but had not read *Moby
Dick.*"

This inversion in Academy illustrates the paradoxical casting of
art from its own *topos* and house. Wise men first met in Plato's grove
in Academe for the worship of the Muses who patronized and inspired poetry and music. The attempt to appreciate and explain
works of beauty soon grew out of this contemplation there. It was, in
fact, Aristotle who with his *Theory of Poetry and Fine Art* defined
the role of Academic criticism. On the one hand, he strove to understand the works of art acknowledged beautiful with the critical and
universalizing tools of philosophy. He hoped in the process of discovering and defining true and great art to help both future creation
and appreciation of art. In order to shape taste, however, it was
necessary for Aristotle to erect criteria which would judge and exclude inferior works of art as well as exalt the superior. He intended
his remarks to have a tentative character, to serve as the starting point
for a growing comprehension of the artistic process. Like many of
the creeds of Christendom,[2] however, Artistotle's work was so well
done that it rapidly achieved canonical status. His taste was canonized with regard to past creation so that in drama, for example,
Sophocles' classic synthesis was absolutized above the primal purity
of Aeschylus and the sophisticated complexity of Euripides. In addition, new works that did not conform to Aristotle's generalizations-
become-statutes were judged not merely inferior but heretical. And
thus was established Academy's tyranny of taste over art.

Many good and true things result from Academic criticism of art:
it may bring an improvement in art as well as in the appreciation
of it, and it means the enrichment of Academy. The primacy of

criticism over creativity in the modern Academy, however, has brought about a distorted situation in which art is either excluded or relegated to such a demeaning role that it has in many cases come to look on Academy as a deadly enemy. It is quite defensible to maintain that the business of Academy is Truth (and truths), and that therefore majors and degrees are not to be given for basket-weaving, home economics, machine tool operation, painting, singing and acting, but rather, in engineering, business administration, art history, musicology, and the literary criticism of drama. The Truth of Academy is, however, intimately related to beauty, and ultimately it is creativity not criticism that is beautiful.

In earlier chapters we have pointed out that there are many who consider the true to be the highest value for the Academy: even Kahler, who has defined the good, the true, and the beautiful as "relative absolutes," insists that truth is the primal value of the three. We have also found many, especially among the social scientists, who regard the question, What is the good for man, in general and in particular? as the definitive one for Academy. There are those, however, who uphold the primacy of beauty. Nor are all of these purveyors of the arts, for we find Frank Pinner, a social scientist concerned with the nature and future of the university, making the claim that "the most pervasive characteristic of all intellectual products, be they scientific theories, historical accounts, or works of art, is their beauty." [3] This is a clear indication that the question, What is the beautiful? belongs in a substantive role in the Academy, and leads us to an investigation of our thesis that this is, in fact, a motivating question defining a family of disciplines in Academe.

Our thesis is not disqualified by the fact that beauty is perhaps the most ephemeral of the three values, the most difficult to define, the most controversial. Scientific methodology may unite the seekers after the true; interlocking common interests in what is good for man may bind together the crafts of conduct; but we are apt to find the compartments of literature, music, and the plastic arts emphatically separated if not at war within Academy precisely because no common ground, no unifying concept of beauty is agreed upon. Therefore, before we can consider the many concrete and practical problems of the arts in Academy, we must look for some more fundamental approach to the question of the beautiful which troubles all

and each. Beauty as an independent value has received many divergent definitions. In itself it has been understood as purity, as perfection, as inner consonance, balance, or harmony, as the quality of
divinity itself. Beauty as the aim or goal of art has been understood
as the *apprehension,* presentation, imitation, and representation of
beauty either in nature or in reality as it ought to be. In art, then, we
have inevitably to do with the human senses, so that the aesthetic
response, for example, is basically a refined sensuality. Consequently,
beauty has different dimensions depending upon the sense to which
a particular art form appeals. Beauty in painting involves light and
color, shape of line and balance of composition. Sculpture further
emphasizes texture and tactile values, while architecture adds the
total sense of a shaped or sculptured space, in which hearing and
even the size of the person experiencing the space are also involved.
The acoustic dimension of hearing brings us both to music and to
speech. In the former, the dimensions of hearing trained to apprehend and distinguish pitch, quality, timbre, or tone color, melody,
and rhythm are brought into play. With the addition of the last two,
we have introduced the " sense " of time so vital to the audible arts
yet largely missing from the space-oriented plastic ones. From
speech, on the other hand, though we lose some of the intense beau-
ties of music and its peculiar power of abstraction, are drawn the
rich varieties of literature and drama. In addition to the sense of
time, and certain other " musical " elements, the arts of speech provide us with more symbolic food for the mind than any other artistic mode. Though the senses of taste and smell are in general less
consciously highly developed than those of sight and sound, they
play a far greater role in the quality of daily living than is generally
acknowledged by aesthetic theory, and the very word " pleasure,"
commonly associated with the " less aesthetic " senses of taste, touch,
and smell, is very important to beauty. " That which is pleasing to
the senses which apprehend it," runs the famous aesthetic formula,
" is beautiful." The distinction between pleasure and pain, then, turns
out to be more useful to aesthetics than to ethics, to which it has so
often been applied. This is especially true if we abstract from pain
that response to tragedy which purges (performs a catharsis) the
emotions by arousing pity and fear.

Even so, these very distinctions which mark out the province of beauty inevitably draw us back into the province of ethics and demonstrate the interrelationship between the questions about the beautiful and about the good for man. Still further, we are drawn into considering the question of the relation of the beautiful to that which is true, since this question of truth in all its forms is the business of Academy as a whole. In discussing the tests of truth in Chapter III, we suggested the thesis that there may be three definitions of truth, none of which is universally comprehensive, but each appropriate to various activities in Academy. We suggested that truth as correctness or correspondence to the facts is primarily but not exclusively appropriate to the sciences, that truth tested pragmatically in various areas of human living is primarily but not exclusively appropriate to the crafts of conduct, and that truth as coherence is primarily but not exclusively appropriate to the arts. It is our present business to find out what this means for the role of the arts in Academy.

The truth of beauty is the truth that coheres. The validity and the limitations of this statement require explication. Logic tends to treat the claim that a set of statements is true if it is coherent as a reduced (or stepped-down) version of the " discredited " claim that truth is perfect correspondence. To be something more than a second-rate or back-door version of correspondence, coherence must be defined as *self*-consistency not demonstrably dependent upon consistency with external reality, be it proximate or ultimate, empirical or ideal. This definition we accept for the truth of beauty. In this way we reject the word " discredited," for it applies only to the failure of coherence to be *adequate* to all Truth. The logician looks for unambiguous truth, invariably reproducible by everyone everywhere at all times. And such truths come in very small packages, available almost solely to the scientist, who may be experimental but *qua* scientist never really adventurous in the realms of the ultimate. Man's hunger for truth is not satisfied by such neat packages — be they of such magnitude as to be had microscopically or telescopically. The truths men hunger for finally are not to be had with the security the logician craves. Therefore when men attempt to coerce belief in their convictions by claiming they cohere so perfectly or correspond so completely with empirical reality that they must be ultimately true, *the logician rightly judges the claim* of that faith to verifiability: discredited, untrue. This means that the fruit of the tree of all knowledge, ranging from good to evil, is, after all, the fatal fruit. Man as man is finite and *non capax infinitum:* he cannot encompass ultimacy. Man, however, can know and prove, within careful limitation and usually with a high degree of probability, the correctness of certain formulations, their correspondence with the facts. Man can also formulate the good for himself in certain situations in a manner proved adequate on the balance sheet of living, that is, by the pragmatic test of truth. These two " kinds of truth " supplement each other and are valuable even though neither alone nor both together *possess* final truth. And we are now claiming that there is a third valid " kind of truth " which complements the others, precisely in Academy: the truth which coheres, the truth of beauty, the truth of art. The definition of beauty as true by virtue of coherence refers to an inner harmony, a self-consistent vision of reality realized in a form available to the senses.

This definition sacrifices some of the ostensible objectivity which has made the classic Greek formulation of art as imitation so appealing. Whether art is an imitation, *mimēsis,* of the pure forms of Plato's perfect world or an imitation of nature with Aristotle, there always seems to be a reality outside of the artist which controls the creation and the appreciation of beauty. Actually, for Aristotle, however, " A work of art reproduces its original, not as it is in itself, but as it appears to the senses." [4] Aristotle, of course, assumed a kind of objectivity, a universality, about man's sense perceptions in which the purely typical is good and deviation from the typical is unessential and inferior. In fact, as Butcher reminds us, " Aristotle's psychology does not admit of such a faculty as a creative imagination, which not merely reproduces objects passively perceived, but fuses together the things of thought and sense, and forms a new world of its own, recombining and transmuting the materials of experience." [5] This phantasia, or creative imagination, on which so much of modern art depends, was of course not unknown to the Greeks but did not play the constitutive role in thought about art. One can well understand why, for the private vision gone wild is the danger of any view of beauty which depends on self-consistency. The question immediately arises: " For whom is this work of art or the vision behind it coherent, balanced, harmonious, in short beautiful? " Obviously for some individual or individuals — presumably the artist, the critic, and some public, either immediately responsive or gradually convinced. This consideration lends importance to our earlier suggestion that the test of truth by coherence is not exhaustive alone, but needs others to complement it.

These complementary tests of artistic truth are, from the perspectives of our time and place, most likely to be found in the area of the pragmatic test of truth rather than in some artificially objective standard. By this I mean to suggest that the creative product must fulfill the coherent vision of reality not only for the creative artist but for others as well. The dictum of Holmes that an idea to be valid must win acceptance in the marketplace of minds applies not only to ethics but also to art. To say this, however, is not to deliver the artist and his creation to their public, be it vulgar or refined. In art, creativity remains primary and appreciation always takes up the secondary place. First of all, this means that what appreciation must appreciate is not itself but the work of art and its beauty. Further, this position fundamentally differs in two respects from that of the school of social determination of art represented by Henry Pleasant's *Agony of Modern Music*. First, the pragmatic test does not reduce art to the least common denominator. In appealing to " the ordinary mortal " it does not submit to a majority vote; it is enough for a significant minority to appreciate an artistic vision and its expression. Second, the pragmatic test by no means implies that " what appeals to society determines " art. We may provide good conditions for artistic creation, but we do not " determine " art as a gambler might " fix " the outcome of a horse race or a prize fight. Society — that inevitably immoral collective abstraction — does not create art any more than a committee thinks. Art is produced by an individual who is a creative artist. The pragmatic test *corroborates* the validity of an artistic vision and its expression through the appreciation of a group of individuals for a work by a creative artist.

After these comments on the validity of a work of art, we must turn to a few brief remarks about the creative vision and the creative process that produced it. The truly creative process is organic, involving at least two living realities: the creative artist and his creature itself. We would not indulge in idolatrous or mystical worship of the creative genius. We would, however, suggest with all the power of metaphor that in the valid artistic realization of a creative vision the work of art achieves a life of its own. The mythological expression of this is found in Pygmalion and Galatea or, perhaps, Geppetto and Pinocchio. The worthy artist is not a haphazard mystic, following a momentary whim. He is also a trained craftsman who handles the tools of his trade with diligence and skill. He will exercise control over his creation, whether his plan is a broad outline or a detailed schedule. As the creation attains its own life, however, the daring artist will allow it great freedom to unfold its own nature and story. Thus, Pinocchio may run away from his creator, and the wise artist allows himself to be surprised and instructed by his own creation and will shape his work accordingly. This may even cause an artist deliberately to leave a work unfinished because *it* simply *will not* " come out." [6] This does not mean that the author, sculptor, or musician is not able to force his materials to fit a predetermined mold if he wishes. Instead, I take it, he cannot *legitimately* do so because his materials are no longer purely passive. The characters or motifs turn out not to move toward the goal or point of convergence the artist had intended. Further, it seems clear that — like a father with a human son — no artist himself fully understands his own validly symbolic creation. This means, of course, that we cannot comprehend a work of art simply by discovering " the artist's intent," though that remains the foundation of legitimate scholarly criticism, and a permanent check upon capricious exposition. There is, almost invariably, more within the work of art than the artist intended, or knew how to create either consciously or unconsciously. And this I take as evidence that the creature of the artist becomes a living " other " with whom he must converse, cooperate, and perhaps grapple in the creative process.

A fine example of this is provided for us by the formally transcendental world of Herman Melville, in which symbol is piled upon symbol without rigid intentional control over their interaction or their relative validity. This is admitted by Melville himself, if one takes seriously his statement in a letter to Mrs. Hawthorne that he had not realized that all of the symbolism of *Moby Dick* hangs together in one great allegory until Hawthorne had pointed it out. Even if this is not accepted, who is to limit and classify as, for example, primary, secondary, and illegitimate, the identification of Moby Dick as an irresistible-unattainable goal, as the embodiment of the mystery of iniquity, and as Melville's understanding of God; or, again, how should we evaluate the facts that Billy Budd *is* an English sailor Melville had known, *is* Adam before the Fall, *is* the innocent broken Christ, the sacrificial lamb of God whose true cross has been venerated in the dock areas throughout Britain, which makes in turn of Captain Vere an unjustly legalistic naval captain, the God who punishes fallen Adam, Pontius Pilate — or perhaps Melville's own father. Such allusions are by no means so obvious in an art whose symbolism is less complex; but as long as art is art it speaks a *symbolic* language in which meaning is ambiguous and intention is of limited interpretative value.

Out of this metaphorical complex grows an important idea: *the work of art must be sensed, and he who senses it must open himself to its coherent truth, a truth that apprehends*. This statement points back once more to the role of the senses in art. We shall often be satisfied to say, " A musical idea must be *listened* to," or " We must learn to *see* a painting," but this use of one sense must be understood to involve all man's sensory powers. " He who senses " the work of art commonly refers to the critic, the appreciator, the public. But our earlier reference to Pinocchio points to the fact that the creative artist must himself be the first listener or viewer of the creation. However consciously he constructs his coherent vision of reality and realizes it, and by whatever means he accomplishes these processes, the artist must pay attention to the coherent truth which is emerging. This is necessary if the work of art is to be valid, to be coherent, to be true to itself.

Then, however, the appreciator and the evaluator must listen too. They must listen not to their own taste or to the comment of the artist or to his psychosocial biography, or to his teacher, his predecessor, his follower, his appreciative or depreciative critics: they must listen to the work of art itself. And in so doing they must not only attempt to penetrate the creation, they must allow themselves to be penetrated by it. *They must open themselves to the truth which apprehends*. The importance of this statement for this entire book would be difficult to exaggerate. To be sure, this view grew up first in the artistic soil of Academy, and it applies first to the art-scientists laboring there, but the craftsman of conduct and the scientist must learn to listen too. This was implicitly suggested when, in Chapter

III, we insisted that the scientist is a scientist by virtue of paying attention to his subject matter and allowing it to yield to the logic, the methodology, most appropriate to it. We must seek the Truth, whether we test truths pragmatically, by consistency with facts, or by the inner coherence of the truth of beauty. Yet our seekings will be feeble and our findings meager unless they are met and controlled by a truth about Truth and a truth about Humanity which finds and grasps us. Only then can a mental mechanic become an intellectual, a true citizen — be he instructor or student — of Academy.

Directly in terms of art this means that creativity, the work of art itself, is primary and appreciation is derivative. To put it still more bluntly, art is the primary necessity, the host, and art-science is a useful parasite on its creativity. This establishment of priority does not demean art-science; it performs many useful functions for art, just as a parasite may for its host. This establishment of priority does not dethrone art-science in the modern Academy where the business of stating truths about truth, goodness, and beauty establishes scholarship supreme. The establishment of priority, however, makes it clear that art and art-science are not related as the chicken and the egg; art-science is dependent on art not only in point of time, but also for its very existence.

Since art-science needs art to exist even in its own home Academy, it seems clear that art-science should foster art in the Academy. It is right that increasingly guest lectureships are provided to bring into the house of intellect the vitality of contemporary poets, painters, and composers. It would seem reasonable that Academy, with the inevitably derivative art-sciences that fit its texture of life, should recognize its dependence on creativity not only that *fixed* in the past but that which is emerging tenuously today. Academy should welcome the artist within its own groves; and it should be the primary function of the artist there to produce works of art so that Academy will be aware of what a creative process is, distinct from the procedures of a science about art.

Considered in their integrity in turn, art-sciences occupy a position among the sciences of Academy as legitimate as any. Their subject matters are discrete and well-defined, a painting and a symphony being far more easily classified than, say, a problem on the border line between economics and political science or physics and chemistry. In addition, musicology and the history of art, for example, each describe an integral *world* of creativity with an independent historical continuity. The methodologies employed are quite familiar in Academy. Above all, the tools of historical science are brought into play, so that a fine arts professor can say: " I am a historian — who specializes in painting." This implies that he has an eye for line and color, for proportion and visual organization, and a joy in aesthetic quality. With these assets, skills, trained aptitudes, in short with this eye, he reads a painting, he gathers data just as the economic or social historian uses his special skills to gather the data which he submits to the historian's craft, sifting, classifying, evaluating, arranging into a pattern of development. In point of fact, the art historian may produce a stylistic scheme for Greek sculpture, for example, as accurate as the Biblical archaeologist's dating of levels in an ancient city by the shards of Palestinian pottery found there. To mention a history of style in art is simply to call attention to one classic scientific endeavor in this field. The art historian may also share with the so-called intellectual historian an interest in the ways of expressing an idea known in art as iconography, he may write a social history of a given period of architecture; and he may need the methods of literary analysis in working side by side with other specialized historians in the documents pertaining to his works of art. Thus, by virtue of possessing a discrete sector of reality as its proper subject matter while handling it with an appropriate methodology, including logical tools familiar to Academy, art-sciences are indubitably valid Academic disciplines.

As a matter of fact, the very readiness with which Academy has accepted musicology, the history of art, and the literary criticism of absolutely everything, has become a great temptation for the art-sciences. Like the social studies, envious of the security of " exact " natural sciences and creating through behavioral psychology a scientific aura all their own, art-sciences are tempted to give the impression and even themselves to believe that exhaustive accuracy is a desirable and achievable goal for them. The very statement that art is inextricably bound up with the human senses — which all aesthetic theory back to Aristotle cannot avoid — seems to open the door for a rigorous and exhaustive *behavioral scientific aesthetics.* If art is a matter of the senses, why not entrust aesthetics to the medical and psychological authorities who measure the range and quality of human hearing and sight? Some real contributions have been made in this area, for example, by Josef Albers in the field of the visual effects of color matching. Then, too, we have the attempts of certain contemporary composers to try the limits of tolerance for aggravation at the psychoacoustical boundary.

When we described the attempt to limit and lend precision to the social studies by using the categories of behavioral psychology to create a monolithic behavioral scientific facade, we suggested that this very attempt excluded much of the wholeness and uniqueness of man from disciplines which must ask after *his* total and particular good. In a sense, in the arts we are not supposed to be dealing with the whole man but with parts of him such as his eyes and his ears. Aesthetics depends upon refined sensuality, we have said, and we sometimes see true art produced on the basis of more painstaking and fundamental studies of anatomy or of light. But the border line is crossed as we move, for example, from the revealing studies of light by the impressionists and the few good early pointillist paintings to the reduction of the pointillist creativity to a technical formula. Forging " art " by formula (and the most precise example is the intricately mathematical music, such as that of Milton Babbitt) may be a highly developed and respectable craft, but it is not art. Why? Again, because we must say that artistic man is more than his senses. But *what* more? Wriggling a bit in our Academic chairs, we must pronounce again the word: " spirit." We do not do so out of slavish admiration for the European Academic tradition which says: " Of course. The liberal arts as such are *Geisteswissenschaften,* sciences of the spirit." We do so rather because in concentrating our attention on works of art we persistently encounter a creative element in man which has no name — not mind, nor feeling, nor genius — as satisfactory as spirit.

Spirit in the classical vocabulary of Academy meant that which was both essential and highest in man, and in spite of all the difficulties surrounding the term alluded to in Chapter III, Academy can hardly dispense with man's spirit without truncating the Humanity it seeks to serve. To use plain words, Academy may or may not believe in God, but it must believe in man. Theology, on the other hand, precisely because it has been convinced by the spirit of God, possesses, or rather is possessed by, the conviction that we are wise to speak of a spirit of man. If man is made in the image of the Maker who has and is the Spirit, man must in some derivative way partake of his freedom and creativity, and this is nowhere so clearly reflected as in man's art. As a result, an art-science that is committed to the struggle to understand the works of its art must somehow reckon with this creative spirit of man, even though it will not suffer confinement within the bounds of the scientifically definable. Once more, and for the last time, we must express what is always to be understood; namely, that our risky affirmation of such a dangerous thing as the free human spirit does not give license for unbridled emotionalism and groundless speculation. All the tools of criticism and of historiography must be applied with rigor and energy, first and last. There will remain questions that science as science cannot answer, both for lack of information and for lack of the right quality of power to attack them. Then the art-scientist must make clear that his technical task has reached its limit. And then he must consciously and openly wrestle with the human spirit. This human spirit includes mind or intellect, but unlike them it is not tied to one organ or system such as brain and nerves. Rather, " spirit " is the verbal symbol for the capacity of the total human being to transcend the self, that is, to make himself the object of his study, in the kind of freedom uniquely given to man among the creatures. And because of spirit, just as we saw in viewing " Theology as a Science " that a science in order to do justice to its subject matter must be more than the sum of all auxiliary sciences that contribute to knowledge about that subject matter; just as we saw in viewing " Theology as a Craft of Conduct " that values must guide such crafts of Academy beyond compiling the contributions of behavioral sciences; so now we see that an art-science to do justice to its art must transcend careful scientific analysis *and itself become — an art.*

As soon as we have said this we suddenly became aware that the presence of the artist in Academy at any period is not really strange after all. There are some disciplines that seem especially to require and to benefit from art: the history that comes alive under the tongue of a storytelling historiographer; the speculative philosopher (to use a " discredited " term for the suspect metaphysician) who creates a symbolic world of values with which to appease man's inveterate ap-

petite for the beyond; the sociologist still inflamed with passion for
social justice, or inflamed anew; the teacher of language and literature who evokes the glory and misery of man's word-centered nature, and thus illumines the problems of humanity. But we have also
known astronomers infectiously intoxicated with infinity and teachers who could make music of mathematics. In fact, as Frank Pinner
insists about all work in Academy: "Whatever we do, whenever it
is well done, it is in some measure a work of art." [7] In short, teaching itself and the study which penetrates the heart of a subject
matter are art. Yet what has happened to the distinction between
art-science and art if the former has become the latter? In a simple
formula: an *art-science* is ultimately more than a *science;* it is also an
art about art. This indicates still more strongly than heretofore the
integral place of art in Academy. Like science, art utilizes observation, analysis, selection, and arrangement of sense data, and, if John
Macmurray is right, artistic observation is even more penetrating and
profound. It is by this process that the " artistic vision," to which we
have so frequently referred, is formed. The artist takes the materials
available to Everyman — to the limit of his sensual sensitivity — and
by filtering them through his sensory equipment, his memory, his
emotions, his imagination, in short his spirit, the artist creates or
receives an artistic vision. This vision, whole or fragmentary, rough
or refined, abstract or concrete, is a completely human possibility;
but until its realization, it remains private, empty of general validity and free of critical control. When this vision becomes the conception for a work of art which is then produced, however, that work
of art is inevitably tested by the artist, the critic, and the general
public.

In order to translate his artistic vision into the concrete work of
art, the creative artist requires a particular language. Rarely does an
artist actually create a new language, though he must make some
artistic language with its tools, its style, *his own,* just as each of us
makes himself at home in his mother tongue by establishing patterns of vocabulary and syntax which add up to his own verbal style.
An artist then takes up tools and materials of a language — brush
and oils or pencil and paper, tempered or twelve-tone scale, rhymed
metrical poetry or stream of consciousness prose — and he normally
accepts, at least as a point of departure for a given work, some

established style (terms like Neo-Romanticism and abstract expressionism are both too particular and too ambiguous to be precise, but they are at least token designations of styles which an artist may adopt and adapt). The artist chooses or develops a language, a style, a handwriting even, because of its power to express his artistic vision. The language may be concrete or abstract, but it will certainly be symbolic, and in the greatest art it will be uniquely appropriate to the artistic vision.

All language, including the languages of art, is symbolic whether the symbolism is literal or propositional, analogous, parabolic, metaphorical, allegorical, or purely allusive, abstract, emotive. And when the work of art is experienced and evaluated the effectiveness of the symbolism of its artistic language must be taken into account. The first test might be one of *clarity,* the question of whether or not the language expresses the artistic vision appropriately — and perhaps also economically. The second test of the symbolism of artistic language is the *richness* which a work of art contains and can communicate. This is partly a question of the state of development of the language used, so that a perfected language and a golden age are mutually determinative, as in the cases of Elizabethan English, Renaissance painting and sculpture, and the Romantic symphony orchestra. But the richness of the personalized language marks the greatest artist of such an age: for example, George Steiner in appreciation of Shakespeare refers to " this mastering response to the sum of all potential meanings and values [which] reached an intensity far beyond the norm." [8] These two tests of language relate to our test of artistic truth, coherence, in quite complementary ways. *Coherence* implies that a work of art must have some kind of balance, some form of wholeness or completion peculiar to itself. This balance may be tragic, jagged, broken. This wholeness may result from an extrapolation of what we see or hear to convergence or equilibrium; yet a roughhewn slave statue of Michelangelo will be more balanced and complete than a photograph of a sunset at Sounion across a glass-smooth sea. Further, however, the language tests of clarity and richness belong to the coherence which is the *true* test of *beauty.* A work of art created in a language must say or do something clearly, and it must do it more richly and fully than can a science or a craft, or it is not art. A potential artist is born when child or man can see something *more* and say so, but no true work of art can be produced until this richness is under the control of clarity. There will be a constant war in art between richness and clarity, a war which both must win; for no work of art is born with its characteristic symbolism until richness and clarity are wed.

In addition to *symbolism,* however, there is a quality of uniqueness proper to the language of art. We have said that the artist " sees something more " and that artistic language expresses this vision " more richly and fully " than those of science and craft. But that is not to claim enough. Each art hews out a language for itself different from that of every other art. This is most obvious when artists are asked to combine their first love with the art of conversation. Who has not known the awkward, tongue-tied, almost listless boy who can paint passionately? The incredible example that proves the point is the sight of a Tennessee Williams fumbling for plausible conversation about the magnificently expressive words he has time and again given his actors. Art seems to speak such unique languages that complete translation from one to another is impossible. We must beware of the work of art that translates too easily; it may not have anything to say. I recall viewing a twentieth-century painting in the company of an art historian. " I like it," we chorused. " Yes, see, x means A," said the other; " and y means B," I replied; "and z means C and that is *all* there *is.*" It was suddenly dull. We had exhausted with our words about it all of the symbolism in what was exhibited as a work of art. The painter had not seen more deeply and his painter's language had revealed nothing more fully than words could tell.

A *beautiful work of art,* then, is *true* or authentic when through use of a particular artistic language an *artistic vision* is realized with a *coherence peculiar to itself.* When the artistic vision is sufficiently profound, the language appropriate to it, and the realization adequately answers the test of coherence, *no other language can fully represent the work of art in translation.* There are inherent incongruities even among languages of the same type, such as tongues. A Semitic language, Hebrew, for example, structured on a scale of emotional intensity, reflects a whole conceptual world which presents a refreshing view of reality to Western minds structured to fit time-oriented speech. Translation from one world to the other, no matter how skilled, can never perfectly convey the magic of its artistic vision. How much less, then, can speech convey the vision of the painter or the composer. Good art history lectures invariably use visual aids and musicologists introduce those of hearing; but these are importations into Academic disciplines which characteristically translate perceptions of reality into written symbols, linguistic or mathematical. This is what we mean when we say that Academy needs more than a science about an art, it requires an art about an art. To concentrate on one field, art history must create a vocabulary, a syntax, a grammar, which will accurately, perceptively, and coherently convey as much as possible of a painting and of the style of a painter in the context of his stylistic tradition. When the art historian does this he is himself an artist of Academy, practicing an art about art. This is least obvious but perhaps most true in the case of literary criticism. Good criticism is a literary art, but it is not a literary art about a visual or a musical one. It is a literary art about a literary art. What literary criticism can do is illustrated by George Steiner's lesson from Shakespeare, who, as he puts it, "used language as a total possibility. . . . The great majority of men use language in an essentially unreflective, utilitarian way; they take words to have a fixed, single meaning. . . . With education and complication of our emotional needs through literature, we are made aware of the polyphonic structure of language, of the multiplicity of intents and implications, at times contradictory, latent in their placing and stress. We grow alert to the fact that none but the most formal or rudimentary of linguistic propositions has a single equivalence." [9] To foster this growth and guide is the function of the educator, of the literary critic. And it is not enough that "the footnotes lengthen; the glossaries grow more insistent" with the more refined discoveries of literary science. The literary criticism that serves the art of literature by pruning away the unworthy and fostering appreciation of the beautiful must itself be an art.

Our discussion so far has sketched the outlines of the derivative arts of Academy but has failed to penetrate the essence of art itself. This perhaps can only be done through a closer scrutiny of the art one practices himself: in this case, the art that is called theology.

THEOLOGY AND THE ARTS

We have repeatedly said that no Academic discipline fits neatly into one category: art, craft, or science. There is scarcely a science that does not disclose a kind of beauty; no study of behavior or of beauty today would yield its claim to be a " true " science; and art divorced from the question of the good can become a dangerous thing. Theology, which many people consign to the role of a guardian of morality, limited to the grove of the crafts of conduct, has been shown to be a science, but theology to be good theology *must* be an *art* as well. To explicate this statement, we wish to show the authentically artistic dimension of theology in three perspectives: first, theology in relation to its art-sciences; second, theology in relation to so-called religious arts; and, finally, theology itself as a creative art.

We have defined theology in different terminologies in the course of our various chapters. As *truth*-oriented, as a *science* whose linguistic propositions are *consistent* with its subject matter, we have said that theology is the human cognitive response to God's revelation of Truth and Humanity in reconciling the world to himself. As oriented toward the good for man, we have seen theology as a *craft of conduct* whose language must be tested *pragmatically* in terms of its relevance to actual man here and now. And we have said very simply that theology is the Church's speech about God. This third defining statement is the most appropriate for considering theology as an art, for theology will be an art if its speech about God has that kind of coherence which marks the beautiful.

The art-sciences of theology are *sciences* and should be *arts about* theology's speech about God. Academy, from time to time, but especially since the end of the eighteenth century, has taught theology that her art-sciences are both the crafts of historiography and the science-art of literary criticism. At the flood tide of enthusiasm for literary criticism and history, each threatened to engulf theology altogether. Concerned by the seriousness of this threat, Karl Barth protested against the attempt to reduce theology to historiography by saying that " church history " owns no right to exist independently at all but that each form of theology, dogmatic, Biblical, and practical, should include its own history within itself. And it would not be difficult or unjust to address the same critique to literary analysis. Our story about discussions of *Moby Dick* based on its commentaries recalls those students of the greatest interdenominational seminaries in America who tell about passing three years of Biblical courses " on commentaries alone," without ever reading the Biblical materials whose expositions were the assigned topic for term papers and examinations. Here, if ever or anywhere, is the unhealthy tyranny of art-science over art.

This warning does not destroy, rather, it highlights the fact that historiography as a derivative servant of the art, theology, is enormously useful, even indispensable to her. No theologian can do without historiography, for the uses of the past are direct and immediate in a living organism as thoroughly historical as the Church and in a living cognitive tradition as committed to the interpretation of history as is theology. Wherever we turn in the life of Christianity, the history of each sector is vital to an understanding of the essential character and current possibilities. This is true of the polity (the internal organization) of the Church, and of its relations *ad extra,* toward other religions, toward other institutions and movements, toward culture as a whole. This is true of Christian worship, of Christian dogmatics, and of exegesis, the interpretation of Scripture. In each case the theologian must employ all the rigor of scientific thinking and all the diligence and skill of historiographical craft to create an artistic representation of a living, developing Christian art.

Exegesis occupies a rather special place among the sectors of theological reality because it demands not only a historical art about the Bible but also a literary one. The theologian as an exegete is concerned not only with what the Bible means to subsequent periods of time — though he can never afford to ignore what the Bible has meant to earlier presumably precritical thinkers such as Augustine, Thomas, and Luther, nor to ignore what the Bible means to his own presumably critical period — but also with what the human authors of the Bible intended to say. As we have already shown in some detail (especially in Chapter III), literary analysis of the Bible is a highly organized and highly respected discipline. No other book has been studied with such joy and agony, or in so great detail. Almost since literary criticism has crystallized into a formal scientific discipline it has been applied to the Bible. Questions of authorship, of date, of vocabulary, of anachronism, of intellectual and literary dependency, have been investigated with seemingly exhaustive thoroughness. Then in addition to these questions of *Literarkritik,* Hermann Gunkel and his students, most radically and notably Rudolf Bultmann, added those of *Literargeschichte* or form criticism. They investigated the history of particular literary *Gattungen,* categories, forms, or types, as they developed over a period of centuries alongside the Biblical tradition, but most especially within it. Their work has become equally indispensable with literary criticism to the art-science known as literary analysis of the Bible. With all its tools this art-science, like " scientific art history " or its counterparts in the study of music and of the other literatures, arrives at something close to the " intention of the artist " in producing the work of art.

" Artist's intent," however, is not enough to know about a work of art. The Biblical exegete must do more than listen to what the artist wishes to say with a work of art, he must listen to the work of art itself, to hear what it says to his *critically trained* sensitivity. This is why Biblical exegesis, if it is to live and to treat the Bible as a living word which can speak to man, must also be an art. Martin Luther, who demanded the freedom and right as one of the most highly trained and skillful interpreters of his day to hear the Bible say then and there, " the just shall live by faith," knew that Biblical exegesis is a true art. Adolf von Harnack, as a historian of Christianity including its earliest period, discovered as a result of his historiography that the Gospel of Jesus had been " the fatherhood of God, the brotherhood of man, and the sacredness of personality," and this he also preached as relevant to his time. For Bultmann, form criticism is no mere scholarly mechanism the proper manipulation of which will unlock the secrets of the Bible. The " existential self-understanding " which is so essential to his theology is part and parcel of his form criticism. The categories, the vocabulary, the " posture," " stance," or attitude discovered in the twentieth century by Martin Heidegger, Bultmann considers an invaluable entrée into the living creative mind of the first century. Each theologian, Luther, Harnack, Bultmann, has made an art of the analysis of Biblical literature. Each *work of art* — let us say,

Luther's writings of 1520, Harnack's *What Is Christianity?* Bultmann's *Theology of the New Testament* — must be judged *scientifically* by the Church for its dogmatic content, and Harnack's effort, at least, may fail this test. It also will be judged by its own and
subsequent times *pragmatically* for its *relevance* to that time. Yet we
would be making a serious error to ignore these literary efforts precisely for what they are from the standpoint of beauty: works of
art. Their appeal, their truth, their power, is directly related to their
inner *coherence,* the *truth* of their expression of an artistic vision of
reality. We see, therefore, that in theology, precisely those works
which hold themselves responsible to analyze the literature of the
Bible are and must be judged as works of art about a work of art.

Literary analysis, however, has produced only a small percentage
of the works of Christian art with which theology ought to concern
itself. *Ars praedicandi,* the art of preaching which has always been
an integral part of the Biblically-oriented artistic culture (*Deuteronomy* is principally a collection of sermons from the seventh century
B.C.), and which Protestantism tends to make into the only Christian art form, is very closely related to exegesis and dogmatics.
Other arts, however, may speak or show the Christian Gospel more
tellingly than exegesis, dogmatics, or the homiletic art, preaching.
They may reproduce the content of the Christian Gospel well or ill,
but great works of art will tell what they have to say coherently
and effectively. Therefore, theology cannot ignore these works of
art; it must judge them scientifically. Theology makes a *serious error,* however, if it judges works of art *only* scientifically. When it
has done so theology has often crushed not merely beauty but sometimes a truth of beauty which has seen more deeply into the nature
of Christian truth than has scientific theology itself. Therefore, theology in its testing of artistic forms of Christian proclamation has
the *obligation* to be an art, to listen to the Christian Gospel *as the
artist has done, before it judges his work of art.* This means that
theology must learn to trust all the human senses, to affirm at least
the possibility that the God who formed all things through the
Word, the Son, can use sight, hearing, smell, taste, and even touch,
to tell his Truth. Protestantism that tends to trust *only* the *hearing*
of the Word must learn that the God who with his own fingers
made man's body of the dust of the earth called *it* good too.

It would require another book to recount how artists have tried to tell the Gospel in paint, wood, metal, stone; on woodwind, brass, and strings; above all, through the human instrument, and how theology judges and misjudges them. This has been badly done on countless occasions. Theology has, however, become increasingly aware of this responsibility and has done this job with increasing seriousness, as in the latest edition of the great encyclopedia, *Religion in Geschichte und Gegenwart*. With apologies for brevity and limited precision, we must here briefly adduce some material exemplary of what we have been saying from various fields of art.

In our survey we will inevitably choose only those works of art which are " interesting " and " useful " to us, but some criteria must be defined to allow these apparently arbitrary choices to earn these accolades. What we are after is " good " art, " good, true, beauty," which has already successfully or might yet conceivably be used to convey Christian conviction. This means two things in the terminology we have developed: first, we are interested in coherent art, art that uses an effective and appropriate language for realizing its vision of reality; second, theology is cast in the role of a member of the community of appreciation. This means that theology must listen to the works on their own terms, to learn whether or not they convey content, and if so, how. Further, theology must sometimes judge not only whether a given creation is good art, but whether it is " good " theology, useful to the Church as a true form of its speech about God. Finally, theology as a part of the community of appreciation must come to art as learner. By observing how valid art works, theology may discover something about how she can create more effective, because more beautiful, speech about God.

The *architectural* projects of principal interest to us in Judeo-Christian history are of course the places of worship. The temple of Solomon, which is stylistically a Phoenician temple plain and simple, sets the characteristic pattern of borrowing. When the Christian churches outgrew the house-church and were free to ascend from the catacombs, they took over not so much the form of the pagan temple as that of the *basilikē,* the house of the *basileus* or king. With Byzantine Christianity the church building took on a cruciform, in this case the form of the Greek cross. Western architecture has repeatedly derived its inspiration from classical Rome, in the Christian Romanesque churches, those of the Renaissance, and various forms of classical revival. Other influences have entered the stream of developing Church architecture as Christians have come into contact with still other cultures, but the principal remaining innovations have arisen within the evolution of Western culture itself. All these styles and each particular example must be judged in terms of their utility. But almost more important to theology and the proclamation of the Christian Gospel are the dimensions of aesthetic appeal and their intensity. How does the shape of the building, its attempt to sculpture space in a meaningful way, affect the individual and the community which expect to find meaning there? Does the cruciform suggest the cross, the nave the ark of salvation, the circular form God's perfection, the modern fish the mystery of Christology? Do simplicity and complexity actually *clarify* and *enrich* the experience of the worshipers? Does the breechless stony mass of the Romanesque fortress of God successfully impart serenity and strength? Does the human spirit soar with the Gothic sweep to the heavens? Does Baroque monumentality inspire confidence or awe? How does light, the symbol for the conqueror of evil and the source of color, the symbol of seeing itself, come into the building and what does it do once there? Does the decoration inspire and illumine or is it a clumsy and repulsive clutter? All these are questions of aesthetics, of art's attempt effectively to convey a vision of reality. And since the vision here in question is a matter of communication or failure, of life and death for theology, it has the right and the obligation to evaluate the effectiveness of the Christian proclamation embodied in ecclesiastical architecture.

The same applies to other plastic arts, of which we shall concentrate on *painting,* for it is the most purely visual of all. Here the question of *symbolic* appropriateness forces its way most abruptly to the fore. How much symbolic power does a style possess, and how much of it can be brought to bear on the content of the Christian Gospel? Is the type and intensity of coloration, the perspective depth, the weight of line, the compositional organization characteristic of a style capable of rendering " natural " or " spiritual " impressions? Is the style flexible enough to cover a broad range of theological reality, or is it only adequate for a limited one, and if so, does its particular capacity correspond to the needs of the present society, or of one from the recent past, or will it create a taste for the future? Again, a theology committed to Truth and Humanity is not free to ignore such questions. In addition, theology may have much to learn from the efforts of great religious visual artistry, simply because it makes clear the interrelatedness between language, artistic style, and various types of symbolism.

The earliest phase of Christian art used highly abstract symbolization, partly because it desired to be cryptic. This art was deliberately esoteric, especially in the catacombs, intended to be recognized by Christians, but not by pagan persecutors. The classic example is the simple one-line drawing of the fish, the Greek equivalent of which is *ichthus*. This word was probably formed by the initials of an early Christian creed: *I*, Jesus; *ch*, Christ; *th, u*, Son of God; *s*, Savior. This naïve, even primitive, art, in which a single line conveys a story, its interpretation and an affirmation of it, is the permanent refutation of the claim that Christian art cannot legitimately be abstract. It was so abstract and so effective that Christian art might conceivably have developed from it into a form of hieroglyphic nonrepresentation. Art, like all culture, sank drastically in the Dark Ages so that the best of it in Carolingian manuscripts and scattered church decoration displays a rather crude and stylized directness with a naïve, elemental power and charm. Where Byzantine culture survived the inundation of barbarian darkness we find important traces of the magnificent vitality and realism of the early mosaics, along with a kind of stylization resulting from the iconoclastic restriction of art to two dimensions, which forced art to symbolic levels of higher abstraction. Romanesque sculpture — one thinks of Moissac in southern France — possessed this same stylization and abstract symbolism together with the wild and rugged vitality of a Christianity in exuberant expansion. Gothic painting, especially in Italy, losing this vitality, moved toward spiritualization. Increasingly, thereafter, realism was victorious, and even though it may well be argued that no art more successfully presents the suprahuman dimension than does the Renaissance, it is not abstract, or stylized, style. In fact, no abstract style has been possible, after the Renaissance, until the dawn of the twentieth century. This means that no matter how many angels and three-dimensional curves the Baroque may give us, and no matter how interested the eighteenth century may have been in miracles, all is rendered naturalistically or at worst hypernaturalistically — louder, brighter, larger than life. Only the invention of the camera seems to have saved painting from degenerating farther into an overrefined literalism of sight. At first, as modern art, liberated from the task of being photographic, became increasingly experimental and abstract, theological critics stolidly announced that this was the death of religious art. But, recalling the high degree of abstraction in the earliest Christian art, we are beginning to realize that not only a Picasso *Guernica* but Chagall's semiabstract late efforts and even an apparently fully abstract Manessier lithograph can be vehicles, symbolic languages for religious truth.

The high degree of abstraction in modern visual artistic symbolism leads us to music, which in all but its textual-vocal form has always been far more highly abstract. We tend to think of music as the characteristically Protestant form of beauty, precisely because the ear seems to have been the only sense organ Luther and Calvin were willing to trust. Long before the Bachs and Händels appeared, however, the Christian Church was singing. She was taught to sing by her mother, the Temple of Israel. Before a score of Puritanisms restricted both Judaism and Christianity, the God of Abraham, Moses, and Paul was served with a rich variety of musical expressions. The song of Miriam, one of the oldest segments of the Bible, is said to have been accompanied by instrumental rhythm and dancing maidens. David, the sweet singer and King of Israel, danced naked before the ark of the covenant as it was brought into the holy city of Jerusalem. " Blessed are the people who know the festal shout," sings the psalmist, and the psalter ends with the whole polyphony of nature, man, and his musical instruments joining in praise to God. We have noted earlier that the New Testament community, too, could be carried away with religious enthusiasm, and this had its musical accompaniment. Among the profoundest, as well as most memorable, expressions of theology in the New Testament are the hymn on love in I Cor., ch. 13, and the hymn of the exalted servant in Phil. 2:5-11, both written or at least handed down by the apostle Paul.

During the Dark Ages, music too suffered a great reduction in variety and complexity, yet the austere beauty of the Gregorian chant or plainsong emerge from this period. In addition, the influence of Augustine was as important for cultural life in general as for theology itself, and music — together with architecture — was most strongly affected. As he used Plato's *Republic* to help shape his vision of the city of God, so Boethius used the mathematical symbolism in the Pythagorean side of the Platonic tradition — the three-in-oneness of the Christian God especially finding echo in this musical-mathematical symbolism — as a key to aesthetics. Thus the ancient classical music theory persisted in a linear-melodic form until the harmonic inventions achieved by the Flemish composers and the studies of proportion, climaxing in the Venetian works, crystallized into the simultaneous-chordal structure celebrated in Renaissance musical theory. This made possible a new comprehensive musical system which, taken as a whole, is still the basis of our present-day music. Some of these theorists stressed the consonance of music not only within itself but with its text, so that it becomes a powerful vehicle for theology in the Masses of Roman Catholicism as well as in the oratorios and Passions of Händel and Bach, and especially in the Lutheran and Calvinist hymnody of the sixteenth, seventeenth, and eighteenth centuries. Because of its highly abstract symbolic character the nonlinguistic music for instruments other than the human voice is, however, of still greater interest to us. Albert Schweitzer, in his dual capacity as theologian and musicologist, has said that for four hundred years after the Reformation only one man understood Luther and he a musician: Johann Sebastian Bach. This refers not simply to the piety reflected in the arias and great choruses of the Passions together with the emotional content of their musical foundation and vehicle. More significantly, according to a theory held by many scholars, the entire harmonic and temporal structure so intricately designed by Bach reflects a consciously worked out musical mathematics based on religious symbolism; and this is as true for organ and orchestral compositions as for cantatas, Passions, and the Mass. It is no wonder that Bach has had as much influence on the musical dimensions of Germanic culture as Luther has had on the German language and family ethic. From the perspective defined by Bach, Beethoven's *Missa Solemnis,* not to mention Romantic religious music, has often been judged too theatrical, and more modern theologians have often turned to pre-Romantic music without text for the aesthetic reflection of theology's proper mood and tone.

The high degree of abstraction in modern artistic symbolism, however, has tended to leave theology in confusion. Christian thinkers who revel in Picasso's *Guernica,* Salinger's family, and the Theatre of the Absurd do not know where to begin with Hindemith, Schönberg, or Stravinsky, except in a tentative way when a religious title is attached. Yet, as is the case with other art forms, the very abstractness of modern musical symbolism can lend itself to visions of truth which attempt to probe beneath the visible-tangible skin of reality. There is a profound awareness of this fact among musicologists, one of whom has said that the whole range of twentieth-century music represents the attempt to describe the demonic. It need not remain so, for the techniques of modern music would seem to have not only sufficient power of abstraction but also the possibilities for synthesis which would make it a worthy witness to the Reconciliation. The danger that always surrounds symbolism with great powers of abstraction, namely, that it will remain too esoteric to *find* an audience, lurks behind the shoulder of the composer who is our contemporary. Yet I would suggest that the very theme of Reconciliation as an underlying foundation for truly probing analysis of modern life might well offer a valuable key. It is possible that some of the composers now coming to full musical maturity may discover ways of creating new coherences, harmonies, balances *out of* — by which I mean *through* not around or in ignorance of — the agonies and nervous vitalities so well portrayed by their immediate predecessors.

When we turn to the literate arts, those of tongue and typewriter, the possibilities seem limitless. Courses and even teaching contracts in the area of " theology and literature " are no rarity in the American Academy. First the T. S. Eliots and W. H. Audens of modern poetry and then the modern novel have been exploited endlessly, both by and without the author's leave. What American theologian worth his salt has not played ball with Salinger, wrestled with Ingmar Bergman — victoriously with *Seventh Seal,* profitably with *Virgin Spring,* heroically with *Through a Glass Darkly* — and dabbled with Paddy Chayefsky. There are numerous departments of religious drama, many doing excellent work, some keeping alive or re-discovering the roots of Christian drama in Medieval and Renaissance modes, some performing good overtly religious current plays from the Coventry porch series through *Murder in the Cathedral*. We would like to turn, however, to the most experimental form of modern theater, that which Martin Esslin has defined as " the Theatre of the Absurd."

"The Absurd" is a concept essential to Existentialism. Esslin claims that Christian Morgenstern's *Galgenlieder* (*Songs from the Gallows*) of 1914 combines a kind of punning *humour noir* with a cosmic fear which gives birth to a " thinking mind " and thus anticipates Martin Heidegger's philosophy of being based on anxiety in the face of the threat of nonbeing (*Sein und Zeit,* 1926). Jean-Paul Sartre's *L'Etre et le Néant* (*Being and Nothingness,* 1943) gives massive formulation to the French Existentialist awareness, and the Absurd plays an important role, especially in certain of his plays. It is Albert Camus, however, who definitively shapes the concept: " A world that can be explained by reasoning, however faulty, is a familiar world. But in a universe that is suddenly deprived of illusions and of light, man feels a stranger. . . . This divorce between man and his life, the actor and his setting, truly constitutes the feeling of Absurdity." [10] " Absurd," as Esslin points out, originally means " out of harmony," in a musical context; but he uses Ionesco's formula to establish the connotation of the term for those modern dramatists he groups in the Absurd Theatre: " Absurd is that which is devoid of purpose. . . . Cut off from his religious, metaphysical, and transcendental roots, man is lost; all his actions become senseless, absurd, useless." [11]

Thus, " Absurd " points to a content, to a serious and profound vision of reality, which hungers for deep and solid satisfaction. Its disciples are the sons who have asked their fathers — men of patriotism, faith in free enterprise and with the name of God on their lips — for bread and have received a stone. The Absurd vision is allied to the Tragic view of life — without the noble dimension. Actually, the Absurd Man is like nothing so much as the Christian drowned in the awareness of Original Sin. When this is said, however, it does not refer to the hereditary aspect of the traditional doctrine. Rather, the Prodigal Son is the man in Original Sin, estranged

from his Father, alienated from his society, lost, broken, destitute in
a foreign land. Further, however, this is an Original Sin far more
terrifying and requiring far more raw courage to face, for *this*
awareness of Original Sin is isolated from awareness of anything
else. The Absurd Man remembers no Original Righteousness " before the fall " and recognizes none of its perduring remnants; he
looks for no Reconciliation, he remembers no Father, no home.
Beckett does admire the *two*-edged saying of Augustine: " Do not
despair: one of the thieves was saved. Do not presume: one of the
thieves was damned." He adds, however: " I am interested in the
shape of ideas even if I do not believe in them. . . . That sentence
has a wonderful shape. It is the shape that matters." [12] Let theology
not be deceived by the occasional use of its symbols; the Absurd
Man is not about to sell out to Christianity. His awareness of " Original Sin " claims to be beyond *all* Christian constructs — creation,
preservation, " the Holy Ghost; the holy catholic Church; the communion of saints; the forgiveness of sins; . . . and the life everlasting " — because it is true and realistic while they are false, illusory,
and dangerously misleading.

Initially, then, the Absurd is a *content,* a message, and a passionately serious one at that. When the Absurd began to tread the boards,
however, in plays of Camus and Sartre, it did so in a rather traditional theatrical *form*. Esslin, therefore, does not include those pioneers of the Absurd in his Absurd Theatre — along with Adamov,
Beckett, Genet, Ionesco, and such related writers as Pinter and Albee — for that Theatre is defined by the attempt ". . . to achieve a
unity between its basic assumptions and the form in which these
are expressed." " In some senses," Esslin continues, " the *theatre* of
Sartre and Camus is less adequate as an expression of the *philosophy*
of Sartre and Camus — in artistic, as distinct from philosophic,
terms — than the Theatre of the Absurd." [13] This new theatrical
convention is marked by common " essential hallmarks " of which
Esslin lists five: " the abandonment of the concepts of character and
motivation; the concentration on states of mind and basic human
situations, rather than on the development of a narrative plot from
exposition to solution; the devaluation of language as a means of
communication and understanding; the rejection of didactic purpose; and the confrontation of the spectator with the harsh facts of

a cruel world and his own isolation." [14] These may now profitably
be illustrated, along with a sixth consideration, namely, the content
of the new world opened up by these rejections beyond the abandoned old one.

The *abandonment of character and motivation* represents a rejection both of the Aristotelian idea that human nature, *ēthos* (character), is both real and known and that it is the business of drama
to be ethical, to unfold character, and also of the Christian-Enlight-
enment emphasis on the individual and his personality. With regard to Beckett's *Waiting for Godot* and *Endgame,* Esslin writes:
"Hamm and Clov, Pozzo and Lucky, Vladimir and Estragon,
Nagg and Nell are not characters but the embodiments of basic human attitudes, rather like the personified virtues and vices in medieval mystery plays." [15] Jean Genet writes of his own *The Maids:* "I
hoped . . . to obtain the abolition of characters . . . and to replace
them by symbols." [16]

The *concentration on states of mind and basic human situations*
brings with it the breakdown of narrative plot. In a real sense this
represents not only a break with traditional drama but a retrover-
sion to the cyclic mythological structure broken and set in motion
almost thirty-five hundred years ago by the prophetic Biblical emphasis on a purpose in history. As Esslin puts it in following the
analysis of Beckett's "characters": "And what passes in these plays
are not *events* with a definite beginning and a definite end, but
types of *situation* that will forever repeat themselves." [17] Yet the formal analogy to the medieval mysteries reminds us that there are in
the Bible important typologies and in the Christian liturgical calen-
dar certain annually celebrated events which partake of the same
formal aspect. It is no wonder that Genet with his "mere symbols"
in a "hall of mirrors" strives to find a credible "rationale for his
mock-liturgy and mock-ceremonial." [18] It is no wonder Ionesco finds
that he and Beckett have formal affinities with the nonhistorical
Wisdom Literature of the Old Testament: "The value of a play like
Beckett's *Endgame* . . . lies in its being nearer to the Book of Job
than to the boulevard theatre or the chansonniers. That work has
found again, across the gulf of time, across the ephemeral phenomena of history, a less ephemeral archetypal situation, a primordial
subject from which all others spring. . . . Yes, it is King Solomon

who is the leader of the movement I follow; and Job, that contemporary of Beckett." [19]

Perhaps the most easily recognizable and yet profound aspect of the Theatre of the Absurd is *the devaluation of language as a means of communication and understanding*. Here again, Aristotle is the enemy par excellence, this time as the symbol of logical order. In Ionesco's *Victims of Duty* the policeman-psychoanalyst stands for the (rejected) proposition that the mysteries of existence can be solved. " As for me," he says, " I remain Aristotelianly logical, true to myself, faithful to my duty, and full of respect for my bosses. . . . I don't believe in the absurd; everything hangs together, everything can be comprehended in time . . . thanks to the achievements of human thought and science." [20] And it is precisely he who communicates and understands — nothing. Harold Pinter's unique mastery of the use of technological language similarly reveals that " in a world that is increasingly deprived of meaning, we seek refuge in being experts in some narrow field of irrelevant knowledge or expertise." [21] That is why Ionesco thinks " words themselves must be stretched to their utmost limits, the language must be made almost to explode, or to destroy itself in its inability to contain its meanings." [22] He is, in short, determined " to destroy the rationalistic fallacy that language alone, language divorced from experience, can communicate human experience from one person to another." [23] Pinter, on the other hand, seems to feel that language is simply not used in real life for purposes of communication: " I feel that instead of any inability to communicate there is a deliberate evasion of communication." [24] On the other hand, this has led to the very useful distinction made by Arthur Adamov as early as 1938 between curable and incurable words. He is deeply concerned with man's spiritual problem, writing: " I am separated. What I am separated from — I cannot name it." He adds in a footnote: " Formerly it was called God. Today it no longer has any name." [25] Thus the crisis of faith is also a crisis of language: " The words in our aging vocabularies are like very sick people. Some may be able to survive, others are incurable." [26] On the other hand, many Absurd artists would join Humpty Dumpty when he says to Alice in Wonderland: " When I use a word it means just what I choose it to mean — neither more nor less. . . . The question is, which is to be master —

that's all." And some have followed Lewis Carroll into the nonsense world, trying to "break the determinism of meaning and significance" by using words as mere emotive sounds intended to help the other tools of stagecraft convey what a certain experience *feels* like.

Almost inevitably a movement desirous of complete freedom from illusions will overtly *reject all didactic purpose*. Thus the Theatre of the Absurd will reject absolutely the Aristotelian-Victorian dictum that a play *must* point a moral. More typical is the statement of Beckett adduced above, " I am interested in the *shape* of ideas even if I do not believe in them," and the statement of one of Genet's *Blacks:* " The time has not yet come for presenting dramas about noble matters." The Theatre of the Absurd is not concerned to *solve* a situation or a problem but to convey it as intensely, as truly, as powerfully, as possible.

Thus, the only conceivable didactic dimension or possibility of indoctrination is the fifth of Esslin's characteristics: " the confrontation of the spectator with the harsh facts of a cruel world and his own isolation." No techniques that can be invented are left unused, no senses or emotions are spared in the process. Edward Albee, both in the frightening dog in *The Zoo Story* and in the use of the imagined son as a bone of contention in *Who's Afraid of Virginia Woolf?* has shown that when all communication is lost, at least conflict can establish a human contact with reality. Yet many Absurd Dramatists would follow Brecht in saying: " So great is our isolation that even conflict is impossible." [27] And still this is not so much a didactic content, a message to get across, as it is a new form of the emotional catharsis of Greek tragedy which makes men, in Esslin's words, " better able to face their time. In the Theatre of the Absurd," he continues, " the spectator is confronted with the madness of the human condition, is enabled to see his situation in all its grimness and despair, and this, in stripping him of illusions or vaguely felt fears and anxieties, enables him to face it consciously, rather than feel it vaguely below the surface of euphemisms and optimistic illusions. And this, in turn, results in the liberating effect of anxieties overcome by being formulated." [28]

In the metaphysical, spiritual dimension which contains more than emotion the Theatre of the Absurd is one expression of the search for a way in which man can live in " a world deprived of a

generally accepted integrating principle." It is ready with Rabelais
to employ the magic of nonsense, which can free man from "the
poverty of sense and its restrictions." It is prepared with Artaud to
return to myth and magic and present a "battle of symbols" to illumine man's deepest conflict. With Ionesco it affirms that "to feel
the absurdity of the commonplace, and of language — its falseness
— is already to have gone beyond it." [29] And with all this Esslin is
in profound agreement, for he feels that "the need to confront
man with the reality of his situation is greater than ever. For the
dignity of man lies in his ability to face reality in all its senseless-
ness: to accept it freely, without fear, without illusions — and to
laugh at it." [30]

This concluding allusion to the *dignity* of man revealed precisely
in realistically confronting his *misery*, points to the reason we have
chosen to spend such a large proportion of our resources on the Theatre of the Absurd. This modern theatre is an art with all the power
of abstract symbolism to transcend the realistic, the obvious, but at
the same time through speech and above all through the minimally
obstructed human presence it can communicate its content more
easily than other forms of abstract art. And what of that content?
Esslin's final statement has a ring reminiscent of the tradition of
Augustine, Pascal, and Reinhold Niebuhr: original righteousness/
original sin; glory/misery; Christian Realism. But again, the very
foundation of Absurdism scarcely allows Esslin's single use of "the
dignity of man," but forces revulsion at the very terms "original
righteousness," "human glory," and "Christian." Absurd courage
will not sell itself to any form of Christian security. Yet its very
concern, passionate, express, and unblinking, for the truth about
man beneath, behind, beyond all conventions of religion, science,
craft, and even art, commends this Theatre to both theology and
Academy in their *common quest* for Truth and Humanity.

The art forms, the styles, and the individual works of art which
have forced themselves upon us in this peculiar order begin now to
form a pattern of opposing tendencies. As we have moved from
past to present in Judeo-Christian art and from architecture to
painting and sculpture to music to drama we have seen, on the one
hand, the intent of the artist become decreasingly religious; and,

on the other hand, we have become increasingly aware that abstract symbolic or artistic language seems more useful in the representation of the search for ultimates. This combination of tendencies is unfortunate, perhaps even catastrophic, since theology ought to be concerned where ultimates are talked about, whatever language is being used. The two opposing movements are certainly conditioned by the history of Western Culture — anyone interested in the history of Western painting before the seventeenth or even eighteenth century must deal, at first exclusively then principally, with art whose subject matter is the Christian Church's speech about God. Within the history of art itself, however, theology has been very slow to give up old conventions and, therefore, art has experimented increasingly and in more and more abstract symbolism in the absence of theology. We do not mean to equate " conventional " with concrete symbolism and " unconventional " with abstract. It happens that at present most of popularly accepted artistic conventions in religious art are concrete: we expect God and angels to look like men, and do not mind a halo here and there to help us pick Jesus, Mary, and the disciples out of a crowd; we expect religious music to have words, nice ones at that, or to be played on an organ, and, at least in the last two measures, to sound like Bach. It also happens in our day that concrete and literal symbolism seems most appropriate to sciences when they *do not* wrestle with ultimates while abstract symbols seem most appropriate to the arts when they *do*. Theology is the last of the arts to give up total dependence on the conventional concrete symbols (both verbal and visual) for ultimate reality which have become broken and empty or, better, with Adamov are seriously ill. In view of a sick language with badly infected symbolic members any art should set about to cure the curable words and symbols and to replace the incurable ones with some which are live and fresh. This theology is not doing with sufficient energy or — artistry.

Theology should be especially grateful, then, to an art which is exploring " religious problems " and testing " religious symbols " more profoundly and more rigorously than is religion. Just as visual art and drama of the sixteenth century painted the problem of evil among the ruins of the medieval synthesis and reinforced the Reformation's awareness of this problem, so the Theatre of the Absurd has the power to shock any complacent twentieth-century theology which will listen. Most important of all are the artistic tools developed by the Absurd Theatre. Perhaps their usefulness has not been fully explored. Some would say they are limited to the creation of an antitheology, that their ability to produce even a crazy-quilt coherence depends on the Absurd rejection of meaning. But if these artistic tools really possess the liberating power claimed for them, and if those who use them are as open to discover what is actual as they claim, then it is possible that the Theatre of the Absurd may yet discover new harmonies and even the Reconciliation to which it is blind, by and to the God whose name it does not know. His Reconciliation to the father from whose love he has completely separated himself always comes as a surprise to the prodigal son. The event that sets his world right side up always seems "too *good* to be *true*." He mistrusts its reality until it grasps him. Thomas to be "true to himself," his senses, his logic, his verifying and falsifying mechanisms, his negations, his fears — must doubt. But doubting Thomas, the Prodigal, the Absurd Man if he is as free as he claims from all old conventionality, free for any truly new reality, can be grasped by the reality of Reconciliation. It remains to be seen whether the Theatre of the Absurd has not at least created the tools of its own transcendence, whether in showing how foolish is all the wisdom of men — including the men of the Church — it has not opened the way for the unveiling of the wisdom hidden in the folly of God.

All this belongs primarily to theatre, to art, to the arts of Academy as they daily demonstrate their courage and willingness to struggle with the ultimate problems of Truth and Humanity. But theology is more than a bystander before this drama. Theology may have something new to learn from the new language of tongue and stagecraft created by the Theatre of the Absurd. Theology should not merely judge but allow itself to be judged by the discovery of fresh paths to truth. Here may be, at least in part, a new language for theology to borrow as theology has always borrowed language, method, the fruits of an art that penetrates reality convincingly. For at this point it must be added that precisely in her role of borrower, selecter, arranger, synthesizer, theology reveals herself as an art.

How Theology Works as an Art

Until now this chapter has concerned itself with the art-sciences used in the making of theology, and with the relation between theology and other arts. Now, in closing, we must concentrate on the inner nature of theology itself — as an art. In earlier chapters we have said, first, that theology must be a science, true to its own subject matter, and, second, may also as a craft of conduct submit its insights into concrete problems involving the good for man to the pragmatic test of relevance to life. In this first case, precisely as the most effective cognitive response to its subject matter, *corresponding* to the experience of God's Reconciliation, theology presents a *coherent* picture and is thus a work of art. In this second case, precisely as the Church's language about God to men seeking their truest good, theology should be *beautiful*. Finally now, in the very terminology we have used to define an art in this chapter: *theology in every age seeks an artistic language with which to concretize its vision of reality*.

The language Biblical and Christian theology has most characteristically chosen has been a language of the tongue. Music, architecture, the sacramental act, and sometimes painting and sculpture have also been employed. When employed, however, they have tried to tell a story, a history, to represent a moving scene, a drama involving persons. And often in theology the story, the words, the tongue, are there alone. When this is true, however, the words have formed *symbols* both *rich* and *clear,* symbols that convey both the sharpness and the fullness of sight and hearing. The troubles attending theology have often arisen and heresy spawned when some theologian has failed to recognize that his science, his craft, is also art. Too often a poetic image or a metaphor has been taken as a scientific proposition; a parable as an allegory with rigid literal correspondence; a hyperbole or bit of irony for sober statement of policy or fact. To understand the world of the Bible is, however, to know a daring, exciting world of artistic creativity where the Truth that apprehends men is in its turn grasped by the human spirit in all its noble, partial, limited ability to reflect and represent the image of God. And it is this world of primal apprehension of God's decisive revelation out of which theology always lives when it strives to find true and relevant forms in which to proclaim the Christian vision of reality. Different ages of theology may adopt languages much different from the metaphorical freedom and power of the Bible itself — Augustine's Neo-Platonism may contribute dualistic clarity and a vast dimension of transcendence, Aquinas' Aristotle may provide order and colossal structure, Luther's German may provide the infinitely varied flavor, both elegant and earthy, that English finds in Shakespeare — but all attempt to witness to the Christ event of God's Reconciliation, the content that finds and judges its form, the content we would not know without the Bible.

Theology, then, is an art, each form of theology a symbolic representation of the Christian vision of reality. This has been recognized precisely in the strictest theological formulations, the *creeds* of the Church, which are often significantly designated: *Symbols*. Though they are intended to be used as the knife-edge on which heresies and orthodox teachings are tested, weighed in the balance, these symbols arise out of conflict and compromise and are products of their times. The very term " symbol " for a creed indicates its temporality and its artistic character. The creeds perform further artistic functions by giving precision and structure, clarity and fitting order, to expressions of faith. This may best be seen in terms of the two uniquely Christian concepts: the doctrine of God and of the redeeming God-man. What had been said in the Bible through dramatic narrative by allusion and suggestion but left in unresolved dialectic is said as the need for the creeds arises in formulas, but these are *symbolic* formulas not mere literal propositions. The Scriptures in Hebrew had spoken of the one God whose Glory, Name, and Spirit were inseparably his, yet could dwell in a place or come upon a man. All this was said but neither there nor in the Greek New Testament do we hear of a Trinity. The messiah (a Hebrew term whose Greek equivalent is " the Christ," in English " the anointed one ") is a man not God (except for what are probably the unexpurgated pagan remains borrowed in Ps. 2:7; 45:6). The Son of Man in late Old Testament apocalypticism (see Dan., ch. 7) is a figure, more divine than human, symbolic of ultimately purified and triumphant Israel. The New Testament speaks of Jesus of Nazareth (especially in the Synoptic Gospels) and the man Christ Jesus (I Tim. 2:5). It speaks of God's Word made flesh and the Son who reveals the Father (John 1:18). It even hymns the Christ, Jesus, who was in the *form* of God, took the *form* of the servant who suffers death and is then most highly exalted (Phil. 2:5-11). But we never hear of the Christological synthesis of two natures in the one person of the mediator. The creeds, however, fuse Hebraic metaphor with philosophic order to create probably the most beautiful and useful keys to Western thought.

This is true from the structural point of view as where the intricate poetry of *The Divine Comedy* is shaped by Dante's deliberate mirroring of the Trinity in his *terza rima form,* and also from that consideration of the *shape* of ideas, of *content,* which modern thinkers like Beckett so admire. Long before Hegel copied it, the creeds had schematized the Hebraic concern for history into a comprehensive Trinitarian movement. Nicaea and the Apostolicum begin with a first article about " God the Father Almighty, Creator of all things visible and invisible," and then proceed via the second or Christological article, the longest, most firmly historical — born . . . suffered . . . crucified . . . dead, buried — and the most peculiarly Christian. They end in a third article with the Holy Spirit and his activity in the present age and into " the life everlasting." It is this magnificent structure which has shaped the outline not only of theology but also of almost every complete philosophy of history, including that of Karl Marx. Modern theology, after a century of rejecting traditional Christian Dogmatics, had to learn this all over again. And so Karl Barth, following a decade of " informal dogmatics " attacking various burning issues of the hour, had to detour through his book on Anselm in order to discover the importance of beauty for theology. This discovery gave a new *shape* to Barth's theology. It was a new awareness that led to perhaps the most complex, comprehensive, and coherent architectonic in the history of theology. Barth's *Church Dogmatics* represents an even better example than Tillich's own *Systematic Theology* of Tillich's basically artistic concept of the " theological circle."

The theological circle is the form of the true or coherent realization of the Christian vision of reality. It cannot finally be evaluated from without. But from within its coherence is so perfect that one can begin at any point and arrive directly at all others. The tone and flavor of a given work of the theological art will be established by the starting point — being, creation, providence with Aquinas and Tillich, spiritual experience with the heirs of Schleiermacher and John Wesley, the Christological beginning with Barth — but the choice of starting point does not prejudice the possible scope or quality of the work. Thus, Barth can from every point of his theological path write a coherent theology from a new perspective until, coming with a maximum of *clarity* and *richness* to the first three books of Volume IV on the Reconciliation, he can use the three offices of Christ and the Trinitarian structure of theology to produce his versions of the three theological possibilities of the Reformation.

CHURCH DOGMATICS, VOLUME IV

	IV, 1	IV, 2	IV, 3
	Barthian-Lutheran	Calvinist-Barthian	Barthian-Anabaptist
The View of the God-man	Christ as Priest	Christ as King	Christ as Prophet
The Problem of Evil	Sin as Pride and Disobedience	Sin as Laziness and Misery (Estrangement from service to and enjoyment of Divine Sovereignty)	Sin as Lie (Rebellion against Truth)
The Form of Reconciliation	Justification (Obedient Lord-as-Servant is Judged, Crucified, Humbled in our place)	Sanctification (In the Servant-as-Lord, We have been exalted to Discipleship as Covenant Partners of Divine Sovereign)	Vocation (We are Called to Witness to the Victory of Light and Truth over Darkness and Falsehood)
The Work of Holy Spirit in Church	Assembly (of the Community of Faith)	Edification (Construction and Instruction)	Sending (Mission)
The Content of Christian Life	Faith	Love	Hope

Here we have a perfect example of a beautifully shaped intellectual conception.[31] Each book of Volume IV is vertically coherent, complete within itself from the point of view of one conception of the Incarnation and Reconciliation. Each topic of Volume IV is (horizontally) part of a coherent pattern. And the entire Volume IV fits within the grand scheme of the freely developing whole of the *Church Dogmatics* from Volume I, Book 1, through the originally planned fifth volume.

Much more than the shape of theology is made beautiful by its special character. Christology and the doctrine of the Trinity, rough-forged and beaten fine in the heat and pounding of the controversies which produced the creeds, are the special, symbolic Christian keys to the kingdom of man's world, its need and its satisfaction. " Trinity " speaks of the God who is *fully one,* united but not solitary.

The *fullness* is symbolically expressed by the three hypostases or subsistences — these terms are at least less *mis*leading than " persons " which suggests separate individuation — known as Father, Son, and Spirit. These three names suggest the inner life of God designated by the dynamic term *circumincessio* (a mutually inter-penetrating movement) rather than by the static *circuminsessio* (a mutual residing within). The inner life of God is further suggested by the description of the Son as " *begotten* before all worlds " *within* God, not as emanating *from* or created *by.* The Spirit, for the Western Church, proceeds from the Father and the Son, a teaching re-producing the New Testament experience of the Christocentrically determined Spirit. (This Son-anchored Spirit is, of course, unknown to the Old Testament which speaks simply of the Spirit of God, as does the Eastern Church.) Barth has reminded us that " spirit " in Greek carries the neuter article, in contrast to Father and Son, which are masculine; as a result he has suggested that the Spirit *is* the relation of the Father and the Son which enables the author of I John to announce that God *is* love.[32]

On the other hand, the *oneness* of God is expressed in the formula *opera trinitatis ad extra sunt indivisa* (the external operation of the Trinity is indivisible). It is not merely the Father who acts stern, re-mote, austere, the Son who expresses compassion, the Spirit who excites and comforts. It is the one God who does all. By *appropriation* it can be said that the Father symbolizes, for example, creativity; the Son, Reconciliation; the Spirit, final redemption; but there is no separation of purpose or activity. This combats not only all Gnostic talk of the Old Testament Creator-God as a demiurge, inferior to the loving Father of Jesus, but also the modalism which produces the "doctrine of progress" philosophies of history (culminating in an "age of the spirit" higher than the other two) from Joachim of Fiore through Hegel and beyond. Thus the symbol of the Trinity gives Christianity the power to express the unity and fullness of its experience of God, both in its relevance to and comprehension of the whole of existence.

The other uniquely Christian theological symbol is the Christological one, which is if anything still more useful. Hebraic man is known by a God he has never seen and from whom he is cleft by his limited nature and his sin. The Incarnation of the Word says that Almighty *God* has taken all these contradictions into himself and thus resolved them. Reconciliation says that "for us men and our salvation" God cared enough to give himself, to *do* the needful, to act. The "impossible" personal union of the divine and the human presupposes, silhouettes, demonstrates all man's problems by forming the basis for his redemption. From atonement, Incarnation plus Reconciliation, Christianity derives also its peculiar knowledge of God and its criteria for ethics, the living of the Christian life.

Thus in Christology and Trinity, theology's two greatest and most unique insights have found their decisive forms and, connected at their fulcrums like twin blades or arms of a scissors or tongs, they have become the principal "machine tools" ultimately responsible for the special character of theological works of art. Their consonance of form and content assures the fundamental coherence which lends true beauty to works which employ them well.

This is not to say that any one theology is final because it has made the best use of the correct tools. A painting, a symphony, a poem, a building, a theology, may satisfy more than the scientific and practical needs of a moment in history. It may also, even primarily, satisfy the aesthetic needs of that moment as well, and of many subsequent moments, too. Yet none of these works of human art is absolute, ultimate, final, perfect. The need for something to see, to hear, to imagine, to live on, and to live by abides; but its satisfaction often requires different languages in different times. Even where forms do not change — line, light, composition, color; pitch, intensity, harmony, tempo; a chair, a bed, a place for fire; the triune God and Christ's person and work — and where goodness, truth, and beauty are shaped by special forms into enduring particular contents, each age must produce its own works of art in its own languages. This is why it is so important that theology remain in Academy in the presence of other arts, each forging a language for its creativity. This is why creative theology in Academy must dare to find new ways of saying "God-three-in-one" and "true God-true man, distinct not separate, related but unmixed" and "created," "sustained," "alienated," "reconciled," "pilgriming," "redeemed." It is the function of creative theology in Academy to discover and to dare, to find and forge artistic tools and to learn to use them in creating the works of theological art. It must do this as its logical duty, its rational worship, its reasonable service (Rom. 12:1) to God. It must also do this for man: it certainly must prove interesting and useful for the man of Academy, but in the first place it must do this for the self-acknowledged Christian man of the Church; for the art of theology, though it belongs in the Academy, belongs to the Church. It is created for the instruction and construction of the Church, which must judge the correspondence of theology with its content. Like any art, theology must hold fast its vision of reality and express this with the tools of its time and craft, but then can only offer the works of its art for the free and sympathetic reception of the men and women who choose to accept.

With these words we hope to have given an account of that second criterion of artistic worth suggested earlier in the chapter. We said that a thing of beauty must, first, express the coherence of an artistic vision; but, second, not only for the artist but also for some significant community of appreciation. In the case of theology, in the Academy and of the Church, the external institutions of criticism and of appreciation are immediately at hand. And so we can turn to certain characteristics of the creative artist and process peculiar to the theological art. Creativity in any form can and should produce excitement and satisfaction for the agent of creation. Yet it is no accident but a happy designation that Barth has now given us in calling theology "the happy science." If Stuermann is right in saying that theology shares *humility* with modern natural sciences, Barth is certainly also correct in characterizing his art by its *joy*. Just as the architectonic form of theology can delight the sense of order, so the content of theology is irrevocably *Eu-angelion, Go*(d)*spel*(1),

Glad Tidings, *Good* News. " God rest you *merry,* gentlemen," is but one of the vast literature of happy phrases which mark as unique the Christmas carols of the English-speaking world. There are many forms of Christian Joy: there are the angels dancing on the clouds above the manger in a bas-relief in Naples; there is the gourmet at the wedding feast in some Cana who discovers God's world tastes good and that there is better to come (John 2:10); there is a man or woman or child at the altar rail to whom the Risen Lord is known in breaking bread with a flash of light like that in Rembrandt's *Supper at Emmaus;* and there is the quiet, sure reflection as Paul sings through the voices and strings of William Byrd: " Christ rising again from the dead, now dieth not. Death from henceforth hath no power on him. Likewise count yourselves dead unto Sin but alive unto God." The theologian as an artist may take his key from one or more of these or from some other form, but a theologian's artistic *œuvre* can have but one primary keynote: that of joy.

In saying this we have spoken, above all, for theology, but have struck a theme fundamental to artistic creativity as such. Now in our final section we wish to speak of the definitive inner attitude of theology and of the wellspring of its vitality and power in a way that speaks to the fundamental nature and problems of all disciplines of Academy. Already the Introduction directed our attention to the recurrent theme that the underlying problem of Academy is its crisis of conviction and that theology exists and comes to Academy as a bearer of conviction. We have attempted, above all in Chapter I but also in Chapters III and IV, to give shape to the content of theology's conviction. We have tried to show that this conviction points to the same Truth and Humanity to which the faith and life of Academy must also bear witness. We have sought to make clear theology's relation to the questions about the *true* it shares with the sciences of Academy, to the questions about the *good for man* it shares with Academic crafts of conduct, and to the questions about the *beautiful* it shares with the arts of Academy. Still we have left unanswered that most vexing question about thought, namely, In what inner way does theology, *as a science, as an art, as a craft of conduct,* arrive at its convictions? Our answer has waited until now because it is most clearly seen from the standpoint of art: *theology arrives at its convictions by attending to its business.*

John Macmurray, among others, has pointed out that although sciences, both natural and social, pride themselves on the power, clarity, and completeness of their observation, they are surpassed by the arts, whose observation is more penetrating, more rigorous and acute. Insofar as *theology* shares this characteristic of art, it first *pays attention* to its vision of reality and then *portrays what it apprehends for all to see.* Or, since theology claims that its only legitimate subject matter is the Word of God, we should substitute another sense perception in our metaphor: *theology* listens *to its subject matter and tells to everyone what it has heard.* Beyond this bare assertion we must make clear but one more presupposition: theology *trusts* that its subject matter really has something important to say. At first sight this statement may seem like the very thing about theology that a critical Academy most often attacks: " Theology is too gullible," it is said, " too credulous for modern scientific men to take seriously." Reinhold Niebuhr spoke for this mood of Academy when in 1954 at Evanston the European theologians wished the World Council of Churches to reaffirm the apocalyptic Biblical vision of the end of history. He said, in effect: " You'll never sell those fairy tales to the American people." Yet the assertion that a discipline *trusts* that it has something important to say is in reality a profound suggestion to all disciplines and a critique of the way in which each is carried out by some of its practitioners. In the Academy as in the Church we are impressed by our achievements and dazzled by the power of our tools. We would rape nature with electron microscope and acoustical telescope, we would choke information out of victimized " subjects " and force our interpretations upon them. And after we triumph over our subject matter we hunger for adherents; we lust to communicate our victory. In this whole process, it is quite possible that we are losing the very objectivity we profess by failing to place sufficient trust in our subject matter.

The scientist has his job to do " on " his subject matter and he has powerful tools with which to do it, but first and last he should pay attention to his content. I would pay honor to the botanist in awe of the life unfolding before him, the psychologist who really listens to the people he interviews, the historian who lets the facts speak for themselves, the musicologist who waits for the tones to strike the inner ear. It is quite possible that true objectivity is far more passive than our aggressive activism in Academy has allowed us to admit. Good, true, beautiful theology listens when the aggressive apostle Paul says, " It is that I am apprehended, not that I apprehend " (Phil. 3:12). Theology, therefore, in telling of its conviction in Academy must speak of the *truth that apprehends.* As we unfold the implications of this statement we must make clear — on behalf of theology, on behalf of art, and on behalf of Academy — that what we advocate really has nothing to do with subjectivity! When we advise dethroning the idol of objectivity from the temple of knowledge, we are suggesting that citizens of Academy should not listen primarily to the whistle, whir, and clank of the mechanisms of scholarship; but the alternative we commend is *not* to lend scholarly ears to prejudices, whims, and fancies within the scholar's head or breast. Instead, we point to a third way: that of listening to one's particular Academic subject matter — a manifestation of the nature of matter-energy, a special kind of human need, a coherent form of beauty — to hear the inner harmonies which are there, independent of our tools and our wishes. This is indeed the most fundamental kind of objectivity, beyond Kant's subject-object chasm. It is that acknowledging of a " thing-known " as a legitimate other which Watson's book on Luther exemplifies for theology in its title: *Let God Be God.*

For the scholar to assume the attitude necessary for this involves something quite difficult, something that resembles nothing else so much as religious conversion. Let those who are repulsed by some too-familiar image evoked by this term join the Beckett for whom the shape of an idea is the important thing. Jesus said that unless a man be converted and become as a little child he shall not see the Kingdom of Heaven. He referred, I take it, to the dimension of innocence which is *open* to the Kingdom hidden from sophisticated eyes by their confining rationales for experience and by the trappings of their knowledge. This applies directly to Academicians. Unless a man can recapture and rediscover and again revitalize his childlike receptivity to what he wishes to know, he is doomed to remain forever outside the gates of the kingdom of the knowledge of Truth and Humanity. But, as difficult as it is to break our hardened habits of objectivism and subjectivism, this perennial outsideness need not persist. Or at least what is impossible with men remains possible with God. Here the experience of Luther can serve as paradigm.

"*Wie kriege ich ein gnädiger Gott,*" he cried: "How shall I lay hold on a God who will be gracious to me?" He strove to exhaustion with all the weapons of Church and Academy, becoming monk and priest, *magister,* doctor, professor, and still this God eluded him — until he stopped speaking to listen and hear that the God he sought had been "long beforehand with his soul," had already been gracious to him in the way that turned his whole world rightside-out. Lutherlike, we in Academy sharpen our tools, we *earn* honors, we *produce* research, we look at the big picture and the little one, we look at other scholars, we may even dare to look at ourselves — and we are not satisfied. One cannot prescribe for all, one must only speak of his own discipline and suggest that others in their own integrity may benefit from what he sees in it. In any case, good, true, beautiful theology must be sensible to, it must really listen, look, taste, feel, it must be *radically empirical* about — not its history or itself but about its material, the Word of God. Thus informed theology — as a science, as an art, and for the sake of its decisions as a craft of conduct — must always listen with new ears to hear the fresh thing its living subject will say. *Faith* is simply theology's name for her *passive,* receptive attitude, her openness to hear. *Spirit* is simply theology's word for the *active* role of the living Word in the movement, growth, development, and the new beginnings of theology. *Language* and *logic* are theology's words for *her* attempt to tell what she has heard, to obey the Word.

All of this describes how theology arrives at the convictions that form the ultimate, objective basis for all her work. Conviction is really a convincedness. Theology is "vinced," conquered, overcome by its subject matter. The theologian is grasped by his Truth which apprehends, and carried along "con," with and by it. And theology, from its own experience as a cognitive activity, would suggest analogous things to Academy in its crisis of conviction. The citizen of Academy need not be condemned to a life of Sisyphus labor, as Camus has put it, or even to spend his days for a little lump of conclusions hard-won after a career of seeking, striving, grasping with the tools and claws of an honorable discipline to get a finger and toe hold in the overwhelming yet elusive mountain of his subject matter. The claws of our craft are always there to be used, no piece of data, no generalization, need ever finally escape them; but

we need not *always* laboriously dig and climb. The time comes too —
first and last and repeatedly — when we must respond to our Academic tasks in a manner best described through a passive metaphor.
The citizen of Academy who would have something true and useful
to say legitimately can and in fact should become a kind of sound-
ing surface, tuned to and connected with the driving force of his
subject matter. In thus becoming " all ears " for it, he experiences it
by a kind of sympathetic vibration, and in being so used by the material subject of his discipline he communicates it to others in
Academy.

This is fundamentally the artistic path to truth, but the lines sep-
arating art from science and both from crafts of conduct are indis-
tinct, if not, indeed, meaningless; for we are dealing with the convictional roots of a discipline, where man and matter meet, where
scholarship and Academic existence have an effect on student and
professor and community. Here they impinge on actual living, the
only aspect of learning that really matters, the one that gives Academy its reason for being. At this level, arts and sciences and crafts
of conduct all seek some genuine contact with Truth and Humanity,
whether it be through questions about the true, about the good, or
about the beautiful. And theology joins them each and all as legitimate and equal partner in this their common quest.

Conclusion

The Common Quest

W E SET OUT to investigate a way in which the Gospel of Jesus Christ may be communicated to people who live the life of the mind in the modern university. We suggested first that this communication is attended by serious difficulty, not simply because Christian thinkers are lazy or incompetent, nor because the Christian view of reality is incompatible with really serious scientific work as it is carried on in the Academic world today, but because that world born of its own convictions is suffering a severe and only partly recognized crisis of conviction. The rift between knowledge about and knowledge of, between the mechanics of mentality and the whole man, between facts and faith of any kind, has been allowed to widen into a chasm tantamount to divorce and to threaten the primary function of the Academic institution. We suggested that Christian intellect comes to the Academic world precisely as a bearer of conviction, and while itself benefiting from life in the grove of Academe it might contribute both formally (as an example of the anatomy of convincedness) and materially (by witnessing to common elements of faith) to the solution of *Academy's crisis of conviction*.

Next we turned to a scrutiny of Theology, as the characteristically Christian form of the life of the mind, to discover exactly what it has been and is, and how it has been related to Academy in the past. Recognizing that Academic nervousness about "believing in something," though everywhere discernible today, is of recent vintage, we attempted to define a theology that might be penetrating and useful today. We learned that on the simplest level theology is not a subjective account of any man's religious experience, but is the common witness of a community of conviction to what it is acquainted with, knows about, acknowledges, and proclaims. In short, *Theology is the Church's speech about God*. This means, on the one hand, that the Church as a whole tests the appropriateness of a given theology to the common witness, even when that theology is forged in Academy. As that form of speech about God which comprises an intellectual discipline appropriate to Academy, on the other hand, *Theology is the cognitive response to God's revelation*. As such, Theology understands itself to be *a humble science* (with Stuermann) and *the happy science* (with Barth). Theology is humble because it is aware both of what it cannot do and of what it can do. The phrase " it cannot do " points to that recognition of its own limitations fundamental to all genuine intellectual disciplines. Theology is not the Word of God, it is the speech of man about God and his Word. The theologian is " nothing more " than man: his speech, his vocabulary, grammar, syntax, his historical-literary critical mechanisms, and his logic are human and subject to critical review by other men. And so the theologian, if he is wise, is humble. He observes, he reads, he reflects, he conceives, he attempts to communicate his discoveries to others — and he listens. Theology is " happy " because the work of the theologian is a *cognitive response* to something which, together with a responsible significant human community, he acknowledges to be reality. Theology is happy in a unique sense because what it *responds* to is good news, the Gospel that God has *reconciled* all men, all things, to himself. Reconciliation is the peculiarly Christian key to Truth which opens the door to a dual awareness of reality. The very fact of Reconciliation implies that there *has been* alienation and estrangement between man and God, between man and his world, between man and man, and that men still orient themselves toward alienation both within themselves and in external attitude. Beyond alienation, however, the decisive reality is that estrangement *has been overcome* on the cosmic scale and that this victory can and *shall be realized* throughout concrete existence. This also provides the Christian key to knowledge of and about Humanity. Man, in the large and in the intimate, has lived against himself too often and too long. The resources of Reconciliation are at hand. Knowing that the mighty Incarnation signifies " the Humanity of God " himself, Christianity knows that *man* can be a new being which shall truly be the measure of all things.

Next, we turned to Academy as the institutional symbol of man's pursuit of knowledge for *its* and *his* own sake. In doing so, we discovered that Academy is above all a place, a place with a shape we tried to describe in a kind of metaphorical topography. Just as Plato's original Academy was an olive grove, so figuratively all subsequent Academies, including our own universities and liberal arts colleges, have been groves or fields for the cultivation of knowledge. The modern Academic grove has expanded into various groves and fields (by which we signify groups of disciplines), which are divided and subdivided into sectors (or regions) of Academy (separate disciplines) and again into tracts or plots, which correspond to specialties within a discipline. In the original grove of Academe several activities were carried on, but all were at first intended to honor the Muses and all were ultimately drawn together by the penetrating and unifying power of philosophy. Thus in giving a figurative topography of that Academy we could have spoken of the whole as one grove of Academe. The same would be true of Renaissance and Enlightenment academies of art or of science. The modern university, however, represents such a diversified agricultural operation that we must speak of the groves and fields and orchards and vineyards of Academe. Each grove, orchard, or field is devoted to different groups or kinds of disciplines, namely, natural science, social study, art. Within a given grove, say natural science, there is a certain community of approach and spirit, and an obviously related set of subject matters, but there are also distinct demarcations between various sectors or disciplines, such as zoology, physics, and chemistry, within the given grove. In turn, each region or sector, for example, chemistry, is subdivided into various discrete areas we have called plots or tracts, namely, organic, physical, and biochemistry. Within our allegory, one variety of a crop is grown on a given tract of land in Academy, other varieties of the same crop are grown on contiguous tracts in the same sector or region, and similar crops requiring similar soil and care and a similar microclimate are cultivated in the various sectors of one grove or orchard or field of Academy. All the groves (fields and orchards) of Academy are united to each other by some form of allegiance to Truth and to Humanity, the classical criteria of Academic cognition, even though their vision and understanding of these " fallen " absolutes may be quite diver-

gent, partial, and even minimal. The very uncertainty about Truth
and Humanity in large segments of Academy today represents the
content of what we have called its crisis of conviction. It is because
of this crisis that we see the contribution of Theology in terms of
communicating its peculiar witness to Truth and Humanity within
Academy.

In addition to the ultimate criteria of Truth and Humanity under
which all of Academy stands, we have suggested that there are three
separate though related classifying values and corresponding tests of
validity which characterize the three groves, or groups of disciplines,
in Academy today. The three classifying values and the three corresponding kinds of motivating questions, relate to the classic Platonic
triad, the true, the good, and the beautiful. The tests of trueness or
validity are the concept of correspondence, the pragmatic test of relevance for practical living, and the test of coherence. As we have
formulated the three divisions of the one modern academy, the *scientific* grove of Academy is defined by its responsibility to questions
in the form: What is the *true?* tested in terms of correctness, or
correspondence to the facts of a particular science. The disciplines of
the *social* field of Academy, which we have called the crafts of conduct, are defined by their responsibility to concrete and specific questions about the *good* for man, and by statements and prescriptions
which can be tested *pragmatically* for their *relevance* to human life
now. The *artistic* grove (or orchard) of Academy is defined by the
questions its disciplines ask concerning the *beautiful,* the answers to
which are tested by the *coherence* of an artistic vision as reflected in
its realization — a coherence, harmony, or balance recognized by a
community of appreciation.

Theology is understood from two points of view: as a discipline
that belongs in *Academy,* and as the *Church's* cognitive response to
the fact of revelation. Seen in this dual perspective, Theology has
much to learn and to communicate in the Academic community of
dialogue. As a discipline of Academy, Theology shares with many
other disciplines the tendency to belong to more than one Academic
grove, field, or group of disciplines. As a particular " ear " and
" voice " in Academic dialogue, *Theology engages with Academy in
the common quest for the contemporary significance of Truth and
Humanity*. In doing so, Theology acts as a human endeavor among

human endeavors. Though convinced that its Gospel, its vision of reality, is true for others as well as for itself, it does not claim to possess Truth and Humanity in any superhuman way. It attempts to bear witness to its peculiar vision of Truth and Humanity as correctly, as coherently, as relevantly as humanly possible, fully aware that other disciplines are doing exactly the same thing. It enters into Academic dialogue by asking the questions about the true, the good, and the beautiful from the point of view of its own subject matter. It asks these questions in company with other disciplines asking the same questions, and assays answers to its own questions and those asked of it. As a science, Theology must listen attentively to its own subject matter: the Word of God, heard primarily in the Bible for Protestant theology. It is important to insist in this connection that Theology attempts to hear God's Word through the critically investigated words of men, rather than to heed men's words about themselves as they think they have been influenced by God. Theology must then attempt to respond cognitively to this subject matter, with words which correspond to its reality. As a craft of conduct, in company with the social disciplines, Theology from time to time dares to attempt prophetic statements. These are statements on the basis of its scientific subject matter which it hopes will prove pragmatically to be relevant to some specific area and to the whole of life today. As an art, Theology attempts to observe, to listen to, to be possessed by the truth of its own coherent Gospel, and to utilize some artistic language to create a coherent and convincing (that is to say, beautiful), realization of that vision of reality.

Theology does all this in dialogue with other disciplines, also busy about their own discrete subject matters, and it attempts to do it with humility and with joy. In the course of this dialogue, the content of which is the Common Quest, Theology has as much to gain as to contribute. Theology has to inform and to be informed in Academy. On the surface level of meaning, this statement signifies that Theology has information to mine and to give about the world of the Bible and of the faith and life of the Church to historical, artistic, and ethical disciplines. It has information to gain from historically-oriented disciplines concerning the political, economic, social, and aesthetic conditions which have surrounded the Christian reality in the past; and from these disciplines, as well as from the natural and behavioral scientific investigators, it gleans accurate analysis of our contemporary scene. This information giving and receiving, as necessary and important as it may be, is, however, always a preliminary activity or by-product of the Common Quest whose form is dialogue in the Academy. Theology is informed by and helps inform disciplines from all three Academic groups in something like the way contiguous soap bubbles shape each other. Sharing a common form, as human cognitive efforts, their growth brings them together, and contact broadens into a shared boundary on which each molds the other. Theology and the Church are strengthened and enriched by this contact, this dialogue. They are shorn of all excuse for ignorance of their time, for intellectual laziness and parochialism. They are challenged to meet the deepest longings and highest achievements of the human mind and spirit. For its part, Theology brings conviction of an intense, strongly characterized and historically tested nature into Academy. It helps Academy to be aware of the nature of human convincedness, of how convictions are attained and tested. It reminds the disciplines of Academy specifically of their mutual commitment to Truth and Humanity, which Academy needs at its center and throughout the whole of its existence. Theology is an ambassador of the Gospel of Reconciliation, precisely by being itself a cognitive, which is to say Academic, response to it. Proceeding as a science, Theology must remain true to its subject matter, and thus with so-called secular science remain scientific, " so long as they [both] acknowledge one another and remember in a self-critical spirit that knowability is but a mode of Being, . . . never Being per se." Creating and appreciating as an art, Theology must maintain its coherent vision and discover fresh and valid forms of realization if it is to communicate the truth of beauty and of joy. Learning to live in each modern world as a craft of conduct, Theology must claim, show, and allow to be tested by living, the relevance of Reconciliation to various particular forms of the question about the good for man, here and now.

It is thus that Theology carries on and encourages the Common Quest with Academy by *cognizing* its vision of Truth and Humanity in the special ways they bear on the questions about the true, the beautiful, and the good for man. It may be that we do not live in a day of great syntheses, when one strong, clear vision of Truth and Humanity can be shared by all. It may, rather, be a time for each to speak his own as clearly, as honestly (and therefore, perhaps, minimally) as possible while all listen and try to catch the pitch, the note of relevance for others. We seek more than that a political scientist should understand the mechanisms of the electrochemistry of thought, or that an Absurd dramatist should know about acoustical astronomy. We would hope that student of government and literary artist would meditate on the implications of what they each learn, and convey their discovery in a form enlightening to others.

Jonathan Edwards stood astride two epochs and married in his speculations new forms of thought with classic convictions reconceived.[1] He was among the first to see the wide-ranging and fundamental significance of both the psychology of John Locke and the physics of Isaac Newton. With what he learned he rethought Theology in the language John Calvin forged two centuries before, this time not so much from the outside in, as Calvin himself had done, as from the inside out. His monumental accomplishment did not end the bitter struggles between Theology and Academy in his day, or seal over the widening chasm between traditional ecclesiastical thinking and the truly secular enlightenment. He did, however, provide a profound understanding of the problems that have plagued the American soul from that day to this, and he suggested directions that offered fresh impetus for both Theology and Academy, directions that in some cases would have proved more profitable if followed more closely and with his own freedom and breadth of spirit. Perhaps the time is not yet ripe for a new Edwards, whose vision of Truth and Humanity is intense and comprehensive enough to allow an incorporation of fundamental motifs from widely separated areas of Academy within one another. Though many intellectuals quail before the mass and diversity of knowledge today, saying that comprehensive synthesis will never again be possible, the success of a Tillich in his dialogues with art and sociopsychic research indicate the human hunger for an overarching conviction. Perhaps Theology and Academy in America do await a new Edwards, who can incorporate, for example, the burning edge of Freud's psychological revolution and the vast dynamic of Einstein's general theory within a theology of Reconciliation, and do it substantially, not in a merely formal way. But even if such a mind, a spirit, a man, arises among us, his endeavor would be nothing else than an intensified form of the Common Quest, as valid in Academy as in Theology, a fresh starting point gained for man's intellectual quest for the present significance of Truth and Humanity.

NOTES

Notes

Introduction: The Crisis of Intellect

1. Interesting use has been made of the distinction both by Christian Bay and by Christopher S. Jencks and David Riesman in contributions to *The American College: A Psychological and Social Interpretation of Higher Learning,* ed. by R. Nevitt Sanford (John Wiley & Sons, Inc., 1962), pp. 735 f. and 984 f.

2. The establishment of an Academy in this country was one of the typical achievements of Benjamin Franklin for the American Enlightenment.

Chapter I: Theology and Conviction

1. The term " dialogue " as used throughout this chapter seems more useful and appropriate than others such as " apologetics," which are commonly used to describe Christian responses to culture. *Internal dialogue* represents the attempt of the Christian Church to understand its own faith in relation to life and thought at a particular historical moment. *External dialogue* occurs when the Church attempts to explain its faith in a persuasive manner to a culture in that culture's own terms.

2. Abelard's own version of the *articulus* ran: *titulus* (thesis), with a positive content; *videtur, quod . . .* (" It is seen, that . . ."), one or more objections or antitheses, contradictory to the thesis; and *sed contra* (" but against this, or these "), which signals the solution, the positive content of which is designated by quotations against the objections. From this developed the complete *articulus:* Title (thesis); *antithesis; sed contra* (usually one affirmative sentence); *corpus articuli* (the author's own opinion); answers to objections. In Aquinas' version of the form, the *objectiones* that follow the thesis and appear to contradict it are usually based on Biblical texts or quotations from other Christian authorities. Often the form of the objections appears to support the thesis while the content contradicts. In the *sed contra* and the *responsio* (Thomas' own *corpus articuli*)

the relationship is usually reversed, form not supporting thesis but content in agreement. Finally, in answering the objections (*ad primum* — or *secundum, tertium,* etc. — *ergo dicendum* . . .) Aquinas directly overcomes the contradictions.

3. For the additions in parentheses, see Karl Heussi, *Kompendium der Kirchengeschichte* (J. C. B. Mohr, 10th ed., 1949), p. 291.

4. John Calvin, *Institutes of the Christian Religion,* tr. by Ford Lewis Battles and ed. by John T. McNeill (The Library of Christian Classics, Vol. XX) (The Westminster Press, 1960), I. viii.

5. This definition excludes Jonathan Edwards and Paul Tillich from consideration.

6. Such a being-intoxicated philosopher as Martin Heidegger is really much more candid than Tillich on this point. Noting in a study of ontology that " being " has become an empty word for moderns, he asserts quite typically: " We do not mean to accept this fact (of being) blindly " (*An Introduction to Metaphysics,* tr. by Ralph Mannheim; Anchor Books, 1959, p. 63).

7. John H. Randall, Jr., " The Ontology of Paul Tillich," *The Theology of Paul Tillich,* ed. by Charles W. Kegley and Robert W. Bretall (Library of Living Theology, Vol. I) (The Macmillan Company, 1952), pp. 160 f.

8. See Charles C. West, *Communism and the Theologians* (The Westminster Press, 1958), pp. 78–111.

9. Paul Tillich, *Biblical Religion and the Search for Ultimate Reality* (The University of Chicago Press, 1955), p. 85.

10. These words of Acts 5:29 are echoed in the declarations of the Synod of Barmen, 1934.

11. We should be quite clear that Paul's folly is theology, for in the almost rudimentary etymological sense *theology is speech about God*. It is unmistakably theology that Paul produces when he speaks " the word of the cross " (I Cor. 1:18).

Chapter II: The Topography of the Academy

1. Karl Jaspers, *The Idea of the University,* tr. by H. A. T. Reiche and H. F. Vanderschmidt (Beacon Press, Inc., 1959), p. 40.

2. *Ibid.,* p. 45.

3. All three quotations are from Jaspers, *op. cit.,* pp. 49–52. Jaspers takes a further, somewhat questionable, step in claiming that to fulfill his role in this birth-drama, the teacher " hides in paradoxes " and " makes himself inaccessible " for the sake of the search in which both are engaged and for the sake of generating and developing the independent human being of the student.

4. See also Arnold S. Nash, *The University and the Modern World* (The Macmillan Company, 1943), written to raise the question of the nature of the university against the background of the same painful pages of Academic history. Nash stresses the inherent weakness of " presuppositionless science " and " pure objectivity " which left the German intellectual, individually and institutionally, defenseless against the demands of political and military power. Nash has no difficulty discovering such documentation as the statement made by a university faculty: " We renounce international science. . . . We renounce the international republic of learning," and others openly calling for an anti-Semitic nationalism.

5. It is most instructive to recall that one of the fundamental advances in modern physics was initiated by Nils Bohr in the course of the rigorous but brief interrogation that made up his own oral examination for the doctoral degree.

6. C. P. Snow, *The Two Cultures and the Scientific Revolution* (Cambridge University Press, 1959), p. 11.

7. Jacques Barzun, *Science, the Glorious Entertainment* (Harper & Row, Publishers, Inc., 1964), p. 16.

8. *Ibid.,* p. 14. Italics added.

9. The technological revolution is based on scientific method, whereas the industrial revolution was built on largely untrained pragmatic inventiveness.

10. *Ibid.,* p. 287.

11. *Ibid.,* p. 190.

12. Campbell Stewart, " The Place of Higher Education in a Changing Society," in Sanford, ed., *The American College,* p. 899.

13. Kent Bendall and Frederick Ferré, *Exploring the Logic of Faith* (Association Press, 1962), p. 25. Italics added.

14. Jaspers, *op. cit.,* p. 68. Italics and translation of Latin added.

15. Christian Theology will, in this etymological context, prefer the word " revelation," and claim that in the final sense Truth is the authentic reality manifested in God's revelation (as persistently suggested in II Cor., chs. 3 to 5). Heidegger, however, rejects the particularity of Christian revelation, as well as that of logic, which would imprison truth in the vehicles of its own vocabulary.

16. Martin Heidegger, *Existence and Being,* ed. by Werner Brock (Gateway, 1949), pp. 308 f. Parenthetical material added.

17. *The Idea and Practice of General Education,* by present and former members of the faculty (The University of Chicago Press, 1950), p. 17.

18. Truth is, for example, for the sake of the truth seeker, as in Christian Bay's statement: " A person is an *intellectual* . . . to the extent that his

mind produces and utilizes the insight . . . that is required for coping
with and anticipating the problems of living a full life and of facing death
with serenity." "A Social Theory of Intellectual Development," in Sanford, ed., *The American College,* p. 978. See also the limiting statement of
Nevitt Sanford on p. 92 below.

19. In spite of the ringing affirmation that includes *humanitas* as a
value for the university in the statement opening this chapter, Jaspers' unconditional value for the university is Truth (p. 85), whereas humanity
is a by-product (p. 92).

20. Stewart, *loc. cit.,* p. 937.

21. Bay, *loc. cit.,* p. 1003. This is a clear example of the tendency noted
by Snow and described on p. 102 below. It is interesting to note that even
Snow's optimistic English scientist shares this pessimistic feeling of the
humanists about personal existence as distinguished from civilization's
progress: "Most of the scientists I have known well have felt — just as
deeply as the nonscientists I have known well — that the individual condition of each of us is tragic. Each of us is alone; sometimes we escape
from solitariness, through love or affection or perhaps creative moments,
but those triumphs of life are like pools of light we make for ourselves
while the edge of the road is black " (Snow, *op. cit.,* p. 6).

22. "Developmental Status of the Entering Freshman," by R. Nevitt
Sanford, in Sanford, ed., *The American College,* p. 281.

23. Frank Pinner, "The Crisis of the State Universities: Analysis and
Remedies," in Sanford, ed., *The American College,* p. 271.

24. Nash, *op. cit.,* pp. 283 f.

25. Elton Trueblood, *The Idea of a College* (Harper & Brothers, 1959),
p. 246.

26. Alexander Meiklejohn, *The Experimental College* (Harper &
Brothers, 1932), p. 246.

27. Christopher Jencks and David Riesman, "Residential Education: A
Case Study," in Sanford, ed., *The American College,* p. 734.

28. Robert H. Knapp, "Changing Functions of the College Professor,"
in Sanford, ed., *The American College,* p. 292.

29. Pinner, *loc. cit.,* p. 966. Karl Jaspers quotes J. Grimm as saying, "Our
universities . . . tend to ignore any radically new piece of work until it
has proved its validity elsewhere. Universities are like gardens where wild
growths are only reluctantly tolerated," and cites Renaissance humanism,
the revival of philosophy and of the natural sciences under Descartes,
Spinoza, Leibniz, Pascal, and Kepler, the Enlightenment, Romanticist humanism, Marxist sociology, and the introspective psychology described by
Kierkegaard and Nietzsche as forms of pioneering cognition that were

forced to be nurtured *outside the university* (*op. cit.*, pp. 75 f.) Thus dissensual knowledge must fight the reactionary mind not only in general culture but often within the sacred groves themselves.

30. Pinner, *loc. cit.*, p. 971.

31. M. Rokeach, *The Open and Closed Mind* (Basic Books, Inc., Publishers, 1960), pp. 400 f.

32. Jaspers, *op. cit.*, p. 53.

33. R. Nevitt Sanford, "Research and Policy in Higher Education," in Sanford, ed., *The American College*, p. 1032.

34. José Ortega y Gasset, *The Mission of the University*, intro. by Howard Lee Nostrand (Princeton University Press, 1944), p. 78.

35. *Ibid.* See also Nostrand's introduction, pp. 19, 30.

36. Jaspers, *op. cit.*, p. 81.

37. *Ibid.*, p. 85.

38. At the university in which I studied under Jaspers, this lower faculty was divided into Philosophy I, consisting principally of humanities, and Philosophy II, made up of mathematics and the natural sciences. As at most European universities, the social studies were not accorded status, what was taught being included under medicine or law, or taught as though it were a "humanity."

39. An interesting and significant attempt to understand the interrelationships of various forms of cognition has been made by the Scottish philosopher, John Macmurray, in *Religion, Art, and Science* (University Press of Liverpool, 1961). He begins from no explicit assumptions about culture or the inherent right of Academic disciplines. Instead, he attempts to analyze the separate meaningful activities of man, and thus discover for each religion, art, and science its own validity within its own proper bounds. By this means he is able to place religion's (and art's and science's) "own inner geography" within "a kind of geography of the whole field of reflection" and relate this to "the geography of human life as a whole." He does so by claiming that man now has three authentic general, unreflective, practical activities. To each such activity corresponds a specialized mode of reflection, with its own appropriate method and somewhat less clearly and satisfactorily, an anthropological center or faculty. Macmurray has attempted to free his analysis from the prejudices of the traditional mind-centered anthropology, and to operate on the definition of the self as an agent. Thus, man produces activities, both unreflective and reflective, of which thinking is but one of the latter.

Macmurray's analysis proceeds with a kind of empirical directness that distills a great deal of Anglo-Saxon common sense, but produces a less neat system than that of Idealistic philosophers who approach their data with a prearranged network of categories. Three massive sentences that paraphrase his argument might, however, give us the shape and tone of his discoveries: (1) Science is that reflective activity which *derives* from technical problems of practical life and *proceeds by* the generalizing reflective activity known as reasoning in an intellectual dimension of self-transcendence to a *knowledge* of the facts that are the basis for the *production* of technology; (2) Art is that reflective activity which *derives* from the problems of valuation of the sense experience of practical life and *proceeds by* a particularizing reflective activity known as contemplation in an organic-emotional dimension of self-transcendence to a *knowledge* of values or intentions (realized as a last step of contemplation in the work of art) to *produce* a refinement of sensibility, an education of emotion, a training of judgment; (3) Religion is that reflective activity which *derives* from the personal relations of practical life and *proceeds by* the participatory reflective activity known as communion (worship's communal, symbolic action as opposed to thought or action is itself religion's reflective activity) in a dimension of self-transcendence arising from the capacity for speech to a *knowledge* of personal relationship that aims ultimately to *produce* world community.

There are many terms in these linguistic equations that are not entirely comparable, and also some things contrary to the nature of Theology as we conceive it and some things irrelevant to the Academy. Yet Macmurray has made a quite significant attempt to understand and explain both the activities of culture and of intellect in terms of a particular view of humanity, and provided us with a geography of cognition in the attempt.

40. Stewart, *loc. cit.,* p. 900.

41. Erich Kahler, *The True, the Good, and the Beautiful* (Ohio State University Press, 1960), pp. 36, 40, 12.

42. Snow, *op. cit.,* p. 9; Pinner, *loc. cit.,* p. 971.

43. Jaspers, *op. cit.,* p. 104. He also, however, sounds the warning we have found necessary to give in our emphasis upon the need for conviction about the bearing of ultimate criteria on all Academic work: " But whoever boasts about his craftsman-like competence and thinks that it suffices to make his contribution valuable is lost in a morass of materials and technique " (p. 41).

44. In all that is said here we must exclude philosophers like Jaspers himself, who persist in the " philosophic " vision that would give the role of unifier to one or more of our " misfit disciplines ": " Integration of the various disciplines joins them into a cosmos which culminates in the vision of unified science, in theology, and in philosophy " (p. 2).

45. Walter E. Stuermann, *Logic and Faith* (Westminster Studies in

Christian Communication, ed. by Kendig Brubaker Cully) (The Westminster Press, 1962), pp. 25 and 22.

46. *Ibid.,* p. 90.

47. *Ibid.,* p. 22.

Chapter III: Theology as a Science

1. Jaspers, *op. cit.,* p. 10. The immediately following quotations are
from the same source.

2. Jaspers, *op. cit.,* p. 12. See the distinction between exactness and
strictness in Heidegger, *Existence and Being,* p. 326.

3. Karl Popper, *The Logic of Scientific Discovery* (Basic Books, Inc.,
Publishers, 1959), pp. 278 f.

4. Barzun, *op. cit.,* p. 287.

5. Heinrich Scholz, "Wie ist eine evangelische Theologie als Wissen-
schaft möglich?", *Zwischen den Zeiten,* 1931, pp. 8–53.

6. Heidegger, *Existence and Being,* pp. 294 ff.

7. Kahler, *op. cit.,* p. 30.

8. See Bendall and Ferré, *op. cit.,* pp. 122 f.

9. *Ibid.,* pp. 123 f. Italics added.

10. Kahler, *op. cit.,* pp. 30 f.

11. Stuermann, *op. cit.,* pp. 95 f.

12. Although the time comes, as in the struggle for Academic freedom
in the German Academy during the Nazi period, when faith in such ultimate criteria as Truth and Humanity must be upheld in Academy by all
disciplines.

13. Logicians may object to the persistent use of the term "cognition"
in the theological context, claiming that it is a word reserved for formal
propositional knowledge. We shall firmly insist that logicians writing in
the English language have appropriated the wrong word when they chose
cognition for this meaning from the Western terminological pairs of words
for knowledge. Cognition denotes "the knowledge of" entailed by personal acquaintance in its etymological relationship with *cognoscere* in
Latin, *connaître* in French, *conoscere* in Italian, and *kennen* in German.
The more formal and remote "knowledge about" is denoted by *sapere* in
Latin and Italian, *savoir* in French, and *wissen* in German. It might be
well to develop some term related to this group for the propositionally
circumscribed knowledge of the logician.

14. See Calvin, *Institutes,* I. vii., esp. par. 2.

15. Heidegger, *Existence and Being,* p. 227. Italics added.

16. Heidegger, *An Introduction to Metaphysics,* p. 101.

17. *Ibid.,* p. 147.

18. *Ibid.,* pp. 155 ff.

19. Heidegger, "What Is Metaphysics? Postscript," *Existence and Being,* p. 355. For Heidegger, on the other hand, the God of whom Christians speak is, after all, a being, derivative of Being itself; in short, he is not God: "Being — this is not God nor the ground of the world. Being is farther than all that is and yet it is nearer to man than any one being, be this a rock, an animal, work of art, a machine, be it angel or God" ("The Letter on Humanism," *op. cit.,* p. 76).

20. See Heidegger, *An Introduction to Metaphysics,* pp. 113 f.

21. See Bultmann, *Das Evangelium des Johannes* (Vandenhoek und Ruprecht, 1957), esp. the Prologue, pp. 8–17.

22. This historical process follows that of the Old Testament in which Israel knows God and knows itself through God's deliverance from Egyptian bondage as the starting point of faith and life, long before the extended sixth-century reflections on creation in Isa., chs. 40 ff., and Gen., ch. 1.

23. Barzun, *op. cit.,* pp. 287 and 305.

24. Surprisingly, this is great Calvin's "back-door error" on the problem of evil. He who is so concerned with God's power and justice, is also so concerned with God's glory that anything which might taint it must be kept away from him. So Calvin's God is "glorified" in the damnation of the reprobate, and the consequent "limited" atonement is a limitation on God's *power* to defeat evil, which now triumphs over some human beings.

25. Stuermann, *op. cit.,* p. 158.

26. The concept of the *diabolos* as a murderer (John 8:44) or one who sins (I John 3:8) "from the beginning" is not clearly related to creation.

Chapter IV: Theology as a Craft of Conduct

1. *Hesed* is here translated "kindness" by the RSV, which usually renders it "steadfast love." The traditional versions render this vital concept rather blandly, sometimes as "mercy," sometimes as "loving-kindness," "favor," etc. It is perhaps best understood in the context of covenant theology as "faithfulness within the covenantal relationship," an impossibly awkward translation.

2. Calvin, *Institutes,* II. viii. 52. Italics added.

3. A summary of the immediately preceding discussion of the good in Biblical terms — as the creation and maintenance of the cosmic order which includes all that is creaturely, as justice and love toward the neighbor, and faithfulness and humility toward God — could arrive at the same result. It would, however, do so less directly and with a less obviously

universal character than does our discussion of evil.

4. George Gaylord Simpson and Anne Roe, " The Evolution of Behavior," *The Behavioral Sciences Today,* ed. by Bernard Berelson (Basic Books, Inc., Publishers, 1963), p. 98.

5. The term has grown rapidly in general acceptance since the University of Michigan began publishing a new social science journal, *Behavioral Science,* and now the movement boasts a center for Advanced Studies in the Behavioral Sciences at Stanford. The aura of success and security surrounding the word " science " has proved useful in winning public acceptance and financial assistance for the social studies.

6. Perhaps we need not go to the extreme of Barzun's rejection: " Every time that thoughtful men have pondered the results of their physical research into man they have been forced to conclude that the tendency of living things is at the opposite from the mechanical " (*op. cit.,* p. 189). The same concern lurks, however, behind the reassurances given by the creators of superhuman " thinking machines ": " Let not this enthusiastic report on the scientific potentialities of simulation research arouse anxieties of the sort raised by the speculations of science fiction writers that machines will take over our civilization and supplant man in the near future. . . . It may, of course, then become possible for us to build machines which will work out solutions to many problems which we now consider distinctively human and to do so in a manner surpassing present human performance. But that this will lead to the machine becoming master and the designer becoming slave seems to me most unlikely. On the contrary, it will free man for novel, creative tasks which are progressively beyond the capability of machines designed by man " (Samuel A. Stouffer, " Methods of Research Used by American Behavioral Sciences," *The Behavioral Sciences Today,* p. 88).

7. Gregory Zilboorg, " The Changing Concept of Man in Present-Day Psychiatry," *Freud and the Twentieth Century,* ed. by Benjamin Nelson (Meridian Books, Inc., 1957), p. 37.

8. Barzun, *op. cit.,* p. 305.

9. " Certainly there are problems that we think about, that we think hard about, where there does not seem to be any test. . . . The test simply may not exist. Ethical questions seem to have that character. By what test do we settle the problem of living a good life?" (George A. Miller, " Thinking, Cognition, and Learning," *The Behavioral Sciences Today,* p. 148.)

10. Berelson, *op. cit.,* p. 7.

11. Lincoln Pettit, *How to Study and Take Exams* (John F. Rider, Publisher, Inc., 1960), p. 19. Barzun puts his finger precisely on the sore spot

of confusion in the behavioral sciences that arises when the *question of values* is legitimately put to a sociologist or an economist, for example, and that worthy is qualitatively unable to answer it with the resources of the *scientist's* arsenal: " The moral is plain: our scientific culture often expects of behavioral science answers to the question What Ought to Be, and the answer often given is a composite report that conceals under figures subjective impressions and shifting measurements of What Is. Leaning on the normal distribution curve we try to compute the greatest good of the greatest number, a response to complexity that is now a habit" (*op. cit.*, p. 173).

12. The limits of the thinking of behavioral scientism are nowhere more patently displayed than in the " Kinsey approach" to human sexuality. Moving to this field from the study of insect behavior (he had earlier been interested in *The Edible Wild Plants of Eastern North America,* but specialized in the evolution of the gall wasp, genus Cynips, taking *The Life Histories of American Cynipidae*), Dr. Kinsey applied similar though more complicated procedures to his human specimens. All his precautions, however, have certainly been inadequate to cancel out the complex psychological factors involved in the volunteering of precisely those people whose behavior ended up as part of the statistical analysis. We can never be entirely sure that all of those people conformed to the rule, as did the insects, and never bragged to a human interviewer about their sexual attainments. It must indeed be granted that Dr. Kinsey's program did in the last analysis involve an attempt to answer the question: What is the good for man in the area of sexual behavior? This is clear from the persistent implication that restrictive laws dealing with sexual behavior should be abolished and replaced by more permissive ones, or by minimal legal prescription. One must be allowed to wonder if this thesis never affected the gathering and assessing of data, in the light of reports by blatantly chaste college girls who were dismissed as unreliable when they volunteered to add their testimony, " to balance that of the notoriously promiscuous ' sleep-around' who rooms down the hall." However, even if the data were ideally accurate and its presentation as unbiased as purported, the valuable information made available does not carry its own message or prescription divorced from ethical presuppositions about what is good for man as man. To be sure, Kinsey freed his data and his data-givers from all morally restrictive categories on the scientific grounds that disapproval inhibits honest replies, but questions of value as such are so different from purely scientific questions that it is almost inevitable for such moral neutrality to imply approval of a *permissive* ethic. *The inference, for example, that man " ought to be" as our data shows him to behave,*

and that laws should be changed to allow him to behave as he obviously wishes to, involves a set of ethical assumptions and is not implicit in the data.

13. Karl H. Pribham, "Neuropsychology in America," *The Behavioral Sciences Today,* p. 111.

14. John W. Riley, "Some Contributions of Behavioral Sciences to Contemporary Life," *The Behavioral Sciences Today,* p. 246.

15. Popper, *op. cit.,* p. 287.

16. Cora DuBois, "Anthropology: Its Present Interests," *The Behavioral Sciences Today,* p. 35.

17. Zilboorg, *op. cit.,* p. 32.

18. Pribham, *op. cit.,* p. 111.

19. Earl S. Johnson, *The Theory and Practice of the Social Studies* (The Macmillan Company, 1956), p. xi. The role of sociology in Johnson's topography of Academy is enhanced at the expense of other disciplines. Within the family of social sciences, sociology, not psychology, is the science of man as man.

20. Rene König, "Soziologie," *Fischer Lexikon,* 1958, p. 7.

21. *Ibid.,* p. 9. Even König envisions circumstances in which sociology, liberated from slavish dependence upon philosophy, can enter into dialogue as an equal partner with it (p. 89). Karl Pribham is able to see such an interchange at work for the mutual benefit of philosophy and biology: "The arguments of the philosophers are taken out of the realm of the speculative and into the laboratory. . . . First, it shows that the arguments of the philosophers were not just 'hot air,' and, secondly, it shows that the naïve materialism which has served the biologist so well thus far must be amplified, if not totally discarded, if his data are to make any sense to him or to anyone else" (*op. cit.,* p. 107).

22. Harry Alpert, "Sociology," *The Behavioral Sciences Today,* pp. 52–64.

23. Stouffer, *loc. cit.,* p. 66.

24. See p. 191 above.

25. George C. Homans, "Small Groups," *The Behavioral Sciences Today,* p. 166.

26. Robert K. Merton, "The Mosaic of the Behavioral Sciences," *The Behavioral Sciences Today,* pp. 270 ff.

27. Sanford, *op. cit.,* p. 1014.

28. *Ibid.,* p. 1019.

29. Johnson, *op. cit.,* p. 122.

30. John Kenneth Galbraith, *American Capitalism* (Houghton Mifflin Company, 1962), p. 31.

31. Johnson, *op. cit.,* pp. 68 ff.

32. Heinrich Rittershausen, "Wirtschaft," *Fischer Lexikon,* 1958, p. 179.

33. The entire process is clearly illustrated by J. M. Bochenski, *Die Zeitgenössischen Denkmethoden,* 1954, who divides and diagrams separately the psychological and the logical process involved. Schematically, two (or some) economic data are reduced to hypothesis 1, and then checked against some relevant data. Hypothesis 2 is similarly derived and checked, using different data. The two hypotheses are then reduced to theory A, from which hypothesis 3 is then deduced (or *re*duced). Hypothesis 3 is then checked against new data relevant to it. In more specific terms, one deduces so-called middle theories out of the highest theories — for example, wage and interest theory from price theory, and then the lower theories, such as discount theory, from these.

34. Rittershausen, *op. cit.,* p. 317.

35. Galbraith, *op. cit.,* p. 12.

36. Exodus 20:17, among other formulations; "Thou shalt not steal" (v. 15), is, of course, also related.

37. Frank H. Knight, "The Limitations of Scientific Method in Economics," *The Ethics of Competition* (Harper & Brothers, 1936), p. 105.

38. Galbraith, *op. cit.,* p. 116.

39. *Ibid.,* pp. 185, 192.

40. Paul A. Samuelson, *Economics, An Introductory Analysis* (McGraw-Hill Book Company, Inc., 5th ed., 1961), p. 403.

41. Galbraith, *op. cit.,* p. 211. Traditionally we congratulate ourselves on the democratic guarantee of individual liberty against misuse of power, especially by the tyrannical state. Yet, as Galbraith puts it, "Power obviously presents awkward problems for a community which abhors its existence, disavows its possession, but values its exercise" (p. 40). This reflects the fact that, "In the nature of man, the alarm over the exercise of such power runs to its use by second persons." We treasure our own freedom to decide, but "a decision which one is free to make rarely impresses one as an exercise of power." We prefer to think that both our political and economic systems are self-contained devices for the orderly utilization of power, and their unhampered operation affords automatic regulation of power and protection against its abuse.

In a curious way we have compromised our confidence in the balance of political power between executive, legislative, and judicial branches of government, by accepting as our image of the commonplace corrupt officials and self-interested pressure groups to the extent that one widespread reaction to an astronaut's decision to run for the United States Senate reads: "I am terribly disillusioned. I thought he was too nice a

boy to get mixed up in such a dirty business as politics." Our faith in traditional competitive capitalism, however, seems more durable. The price-
market governor, we still say, will control and regulate economic power,
will see to the production of the right goods, and provide the power for
all good people to procure them and to avoid both depression and inflation
unless interfered with by monopoly. Conservatives hold that any form of
limiting the free use of capital by fixing wages at a high level, prices at a
low one, and by "confiscatory" taxation is a *monopolistic organization of
government power,* and that the supply side of the market must be protected from it and from similar *organizations* of *power* by *labor,* or even
by *consumers,* if capitalism is to work its miracles. Liberals have identified
the villain as the *monopolist of supply,* who can upset the equilibrium by
fulfilling as much of the demand as he chooses at unfairly high prices,
and they have counseled some extended form of antitrust control on business. Theoretically, for the liberals the Keynesian solution to depression by
government intervention should solve the problem, but as Galbraith has
shown, the Keynesian formula is inadequate on the inflational end of the
cycle, precisely because Keynes too has failed to deal satisfactorily with
the problem of power.

42. "Introduction," *Political Behavior, A Reader in Theory and Research,* ed. by Heinz Eulau, Samuel J. Eldersveld (The Free Press of Glen-
coe, Inc., 1956), p. 3, as are the references immediately following.

43. Graham Wallas, *Human Nature in Politics* (A. Constable and Co.,
Ltd., 1908), p. 35.

44. Charles Edward Merriam, *New Aspects of Politics* (The University
of Chicago Press, 1925), p. 136.

45. Zilboorg, *op. cit.,* p. 38.

46. Heinz and Eldersveld, *op. cit.,* pp. 32 and 3 f.

47. Berelson's article, "Democratic Theory and Public Opinion," originally appeared in *Public Opinion Quarterly,* Vol. 16 (Princeton University
Press, Fall, 1952), pp. 313–330. Whenever a religious thinker draws from
such a basis an opinion that is optimistic rather than pessimistic, he is immediately charged with being a careless Pollyanna. Berelson, however,
demonstrates that effective consensus is often a reality even where dogmatic conformity is not eagerly offered. In addition to its application to
other ethical areas, this principle would often be helpful in explaining a
religious situation. Christians, for example, are often attacked as hypo-
crites because they agree with difficulty on theological formulations and
allow a latitude of interpretation of theological symbols considered un-
forgivably lax — especially by those *outside* the Church. Though it does
not describe an ideal *goal* of Christian Dogmatics, the following applica-

tion of Berelson's statement to the religious institution, for example, might prove not without usefulness in the face of the pessimism about the current and future state of the Church: "An effective *religious institution* must rest upon a *dogmatic and* moral consensus. . . . A seeming consensus which is accepted at its face value is far better than no consensus — and a seeming consensus is sometimes reflected in loyalty to the *same creedal statements and liturgical symbols* even though they carry different meanings." (The italicized words are religious substitutes for Berelson's political terms. When we say here that religious symbols "carry different meanings," we intend to indicate that they evoke enormously varied responses in terms of intensity and degree of acceptance, as well as level of sophistication and specific imaginary content.)

48. David Easton, *The Political System* (Alfred A. Knopf, Inc., 1953), p. 317.

49. O. H. v. d. Gablentz and E. Fraenkel, "Staat und Politik," *Fischer Lexikon,* 1957, p. 348.

50. Easton, *op. cit.,* p. 146.

51. See, for example, H. D. Lasswell, *Politics: Who Gets What, When, How* (Meridian Books, Inc., 1958). Similar creative modern insights concerning power are to be found in the work of Hans Morgenthau, whose "Love and Power," *Commentary,* March, 1962, contains insights reminiscent of those which inform Paul Tillich's *Love, Power and Justice.*

52. Lasswell, *Power and Personality* (W. W. Norton & Co., Inc., 1948), p. 10.

53. This latter point accounts in part for the prophetic agony of Jeremiah (chs. 20:7-18; 23:9 *passim*). This agony involved not only rejection and persecution by his contemporaries, but in a deeper sense his sympathetic suffering for the nation under judgment and as Niebuhr says, his awareness of being himself under the same judgment. In addition to these dimensions (expressed in vs. 16 f.), ch. 23 contains attacks on the false prophets who participate in the immoralities of their own time and who pander to it with prophetic gimmicks (in Jeremiah's day, dreams, as in Amos' day, the Baal cult).

54. In our account we are ignoring the historically dubious destruction of Sennacherib's army by an instantaneously fatal plague in Isa. 37:36 and II Kings 19:35.

55. Much is owed to Prof. Paul Lehmann, of Union Theological Seminary, New York, for the application of the navigational metaphor to ethical deliberation. Neither he nor others, as far as I know, use the term "criterial" for the third ethic. He uses the term *koinōnia,* the Greek

designation for the Christian *community,* or *contextual* ethic for the third. Others use the term "contextual" practically as a synonym for "relativist" (in anthropology, "contextual" refers everything to a single self-contained society as opposed to the cross-cultural or comparative approach); "situational" is a similar term often used by existentialistic thinkers. Both "contexual" and "situational" when used this way tend to lean too strongly in the relativist direction, emphasizing the momentary complex of problems to the neglect of transcendent criteria or values. Lehmann, on the other hand, like Barth and latterly even Tillich, emphasizes the *Church* — or *koinōnia* — as the necessary *context* within which men of *conscience* exercise an ethic. (See his *Ethics in a Christian Context;* Harper & Row, Publishers, Inc., 1963.) Still, I prefer the term "criterial," which points first to the fixed stars of ethics rather than to the historical relativities constantly uncovered with such analytical acumen by the many disciplines of Academy.

56. See p. 323n9 above.

57. See pp. 239–240 above.

58. Though we are *unjust* — unrighteous, sinful — and God's *justice* condemns sinfulness, in redemption through Christ Jesus, God himself is proved just — *dikaios,* righteous — "and the *justifier* of him who has faith in Jesus." This is one of the passages whose parallel structure is clearer in the King James Version than in most modern translations.

59. We have preserved the old English word "meet" (to satisfy a need of demand) to call attention to an answering, a co-respondence of one sex to the other.

60. So that for a Christian man to copulate with a prostitute is "to take the members of Christ and make them the members of a prostitute" (I Cor. 6:15b).

61. Though David and Jonathan are approvingly said to have loved each other with a love "passing the love of women" and the Fourth Gospel speaks repeatedly of the disciple whom Jesus loved, the affection expressed by a kiss (I Sam. 20:41 and elsewhere; cf. also the holy kiss of the New Testament, Rom. 16:16; I Cor. 16:20; II Cor. 13:12; I Thess. 5:26; I Peter 5:14) does not necessarily suggest homosexual practice in a book that never hesitates to announce a sexual act (although there is evidence in early sources that because of the holy kiss practiced during the security of early Christian worship, the Romans considered Christians sexually immoral). On the contrary, homosexuality is expressly condemned in both the Old Testament (Lev. 18:22; 21:13), where it is the sin that makes Sodom the symbol of evil (Gen. 19:5-8; 24 f.), and the New

Testament, where we find Paul insisting that Christian converts give up the reprehensible practice of homosexuality (Rom. 1:26 f; I Cor. 6:9-11; cf. Lev. 18:27 f.).

62. In Gen. 19:38, the inferiority of the offspring produced by incest speaks dramatically against it: Lev. 18:6-18; 21:11 f., 17-23; Deut. 22:30; 27:20-23.

63. We must bear in mind that the one-flesh relationship, though recognized by society through law and sanctified by religion, is consummated privately by two individuals, one or both of whom often say: " I'm marrying him (or her), not his (or her) family! " This assertion may indeed be necessary, for some marriages only work well when the couple declares its independence of one or both families that threaten to choke the marriage with too much " assistance."

64. In addition to its deviation from the one-flesh norm, we would list among the effects of homosexuality the physiological-psychological unrealism and the evasion of the responsibility that makes a man a man.

Chapter V: Theology as an Art

1. Like that of the scientist and the prophet, the predicament of the artist within society and among his critics is not a strictly modern one. One recalls the agelong battle of the playwright and the player to rise above the level of the criminal in public esteem, further, that it was Michelangelo who finally raised the public image of the artist above that of the artisan in art-conscious Italy, and finally the repeated, rather subtle invective of a Henry Fielding, to name one of a protesting host in the history of creative writing, against the critics of his day.

2. I think especially of the creeds of the Reformation, many of which *acknowledged* their relevance to the problems of *one* time and place in Christendom, but the same applies to Nicaea in spite of its controversy.

3. Pinner, *loc. cit.,* p. 967.

4. S. H. Butcher, *Aristotle's Theory of Poetry and Fine Art* (Dover Publications, Inc., 4th rev. ed., 1951), p. 127.

5. *Ibid.,* pp. 126 f.

6. This is, of course, but one of many reasons for the noncompletion of an artistic creation, as in the enormously complex problem of the " unfinished " or " unfinishable " in Michelangelo's *œuvre,* for example.

7. Pinner, *loc. cit.,* p. 968.

8. George Steiner, " Why Man, He Doth Bestride the Narrow World like a Colossus," *The New York Times Book Review,* April 19, 1964.

9. *Ibid.*

10. Martin Esslin, *The Theatre of the Absurd* (Anchor Books, 1961), p. xix. This translation given by Esslin is slightly preferable to that of Justin O'Brien in Camus, *The Myth of Sisyphus and Other Essays* (Vintage Books, Inc., 1959), p. 5.

11. Eugène Ionesco, "Dans les Armes de la Ville," *Cahiers de la Compagnie Madeleine Renaud–Jean–Louis Barrault,* Paris, No. 20 (October, 1957), quoted in Esslin, *op. cit.,* p. xix.

12. Beckett, in Esslin, *op. cit.,* p. 20, quoting from Harold Hobson, "Samuel Beckett, Dramatist of the Year," *International Theatre Annual,* No. 1 (London: John Calder, 1956); also in Alan Schneider, "Waiting for Beckett," *Chelsea Review,* Autumn, 1958.

13. Esslin, *op. cit.,* p. xx.

14. *Ibid.,* p. 167.

15. *Ibid.,* p. 39. Already in 1915 Nikolai Evreinov's *The Theatre of the Soul* portrays the mortal conflict *inside a human being* between his rational and his emotional self, a drama reminiscent of Paul's portrayal of the spiritual struggle between the spirit and the flesh, or the old man and the new — *within me.*

16. Genet, letter to Pauvert, quoted in Esslin, *op. cit.,* p. 151.

17. Esslin, *op. cit.,* p. 39.

18. *Ibid.,* p. 160.

19. *Ibid.,* p. 248.

20. Ionesco, *Victims of Duty,* in *Plays,* Vol. II (Grove Press, 1958), p. 159, quoted in Esslin, *op. cit.,* p. 103.

21. Esslin, *op. cit.,* p. 213.

22. Ionesco, "Expérience du Théâtre," *Nouvelle Revue Française,* Paris (Feb. 1, 1958), p. 262, quoted in Esslin, *op. cit.,* p. 132.

23. Esslin, *op. cit.,* p. 134.

24. Pinter interview with Kenneth Tynan, quoted in Esslin, *op. cit.,* p. 207.

25. Arthur Adamov, *L'Aveu* (Paris: Éditions du Sagittaire, 1946), quoted in Esslin, *op. cit.,* p. 48.

26. *Ibid.,* p. 49.

27. Bertolt Brecht, *Im Dickicht der Städte, Stücke I,* (Frankfurt: Suhrkamp, 1953), pp. 291 f., quoted in Esslin, *op. cit.,* p. 272.

28. Esslin, *op. cit.,* pp. 303 f.

29. Ionesco, "Le Point du Départ," *Cahiers des Quatre Saisons,* Paris, No. 1, quoted in Esslin, *op. cit.,* p. 93.

30. Esslin, *op. cit.,* p. 316.

31. A similar table could, of course, be drawn for the *Systematic The-*

ology of Paul Tillich, the other magnificent conception of the theological art in the twentieth century.

32. This idea was formulated by Augustine as a relational *vestigium trinitatis* in which Father : Son : Spirit = Lover : Beloved : Love, the love which unites them.

Conclusion: The Common Quest

1. Perry Miller, *Jonathan Edwards* (Meridian Books, Inc., 1959), has brilliantly demonstrated Edwards' penetrating insight into the minds of Locke and Newton. As was almost inevitable, Miller, who is interested in Edwards as a literary artist, has failed to appreciate that Edwards' theological synthesis represents an intellectual accomplishment of equal stature.